Photos by Jim O'Brien

Happy Birthday 2009!

to Mike,

Enjoy my stories
and your own memories.
This will remind you of
your own involvement
with sports. "Doc" and
Walt wanted you to have
this and offer it with love
and pride,

Best wishes,
Jim O'Brien
3-22-2009

"Pittsburgh is a place I really enjoy. There are a lot of similarities to where I grew up in Cole Harbour (Nova Scotia), starting with the people. I relate to the people in Pittsburgh. They're just working-class people. When I came there, the way they have treated me — it was very sincere. I appreciated it."

—Sidney Crosby,
Captain, Pittsburgh Penguins

Pittsburgh
Proud

Jim O'Brien

CELEBRATING THE CITY'S
RICH SPORTS HISTORY

by Jim O'Brien

Dedication

Foremost, for my wife Kathleen and our daughters, Sarah and Rebecca, who know many of these stories by heart.

For all the Pittsburgh sports figures, past and present, who brought pride and positive recognition to the city, especially Ernie Holmes and Dwight White, Steelers' stars of the '70s, who died in 2008.

In memory of Myron Cope, a journalist with a gift for words and the personal integrity to get it right.

In memory of some of my patrons who made it possible to pursue writing and publishing these books about achievement in Pittsburgh.

This book is dedicated to Bill Baierl, Mel Bassi and Jack McGinley Sr., who were always there when I needed them.

It's also for Steve Previs, a loyal patron who taught us how to sell and how to stay optimistic. To all of my present patrons. To Beano Cook, who introduced me to all the great sportswriters in America.

To Richard Caliguiri and Bob O'Connor, two former mayors of Pittsburgh, who took an interest in and promoted my books as "civic treasures," in O'Connor's words. To Luke Ravenstahl, who follows in their footsteps and offers the same kind of encouraging words. To Jim Roddey and Dan Onorato, two other Pittsburgh political leaders, who care greatly about this community and its history.

To the gang at Geyer Printing and Cold-Comp Typesetting who work hard to do it right.

To the faithful readers…thanks for caring and sharing.

To all those I interviewed for my book series. Thanks for your time and thoughts. And, finally, happy 250th birthday to Pittsburgh. I'm proud to be a Pittsburgh guy.

— Jim O'Brien

Copyright © 2008 by Jim O'Brien

All rights reserved
Published by James P. O'Brien — Publishing
P.O. Box 12580
Pittsburgh PA 15241
Phone (412) 221-3580
First printing, August 2008

Manufactured in the United States

Printed by Geyer Printing Company, Inc.
55 38th Street
Pittsburgh PA 15201

All signatures in this book are reproduced from originals provided with permission.

Typography by Cold-Comp
91 Green Glen Drive
Pittsburgh PA 15227

ISBN 1-886348-14-6

This book is dedicated to the author's wife, Kathleen Churchman O'Brien, and one of their biggest boosters, the late Bill Baierl.

Acknowledgments

David McCullough, a Pulitzer Prize-winning author and historian with western Pennsylvania roots, was asked what we can learn from the past. He replied, "That there is no such thing as a 'self-made man or woman' — we all are influenced by people around us. And that integrity and character do count in the long run."

I have been fortunate to have met and interviewed and learned from so many outstanding individuals, most of whom have been associated with and excelled in the world of sports. I am grateful for those who were generous with their time and thoughts, stories and insights

Significant financial support has been offered by the following: Armand Dellovade of A.C. Dellovade, Asbury Heights, LD Astorino/Horizon Architects, Atria's Retaurant & Tavern, Greg Babe of Bayer Material/Science, Bill Baierl and now his wife Carol Baierl and his cousin Lee Baierl of Baierl Automotive, Rich Barcelona of Bailey-PVS Oxides LLC, Blue Cross of Western Pennsylvania, Bowne of Pittsburgh, Miles Bryan of Bryan Mechanical, Don Carlucci of Carlucci Construction, Mel Bassi of Charleroi Federal Savings, Ralph J. Papa of Citizens Bank, Compucom, James T. Davis of Davis & Davis Law Offices, Eat'n Park Restaurants, James S. Hamilton of Federated Securities, Inc., Frank B. Fuhrer Wholesale Company, David J. Malone of Gateway Financial, Jeffrey P. Berger and Richard Mullen of H. J. Heinz Company, Hoddy Hanna of Hanna Real Estate Services, Bill Tillotson of Hefren-Tillotson, Elsie Hillman, Thomas B. Grealish of Henderson Brothers, Steve Fedell of Ikon Office Solutions, William V.Campbell of Intuit, Iron & Glass Bank, Andy Russell of Laurel Mountain Partners, LLC, Jack Mascaro of Mascaro Construction, Joseph A. Massaro Jr. of the Massaro Company, Robert Santillo and Danny Rains of McCarl's, Dave Jancisin of Merrill Lynch, Jack Perkins of Mr. P's Restaurant in Greensburg, Inc., Jack Piatt of Millcraft Industries Corp., A. Robert Scott of *Point*, Angela Longo of National City Bank, Lou Grippo of the Original Oyster House, Dan R. Lackner of Paper Products Company, Inc., PPG Industries, Tom O'Brien, James Rohr and Sy Holzer of PNC Bank, Pittsburgh Brewing Company, Robert J. Taylor of Taylor & Hladio Law Offiices, Jim, Barbara and Ted Frantz of TEDCO Inc., Bob Randall of TRACO, Inc., Schiefferlin & Somerset, Thomas J. Usher and John Surma of U.S. Steel Corporation, Clark Nicklas of Vista Resources, Inc., Kenneth Codeluppi of Wall-Firma, Inc., Western Pennsylvania Caring Foundation, Jack McGinley of Wilson-McGinley Co., Rudy Zupancic of Giant Eagle.

Others who have worked with me: Dr. Edwin Assid, Ron Livingston of Babb, Inc., Chuck Belliotti, Dale Blaha of Altany, Loynd & Lindquist, Inc., Richard S. Bontz of Bontz Chevrolet, Jon C. Botula, Tom Ceponis, Dr. Phil Dahar, Don DeBlasio of DeBlasio's Restaurant, Dan Bartow of Legends of the North Shore, Art Cipriani, Dave and Frank Clements, Joseph Costanzo Jr., Ralph Cindrich, Todd Cover, Judge Jeffrey Deller, Dr. Patrick J. DeMeo, Herb Douglas, Foge Fazio, Kim Geyer, Linda Gelorme, Zeb Jansante, Kevin Joyce of The Carlton, Gregory L. Manesiotis, Robert F. McClurg, Dennis Meteny, Linda and

Frank Meyer, George Morris, Jerry Morrow, Judy O'Connor, Andy Ondrey, John Paul, Jim Render, Jim Roddey, George Schoeppner, Len Stidle, Barbara Stull, Tyrone Ward, and Don Yannessa.

I want to thank the following individuals for their loyal support: Tony Accamando, Dennis Astorino, Louis Astorino, Eugene J. Barone, Aldo Bartolotta, Howell Breedlove, Suzy and Jim Broadhurst, R. Everett Burns of E-Z Overhead Door Co., Susie Campbell, Lee Prosky-Carter and John Carter, Renny Clark, Ray Conaway, Gayland Cook, Jay Dabat, Greg Dearolf, Judge Jeffrey A. Deller, Tony Ferraro, Gregory W. Fink, Bob Friend, Dr. Freddie Fu, Dan Goetz, Marshall Goldstein, Bob and Frank W. Gustine Jr., Mike Hagan, F. Edwin Harmon, Donald J. Hastings, Karen Horvath, Jeff James, George Jordan, Bob Keaney, Daniel Koller Jr., Andy Komer, Robert Lovett, Jim McCarl, Mac McIlrath, Nancy and Pat McDonnell, Carl R. Moulton, Pitt Chancellor Mark Nordenberg, Jim Droney of Mt. Lebanon Office Equipment, Ron Parfitt, Joseph Piccirilli, Matt Polk, Charlie and Steve Previs, Pro Football Hall of Fame, Joe Reljac, Arthur J. Rooney Jr., John Rooney, Patrick J. Rooney, Ed Ryan, Patrick J. Santelli, Fred Sargent, Vince Sarni, Vince R. Scorsone, Rich Snebold, Tom Snyder, Stanley M. Stein, Steve Stepanian, Tom Sweeney, Joyce Stump, Dick Swanson of Swanson Group, Ltd., W. Harrison Vail, Larry Werner, John C. Williams, WQED Multimedia, John Zanardelli

Special assistance has been given to me by Debbie Keener of Reed Smith Shaw & McClay, Joe Gordon, Beano Cook, Sally O'Leary, Dan Hart, Jim Trdinich, Doug Huff, Kevin Evanto, Gigi Saladna, Mark Fisher, Celeste M. Welch, Dave Lockett, E.J. Borghetti, David Arrigo, Beth Ann Conway, and Deanna Caldwell and Bill Keenist of Detroit Lions.

Special thanks goes to my friends, Walt Becker, Joan and Tom Bigley, Kelly Bird, Rocky Bleier, Rudy Celigoi, Jack Chivers, Rich Corson, Herb Douglas, Carl A. Dozzi, Stanley Druckenmiller, Jim Duratz, Dan Frank, George Gojkovich, Frank Haller, Terrence G. Hammons, Jr., Ted Harhai, Dr. Haywood A. Haser, Harvey and Darrell Hess, Bill Haines, Samuel M. Hillard, Baldo Iorio, Tommy Kehoe, Joe Landolina, Patrick T. Lanigan Funeral Home. Dick LeBeau, Joseph Lohman of New York Food Company, Pete Mervosh, Bob Milie, Valierie Milie, Jack McGinley Jr., Gene Musial, John D. O'Connor & Son Funeral Home, Tom O'Malley Jr., Jacque Perkins, John Pelusi, Anthony J. Plastino II, Alex Pociask, Joe Pohl, Bill Priatko, Bob Shearer, Al Tarquinio, Ron Temple, Marty Wolfson, and Dr. Matthew Zirwas.

Gerry Hamilton of Oakmont handled the proofreading for this book, and Kim Maiden provided kind assistance in many ways.

I was able to get started in self-publishing thanks to the interest and cooperation of Stanley Goldman of Geyer Printing and Ed Lutz of Cold-Comp Typesetting. They wanted to help me and offered favorable terms. I continue to work with both of those firms today, under different leadership, but with the same spirit of cooperation and pride.

Bruce McGough, Tom Samuels and Keith Maiden are great to work with at Geyer Printing — Keith is especially helpful — and I enjoy working with Denise Maiden, Cathy Pawlowski and Rebecca Fatalsky of Cold-Comp Typographers. They're a winning team.

Pittsburgh and Southwestern Pennsylvania are rich in sports history and tradition. I want to congratulate and commend Jim O'Brien, our region's premier sports historian, for authoring *Pittsburgh Proud* on the occasion of our region's 250th Anniversary. During this year of reflection and celebration, it is fitting that we recognize and remember the significant role that sports and athletics have played in making the "City of Champions" what it is today.

Pittsburgh fans are known around the world for their strong dedication and passion for both amateur and professional sports. Our local teams are not just a source of excitement and entertainment, they are a source of pride and connectivity. People throughout the nation and around the globe stay connected to our region through our college and pro teams.

First-rate sports and athletics enhance the quality of life for residents and make our region an attractive place to live and invest. In addition, sporting events play a valuable role in our region's economy. The arenas and stadiums our local teams call home generate numerous jobs and create significant revenues, and businesses near these facilities also benefit greatly.

Recent special events, such as the Bassmaster Classic, Major League Baseball All-Star Game, the U.S. Open and Stanley Cup playoffs, brought in tens of thousands of fans from all over the country, giving local hotels, restaurants, bars and retailers valuable business.

Pittsburgh has always been one of America's great sports towns, and we will continue to be long into the future.

Dan Onorato
Allegheny County Executive

Former Steelers' star Jerome Bettis is congratulated by County Executive Dan Onorato after Super Bowl XL triumph.

Books By Jim O'Brien

COMPLETE HANDBOOK OF PRO BASKETBALL 1970-71

COMPLETE HANDBOOK OF PRO BASKETBALL 1971-72

ABA ALL-STARS

PITTSBURGH: THE STORY OF THE CITY OF CHAMPIONS

HAIL TO PITT: A SPORTS HISTORY OF
THE UNIVERSITY OF PITTSBURGH

DOING IT RIGHT

WHATEVER IT TAKES

MAZ AND THE '60 BUCS

REMEMBER ROBERTO

PENGUIN PROFILES

DARE TO DREAM

KEEP THE FAITH

WE HAD 'EM ALL THE WAY

HOMETOWN HEROES

GLORY YEARS

THE CHIEF

STEELERS FOREVER

ALWAYS A STEELER

WITH LOVE AND PRIDE

LAMBERT

FANTASY CAMP

STEELER STUFF

PITTSBURGH PROUD

To order copies of these titles directly from the publisher, send $26.95 for hardcover edition. Please send additional $3.50 to cover shipping and handling charges per book. Pennsylvania residents add 6% sales tax to price of book only. Allegheny County residents add an additional 1% sales tax for a total of 7% sales tax. Copies will be signed by author at your request. Discounts available for large orders. Contact publisher regarding availability and prices of all books in Pittsburgh Proud series, or to request an order form. Some books are sold out and are no longer available. You can still order the following: Doing It Right, Hometown Heroes, Glory Years, The Chief, Lambert, With Love and Pride, Fantasy Camp, Steeler Stuff and Pittsburgh Proud.

Contents

View from Chicago
Mike Ditka remains proud of Pittsburgh connection

"I'm just an ordinary guy."

Jim O'Brien

Sometimes you have to spend time in another city to truly appreciate Pittsburgh and its rich sports heritage. I took a break and traveled to Chicago for a week's stay in mid-June, 2008.

My wife Kathie and I drove there — stopping in Columbus, Ohio on both trips to see our daughter Sarah and her family — from our home in Pittsburgh. It's three hours to Columbus and another eight hours to Chicago. We were visiting our best friends, Sharon and Alex Pociask, who live in Crystal Lake, about 50 miles northwest of Chicago.

The Chicago Tribune was holding its annual Book Fair that weekend, and we had tickets for sessions featuring Studs Terkel and Scott Turow, two of Chicago's most popular literary treasures.

I had also made arrangements through Pat McDonnell to have dinner that same Saturday night at Mike Ditka's Restaurant and to interview Ditka, whom I have always regarded as the quintessential Pitt athlete. Ditka is a Chicago icon, but he remains a Pittsburgh guy.

McDonnell, the owner of Atria's Restaurant & Tavern chain, manages Ditka's two restaurants in Chicago. They told me they planned to convert the Atria's in Robinson Township into a Mike Ditka's Restaurant in the fall. That's the closest one to Ditka's hometown of Aliquippa. Terkel and Turow both talked about their writing for an hour. Turkel is 96 years old and said this would be his last public appearance. He is now deaf and requires a wheelchair but he managed to make sense for nearly sixty minutes. He'll have a new book out for Christmas. Turow, who writes crime thrillers, is also licensed to practice law.

As a bonus, we got to meet two of Chicago's all-time best baseball players, Billy Williams of the Cubs and Billy Pierce of the White Sox. They had good things to say about Roberto Clemente and Bob Friend and other Pirates of the past when we talked.

Ditka, who is 69, called to say he was running late. The weather was bad and the traffic was terrible, he told one of the hosts at his restaurant to tell us. We were waiting in the upstairs bar of his two-story restaurant at 100 East Chestnut Street, just off Michigan Avenue. "There isn't a manlier restaurant in town than Mike Ditka's," according to *Chicago* magazine.

The Windy City was really living up to its nickname. In fact, there was a tornado warning. There was flooding throughout the Midwest, especially in Iowa that weekend. There are some who've dealt with Ditka through the years that would say waiting for his arrival is akin to a tornado warning. His face was reddened by the sun and wind when he arrived. Ditka still stands tall, but he walks like a man who's had a hip replacement and has bad knees, with a bit of a rolling motion.

11

Alex Pociask said Ditka had the kind of large hands that his father had when he worked a dairy farm in Wausakee, Wisconsin. Sharon Pociask couldn't get over the size of Ditka's ring. It was the one he won when he coached the Chicago Bears to a Super Bowl title in 1985. "I'm just an ordinary guy who caught a few breaks along the way," Ditka likes to say.

His restaurant is a sports museum. It's mostly filled with framed photos and memorabilia of Chicago sports stars from the Bears, Bulls, Cubs, White Sox and Black Hawks, but Pittsburgh and Western Pennsylvania are well represented throughout its massive passages.

Stan Musial of Donora — Ditka's boyhood hero — and Arnold Palmer of Latrobe are depicted in painted murals on the walls upstairs. They are there along with George Halas, the boss of the Bears, and Vince Lombardi of the Packers and Tom Landry of the Cowboys, all heroes to Ditka. Dan Marino, Terry Bradshaw, Bobby Layne, Ben Roethlisberger, and Mike's buddy George Blanda are pictured elsewhere.

There's a montage of Steelers from the '70s, including Bradshaw, Ham, Lambert, Blount, Russell, Bleier, Harris and Greene. Dwight White is in that picture. Ditka and I spoke about White, hearing that weekend that the former Steeler' defensive lineman had died at age 58 following back surgery. It always hurts to hear news like that. Ditka has been a strong voice in fighting for better health benefits for the NFL players of the past who aren't as well covered as the contemporary players. "We owe it to those guys to help them," said Ditka.

Ditka says he'll always have a soft spot in his heart for Pittsburgh. "I was born there," he said, "and I'll probably die here. The people are a lot alike in both cities. They're hard working and they're genuine, and they love their sports."

Chicago is pitching for the 2016 Olympic Games. It had just been named the best sports town in America by one rating service.

Ditka is delightful. He knows how to play the part of Mike Ditka. He's got it down pat. A young man was standing by our table for ten minutes, waiting for an opening to get a glass signed by Ditka. "I hate to interrupt you, Mr. Ditka, but could you please sign this," the young man finally blurted out.

"Get the hell outta here!" Ditka snapped at him. It was pure Jack Lambert. It was Ditka. Then he smiled and embraced the young man and pulled out one of the Sharpie pens in his pants and signed the glass. You can buy such glasses and plates and T-shirts, cigars and wine at a stand in the lobby. You can get information about Mike Ditka's resort hotel in Orlando there, too. Or flyers about the Mike Ditka line of clothing. There's an assortment of Mike Ditka photos for sale.

"We're doing okay, but you have to keep at it," declared Ditka, who also works as an NFL analyst on network TV in the fall. "I think I know a little bit about football after all these years," he added.

Looking back on his approach to sports and life, Ditka said, "Every thing was competitive. My whole life was based on beating the other guy, being equal to, showing that I could be as good as anybody else. That's the way I grew up. I don't know if that's good or bad."

But that's Mike Ditka, da coach. He is so real.

STUDS TERKEL
"I'm interested in life."

SCOTT TUROW
Writes crime thrillers

Author met Mike Ditka at his landmark restaurant on Chestnut Street in Chicago, just off Michigan Avenue. Note George Halas, Vince Lombardi and Tiger Woods on mural behind them. Ditka's boyhood hero, Stan Musial, is on that same mural.

Pittsburgh Proud . . .

My love of sports began as a young boy, playing football and baseball with my brothers in our backyard. What began as childhood games grew into a love of competition that continued through grade school, high school and college. I truly believe that my involvement in team sports helped lay the foundation for my successes in life.

Growing up in the City of Pittsburgh, sports were a part of everyday life. The super teams of the 1970s put Pittsburgh on the map for its galaxy of sports superstars, and in doing so, changed the way the world looked at Pittsburgh. We were no longer the "smoky city." We were the City of Champions. It made us all proud to be Pittsburghers.

I remember being 18 years old and playing in the WPIAL baseball finals at Three Rivers Stadium. I stood in awe, knowing that I was playing on the same field where Franco made the "Immaculate Reception," where Willie and "the family" played, where history was written time after time.

Although Mario and the Penguins ushered in the 1990s with two Stanley Cups, most of the '80s and '90s were about rebuilding. Our sports teams were rebuilding and so was our City. It was a magnificent transformation, reinventing ourselves from the glories of our past to embrace the opportunities of the future.

Today, Pittsburgh is at the forefront of the nation. In 2007, we were named America's Most Livable City. We have safe and vibrant neighborhoods, outstanding medical facilities and universities, and new high-tech companies. We are a leader in "green" building. Everywhere you look, you can spot new development.

We have a new set of superstars. Exciting players like Ben Roethlisberger, Sidney Crosby and Freddie Sanchez. Just like me, a young Mayor, these young athletes represent a fresh, active Pittsburgh for the future. In our own ways, we are once again changing the way the world looks at our great City.

14

As we celebrate our City's 250th Anniversary, it is appropriate that Jim O'Brien has released *Pittsburgh Proud: Celebrating the City's Rich Sports History*. This is Jim's 23rd book and his 20th on Pittsburgh sports achievement. All of his local books have been printed at Geyer Printing here in Pittsburgh. Together they are a terrific team of their own, recording a unique look at Pittsburgh's transformations.

I am truly honored to have been asked to write this message. I love this City, and as I reflect on the past and look to the promises that our future holds, I am, and will always be, Pittsburgh Proud.

Luke Ravenstahl
Mayor, City of Pittsburgh

Mayor Ravenstahl offers key to the city to Myron Cope upon his retirement as Steelers' color/analyst.

That's my boy. Steelers' owner Art Rooney Sr. groomed his oldest son Dan to direct the team's fortunes. "The Chief" wanted the Steelers to remain his family's business.

Art Rooney Sr. points out his favorite players to Dwight White at Three Rivers Stadium office, including Byron "Whizzer" White. Dwight White was one of his favorites, too.

Dan Lackner
Offers the best story I ever heard
About Art Rooney

January 17, 2007

I go to many funerals because Art Rooney, the founder and owner of the Steelers, taught me why I should be there. He said you didn't go to stare at the dead but rather to share with the living. He said it was more important to go to a funeral when a friend lost a loved one than it was to go to the funeral of that friend.

It makes sense, like Mr. Rooney did on so many subjects. I have friends who feel otherwise, but none of them are in the Pro Football Hall of Fame or have become canonized as saints in our fair city.

I thought about Mr. Rooney when I paid my respects on Friday, January 12, 2007 at the funeral of Father Francis Lackner. The visitation was at the Laughlin Funeral Home in Mt. Lebanon. Father Lackner had lived in retirement at the nearby St. Bernard's Catholic Church complex and at the end at Marian Manor in Green Tree. He had been the pastor for many years at St. Margaret of Scotland in Green Tree.

I had only met and spoken to Father Lackner perhaps two or three times. He knew my sister, Carole Cook, and her daughter, Reisha Marie. "How's Mary Carole and Reisha doing?" he asked when he saw me. His brother Dan has been a friend and booster of mine for many years. Dan Lackner is the president of Paper Products Company in the Terminal Building on the city's South Side. Dan's wife Lois is from my hometown of Hazelwood. She went to St. Stephen's School with my sister. One of their sons, Rich, is the successful football coach at Carnegie Mellon University.

Dan Lackner helped out in the offices of the Steelers when he was still a student at Central Catholic High School in Oakland. He recalls that he and Rege Cordic got out of school 20 minutes early each day so that Dan could get to the Steelers' offices and Rege could get to KDKA Radio where he would become an on-the-air star as a young man, and eventually make his way to LA and even Hollywood.

Lackner learned a lot about Art Rooney in those days. Once, a few years back, when I was having lunch with Lackner at Bruschetta's on the South Side, he told me a story about Art Rooney that may be my favorite Art Rooney story. It tells you everything you need to know about why Mr. Rooney was so special.

Dan Lackner, who was 80 at the time of our luncheon meeting, and still goes to the office most mornings, remembers going to the funeral of Kathleen Rooney, the wife of the Steelers' patriarch, at Devlin's Funeral Home on the North Side.

"No sooner had I stepped inside the door of the funeral home," recalled Lackner, "than this guy comes down the hallway and calls out to me. We'd gone to school together at Central Catholic many years before. His name was McNamara. Joe McNamara. He told me his father of the same name had died at the VA Hospital and was laid out in the next room. 'All his friends are gone, and I didn't know whether to have a funeral for him or not,' said his son. 'But I decided to do it, so here we are.' He told me his father had been a city fireman and had lived on Dawson Street in Oakland.

"I went with him to pay my respects. There was nothing in the room but the casket and a kneeler. That was it. It was a sad scene.

"He told me they were only going to be at the funeral home for one day. When I left to pay my respects to Kathleen Rooney I bumped into Art Rooney in the lobby. He said, 'Dan, who were you talking to back there?' I told him about my boyhood friend and his father. He said, 'C'mon, let's go back and pay our respects.' So we went back together and I introduced him to my old friend whom I hadn't seen in years, Joe McNamara.

"Mr. Rooney talked to him for awhile, offered his sympathy, and I could tell it meant a lot to McNamara. Art signed the book and took a prayer card with him. He went to more funerals than anyone in Pittsburgh did, and he always took one of those prayer cards with him when he left.

"As we're coming out of the room, a big, powerfully built black man is coming through the main door, carrying a big basket of flowers in each arm. Art called out to him, 'Where are you taking those flowers?' The man said they were for Mrs. Rooney. Art said, 'We have enough flowers. You take them back to our friend McNamara.'

"I saw Joe Greene and I think Terry Bradshaw coming in behind the man carrying the flowers. Mr. Rooney sent them back to see his friend McNamara.

"In the door comes Tom Foerster, the former County Commissioner, with his friend, Pete Flaherty, the former mayor of Pittsburgh. Mr. Rooney greets them, accepts their condolences and tells them, 'Don't forget to go to the back room and pay your respects to our friend McNamara.'

"Foerster shoots Rooney a look. 'What McNamara?' And Rooney responds, 'Our friend McNamara, the fireman.'

"And Foerster says, 'I don't know any fireman named McNamara.'

"And Rooney rather testily tells him, 'Yes, you do! The one from Dawson Street! Out in Oakland!'

"And Foerster gives in and says, 'Oh, that one.' And he and Pete Flaherty go back to the other room. So Art had everyone pay their respects 'to our friend McNamara' and sign the visitors' book. It went on like that the rest of the day. When I came back the next day my friend McNamara was still there. He said, 'We decided to stay another day.'

"I went into the room once again to see his father. You could hardly see Joe McNamara. The room was full of flowers. It looked like one

18

of the greenhouse displays at Phipps Conservatory in Schenley Park. He showed me the visitors' book and so many famous Steelers, such as Joe Greene and Mel Blount and Terry Bradshaw, had signed the book. Pete Rozelle, the NFL Commissioner, and Al Davis, the owner of the Oakland Raiders, had been there, too. Everybody who was anybody in the National Football League had signed the book. That's just the way Art Rooney was. That visitors' book might be worth something today."

Dan and Rich Lackner are proud team.

Photos from Lackner Family collection

Father Francis Lackner

Dan and Lois Lackner are loyal CMU football fans.

Steelers fans

Showing their true colors
in black and gold jerseys

November 9, 2005

I spend a lot of time at area shopping malls. I sit at a table in front of the bookstores, selling and signing my books. I have a waist-high view of passersby, and I see more bare stomachs—even in November—than most medical internists in town. I also see more Steelers' jerseys than ever before.

When the Steelers beat the Baltimore Ravens on a Monday Night Football feature on Halloween, TV announcers Al Michael and John Madden said they thought there were more Steelers' fans wearing team jerseys than at any other NFL stop. They also commented that you see a lot of Steelers' fans wherever the team plays on the road. "They travel better than just about any other NFL team," remarked Madden.

I would agree, after spending that Monday evening at Station Square where nearly everyone—men and women and the smallest of children—was wearing official Steelers' jerseys. And it wasn't because it was Halloween. They always put on their uniforms on game day, whether they are at the game or watching it on TV. They were coming out of the stores that sell Steelers' stuff with two and three shopping bags' worth of new gear.

I saw three men walking by, LLOYD 95, POLAMALU 43 and GREENE 91. I wanted to stop them and tell them there was no way that the pleasant and good-natured Troy Polamalu would ever travel in the same company as Greg Lloyd and Kevin Greene, two licensed terrorists.

Not many are wearing MADDOX 8 and STEWART 10 anymore, but I did see one fellow at South Hills Village who had pasted GERELA over the STEWART, turning it into a real retro jersey.

The most popular jersey by far, of course, is ROETHLISBERGER 7, with WARD 86 and BETTIS 36 right behind. RANDLE EL 82 is also a big seller. I felt sorry for the guy wearing ZEREOUE 21.

I felt even sorrier for the parents of the teenage girl that I saw Sunday at The Mall at Robinson Township wearing a Philadelphia Eagles' jersey with T.OWENS on the back. Bet she gives her parents a difficult time. Why would anyone want to wear the jersey of that jerk? He may be the best pass-catcher and productive receiver in the NFL, but he is a selfish troublemaker who tears the team apart.

At Century III Mall, I saw a young teenage boy giving his grandmother a lot of sass. He was wearing R. LEWIS of the Baltimore Ravens. Why was I not surprised that he appeared to be a young brat?

Popular players come and go with the Steelers' fans. Stewart was once so popular, and so was Maddox. But fans turned on them in a hurry when they had their difficulties. Even people employed by the Steelers have been publicly critical of Maddox on the local airwaves.

I've gotten to know Cliff Stoudt well over the past five or six years, and you couldn't ask for a better guy. Yet Stoudt got so much grief from the fans in his last days here. That's wrong.

The storied Bobby Layne might be in the Hall of Fame, and he was as gutsy a quarterback as there ever was in the NFL, but he was never the man that Stoudt and Maddox have been. Or Mark Malone for that matter. Sometimes we are quick to rush to harsh judgment on these guys, and we're particularly tough on our quarterbacks.

I don't think fans watch the game anymore. They think they're on the team. Every fan that has a fantasy football team thinks he or she can coach in the NFL. People don't know how to watch a sporting event anymore. They have gotten their roles confused.

Sportscaster John Steigerwald says, "Fans have become fans of being fans. They think they're part of the show."

I think everyone should get his or her own game, whether its bowling or badminton, basketball, tennis, platform tennis, volleyball, bridge, horseshoes or Texas Hold-Em Poker. Put yourself and your own name on the line. Find out how it feels to be under pressure to win or lose. On the job, see if you can't get more sales, see if you can't be more successful. Whatever you're doing, do it better. What's your record this year? There isn't a Steelers' jersey in our house. We root for them, of course, but we don't rely on the Steelers or any other sports team in town to make our day, or to determine how we feel on Monday. Get your own game. Use your own name. Just do it.

Jim O'Brien

Susie "Crazy Woman" Campbell of Coraopolis is flanked by two Steelers' fans with faces painted black and gold. Ms. Campbell has contact lenses with Steelers' insignias on them, and lots of costume jewelry to match. "Super Dave" Manning, at left, and Travis Reynolds travel from South Carolina to see Steelers in action.

Steelers' fans don't want to be mistaken in their loyalty.

Joe Montana fan (16) in red and white is flanked by two Steelers' fans with gold locks and black shirts and sunglasses at Hometowne Sports at Station Square.

There is always more than one Santa Claus in the crowd at Steelers' games in December.

Photos by George Gojkovich

Steelers' receiver Nate Washington gets wild reception from home field fans after touchdown catch in 2007 season.

Pierre Larouche
From Mario to Sid the Kid

Jim O'Brien

*"He was so handsome
and charming."*
—Cindy Larouche

The view from the deck at the rear of Pierre Larouche's home in Scott Township is spectacular in the spring. The sylvan setting is full of fruit trees and shrubs and they are sprinkled with pink, white and yellow flowers. "You don't even know you're in Pittsburgh," allows Larouche.

He and his wife Cindy are comfortable there. Cindy grew up in nearby Dormont. She met Pierre when he was a young player with the Penguins. He was 20 and she was a few years older. "We met at the Gaslight in Shadyside and I was smitten with him right from the start," she says with a smile. "I was the older woman and I took advantage of his youth. He was so handsome and charming and fun."

He still is. He has a few more nicks and scratches on his mug than he did when they first met, but he still has that devilish smile. That's why he is perfect for his role as a goodwill ambassador for the Penguins. He represents the team well at fund-raisers of all sorts and autograph signings. He's a scratch golfer, has picked up some good prize money on the celebrity golf tour, and escorts sponsors and well-heeled customers of the Penguins on golf junkets. I've had two friends who had similar roles with major corporations. It beats working for a living.

He's Mario's man, a close friend of the Hall of Fame hockey star who wiped out most of Larouche's amateur and Penguins' scoring records. Lemieux and Larouche are both loyal guys.

Larouche was one of the great scorers in the history of the National Hockey League. He was the No. 1 draft choice of the Penguins in the 1974 amateur draft. He scored 53 goals with Pittsburgh in 1975–76 and 50 with the Montreal Canadiens in 1979–80. He was the first player to score 50 goals for two different NHL teams.

At the time he was with the Penguins, he was the youngest player to hit the 50-goal plateau. His record was broken by Wayne Gretzky in 1980. It took the great ones to remove Larouche from the record books. Now 52, he played for the Penguins, Canadiens, Hartford Whalers and New York Rangers. He could skate and score with the best of them. He had a good time doing it and they called him "Lucky Pierre." The name still fits him as snugly as his hockey skates.

The view from Lemieux's owner's box above Mellon Arena is a good one, too. Pierre and Cindy can often be found there. She's the tougher of the two, he concedes. She has survived two cancer scares and remains vigilant about her health.

At one of the early Stanley Cup playoff games, Larouche was shown on TV in that box. The Steelers' Ben Roethlisberger was a guest

Cindy and Pierre Larouche are at home in Scott Township.

Photos by Jim O'Brien

Sidney Crosby continues in tradition established by Mario Lemieux.

that night, as were two future Baseball Hall of Fame pitchers, Tom Glavine and John Smoltz of the Atlanta Braves. Dan Marino was a guest at a later game. They all play in those celebrity golf outings around the country. The outstanding sports stars live the good life.

"I do stuff Mario wants me to do."
—Pierre Larouche

I visited the Larouche home on Monday, April 28, 2008, a cold, dank day, but they brightened the occasion with their friendly spirit, and easy conversation. "We've got a lot of talented young players, and a mix of solid veterans," said Larouche then. "I like our chances of winning the Stanley Cup. I don't know if we'll do it this year, but I think if we can keep this team together we'll win a few Stanley Cups before we're through."

Larouche lauded the likes of Sidney Crosby, Evgeni Malkin, Jordan Staal, Ryan Malone and Marc-Andre Fleury, the great addition of Marian Hossa, and the way Michel Therrien has kept this team together through some early-season adversity.

Crosby is too young and Malkin doesn't speak much English to be able to explain the significance of what the Penguins are experiencing, and how this team's rise fits into the sports legacy of the oft-troubled franchise and the winning sports tradition of this city. But Larouche has been around long enough to know what it means, and how great this experience has been. Larouche is still a lovable rogue.

"Most of the guys on the team aren't old enough to have any experiences to share," said Eddie Johnston, the former coach and scout of the Penguins, who lives with his wife Diane a block away from my home in Upper St. Clair. "Pierre's been around and he's a good story-teller."

It takes one to know one. Johnston was the last NHL goalie to play every game in a season, when he was with Bobby Orr and the Boston Bruins, and in his early days he didn't wear a mask. He shudders when he considers those combat years. But he boxed in gyms, even as a visitor in prisons, when he was a young man in Montreal. So he was a tough guy. And he was smart enough to hold onto the Penguins' No. 1 pick and draft Mario Lemieux in 1984. I love E.J.'s stories. Eddie and Diane are delightful company. So were Cindy and Pierre Larouche, even though Cindy is challenged and weakened by her cancer. She's a battler in the Eddie Johnston mold. If Cindy is concerned about her well being she masks her feelings well.

Pierre Larouche missed out on the Penguins' back-to-back Stanley Cup championships at the outset of the '90s, but he was with the Canadiens when they won consecutive Stanley Cups in 1978 and 1979. He knows the feeling.

When I told him I didn't think it was good form for the fans here to boo Jaromir Jagr every time he touched the puck in the Penguins' playoff series with the Rangers, Larouche laughed. "It's a normal reaction,"

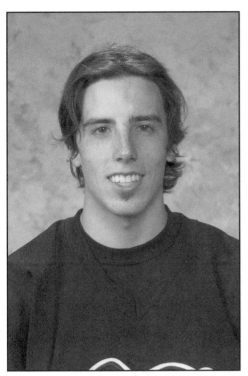

MARC-ANDRÉ FLEURY
Great young goalie

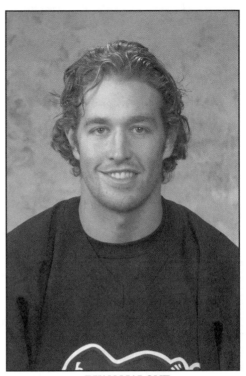

RYAN MALONE
Hometown hero now in Tampa Bay

JORDAN STAAL
It's in the blood

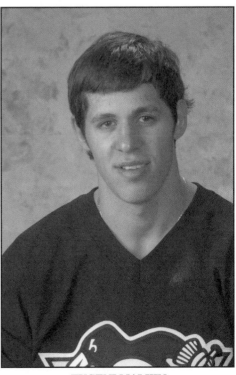

EVGENI MALKIN
From Russia with love

he said. "They're mad that he left. He was a big part of those championship teams, right up there with Mario. He was great here. They loved him here. But they hate him coming back with another team. They did the same thing to me when I came back with other teams. They hated me playing for the opposition."

Larouche looks at today's players with some degree of envy. "They're a lot bigger and stronger and faster, better trained and better paid," he said. "I don't know if they have as much skill as some of the great players we've had through the years. They don't carry the puck as much. That's gone. The deking is gone. I remember Bobby Orr used to be able to kill a penalty all by himself because nobody could get the puck away from him. He'd wear you out."

Larouche looks around the clubhouse—and former GM Jack Riley made a similar observation—and sees all the training equipment that wasn't there when he was playing. "Guys are riding the bike after a game to stay strong," he said. "They just started lifting weights when I was with New York. They start right after practice doing that now.

"I loved playing in New York. People in Pittsburgh knock New York, but they don't have any idea of what it's like to live and play there. They have great hockey fans, and the press there treated me really well. I stayed there for seven of my 14 years in the league and I loved it. There's nothing wrong with New York. There are some super friendly people there."

Larouche still has a fund-raising golf tournament there. Larouche was looking forward to the 20th edition of his Child Abuse Prevention golf tournament at the Ardsley Country Club at Ardsley-on-the-Hudson. That's an interesting involvement because the Larouches have no children.

Larouche looked around his surroundings. He has a nice, but unpretentious home. It's nothing like the mansions that Lemieux and Jagr owned in the South Hills during their playing days with the Penguins. Larouche doesn't live far from Jack Riley, who has resided in the Birdland section of Scott Township ever since he came to work for the Penguins back in the mid-60s. "Ever since 1974, I have thought of Pittsburgh as my home," said Larouche. "My wife's family is still here."

It's no wonder Pierre Larouche was popular with the press. He is comfortable in the company of writers or sports broadcasters and TV types. He is quotable and colorful. Cindy brought out a book called *A Year in the Sun*, by George Vecsey of the *New York Times*. I knew him well during my nine years in New York in the '70s. Vecsey begins a story about Larouche this way:

"I've always had a soft spot for the talented scamps of sports, the outlaws, the breakers of rules who kept the games from belonging to the authoritarians and the bureaucrats.

"Today I have a luncheon appointment with one of those charming rogues, Pierre Larouche of the New York Rangers, one of the most deft offensive players in hockey. I've met Larouche—long hair, squeaky voice, appealing Quebec accent, sly and funny and charming to a visiting columnist. A wildman, at least when he was younger. Impossible to coach. Traded three times. Lucky Pierre."

Larouche smiles at the description. "That can't be me," he says with a schoolboy grin. "Maybe that used to be me."

"Sid saved hockey in Pittsburgh."

He was gifted, to say the least. Larouche played junior hockey with the Sorel Eperviers of the Quebec Major Junior Hockey League. Sorel is the hometown of Mark-André Fleury. During the 1973–74 season, Larouche won the Jean Beliveau Trophy as the league's top scorer, with 94 goals, 157 assists, for a total of 251 points. Ten years later, Lemieux would break that Canadian Hockey League record with 282 points.

When he was with the Canadiens, Larouche scored 50 goals in 1979–80. He broke Beliveau's team record for the most goals (47) by a center. Beliveau was present when Larouche scored the 48th goal. I told him one of the highlights of my life as a sportswriter was meeting Beliveau and Maurice "The Rocket" Richard in the press room at the Montreal Forum. Richard once scored 50 goals in a 50-game season, but he was a right winger with a left-handed shot. He ran over people. Back then, you played against five teams. When they played an 80-game schedule, you played each team 16 times. They used to travel on the same trains at times and they'd get into a fight on the trains.

"They were both heroes of mine," allowed Larouche, referring to Richard and Beliveau. "If you grew up as a French-speaking Canadian and loved hockey you had to admire those men."

Crosby, the captain of the current Penguins, wants to learn about the history of the Penguins and the National Hockey League. He asks questions in that respect of Riley and Larouche. "He's respectful of those who came before him," relates Riley. "He's not like some of the young players today. He doesn't blow off an old-timer. He is really interested in what you have to say." Larouche goes back to the days when hockey players didn't wear helmets. His flying dark hair added to his handsome appearance. If Sid "The Kid" Crosby were to play that way the young women fans at Mellon Arena would require smelling salts to bring them back from swooning in the stands.

"The Kid comes here, and he changed everything," said Larouche. "If we don't have him, we might not have pro hockey in Pittsburgh right now. The Pens had plenty of problems after Mario wasn't playing anymore. He was looking for a buyer, but nothing was happening.

"When the Pens got ball No. 1 in the draft three years ago it saved hockey in Pittsburgh, just as Mario had done as a player and then as an owner. Sid loves the game and it shows when he plays. He's a great kid and he's a great hockey player. Without him, I don't think the team would be here. That lottery pick saved the day for hockey. It was the greatest thing since they got Mario.

"That's a great team they've got here today. You've got to give Craig Patrick some of the credit. He was my coach when I went to Hershey briefly during my days with the Rangers. We go back a long way together. He drafted most of these great young players. He had good judgment about players' abilities. Fred Shero has done a super job fitting the pieces together since he took over as GM.

"Max Talbot is good for the team. He and Fleury speak French. Sid speaks French. They're so happy to be together. That's why they're so good. They love each other. It's all going to come down to money and how much there is to go around. It will be tough to keep this team together. You can't keep them all. Hopefully, we can keep the core, Crosby and Malkin. I don't think Malkin has the overall game that Sid has, but he sure can get the puck and score goals. Rocket Richard was like that. Beliveau had better all-around skills, but Richard lived to score.

"If they stay together, this team could string some Stanley Cups together. For sure, they're going to be electrifying for ten years if they keep the nucleus. I could see them winning three or four Cups out of those years. Malkin is more flashy. It seems like he carries the puck more than Sid does. Sid has a notch up on him when it comes to playmaking."

Asked to compare them to his pal, Mario Lemieux, he responded, "I hate to compare players. Mario's one of a kind. It's a different time. The game is different. It's too early in their careers to compare them to the greats. Players like Mario and Gretzky and Orr and Guy Lafleur and Mike Bossy will always be among the greatest to play this game."

Pierre Larouche wasn't far behind. "I think I was a great passer," he said. "I was fast. I could face-off and steal the puck. I enjoyed setting up players. Stan Mikita was my boyhood idol. I liked the way he played. How many kids get to play against their idol? (I told Larouche that Mikita was also the boyhood idol of former Steelers' star Mike Wagner, who grew up in suburban Chicago.)

"I'm still lucky Pierre. I do public relations for the Penguins. I do stuff Mario wants me to do. I take sponsors on trips to Florida in the winter and play golf with them. That's good work when you can get it. I do autographs at charity events. I do some corporate sales. If Mario needs things done I do them. We've been friends a long time."

"This is a good city for me to play in," says hard-charging Sidney Crosby, who tied Henrik Zetterberg of Red Wings for 2008 playoff scoring lead with 27 points.

Photo by Matt Polk

Coping with Myron
Memories from Annapolis to Fort Greely, Alaska

"Kid, ya gotta sit down and start writing."

March 6, 2008

Jim O'Brien

I met Myron Cope for the first time when I was 14 years old. Cope was covering the Golden Gloves Boxing Tournament for the *Pittsburgh Post-Gazette* which sponsored the event for its Dapper Dan Charities. I was covering the tournament for the *Hazelwood Envoy*, the bi-weekly newspaper in my hometown.

Cope was 29. He was an under-utilized writing talent that sports editor Al Abrams kept under wraps in the office most of the time. The *P-G* was located in a building that was torn down just a few years ago, at the corner of Grant Street and the Boulevard of the Allies. It became the Public Safety Building after the *P-G* moved down the boulevard to The Pittsburgh Press Building. *The Press* is gone, too. Cope loved boxing. He'd done a little boxing in his youth. The Golden Gloves was his Super Bowl back then.

It was the biggest event I had personally covered at that time, too. Our local team, the Glen-Hazel Boys Club, won the team title in the Golden Gloves 11 out of 12 years during this period. Cy Obremski, who managed the Glen-Hazel team, took me with him to the tournament in 1956. He taught me how to box along the way.

I saw Cope scurrying about the locker room in the Pitt Field House, carrying a small portable typewriter. He was five feet four inches tall, and he was taller than I was at the time. I think he liked it better that way. I went over to him and stopped him from scurrying.

"Mr. Cope," I said, "what do I have to do to become a writer?"

He cocked his head sideways and snapped, "Kid, ya gotta sit down and start writing!" Then Cope continued scurrying.

Now read that Cope comment once more and this time say it with your best imitation of Cope's voice.

"Kid, ya gotta sit down and start writing!"

That should put a smile on your face.

It was simple enough, but it was, indeed, the best advice I ever received about being a writer. Many people meet me in shopping malls these days when I am signing my books and they tell me they're thinking about writing a book. But most will never do it. They don't have the discipline and maybe they're just not writers.

When Cope retired from the Steelers' broadcast booth, Myron said a lot of mothers told him through the years that their kids knew all the statistics and wanted to be sports writers or sports broadcasters when

Myron Cope provided color commentary for Steelers' games for 35 years before retiring in July 2005 because of health challenges.

Cope changed crowd behavior at sports events forever when he created "The Terrible Towel."

The voices of Pittsburgh sports, from left to right, are Lanny Frattare, Myron Cope, Mike Lange and Bill Hillgrove as they appeared at annual Sports Night Dinner at Thompson Club in West Mifflin in 2002.

they grew up. "That's not enough," he growled. "You gotta have talent. There's more to it than knowing numbers. It's a gift."

The great Honus Wagner once said, "There ain't much to being a ballplayer…if you're a ballplayer."

I was lucky enough as a young man to get to meet and spend time with Myron Cope. I learned a lot from him. I admired him. But we had different views about a lot of things. We were not always on the same page. I found him difficult at times. I must confess here that we were not close or personal friends. We were not intimates, though many people think we were. I want to be honest here.

He was always kind and good to me when he could be of help. When he had his sports talk show, he always interviewed me a good hour whenever I'd have a new book out. He insisted I do his show first. Cope was always the competitor. He always read the book and had it marked up, and had post-it notes scattered throughout. He'd flip through it during the interview. He always did his homework and was prepared to do an interview. That was appreciated.

There was a private side to him, and there were some things he was reluctant to discuss. In the end, we simply shared some moments in time, and had some common bonds. There was an association and a mutual respect that lasted more than 50 years. We never argued and we never owed each other any money. That's pretty good.

I'll never forget this one night in a ballroom at the Sheraton at Station Square. We were on the same program to raise funds to assist two Steelers who needed some help, namely Mike Webster and Steve Courson. The evening was billed as "A Farewell To Arms," the title of an Ernest Hemingway war novel. The banquet banner was a reference to the biceps and muscular builds of the two Steelers' linemen who were being roasted. They always wore jerseys that revealed their arms, no matter how cold the weather. I was the emcee and I saved Cope and Ray Mansfield for last. They were usually great storytellers and they were funny. Both had too much to drink by the time they got to the podium and it was a disaster in both cases. Neither one of them knew when to say, "Thanks and good night."

Cope brought along a copy of Hemingway's book, *A Farewell to Arms*, and he started reading from it. He wanted to do something different, he later disclosed, from his normal story-telling and Cope brand of humor. It didn't work. The audience had already been there too long, and Cope was dying up there, putting everyone except himself to sleep. I thought I had to do something to save the show and to save Cope. The late Bob Prince used to toss up his pocket-handkerchief to signal that someone had spoken too long. I decided to do something different. I was fearful of offending Cope, whatever I did, and I didn't want to incur his criticism or wrath. I respected him too much to hurt his feelings. I fretted about what to do, or if I should do anything and risk Cope's annoyance.

34

I got up while Cope was continuing his reading and I went to the far end of the dais where Jack Lambert was sitting and frowning. "What the hell is he doing?" Lambert asked when I approached him. Well, he said something like that anyhow.

"Listen, Jack," I replied. "You have to do us all a favor. When I get back to my seat I want you to come over and grab Cope and throw him over your shoulder and carry him off the stage."

Lambert liked the idea, and smiled with a leer. You'd have thought I was suggesting he mug Earl Campbell instead of Myron Cope. A minute or so later, Lambert left his seat and came to the middle of the dais. Cope looked up at Lambert, surprised to see him standing at his side. Cope looked confused, caught off guard. "What's up, Splat?" Cope inquired.

Without a word, Lambert lifted Cope like a sack of flour and tossed him over his right shoulder. He carried Cope off the stage. Myron was dangling, and making one of his strange sounds as they moved along. Cope was going along with the gag, ever the showman. Lambert took him into the kitchen. That was the way the program ended. The crowd went crazy. Anyone who was there that night will never forget Cope's exit.

I left the dais and joined my wife Kathie in the back of the room. I was concerned about how Cope would respond to what we did. Cope came out of the kitchen, smiling like crazy. He said hello to Kathie — he was always the gentleman — and he said, "Your husband done good. You betcha. I was dying up there and I didn't know how to get out of it. Jim did, thank God, he knew what to do."

I was so relieved to hear Cope's comment. He not only forgave me; he was giving me a compliment.

This is the time of the year when I remember Myron's advice about a lot of things all over again.

"Kid, ya gotta sit down and start writing."

After being out every day, all day, for about 30 days during the holiday season I am whipped when January and then February arrive. It is difficult to find the discipline to sit down and start writing my next book. But if I am going to have a book this year I had better sit down and start writing. Like now.

When I am writing, Myron Cope comes to mind a lot. I'll go back and change a word or two, get the verb tense right, fix something. I don't get the grammar right all the time, but I try. I care. I don't want to offend Cope's critical eye. He was a wonderful writer before he became a radio sports commentator and broadcaster and then a color man for Steelers' radio broadcasts. Before he became the Myron Cope that most Pittsburghers know so well. I think of advice Roy McHugh, his friend and editor, offered as well. McHugh remains Cope's biggest fan.

Myron Cope was a wonderful writer, more than anything else. He was a stickler for proper grammar and usage of the English language. He was critical of stuff he saw in the city's newspapers and he'd point out improper grammar and usage to all of us writers. He worked hard, dug deep for stories, and took pride in his professionalism and integrity. Anyone who was paying attention had to profit from Myron's efforts. He was a great role model. If you were in his company you were having fun. I make mistakes, I know, but I do try to get it right.

When Bill Hillgrove tells me, "You're always working." I take that as a compliment. Cope would approve of that. Cope was a working journalist who was always out to beat the competition. He cultivated behind-the-scene sources and insiders who provided him with stories.

Myron Cope, of course, died last Wednesday morning (February 27, 2008) at the age of 79. If you didn't know that you must have been hiding in a cave or given up newspapers, radio and TV for Lent.

His good friend, former Steelers' publicist Joe Gordon, had been with Cope most of his hospital stay. Gordon has been a loyal friend in a quiet manner. ("It ain't charity," Art Rooney Sr. liked to say, "if you talk about it.")

When Gordon was asked if he could believe the outpouring of news stories and public affection for his friend in the wake of Cope's death, Gordon said, "I'm a little surprised. If I knew it was going to be like this, I might have announced his death a day earlier so Myron could have enjoyed the response."

Another long-time friend and admirer, Beano Cook, couldn't get over the local and national response to Cope's passing. "If the President of the United States had died the same day," commented Cook, "his story would have appeared below the fold in the Pittsburgh newspapers!"

Cope and I were friends. We weren't best buddies or anything like that, so I don't mislead you or overstate our relationship. I was never someone he'd call to meet for a drink. But a lot of people knew I knew him better than most, and asked me how he was doing. I relied on Gordon to get updates. He was his best buddy.

I got to know Myron Cope better because of Beano Cook. Cook was the sports information director at Pitt when I went to school there in 1960. I had just graduated from Taylor Allderdice High School. Cope was an Allderdice and Pitt alumnus. He had been the sports editor of *The Pitt News*, the campus newspaper. Cook likes to boast that when he took the job at Pitt, the three writers covering the Pitt football team were Cope of the *Post-Gazette*, Roy McHugh of *The Pittsburgh Press* and George Kiseda of the *Pittsburgh Sun-Telegraph*. "There weren't three better writers covering one college football team in the country," claimed Cook. They were all great role models.

"How are we going to get the scores?"

I became the sports editor of *The Pitt News* as a sophomore and kept the position for two years. It was during the 1962 season, my second as sports editor of *The Pitt News* and my fifth and final year as the sports editor of *The Hazelwood Envoy*, that Cook asked me if I could drive Cope to and from the Pitt game at Navy. Cope had been the editor of *The Forward*, the Allderdice newspaper. I was not permitted to be on the staff because the sponsor, Miss Diantha Riddle, said I couldn't write for *The Hazelwood Envoy* at the same time. Like I was going to scoop *The Forward* on news stories. When I went to Pitt, there were several outstanding writers and editors on *The Pitt News* who went to Allderdice but were never on the school paper there. That was some solace. Take that, Diantha Riddle.

I had a new Karmann Ghia sports car. Don't ask me how I could afford such a fancy car back then? It had a Volkswagen engine and a sleek Italian-fashioned body. It was anthracite gray on the bottom and pearl white on the roof. I drove my mother and a niece to the World's Fair in New York in that Karmann Ghia.

We weren't far into our trip to Annapolis to see Pitt play Navy when Cope discovered one thing the Karmann Ghia didn't have. "You don't have a radio!" he blurted. "How are we going to get the scores?" Cope was carping about the absence of a radio most of the trip to Annapolis. And back. Cope could complain with the best of them. He could get ornery and cranky in a hurry.

We went out to a Red Bull Inn that evening in Annapolis. We were both single at the time. No one in Annapolis knew Myron Cope. This was before he became a radio personality in Pittsburgh and not too many people in Pittsburgh could have picked him out of a police lineup then either. He had the same voice, mind you, but no reputation in Annapolis or any other port on the East Coast.

As soon as we stepped inside the Red Bull Inn, Cope canvassed the joint and spotted two women sitting at the middle seats of the bar. I saw that there were about 35 men at the bar.

"Hey, look, there's two girlies over there!" Cope cries out.

"Yeah, and there's 35 men," I respond. "They're all better looking than you and me. We have no chance."

"Nah, let's go over and talk to them," Cope comes back.

There were two empty seats to the left of the two women. I took the seat farthest from them. Cope was close to one of them. It turned out they were sisters. Not nuns, mind you, but sisters. Cope said hello and introduced me to them. I concentrated on my glass of beer, and let Cope do all the talking. He must have been charming.

In about a half-hour the two women went to the rest room. Cope started stomping one of his feet on the floor, like Thumper in one of those animated Disney films. I learned later from a friend of his that Cope would stomp his foot when he got excited. They called him "Thumper." That name came from a pink-nosed rabbit that was a friend of "Bambi" in an animated Disney film that came out in 1942, the year I was born. Remember Thumper and Flower, the friendly skunk?

Getting back to the Red Bull Inn...

"I think they're going to go out with us," said Cope. "One of them knows a place where we can do some dancing."

Sure enough, the two women smiled and said we could go to this nightclub they knew in the neighborhood. Cope got the older sister and

I the younger one. Cope was quite the dancer and I always enjoyed dancing as well. Cope informed us that he had gone to dancing school when he was a kid. The school was in East Liberty and it was owned and operated by Gene Kelly's mother and his brother Fred. Yes, that Gene Kelly, the star of stage and screen, the star of "Singin' in the Rain."

Cope could see himself in that same role. You betcha.

"If I had stayed with that," Cope told me, "you never would have heard of Gene Kelly." There was nothing modest about Myron even then.

When we returned to Pittsburgh the next evening, we went directly to Dante's, a bar on Brownsville Road on the Brentwood-Whitehall border that was frequented regularly by members of the media and members of the Steelers. There will never be a set-up quite like it again.

The Steelers don't hang out with Steelers these days, let alone sportswriters and sportscasters. I started going to Dante's when I was 19. My brother, Dan, who was five years older, took me there. They thought I was older because I was the sports editor of *The Pitt News* and that had always been a position for seniors.

Bobby Layne and his buddy (and bodyguard) Ernie Stautner usually held court in the back room, and other Steelers such as Lou Cordileone, Myron Pottios, Gary Ballman, Tom "The Bomb" Tracy and others would be at the bar.

When Cope and I arrived at Dante's that night, he said hello to Danny Sartorio, the owner, and the guys at the bar. He turned to me and announced, "Bobby Layne's in the back. Let's go back there."

I declined. Layne could give a young writer a hard time. It was part of his personality. He gave a lot of people a bad time, but he was emboldened to do so because Stautner was at his side. Stautner was one of the toughest guys in the National Football League.

"You go drink with Bobby Layne," I told Cope. "I'm staying out here."

"Bobby Layne is the Leif Eriksson of pro football players," Cope came back. "And you're passing on this opportunity to be with him?"

"You go drink with Leif Eriksson," I told Cope. "I'm staying out here."

Cope shook his head, giving up on me, and retreated to the back room.

I remember going to Dante's one night with my brother Dan and our dad, also Dan O'Brien. I always looked after my dad and I told him to pace himself, that we were going to be there for the evening and we wanted to have a good time.

As soon as he sat down, he told the waitress, Helen Kaufman, to get him an Imperial and an Iron City. That was a shot and beer. The staple of the Pittsburgh working man. I abandoned by brother and dad for about an hour and went elsewhere in the room to socialize with some Steelers and sports guys.

Myron Cope called Bobby Layne "the Leif Eriksson of pro football."

Ernie Stautner served as Steelers' assistant in 1963–64.

Art Rooney presented Stautner for induction into the Pro Football Hall of Fame in Canton, Ohio in summer of 1969.

My brother comes over to me later, all heated up. "Ernie Stautner's picking on Dad," he said, "and we're not gonna put up with that!"

I grabbed my dad by the back of his coat, and pushed my brother toward the door with the other hand. "The hell we're not," I said. "Let's go; we're going home."

I remember a night when Cope crashed into a telegraph pole on the way home from Dante's and was taken to a local magistrate. Cope cursed the magistrate and even spat at him for good measure. They told that story for quite a while in Brentwood and Whitehall. Cope could be obstreperous when he was drinking. He had that Napoleon complex, a little guy who talked a big game.

"Our dear friend Myron Cope passed away today." — KQV's P.J. Maloney

Myron Cope was quite the showman. Cope became a successful free-lance writer and his work appeared in the best national magazines, such as *The Saturday Evening Post, True* and *Sports Illustrated.*

This memory and others connecting me with Cope came back in a rush as I reflected on our relationship after hearing of his death. I was writing when I heard the news that gray morning. That seemed right. P.J. Maloney, the morning host on KQV's all-news format, said he was saddened to pass along the news that Myron Cope had died earlier that day.

I knew it was coming, but it still stunned me. Maloney and Eric Hagman, KQV's sports reporter, then exchanged personal thoughts and stories about Cope. I called my wife Kathie at Allegheny General Hospital, where she is a social worker in the Cancer Center, and shared the news. She always got a kick out of Cope, and knew I'd be saddened by his passing.

I had been tipped off by a little birdie that Cope's condition had deteriorated. Two weeks earlier, when I was signing books at the Pittsburgh Mills in Frazer, Pennsylvania, not far from Tarentum, a woman walked up to my table and told me that Cope wasn't faring well at UPMC's Presbyterian Hospital.

She pointed to a little girl at her side and said, "Her mother is my best friend and she's a nurse at the hospital. She says the cancer has spread to his brain. She says his neck hurts him, and that it's sensitive to the touch. When the nurses try to apply anything there he bites at them. Maybe he doesn't know what he's doing. He's not at death's door, but he's getting closer."

Cope couldn't have done better than having Joe Gordon at his bedside even if Florence Nightingale were still around.

Our friend Gordon was always guarded in his comments about Cope's condition. I'd talk to him on the telephone from time to time during Cope's last stay and he'd say something like, "He's better today." Or, "He wasn't so good yesterday, but he's bounced back. He's a fighter." Or, "He's had a good stretch of a few days."

Cope was thought well enough to go to his residence at the Convenant of South Hills in Scott Township, and that's where he died. Cope had been doctoring on a regular basis for several years. "For him, it's like taking your car in for an oil and lube," Gordon said one day, laughing a little at his own glib line. I had written to Cope when he was in his apartment at The Covenant of South Hills, requesting an interview. He sent me a nice hand-written card, as he always did in response to any written correspondence, and said he was too busy, and not quite up to it, but that we could get together at a later date when he felt better. I still have the card, written in his hand, and I will keep it in my MYRON COPE file. When I flip through its contents, with many photos and clippings, a lot of good memories come rushing back.

I remember being with Cope at a press conference in Pittsburgh prior to Cassius Clay's fight with Charlie Powell, a former receiver with the Oakland Raiders, at the Civic Arena. Clay KOd Powell in the third round of that fight on January 24, 1963. Clay would change his name to Muhammad Ali in 1964 when he became a Muslim.

The press gathering was held on January 17, 1963 at the Sherwyn Hotel, now the main building for Point Park University. WWSW Radio had studios on the top floor where Joe Tucker conducted several sports news shows a day. The hotel was Clay's training quarters and he conducted workouts there and at the nearby YMCA. Bill Burns of KDKA-TV interviewed Clay each day and the young Clay would carry on, and entertain everyone with his poetry and boastful ways. Burns had never met a boxer with more moxie and showbiz.

It was Cassius Clay's 21st birthday and there was a cake with candles to celebrate the event. Cope had gone to Louisville, Clay's hometown, and Miami, where he trained and often fought, to interview him for a magazine story. The story would win a national writing award. Clay kept referring to Myron Cope that day at his party as "Mickey Rooney." It got a lot of laughs and Myron loved the attention.

Broadcaster Howard Cosell would later call Cope "the diminutive one." When Roy McHugh told Cosell that Cope had become a celebrity, Cosell, ever the acerbic one, snapped, "In Pittsburgh." Cope wrote a story on Cosell for *Sports Illustrated* that won a national award, and still appears in many "Best Sports Stories" collections. Cosell owed Cope more than his smart-ass comeback to McHugh, but that tells you something about the insecure Cosell as well. I got to know him well during my stay in New York, and he could be nice and he could be mean and petty. In the end, he was just mean and petty.

Clay loved Pittsburgh and made inquiries about buying a home in Mt. Lebanon. When the word got out about that some of his potential neighbors complained and he backed off and instead bought a home in Cherry Hill, New Jersey, just across from Philadelphia.

Beano Cook and I started a newspaper in 1963, my senior year at Pitt, called *Pittsburgh Weekly Sports*. Cope wrote a column for us for

41

$100 a week. That was more money than I was making for editing the newspaper. Cook knew Cope well, and he got to know Cosell well when he went to work in the publicity department of ABC Sports in New York. Cook knew all the top people in the sports media. Cook helped launch my career. He once proclaimed, "I made you." I have a letter from Cope refuting that claim. I was drafted into the Army at the end of 1964. I ended up at Fort Greely, Alaska — the Army's cold weather testing center — by 1966. Cope was a regular correspondent during my days in Alaska.

Last month, my wife Kathie asked me, once again, to clear out some of my files. As I was going through one file cabinet, I came across a folder marked WRITING. In it, I discovered all this correspondence I had generated with some of the nation's leading sportswriters while I was in Alaska. I was still writing and editing *Pittsburgh Weekly Sports* from Alaska, with the help of friends in the business back in Pittsburgh. I found about ten letters that Myron Cope had written to me in 1966. They were almost in pristine condition.

One can gain insight into the way Cope approached his work, and his thoughts about writing and about newspapers in those letters. I will treasure them. I took them with me when I went to Cope's funeral at the Slater Funeral Home in Green Tree last Friday. I shared them with some of his friends. He was never satisfied with his stories, that comes across loud and clear in his correspondence. Like Red Smith, the Pulitzer Prize-winning writer in New York, Cope sweated blood when he was at the typewriter. Cope, to the end, shunned the use of a computer. In more recent years, Cope said it was a chore to complete his wonderful memoir, *Double Yoi*. He'd been away from the writing game too long. With the help of a great editor and encourager in his close friend Roy McHugh, Cope completed the task. It was worth the effort. If you have not read it, get a copy and, as Cope might say, "You gotta sit down and read it!"

I felt honored to be among the 150 or so people who had been invited to the funeral service. Somehow those who were invited managed to keep it a secret. Otherwise, there would have been a mob scene with Myron Cope's adoring fans flocking to the scene. Some of them were diverted Downtown at the same hour at a memorial service to mark his passing. His fans were waving Terrible Towels in Myron's memory outside the City-County Building. I think of Cope when I'm watching sports on TV and the crowd is waving some kind of towel or cloth. It's Cope's contribution to sports.

Cope was good at writing letters. He answered all his mail when he had his radio show in Pittsburgh. He made every caller feel like he or she had done him the biggest favor in the world by calling him.

As I said, anyone paying attention should have learned a lot from Myron Cope. He was a little guy who became a giant in the world of sports. He found a way to live a dream life. Nobody had more fun. Pittsburgh was a better place because he passed our way. "I don't know anybody who got more out of life than Myron Cope," Stan Savran would tell the gathering at the 2008 Dapper Dan Sports Dinner & Auction.

Rabbi Alvin Berkun, the respected rabbi emeritus at Tree of Life Synagogue in Squirrel Hill, presided over the service at the William Slater II Funeral Home in Green Tree. He called Cope "a proud Jew."

He said, "Myron often said he wasn't a religious person, but he was religious because of the life he led." I thought the rabbi got that right. Myron Cope was Myron Sidney Kopelman when he was a student at Taylor Allderdice High School. But an editor at the *Post-Gazette* got him to change his name because he thought there were too many Jewish-sounding names among the paper's bylines at the time. But Myron made a point at times to let people know he was Jewish.

A friend of mine who is Jewish wanted to know all about the service. He said he had to smile when he saw a big photo across the front page of the *Pittsburgh Post-Gazette* showing Franco Harris and Andy Russell, the two celebrity pallbearers, wearing yarmulkes.

Cope went out with style and in the company of his closest friends and admirers. He was sorry he couldn't stay and have a toddy with them.

The author Jim O'Brien, as a 19-year-old sophomore sports editor of *The Pitt News*, stands on sideline with Myron Cope, who held the same position in his student days, at Pitt football camp at Allegheny College in Meadville in August, 1961. Cope was a senior at Pitt ten years earlier.

These Pirates were honored
to be chosen All-Stars

"You were picked by your peers."
— Dick Groat

July 12, 2006

O ne of the many benefits from this All-Star Week was to learn more about this city's rich baseball heritage. I had an opportunity to talk to three of Pittsburgh's most popular and enduring baseball stars before Tuesday's All-Star Game at PNC Park.

Frank Thomas, Bob Friend and Dick Groat all said they were "honored" to be chosen to play in the All-Star Game in their glory days. Their attitude contrasts greatly with some of today's outstanding players who would rather stay home.

These three men merited more attention and involvement in this week's All-Star activities than many that were in the spotlight.

"It was an honor because you were picked by your peers," said Groat. "It's a sham now the way they have turned it into a popularity contest with the fans voting. Ballot box stuffing is not only allowed, it's encouraged."

Thomas and Groat both grew up in Pittsburgh. Thomas lived near Magee Women's Hospital, where his father worked in the laundry service, not far from Forbes Field. Groat grew up in the eastern suburb of Swissvale. Friend was from West Lafayette, Indiana and was one of five members of his family to graduate from Purdue University there. He is still a Hoosier, but he's been a "Pittsburgh guy" for about 55 years.

Hold onto your box seats because Thomas turned 80 last month, and Friend and Groat are both 75. Thomas played in three All-Star Games, in 1954, 1958 and 1959. He was the Pirates' most productive home run hitter between Ralph Kiner and Willie Stargell, and was, indeed, the Pirates' star player in the mid-50s.

He remembers Leo Durocher, the manager of the Giants, telling him, "You belong in the All-Star Game." He remembers telling Willie Mays of the Giants, "You're the greatest baseball player I've ever seen."

When Thomas lived in Green Tree after he retired from baseball, he played slow-pitch softball for the Main Hotel team in Carnegie. They still talk about some of his prodigious home runs in that sandlot circuit. He and Friend and Groat still play golf in many local fund-raisers.

Friend and Groat have great memories of their All-Star experience as well. They were among eight players on the Pirates' 1960 World Championship team to be selected to play in the All-Star Game that year. There were two All-Star Games each summer from 1959 through

Bob Friend greets former teammate Frank Thomas at Western Chapter of Pennsylvania Hall of Fame dinner at Sheraton North in Warrendale.

Photos by Jim O'Brien

Ol' Buccos Nellie King, Bobby DelGreco and Dick Groat get together at sports dinner in downtown Pittsburgh.

1963, with proceeds from the extra game enhancing the players' pension fund.

Friend played in three All-Star Games and had a 2–1 pitching record. He was the first player from the Pirates to be the starting pitcher and that was in the 1956 game at Griffith Stadium in Washington, D.C. He struck out Mickey Mantle and Yogi Berra of the Yankees and Ted Williams of the Red Sox in a three-inning stint.

He struck out Williams with the bases loaded. He threw him an inside curve on a 3–2 count. Friend remembers Ed Bailey, a catcher with the Cincinnati Reds, coming out to the mound and telling him Williams would "be sitting on a fast ball," and suggested a low inside curve.

Friend followed Bailey's advice and struck out Williams. Fifteen years later, Friend was walking through an airport in Atlanta with his young son, Bobby Jr. He saw Williams approaching. He introduced himself. "I don't know if you remember me, but I'm Bob Friend of the Pirates."

Williams, who was regarded as one of the greatest hitters in the history of the game, looked Friend over and said, "I remember you. I never thought you'd curve me."

Groat played in four All-Star Games with the Pirates, and three with the St. Louis Cardinals. He was upset that Pirates' GM Joe Brown had traded him to the Cardinals. "In 1963, with the Cardinals, I drew more votes than any player at any position," recalled Groat. "The entire starting infield was from the Cardinals. Bill White at first, Julian Javier at second, me at short, and Ken Boyer at third. That gave me great satisfaction."

Groat had another story. "When I made the team in 1960, Mickey Vernon played and coached on that team. He was a great hitter in the American League before he came to the Pirates. He knew I had great admiration for Ted Williams.

"He made me promise that I would introduce myself to Ted Williams at the All-Star Game. When I spotted Williams at the batting cage before the game, I was too scared to approach him by myself, so I got my roomie Bob Skinner to go with me. Williams couldn't have been more obliging. He even missed a turn in the batting cage to talk to us. He knew more about our hitting styles than we did about him."

Groat also got to play with Stan Musial of Donora in his last season in the big leagues in 1963. Musial and Mays were in 24 All-Star Games and had many great achievements in those mid-summer contests. "Musial was a great player and an even greater person," said Groat. I once asked Ralph Kiner what kind of guy Musial was and Kiner said, "Like Frankie Gustine ... with a better batting average."

Now that the All-Star Game here is gone, and the World Cup is completed, Pittsburghers can get back to ignoring the Pirates and soccer at the same time. We can look forward to the U.S. Open Golf Tournament coming to Oakmont next summer.

46

Henry Aaron
Revisiting the classy
baseball hero in his Atlanta home

"I can't change my ways."

A much-publicized pursuit of an all-time home run record (755) by Barry Bonds has brought Henry Aaron back to the news front. I pulled a treasured magazine out of the middle of a stack of sports magazines in my office closet the other day that featured a profile of Henry Aaron on the cover—at bat for the Atlanta Braves. It was the July 1968 edition of *SPORT* magazine.

I had written a profile of Henry Aaron for *SPORT* that spring. It was my first cover story assignment by *SPORT*, and I was quite excited about that. Some sports writers I long admired had stories in that issue. I visited Aaron in his home in Cascade Park, a fashionable suburb in southwest Atlanta. He sat on a sofa in his living room and talked to me for several hours. There was a quiet dignity about him, even then.

His home was a ten-room colonial dwelling. He and his wife Barbara had four young children. The couple would later get divorced. They seemed happy when I was at their home.

Henry Aaron was known as a difficult interview. I have always prided myself on getting good stories from athletes regarded as difficult interviews, such as Bill Bradley, Wilt Chamberlain, Franco Harris, Joe Namath, Chuck Noll, Dave Parker, to name a few.

Aaron had been hurt by slings and arrows and it showed in his dark eyes. He carefully considered every word he spoke, and he spoke in low tones. He was thoughtful, and at times quite profound. Most of all, he was honest. It was obvious he didn't like to talk about himself.

I was 25 at the time and Aaron was 34. He had hit 481 home runs going into that 1968 season. I had been married less than a year to Kathleen Churchman. We were living in a two-bedroom apartment in Pittsburgh's East End. The Pennley Park Apartments were relatively new. One of our neighbors, two floors above us in an adjoining wing, was Roberto Clemente, the star performer for the Pittsburgh Pirates.

Aaron and Clemente were often compared. They were the two best rightfielders, respectively, in the National League. They succeeded Carl Furillo of the Brooklyn Dodgers in that respect. Stan Musial of Donora played left field and first base, but he also saw service in right field for the St. Louis Cardinals and was one of the best in the business.

The cover line for my piece was "HANK AARON: What It's Like To Be A Neglected Superstar." Like Clemente, he didn't get as much national attention in the media as Mickey Mantle and Willie Mays.

Aaron was aware of his own ability. Who knew then that before he was finished, Aaron would surpass the numbers of Mantle and Mays and even the great Babe Ruth?

"I can't change my ways," Aaron told me, almost apologetically. "I play in my own natural way. I know I'm not flashy. I don't try to be. I have good clothes, and I dress well, but not flashy. I want to be remembered as just plain Henry Aaron."

He always referred to himself, and still does, as Henry Aaron, not Hank Aaron.

I learned a lesson in doing this profile of Henry Aaron that has stayed with me the rest of my life, like Bill Mazeroski's home run to win the 1960 World Series.

Before I turned in my manuscript, I asked Roy McHugh, then the sports editor of *The Pittsburgh Press*, to check it over. Myron Cope had the highest regard for Roy McHugh's writing and editing skills, and I followed Cope's cue in having McHugh give my manuscripts a look.

"Show me that you were there, that you were in his home," McHugh advised me. "Set the scene. Let the reader know you were there."

Ever since, I have set the scene for every magazine story I've written. You don't have to be a playwright to employ that technique.

I've been fortunate in my lifetime to spend time in the homes of some of the most famous home run hitters in baseball history. I twice visited the home of Bill Mazeroski out near Greensburg. He and Bobby Thomson of the New York Giants hit two of the most famous home runs ever. I once interviewed Thomson ("The Shot Heard Round the World!") in the company of Mazeroski at an autograph signing session at Robert Morris University.

While traveling with the New York Yankees in the mid-80s, I visited the boyhood home of Babe Ruth in Baltimore. I once had too many drinks in the company of Babe Ruth's wife, Claire, after an Old Timers' Baseball Game at Yankee Stadium. Lou Gehrig's wife, a more stoic sort, shared the same table. I've been lucky that way.

When I visited the home of Bill Mazeroski, he and his wife Milene and their dog Muttley were sitting on the porch waiting for me. It seems right somehow that Maz had a dog named Muttley. It was a cold, dank day and they wore sweaters. They said they didn't want me to drive by and miss their home on a back road near a farm. So they were keeping an eye out for me. That memory tells you much about the Mazeroskis. I can't imagine too many modern day players doing that.

I'll be 65 later this month and Aaron is 73. I can still see him as he was at 34. "The way I see it," said Aaron, when asked why he wasn't more outspoken, "my responsibility lies on the field. It doesn't go to speaking out in newspapers. My record speaks for itself. I'll never change."

That's probably why he doesn't talk much about Barry Bonds, who'll be opposing the Pirates this weekend in San Francisco and in a make-up doubleheader here in Pittsburgh this Sunday. Talking has never been Henry Aaron's strong suit. "I'm a good listener," he told me.

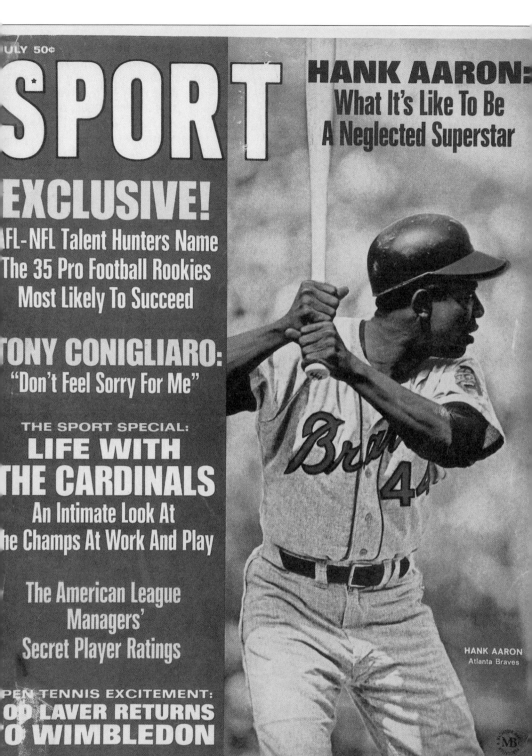

JULY 50¢

SPORT

HANK AARON:
What It's Like To Be A Neglected Superstar

EXCLUSIVE!
AFL-NFL Talent Hunters Name The 35 Pro Football Rookies Most Likely To Succeed

TONY CONIGLIARO:
"Don't Feel Sorry For Me"

THE SPORT SPECIAL:
LIFE WITH THE CARDINALS
An Intimate Look At The Champs At Work And Play

The American League Managers' Secret Player Ratings

OPEN TENNIS EXCITEMENT:
ROD LAVER RETURNS TO WIMBLEDON

HANK AARON
Atlanta Braves

In 1967, Aaron was angered at an Atlanta luncheon when Roberto Clemente was introduced as the man who beat out Aaron for the right field job in the All-Star Game. "I got more votes than Clemente," said Aaron. "I played left field because Walter Alston (the National League manager) asked me to."

The next day, Aaron hit two two-run homers and two singles in four at-bats against the Pirates. He also threw out Clemente when the Pirates' star tried to take third on a hit to right. The competition between Clemente and Aaron was obvious.

No one could foresee that Clemente's career would be tragically shortened when he was killed in an airplane crash in his native Puerto Rico on New Year's Eve, the last day of 1972. Clemente would have been 73 years old during the 2007 season.

Aaron played 23 years to Clemente's 17. Aaron's lifetime batting average was .305 compared to Clemente's .317. Aaron had 3,771 hits to Clemente's 3,000. Aaron had 755 home runs to Clemente's 240. Aaron had 98 triples to Clemente's 166. Aaron had 240 stolen bases to Clemente's 83.

"If I had played in New York," Aaron told me that day at his Atlanta home, "I believe I would have made $2 million (overall). But money isn't everything. What did it do for Roger Maris? It kinda messed up his life. I'm kinda reserved, you know. I'm a hard person to get close to. I can ride a plane from here to Los Angeles and not talk to anyone. I come home, and maybe I won't say anything to my wife for a while, and she might think I'm mad at her. But I've never been a big talker, and maybe if I had all them newspapermen and TV guys around me all the time, I would have probably got perturbed and said some things I'd later regret.

"I just want to play the game. That's what I'm focused on, what I'm doing on the field. I give it my all when I'm out there, and I do it every day, every year. It works for me."

Henry Aaron was a big hit with Braves' teammates Warren Spahn and Chuck Tanner.

She saw Babe Ruth
hit his last three home runs here

I saw Kathryn Groninger-Rowsick standing with the aid of a walker in the narthex at Westminster Presbyterian Church on Saturday, January 5, 2008 prior to a memorial service in honor of Betty Casey Prince, the wife of former Pirates' broadcasting legend Bob Prince. I went over and said hello, and reminded her of our previous meeting at South Hills Village four years earlier. I knew she couldn't see that well, so I wasn't sure she could actually see me or remember me. She seemed pleased that I remembered her. She and Mrs. Prince got to know each other when they were living at Friendship Village, a retirement and assisted-care residence in Upper St. Clair.

May 26, 2004

A beautiful blue-eyed woman walked up to me at Waldenbooks at South Hills Village where I was signing my books. "So you're a sports author," she said. "So how much do you know about Babe Ruth?"

"More than the average bear," I replied. "And I know enough to know you were at Forbes Field the day he hit the three home runs."

Her soft blue eyes blinked in response. "How did you know that?" she inquired.

"Because no one in Pittsburgh asks me about Babe Ruth unless they want to talk about that feat at Forbes Field," I said.

That's how I met Kathryn Groninger-Rowsick a few weeks ago, and that's why I like to do so many signings. I am always meeting interesting people who have interesting stories or photos to share.

This woman was using a walker and, at times, a cane to get around. She was dressed very well, that rare woman who actually gets dressed up to go shopping these days. She had applied her makeup with care, and was wearing attractive earrings. Her hair had been styled. She blushed when I told her how nice she looked.

She helped herself to a seat next to me — I had failed to offer her the seat — so she could tell me her story. Yes, she was at Forbes Field in Oakland on Saturday, May 25, 1935. That's the day that Babe Ruth, playing for the Boston Braves, on the last Sunday of his career, came to bat four times against the Pirates and hit a single and three home runs.

The last home run — the last one of his career, No. 714 — flew over the roof of the double-decked grandstands in right field. Pirates pitcher Guy Bush said years later, "I never saw a ball hit so hard before or since."

Mace Brown, a rookie pitcher for the Pirates, was surprised when Ruth jogged to the Pirates bench after that last home run, and sat down next to him. "Whew, that last one felt good," Ruth told Brown. I visited Mace Brown three times in his home in Greensboro, N.C. and he told me that story on more than one occasion. Then Ruth retired for the rest of the game, exiting the ballpark through the Pirates' dugout and locker room. The following week, he retired as a player. He was simply worn out.

When I told my wife about meeting Mace Brown, she told me that members of his family often called her father "Mace". She never knew why. She asked her dad about that and he said he got the name when he was pitching in sandlot games when Mace Brown was with the Bucs.

Ruth's first home run that day went into the lower deck in right field, his second sailed into the upper deck. His third was the first one ever to be hit over the right field stands. It was only the second time Ruth had hit three home runs in a single game. What a way to go out!

Kathryn Groninger-Rowswick, who is 83, can prove she was there. She had her picture taken with Babe Ruth that day. She has a copy of that photo, and so do her three grandsons. She had previously lived in Whitehall and then Bethel Park. She now lives at Friendship Village, a residence for seniors in Upper St. Clair. One of her long-time friends, Betty Prince, also lives there. The wife of the late Pirates' broadcaster, Bob Prince, Betty suffered a stroke a week after I spoke to Kathryn, and she is recovering at Friendship Village. Kathryn said she has known Betty since 1960, the year the Pirates won the World Series.

That's when Bill Mazeroski hit the only home run at Forbes Field that rivals Ruth's heroics there.

"I was Kathryn Breitweiser back in 1935," said my new sidekick at Waldenbooks. "I was working in the circulation department of the old *Sun-Telegraph* newspaper. Our building was where the U.S. Steel Tower is now. We had a contest for newsboys to sell new subscriptions and one of their rewards was to get to go to a Pirates game at Forbes Field. My boss, John L. Boyle, needed some chaperones and asked me to do that. I agreed to accompany the newsboys along with some other women in our office. Sally Moore and Armelia Hohman went with us. That's why I was there. I even had my picture taken with Babe Ruth at home plate.

"We had quite a few carriers and they all got baseballs given to them. Can you imagine what that must have been like?"

One just never knows what they're going to witness on any particular day at the ballpark. I went to the Pirates' game last Sunday at PNC Park. It was a perfect sunny day for a ball game. The Pirates had won seven out of their last ten games, yet they drew fewer than 15,000. It was a wonderful baseball game, even though the Pirates lost by 2–1. It came down to the final out.

The week before I saw a few minutes of Randy Johnson's perfect game for the Arizona Diamondbacks against the Atlanta Braves. I turned to another TV show because I had no idea Johnson was going to retire 27 out of 27 batters. I wish I had watched the whole game.

Kathryn Groninger-Rowswick watched Babe Ruth's last game at Forbes Field, which is still one of the most remarkable performances in all of baseball history. "He was a perfect gentleman," she recalled. "He

Babe Ruth of Boston Braves is flanked by Charlie Dressen of Cincinnati Reds and Bill McKecknie of the Braves.

Boston Braves' Babe Ruth hits a home run against the Brooklyn Dodgers in an 8-1 setback on April 21, 1935, a few weeks before his finale at Forbes Field.

tipped his cap, and he said, 'It's nice to meet you, Ma'am.' I'll always remember that.

"One of our newscarriers was a black young man. Babe Ruth rubbed the boy's head because he thought it would bring him good luck. That's the way people thought in those days. You wouldn't do that today. Then again, considering what Babe Ruth did that day, maybe it worked.

"My father was a big sports fan and he took us to the games, and I've always been a big fan. Your memory starts to go when you get to be my age. I'm legally blind. But I can still see Babe Ruth. It's great when your memory goes back to things that were wonderful."

Babe Ruth of New York Yankees with another power hitter, Jimmie Foxx of the Philadelphia Athletics, before American League contest at Yankee Stadium.

Bruno Sammartino meets Johnny Majors

Sports stars shine at a Christmas party

"Art Rooney offered me a tryout with the Steelers."
—Bruno Sammartino

December 19, 2007

I was sitting across a kitchen table from two of the most popular sports personalities in Pittsburgh history. Bruno Sammartino and Johnny Majors sat side by side, but did not know, at first, each other's identity. I was not aware that they had never met before.

Sammartino was once the world's heavyweight wrestling champion for an 11-year reign, and Majors was a star tailback at Tennessee and turned Pitt's football program around in the '70s and directed the Panthers to the national collegiate football championship in 1976.

Both are now 72. They were among the invited guests at Armand Dellovade's annual Christmas party in Lawrence, a little Washington County community that abuts Peters Township and Upper St. Clair and Bridgeville. It may be the best Christmas party in the Pittsburgh area.

Dellovade's palatial home is lit up like Palisades Park, and there's always an eclectic gathering of his good friends, many from the sports world. Dellovade is so generous when it comes to looking after his pals.

Sammartino was holding court at the kitchen table, telling one story after another. He has always been an engaging guy, well-read with good taste in music and culture, yet humble to a fault. He said he still works out at his North Hills home each morning for an hour-and-a-half to two hours.

When Majors joined the table with his wife, Mary Lynn, he sat silently for awhile, eating some seafood. When I mentioned that Johnny Majors was also a great storyteller, Sammartino said, "You know, I never met Coach Majors."

Majors smiled and extended a hand. "Well, you're meeting him now," he said to Sammartino. Then the two exchanged compliments, saying how much they admired the other. It was a special scene.

This was the day that the Heisman Trophy winner for the 2007 season was announced—Florida's sophomore quarterback Tim Tebow took home the famous trophy—and it brought to mind that Tony Dorsett had won the award while leading Pitt to the national title in 1976.

Many football fans don't realize that Majors was runner-up to Paul Hornung of Notre Dame in the 1956 balloting. Hornung was the quarterback for the Fighting Irish and accomplished the feat even though the team had a 2–8 record. Tommy McDonald of Oklahoma and Jim Brown of Syracuse trailed Majors in the voting.

Sammartino had said earlier that, after all his years in Pittsburgh, he had never met Bill Mazeroski, the star of the Pirates' 1960 World Series victory. "I met Roberto Clemente," he said, "and I met Arnie Palmer."

Sammartino and his wife Carol flanked their son Danny at the table. Danny is a hair stylist at a downtown salon. Bruno told stories about how he and his mother had to flee to the mountains in Italy when the Nazis took over their town. They ate snow and anything they could scrounge up to stay alive. He was a frail child and nearly died. The family immigrated to America from Abruzzi in 1951 and settled in Oakland, near the home on Parkview Avenue where Danny Marino would grow up.

"I played a little football at Schenley High, but I was mostly into weightlifting at the YMHA on the Pitt campus," recalled Sammartino.

I bump into many Pittsburghers who boast that they used to work out in the same gym as Bruno did in his boyhood.

"Art Rooney offered me a tryout with the Steelers," said Sammartino. "I asked him how much money I could make. He said about $6,500. A wrestling promoter came after me at the same time, and told me I could make $35,000 for starters. I was a dumb kid from Italy, but I knew that was a better opportunity."

Sammartino turned pro as a wrestler in 1959. He went on to worldwide fame and popularity. When I worked in New York in the 1970s, Sammartino had the distinction of attracting more sell-out crowds to Madison Square Garden than any other performer. They used to schedule his outings on the same day that welfare checks went out in New York. He not only packed the Garden (18,000 plus), but also the Felt Forum below where several thousand would watch the wrestling competition on closed-circuit TV.

Sammartino made more money than any Pittsburgh-based athlete in his day, drawing over $100,000 in the late '60s, over $200,000 in the mid-70s, and as much as $300,000 in the late '70s. He was known to more people around the world than Terry Bradshaw, Willie Stargell, Joe Greene, Dave Parker, or even Arnold Palmer. He owned a Rolls Royce in 1971, long before any other local athlete had such a luxury automobile.

He said there were weeks when he wrestled five or six nights. "We wrestled in those boxing rings and they didn't have much padding," he related. "When you were body-slammed it took a toll on your body, believe me. But I never took so much as an aspirin."

That's why Sammartino is so critical of today's wrestling scene where steroids are used more commonly than in baseball, where's there been so much controversy over the issue, and where it's much more violent. "It's become a real sham," he said. "I want nothing to do with it."

Two of Pittsburgh's most popular sports idols, Bruno Sammartino and Bill Mazeroski, meet for the first time at 2008 Dapper Dan Dinner & Sports Auction at David L. Lawrence Convention Center on April 1.

Former Pitt football coaches Foge Fazio and Johnny Majors admired mural at Heinz Field showing 1976 Heisman Trophy winner Tony Dorsett when street was named after him near sports venues on North Side.

I was mesmerized by Sammartino's stories. He remains one of the most familiar sports and entertainment celebrities in the city. He is always a popular attraction on the dais at the Dapper Dan Dinner & Sports Auction. I have always been impressed with his humble nature and his honest storytelling. I can remember seeing him on Studio Wrestling with "Chilly Billy" Cardille doing the ringside announcing, or seeing him wrestle at what was then the Civic Arena. He was a big draw there, too. Izzy Modell would be the referee for the bout.

When I was working in New York, I went to interview Sammartino one night when he was wrestling at Nassau Coliseum. When I was in the locker room beforehand, he introduced me to "Gorilla" Monsoon, Andre the Giant, "Haystack" Calhoun and some other pro wrestlers. Wrestling aficionados will know that was quite a grapplers' lineup.

I sat at the ringside press table as I would if I were covering a boxing match. There was so one else sitting at ringside for this wrestling show. No one really covers a pro wrestling match. During his match, Sammartino dropped his opponent onto the table in front of me. I think he wanted to make sure I was paying attention. Sammartino smiled at me when I looked up to him in the ring. "How's that, Jimmy?" he bellowed. These thoughts were running through my mind as I sipped a cold drink at Armand Dellovade's party.

"Aren't you going to get something to eat?" my wife Kathie inquired after a half-hour at the kitchen table. I didn't want to move. I was enjoying the company I was keeping. It brought to mind a scene at 5410 Sunnyside Street.

I was sitting at the kitchen table in my boyhood home in Hazelwood. I was probably ten years old at the time. I was helping my brother Dan deliver the *Post-Gazette* each morning, six days a week. I was reading the sports section. I was fascinated by newspapers and magazines. I had asked my mother to buy me a toy printing press when I was eight years old as we were Christmas shopping. We bought the printing press at Murphy's Five & Ten Store.

Al Abrams, the sports editor of the morning daily, wrote a column all six days. He mentioned sports figures such as Stan "The Man" Musial, Jim Finks, Ralph Kiner, Billy Conn, Fritzie Zivic and all kinds of characters—he called them Dapper Dans and Dapper Dollies—he met at different venues around town. I recall the likes of Archie "Tex" Litman, Count Phil Petrulli and Lou Mangieri, "the Japanese Ambassador" and "Pittsburgh Phil" Gefsky. Abrams visited places in Florida and Arizona and New York and Chicago, and wrote about the sports stars he met.

It seemed like a good gig. As I looked about the rooms at Armand Dellovade's party, and saw former Pitt coach Foge Fazio, and former Pitt football players such as John Pelusi and Dave Jancisin who had played for Majors, and Jon Botula and Foge Fazio who had played for John Michelosen, and how they had all gone on to become big success

Regards
Billy Conn   Ralph Kiner

58

stories in the Pittsburgh business world, I knew that Al Abrams had sent me in the right direction.

This is, indeed, a good gig.

P.S. I had an opportunity at the 2008 Dapper Dan Dinner & Sports Auction, held at the David L. Lawrence Convention Center on Tuesday, April 1, to introduce Bruno Sammartino to Bill and Miline Mazeroski. I took a picture of Bruno and Maz together for the first time for this book.

Jim O'Brien

Franco, Rocky and Andy
Reflect on their glory days

*L*et's observe a moment of silence in memory of Myron Cope.
Picture him as you remember him. Have him saying something
that sticks in your mind, or have him singing his annual holiday
season song. Do your best imitation of his distinctive voice. Are you smiling? You betcha!

I was sitting at a round table with the best of company. On my
right was Franco Harris with his wife Dana. To their right were Rocky
Bleier and his wife Janet. Across from me were Andy Russell and his
wife Cindy. Think about that Steelers' trifecta. They will always be
hailed as gridiron giants by Pittsburgh fans. Franco, Rocky and Andy.
Any self-respecting Steelers' fan doesn't need their last names to know
these men. They remain three of the most popular Pittsburgh Steelers
of all time. I recognize that. They have stood the test of time. They have
made significant contributions to our community. They still make us
proud. As I sat there, talking with them, swapping stories, reminiscing,
it struck me how a Steelers' fan might feel to be sitting in my seat. I
always feel that way when I am in the company of an admired sports
star, whether it's Arnold Palmer, Bill Mazeroski, Mario Lemieux, Bill
Dudley, Joe Greene or Mel Blount. And I didn't have to pay a license fee
for my seat. It wasn't business as usual.

This was at a bereavement luncheon on Feb. 29, 2008, that followed a private funeral service to say goodbye to a dear friend and
colleague, Myron Cope. We were in a banquet room on the eighth floor
of the Best Western Hotel in Green Tree. It was about two miles away
from the William Slater II Funeral Home where a funeral service had
been held two hours earlier for Myron Cope, the Steelers' celebrated
broadcast analyst and color man. His son, Danny, 40, and his daughter,
Elizabeth, 38, were seated at a table in the middle of the large room.

I hadn't seen Danny since he was a toddler. He sat in silence the
entire luncheon. That's been his life. His father was known for his voice,
and Danny doesn't talk. He was in the restroom when I went there and
when he came out a woman was waiting for him and helped him fix
his pants properly. I'd seen Liz from time to time. She is an attractive
young woman, but she's been challenged to find herself and establish
her own identity. She told me she'd like to do some writing.

A month later, she would appear, along with her brother, on a
TV interview on WPXI-TV with Peggy Finnegan. It was the first time
Danny had appeared on television. "He's the man behind the Terrible
Towel," allowed Liz. "I wanted people to see who inspired that symbol
that represents so much more than the Steelers or sports in this
town."

Nearly 40 per cent of all retired football players
have degenerative arthritis.
—According to survey by
NFL Players Association

I wondered what Myron would think about all this. Some of his friends questioned the decision. The television station had promoted the appearance to great extent. It was an exclusive. Peggy Finegan was sensitive to the fact that Danny had never appeared on television when his father was alive, and asked Liz, "Why now?"

She spoke of her father's deep interest in his children and how much she was going to miss her Daddy. There was no doubt that Myron Cope cared deeply about his family, to hear Liz speak with such enthusiasm about him and their special relationship.

Cope used to upset many of his female listeners the way he spoke of them, often referring to them as "girlies."

I remember sitting with Liz and her mother, Mildred Cope, at a YMCA Scholar-Athlete Dinner at the Hilton years earlier. Myron was being honored as the Man of the Year. When he was speaking, he pointed to Mildred and said, "She's from the old school where women are mentioned in the newspaper on three occasions: when they're born, when they get married, and when they die."

Mildred just wagged her head. She'd heard it before. Anyone who knew her knew she didn't agree with Myron on that note. Like me, he was lucky to have a wife who looked after him. When she died, I remember the sign at the doorway of the funeral home read: MRS. MYRON COPE. Friends of hers, Cynthia Wagar and Audrey Reichblum, told me that's the way Mildred would have wanted it. I wonder about that.

Myron's three sisters, all less than five feet tall, were at the same table as Liz and Danny at the bereavement luncheon. I never knew he had three sisters. I had a chance to talk to Myron's sisters and tell them what a good mentor and model Myron was for anyone who was a writer or journalist. I was told Myron took good care of his sisters.

The last time I had seen Cope was a year earlier when he made a surprise appearance to pay tribute to Steelers' owner Dan Rooney at the Dapper Dan Sports Dinner at the Convention Center. I recalled that I was stunned by Cope's physical appearance, how frail and weak he looked. I was impressed that Andy Russell got out of his seat and assisted Cope in crossing the platform when Russell recognized that Cope was having some difficulty. The lighting was poor and Myron was walking unsteadily with the aid of a cane. His voice was strained and he had trouble expressing his thoughts. I spoke to him as he was leaving and wished him well. He smiled. It was the last time I saw him.

Danny Cope was always thought to suffer from autism, and Myron raised much money through the years for the Pittsburgh Chapter of Autism Society of America, only to learn later that Danny had suffered brain damage at birth and was not autistic as originally diagnosed. Danny lived at the Allegheny Valley Complex in Robinson Township that cared for youngsters and adults with mental and physical challenges. I first saw Danny when he was an infant in a playpen and Myron and his wife, Mildred, were living in Scott Township. They had suffered the loss of an infant daughter early in their marriage.

Myron Cope had succeeded Bob Prince as the prime fund-raiser for Allegheny Valley School, turning over the profits from the sale of the Terrible Towel to the school. Rege Chaump, the president and CEO,often pays tribute to Cope's contribution to the Allegheny Valley School system. Ironically enough, Cope suffered from the same ailment as the Pirates' esteemed broadcaster, dealing with throat and neck cancer in recent years. The cancer had spread to his brain, the same affliction that caused the death of Mayor Bob O'Connor two years earlier. Cope succumbed in the end to respiratory problems resulting from the effects of earlier surgery on his throat. A doctor had accidentally nicked his vocal chords on one of the early operations and it resulted in a lawsuit and a suspension of the doctor's privileges in the hospital He had botched it, you betcha.

Franco and Andy had been among the six pallbearers at the funeral. They had accompanied Myron to the Chartiers Cemetery for the burial. They had been wearing dark blue yarmulkes at the service, but had put them away. Franco's yarmulke had sat up high on his head. Cope's casket — in the Jewish tradition — was closed. It had been draped with several Terrible Towels and a Steelers' jacket. I spotted several former Steelers at the service. It was a private service and there were only about 150 people present to offer their respects. I saw Mike Wagner, Mel Blount, Randy Grossman, Lynn Swann, Tunch Ilkin and Craig Wolfley at the service. I saw media stalwarts Stan Savran, Bob Smizik, Roy McHugh, Sally Wiggin and Gerry Dulac.

Dan Rooney and his wife, Pat, were present, along with Art Rooney II and his wife Greta. Art Rooney Jr. was across the aisle from where I was sitting with my friend Bill Priatko, who had played football at Pitt and with the Steelers and was a pen pal of Myron's. They both had a son with a disability. Mary Regan and Joan Regan were across the aisle. Pat Rooney is their sister. Mary had been the secretary for Art Rooney Sr. for over 40 years. Bill Nunn, one of the team's most valuable scouts, was nearby. There were many people who had worked with Myron during his WTAE Radio days, including John Conomikes, an executive with the Hearst Corporation, who had supported the idea of having Myron Cope doing commentaries and such on the radio, despite having a raspy voice that took some getting used to, and was certainly different from most radio broadcasters.

A friend, Frank Haller, was one of the pallbearers. Haller had been a creative writer in the advertising game in Pittsburgh when I first met him. He had written a column for the newspaper, *Pittsburgh Weekly Sports*, that Beano Cook and I started in 1963. Haller had been a neighbor of Cope when Cope was first living in Scott Township.

Cope had come back to the neighborhood in recent years when he moved into The Covenant of South Hills, where he had assisted care in his last months. Haller had driven Myron to many of his doctors' appointments and other meetings on his busy calendar. Haller also had a son who was mentally challenged so he and Myron had a common bond from the beginning of their special relationship. Haller helped him and Foge Fazio coordinate their annual golf outing to raise funds for the local chapter of the Autism Society. Haller and Fazio continued the fund-raiser after Cope's death in 2008.

Former ad exec Frank Haller has his copy of *Always a Steeler* signed by 7-time Pro Bowl linebacker Andy Russell at booksigning party at Atria's Restaurant & Tavern in Mt. Lebanon.

Photos by Jim O'Brien

Andy Russell enjoys a good laugh with his former coach, Chuck Noll, and insurance broker Chuck Puskar at Russell's celebrity golf outing at The Club at Nevillewood.

Cope had been involved in a fender-bender on the South Hills side of the Fort Pitt Tunnels that led to his last driving suspension. I was driving into the city that day, and saw some cars in a grassy strip between the merging lanes. I thought I saw Cope standing in the midst of the mess — looking like General Custer at Little Big Horn — as I shot by. I was running late for a doctor's appointment. He looked a little frazzled and bewildered. He'd been taking medication for his back ailments at the time, and he didn't have feeling in his feet. He didn't press the brake pedal hard enough and that caused him to bang into the car in front of him.

I called Joe Gordon later to find out if that had been Cope, indeed, that I thought I saw, and Gordon told me it was our buddy. He said he was okay. Cope wasn't perfect, but no one enjoyed life more than he did. And he made it more fun for the rest of us. I think everyone who was at his funeral felt special. They were all going to miss Myron.

"How do you explain Myron Cope to anyone?" — Franco Harris

Myron's close friend, Joe Gordon, the former public relations director of the Steelers, had made all the arrangements for the funeral. And he did this over the telephone from Florida, where he was wintering with his wife, Babe. If Gordon missed anyone, forgive him the oversight. Gordon was good at seeing that things were done right. That's why he was respected and regarded as the best p.r. man in the National Football League during the glory days of the '70s. I remembered that he had looked after arrangements in a similar manner when Mike Webster died of a heart attack. Franco had offered one of the eulogies at the funeral service. He drew some smiles when he asked those in attendance, "How do you explain Myron Cope to anyone?"

It was Cope, after all, who took a cue from one of his faithful callers on his WTAE Radio talk show and referred to Franco's game-winning heroics in the 1972 AFC playoff game with the Oakland Raiders as "the Immaculate Reception." Cope was reluctant to do so at first lest he offend his Catholic listeners. One of them told him it would be okay and that was good enough for Cope. And it wasn't Bishop Wuerl.

This memory prompted Franco to say, "From my rookie season on, Myron and I were joined at the hip. Well, let's say, hip and shoulder."

Franco's observation lightened up the mood of the room.

It was a reference to Myron's diminutive size. But Franco always knew that Myron was a giant in his own game, and that he was nearly as much a part of the Steelers' story as the Rooneys.

Art Rooney II, the team president and the grandson of Art Rooney Sr., said that Myron made football more fun. He didn't always take it as seriously as some of the Steelers' hierarchy did. "He helped keep things in perspective," related Rooney. He credited Cope for creating the kind of incredible following for the team that became known as the Steeler Nation.

"You're always working."

Sitting with Franco, Rocky and Andy was a special way to spend an otherwise difficult morning. A heavy snowstorm had hit Pittsburgh just before the funeral service got underway and it made traveling a challenge for everyone in attendance. Some thought it was Myron's final joke on everyone, or that it was simply Steelers' weather and appropriate for the occasion.

There had been a tribute to Myron in midtown at noontime, with hundreds of fans waving their Terrible Towels in front of the City-County Building with Mayor Luke Ravenstahl and County Executive Dan Onorato presiding over the gathering. Dan Rooney had been delayed getting to the funeral service because he attended the downtown event and because traffic had been slowed by the snowstorm.

It's been too many years since Franco, Rocky and Andy starred for the Steelers. There is gray in the hair that remains on their heads. Once they were reluctant to examine their lives and offer commentary about what they were doing on the football field. Now they need to know more about just what that experience was all about.

Now they are asking most of the questions. Franco was an especially difficult interview during his playing days. He had a dressing stall in the far corner of the team's locker room at Three Rivers Stadium, and he was there by choice. Whenever I'd come over to talk to him, notebook and pen in hand, he'd smile and wag his head. Like why do you insist on torturing me with your questions? You'd have thought I was bringing him a dose of castor oil to swallow. He'd talk, but in short sentences, most of which began, "You know." I think Franco was the first Pittsburgher to pepper his thoughts with "you know" pauses and it became fashionable. I'd ask him, for example, about his feelings about passing Joe "The Jet" Perry of the 49ers in the career rushing stats and he'd say something like, "I hear he was a great one, you know, I gotta read up on him. If it happens it happens. I'll reflect on those sort of things when I'm old and retired."

He was always pleasant, mind you. He just didn't like to talk about himself. He was somewhat shy in that respect. He never wanted anyone to write a book about him. Rocky and Andy were always more comfortable in a crowd, masking their insecurities perhaps with great grins and firm handshakes, and familiar bromides. They had their own hang-ups, I have since learned. Franco didn't feel right comparing himself to Jim Brown or Joe Perry or O.J. Simpson, that's all.

Years later, sometimes I'd be signing books at Ross Park Mall and Franco Harris would happen by. He'd stop by, covertly, poking his handsome head out from the wall to where I could see him, then smile and extend a hand, and put a finger to his lips so I wouldn't identify him to anyone around me. He just wanted to say hello. He didn't want any fuss. But he didn't want to pass without a word either.

> *"I really believe the game is the important thing. That should be our principal concern. We're in the football business."*
> **—Dan Rooney, Chairman of the Board Pittsburgh Steelers**

When I was covering the Steelers in the early '80s for *The Pittsburgh Press*, I was trying to recruit some players to appear at a father-son sports dinner at The Press Club downtown. Franco came into Joe Gordon's office one day and spotted me. "Jim, I will come to your dinner," he said. "I don't want to eat. I'll be there at 7 and stay for an hour and sign anything anyone wants me to sign. Is that okay?"

It was just peachy, as Myron might say. There were 40 Pittsburgh-based sports celebrities who came that evening, but none of them was as big a hit as Franco Harris. He arrived on schedule and departed exactly an hour later. He never stopped signing autographs — or smiling that bemused smile of his — the entire time he was there. That hour was what his friend Rocky Bleier calls "Franco's time."

I've gotten to know Franco better and on a more personal level in the past five years. Harris chaired a "championship committee" that I served on to establish a sports museum at the John Heinz History Center in The Strip. He always came to the meetings with a prepared agenda and got things accomplished. He was impressive. Gordon was on that committee as well. Since then Franco has agreed to serve on a panel overseeing the "Pittsburgh Promise" scholarship program for students in inner-city public schools. He appeared at many of the commencement exercises at city high schools in June 2008.

I usually took advantage of Franco's presence by pulling out a notebook and pen, or to take a picture of him with my camera. He'd just grin. "Jim, you're always working," he'd say, scolding me in his own way. "Is this going to be in your next book?"

Franco Harris had come a long way from Mt. Holly, New Jersey and the Fort Dix military installation nearby where he once lived. He had confessed to Rocky Bleier that he'd been so fortunate for what his football career had provided him. He told Rocky that his dad had been a career military man, and that's all he knew. He thought that some-day he'd be a soldier too. He had no idea he'd be doing that soldiering for the Pittsburgh Steelers. I remember the first time I ever heard of Franco Harris. The Pitt football coach, Dave Hart, was telling me that he'd just missed out on landing this kid from Mt. Holly, New Jersey, who was instead going to Penn State. I thought he said his name was Frank O'Harris. Now Franco, Rocky and Andy were all more comfortable with themselves and their thoughts. They were more willing to share their stories, talk about their accomplishments, and ask about things they weren't sure about. What amazing careers they had all enjoyed. They knew I would be selective about what I would write. I wasn't out to undermine anyone.

Sam Zaccharias, a long-time friend and business associate of Russell, was seated at the same table, to my left. He was with his wife, Anne. They had just gotten married a few months earlier. Sam had been in my class at the University of Pittsburgh. His first wife, Sophia, had been in my English classes. She had died, suddenly, during the holiday season a few years earlier. I had seen her a few weeks before she died. She looked lovely, as usual, vibrant and in good spirits. She came over to where I was sitting and offered a holiday greeting and

Myron Cope receives award from Andy Russell at Thompson Club in West Mifflin.

Myron Cope helps writer friend Roy McHugh mark his 90th birthday at Tambellini's in 2006.

Photos by Jim O'Brien

Myron Cope presents former Steelers' receiver Ray Mathews the Man of Yesteryear award at Thompson Club in April of 2001.

a kiss on the cheek. She always made a fuss over me. We had a bond besides that English writing class we'd shared. She was from Braddock and I was from Hazelwood, so our backgrounds were similar. She was pleased that I had become the writer I wanted to be when I was a student in her class at Pitt.

Her death was difficult for Sam and Andy to accept. They missed her dearly. She was a great gal.

Sitting next to Zaccharias was Chuck Puskar. He was in the seat to my immediate left. Puskar had been a partner with Ray Mansfield in the insurance business, operating out of an office in Canonsburg. Mansfield had been Russell's closest friend among his teammates on the Steelers. They traveled the world together searching for new adventures and challenges. Puskar still talks about Mansfield a lot, and seems lost without him.

Russell reminded us of how he used to question Cope's football knowledge. He knew Cope knew his football history and had all his stories, but he'd say, "You don't know what a Cover Two defense is."

Cope would come back strong and tell Russell, rightfully so, that no one cared about a Cover Two defense. He didn't want to bore his listeners to death. He wanted to entertain them, inform them, and keep them interested in the action. Cope was colorful. He was never an analyst. Andy tends to over-analyze everything, the way Merril Hoge and Ron Jaworski often do on network television.

Bleier was just listening and smiling during most of this conversation. He didn't stay as long as the others. But Bleier is always easy company. "I just want everyone to like me," he says. "I'm not sure what's behind that."

Rocky shared a story with me a few weeks earlier that had stayed with me. He said a friend of his told him, "You know I always wondered what people thought about me. Now I realize that they're not thinking about me."

"I seldom ran the play the way it was drawn up."
— Franco Harris

Andy Russell was now 66. Rocky Bleier was a week away from his 62nd birthday. Both were grandfathers. Franco Harris would have his 58th birthday two days later. I was 65. I was a senior at Pitt when Andy Russell was a rookie with the Steelers and they were playing their home games at Forbes Field. They would move to Pitt Stadium a year later.

Russell was working in high finance, a managing director at Laurel Mountain Partners, L.L.C., merchant bankers with offices at 625 Liberty Avenue, formerly the Dominion Tower. Bleier was still traveling the country commanding nice fees as a motivational speaker. His story of a comeback from wounds suffered in combat in Vietnam to make and then star for the Steelers still played well with corporate types who were looking for something to spark their enthusiasm and work ethic. Russell and Bleier both got started on their business careers while they were playing for the Steelers. Andy gave up football when he was making more money on the side than he was with the Steelers. Franco was the president of Super Bakery, which produced special high nutrition donuts for school children's government-sponsored breakfast programs and had an office in the North Hills.

Russell, who did a two-year stint as an officer in the U.S. Army, is credited with 14 years in the NFL. Bleier is credited with 13 years and Franco, who finished up with a half-season in Seattle, is also credited with 13 years.

Russell was living in a beautiful home alongside the 18th hole at The Club at Nevillewood. Bleier had just moved from one home to a larger home in Mt. Lebanon's Virginia Manor neighborhood. He needed a bigger home since he and Janet adopted two little girls from the Ukraine a few years earlier and needed more room. Franco had a home in Sewickley, not far from the homes of his teammates Lynn Swann and Jack Ham.

So, needless to say, they were all doing well.

Franco was talking the most. Franco and Rocky later told me that Franco was more confident these days, more likely to start a conversation. He had come over to where I was standing in the room getting a can of Diet Coke and he had initiated a conversation. That led to me joining him at that table.

Franco offered insights into his running style. "I was 6–3 and I thought that gave me an advantage in seeing the opposing side," he said. For the record, he was always listed as 6–2 in the press guide and game program, which seems right.

"I don't think I was the size they were looking for, at first," he continued. "I heard Noll wanted someone else, someone stockier like the big running backs of that era."

Chuck Noll favored Robert Newhouse, who became a fine back for the Dallas Cowboys, but not the Hall of Fame back that Harris turned out to be. "I started picking up my reads before I even got the ball," said Harris, initiating a lengthy reflection on his running style. It was fascinating football insiders' stuff.

"I seldom ran the play the same way it was drawn up. If plays went the way they were drawn up every play would go for a touchdown. The defenses foul things up. They move around and they disrupt everything. I wanted to see where they were, not where they were supposed to be."

He smiled at Andy and explained. "I don't think I ever ran the 19-straight play the way I was supposed to. I looked for openings. And when I found one I'd go that way. If I ran it ten times I might run ten different ways."

Steelers' offensive linemen of that era told me that they had to block differently for Franco than they did for Rocky. "When Rocky got the ball and he was supposed to come behind you that meant he'd be on your ass in a second or two, and you better plow straight ahead. Rocky would be where he was supposed to be. With Franco, even if he wasn't supposed to run the ball behind you it was a good idea to try and hold your block a little longer. Any second, he might be coming back your way. It worked for both of them," said guard Gerry "Moon" Mullins.

There were games when they both rushed for more than 100 yards and at least one season when they both rushed for more than 1,000 yards. They were quite the backfield tandem.

Steelers' fans have fond memories of the two-back offense when Franco was paired with Rocky. Franco had been effective with Preston Pearson as well, but Pearson wanted to be the featured back and that caused some difficulty with the coaches.

Dick Hoak, who was the backfield coach at the time, told me he noticed that Franco was more productive when he had Rocky in there because Rocky was a better blocker, and more willing to accept that supporting role. I talked to Hoak, who had retired the year before, at DeNunzio's Restaurant in Jeannette before going to see Terrelle Pryor play for the Jeannette basketball team in a PIAA playoff game with Kane at Hempfield High in February of 2008.

"I was fortunate to become the backfield coach with the Steelers the same year (1972) that Franco came to the team," said Hoak. "He didn't impress people right away because Franco didn't look good when guys were going at half-speed like they did on the practice field. He was at his best when everybody was going full-speed.

"Franco had a unique running style. He was quick. He'd find an opening and he could accelerate fast and get through it. He did it his way and his way worked. It was a privilege to coach him."

"Easy, Fats. Easy."

Randy Grossman was at another table at the luncheon. He was the first Steeler I spoke to when I showed up at the Best Western. We started sharing some stories about Ernie "Fats" Holmes, who had died a month earlier. I introduced someone to Grossman and told them he had a dry sense of humor that he discovered late in life.

"I was always funny," Grossman came back. "You just didn't know it." Grossman could hold his own with Terry Bradshaw and Rocky Bleier for being a good emcee at Steelers' reunion parties or fund-raisers.

I remembered a funny story Grossman had told me about getting together with Holmes at a team reunion a few years back. "I asked Ernie what he was up to," said Grossman, "and he told me he was studying to become a Baptist priest. I said to Ernie, 'You know, Ernie, I'm not of the faith, but I don't think Baptists have priests.'"

Grossman told me a new story. He said that he and Mike Wagner and Ernie had been honorary captains for a game dedicated to the Steelers of the '70s during the previous season in which the Steelers celebrated their 75th anniversary season.

Former Steelers' coach Dick Hoak joins quarterback Charlie Batch at DeNunzio's Restaurant in Jeannette on March 1, 2008.

Joe Gordon checks out some yesteryear prices — 20 cents for a Swiss cheese sandwich — at Atria's Restaurant & Tavern in Mt. Lebanon.

Photos by Jim O'Brien

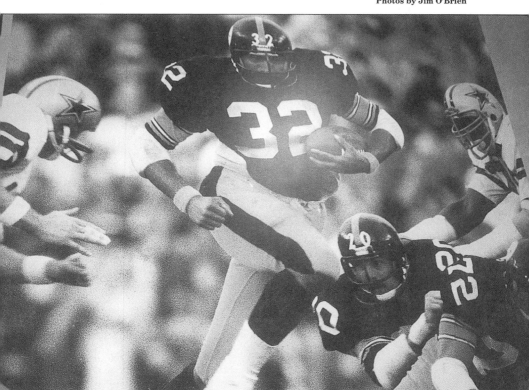

Franco Harris (32) and Rocky Bleier (20) are featured on front of mural at Heinz History Center's Western Pennsylvania Sports Museum.

You may remember how Holmes got into trouble with the law during his playing days by shooting at a police helicopter that was hovering overhead in Youngstown, near the Ohio Turnpike. Holmes ended up spending time at Western Psychiatric Institute in Oakland being treated for his mental breakdown.

He once complained to teammate L.C. Greenwood, who was asked to visit him by owner Dan Rooney, "I got to get out of here. Everyone here's crazy."

Grossman told me this story:

"Before we went out onto the field, we're standing in a hallway, and Ernie is talking to me and Mike. He says, 'I'm really into hunting now. I've become a really good shot.' Mike and I just looked at each other and rolled our eyes.

"Later, we're standing out at midfield at Heinz Field," continued Grossman. "It's me and Mike and Ernie. Then three Army helicopters swooped in overhead during the playing of the National Anthem. Mike looked at Ernie and said, 'Easy, Fats. Easy. Don't get too excited.' Only guys who've played and lived together in a football setting can still have fun over a teammate having a nervous breakdown. It makes you wonder."

One day I was standing next to Rocky Bleier and I realized we're about the same size. I'm only 5-8½ and he can't be more than a half-inch taller than I am. "All my life coaches told me I was too small to play football," I told him. He stuck a stiff finger into the center of my chest in response to my remark and said, "Your problem, O'Brien, is that you believed them."

These guys never stop inspiring and motivating people. They have great attitudes and approaches to life and one can learn from them.

I had a chance to chat with Andy and Rocky in the weeks that followed the funeral, and I found notes in my files on a Franco interview I'd done years before, and here's what they had to say:

Ernie "Fats" Holmes swaps stories with Mike Wagner, sitting near John Stallworth and Rocky Bleier, for "team photo" at the Mel Blount Youth Home All-Star Celebrity Roast at Downtown Hilton.

"Let's get together."

It took me a while to appreciate the way Franco Harris could run with a football. I remember us veterans being critical of him when he first came to camp. He just didn't look that good. One day we were holding a scrimmage and he came out my way on the wing. I was at outside linebacker and I had a clear shot at him. I told myself, 'Now I'm going to put a real hit on this rookie.' I came at him hard and I hit the ground with nothing in my hands. He just made a move and left me hanging out there. That's when I first realized that Franco was something different, something special.

When you're at linebacker, you're looking into the backfield and trying to figure out what's coming your way. You know the down and yardage situation. You know what they like to do in those situations. You've studied the film and you know their tendencies. It can be quite the cerebral challenge. I thought that was one of my strengths.

Franco was a running back who was doing just as much thinking about what the opposition might do. He was trying to figure out where you might be going. He was unique. Jim Brown didn't do what he did. Brown tried to run over people and he was pretty good at it.

Franco would hit a hole and then back up. He'd stop in the middle of his move. He might dart outside, or move through another hole next door. He had an ability to do that. He had great quickness. He didn't have the speed of a Tony Dorsett, but he was deceptive and could find daylight.

They are always timing football players in the 40-yard dash. I think it's more important how fast you can run five yards, how fast you can explode in five yards. After all, how often does anyone run 40 yards in a football game?

I remember Rocky was selling insurance in the off-season in Chicago after he'd come back from Vietnam and had been with the team a few years. His Notre Dame connections are strong there. He was concerned about his status with the Steelers. Chuck Noll had told him he ought to retire.

Rocky didn't know what to do. He called me during the off-season and told me what was going on. He told me that Noll had essentially told him not to come back. I could feel the pain in his voice. This was before Rocky became a real productive running back for the team. The first year he was with the team when he came back from Vietnam he didn't play. He was just rehabilitating himself. The next year he played on special teams.

He was not really playing much in the backfield. It wasn't until 1971 that he really made his move.

I told him he ought to report to camp and make Noll cut him. I told him that the people in front of him could get hurt, or that he could get traded. But I told him he shouldn't just quit.

Rocky started lifting weights in earnest and he built himself up to a rock solid 235 pounds. When he came to camp, he ran the 40 faster than anyone else. It was unreal. He ran a 4.5. Who would have thought he could do that?

The fastest guy on the team, by the way, for five to ten yards, was Jack Ham. He made tackles that Lambert and I could only make if we were stretched out. Ham was the fastest striker. Franco could explode too. He had quickness and vision.

Preston Pearson was ahead of him. He was awesome. He could do everything. Preston got his nose out of joint because he wanted to be the No. 1 runner. Franco was the featured runner. So Preston stopped blocking for Franco. You could see it on the film.

Dick Hoak (the backfield coach) made a comment that when Rocky was in there Franco was picking up first downs. All of a sudden, Preston is on the bench and Rocky is starting. Rocky had this explosiveness for five yards. It came from his weightlifting.

In 1974, Rocky makes a big play in the fourth quarter to score a touchdown against the Vikings in the Super Bowl in New Orleans. Now he's a star.

He and Franco complemented each other in the backfield. Franco has grown as a person. He's the one who calls to set up a dinner with some of our teammates. When some of us are at the Super Bowl on our own, he'll be the one who calls in advance and sets up a luncheon or dinner for us to get together somewhere. He's good at getting everybody together. 'Let's have dinner.' Or, 'Let's have lunch.' He wants us to take time out to bond and to stay together. He makes it happen. I don't do it; I don't think about it. He makes a point to get us all together.

I was watching something about Franco on television the other day, and it showed him in his football-playing days at Penn State. He wore number 34 then. Of course, when he came to the Steelers he couldn't get 34 because I had it. They wouldn't give a number that a veteran was wearing to a rookie. So he got 32. I never realized that he had to change numbers when he came here because I had his number. Seems funny now.

Rock has always been very open to relationships. He makes a living speaking about the game and his teammates. What he learned from the experience. He enjoys getting together with the guys. Rock enjoys getting together with anyone.

Looking back, it wasn't all wins. We lost, too. We didn't always win the challenges. You see that Buddy Dial just died, at

71. He was a teammate of mine when I first came to the Steelers. He was a great pass-catcher and a good guy. He was a lot of fun. He was a good teammate. Now he's gone. It makes you think. We just lost Ernie. I lost my closest friend, Ray Mansfield, too many years ago. We experienced so much together, especially off the field. We had the same mindset, the same interests, and a lust for mountains to climb. Steve Furness is gone, and a few guys who weren't here that long are gone as well. It gets you thinking. (Dwight White, also successful in the investment business, died in June, 2008, of a blood clot after back surgery. He was 58.)

I remember when Noll first came to the team in 1969. He denies this story now, but I remember we had a team meeting and he told us that most of us would be gone in a year. He said it wasn't because we didn't care or didn't try. He told us we just weren't fast enough, that we just weren't good enough.

Only five of us were still on the team when we made the playoffs the first time. That was me, Mansfield, Rocky, Sam Davis and Bobby Walden. Just five survived the coming of Noll.

So we had a special bond. It's important for us, I think, to stay close. That's why I wish Jack Lambert would come around. I have always said that Lambert was the best middle linebacker of our era, better than Butkus and Nitschke. I think Ham was the best linebacker of the bunch on our team.

We missed Jack when we had the 75th anniversary reunion. He would probably tell you he was watching one of his kids' teams playing that day. I know how important that is to him. One time, when he was with us, I said, 'Who would have thought Jack Lambert would be the best father among us?' Jack snarled at me and asked, 'What do you mean?' You know how he'd say something like that. I said, "Hey, Jack, it's a compliment." I hear he mows the grass and lines the fields where his kids play. He umpires. He helps any way he can. And he's home a lot. I respect that. But I wish he would feel as strongly about staying close to his teammates on the Steelers. That's important too. We'd like to see him. We shared a lot together. We achieved a lot together.

Former Steelers running back Franco Harris and Jim Duratz, a cable TV executive from Meadville, met on an airplane traveling to Chicago where both were scheduled to attend the Italian-American Sports Hall of Fame Awards Dinner. Reflecting on "The Immaculate Reception," Franco offered:

"I played so much football in my life, and all I'm remembered for is a busted play. That doesn't seem right."

Franco Harris:

"There were no extras"

I always thought I was an all-right guy. But there was talk when I was still at Penn State that I might be blackballed from the NFL. I wanted to find out where that was coming from. Joe Paterno was on vacation, out on a boat somewhere. I tracked him down and called him, and asked him if he was saying anything negative about me. He assured me he wasn't.

But it was going around that I might be a problem. I remember wanting to send the Steelers a telegram not to draft me, because I didn't want to go where the fans threw snowballs at the players. But the guy who was my agent told me not to send the telegram because I probably had a bad rap now, and it would just make it worse. I got a call that the Steelers had drafted me, and I was in shock.

I think the Steelers thought I might be lazy, and that image persisted after my first week in training camp. I'm still trying to figure that out. After the first exhibition game, the coaches came up to me saying, "Good game," like they didn't expect it from me. It was hard to believe that they were disappointed in the first week of practice. Maybe it was because I didn't allow people to beat on me.

I always feel that the easiest thing you can do is run into somebody. If it's a matter of winding up in the same place, I'd rather not get hit than get hit; chicken as that may sound.

I was always watching runners run. We'd be studying films, supposed to be watching defenses, and I'd find myself running along with the runner, putting myself in his shoes. Lots of running backs were faster than I was on a straight-ahead run, but not in the first 10 or 15 yards, dodging people and being quick about it. I'd be watching where other backs' feet were, how they moved their hips. I saw a certain move I liked, and I'd run it over and over again in my mind, and I'd try it.

I considered O.J. Simpson the best running back. I liked to look at myself in the same light. He, to me, had so much natural ability. I knew there was no way I could touch him in that respect.

In some ways, I was luckier than he was. Being on a team that wins the Super Bowl, not just once but four times. I had the good fortune to be with a winner, and not have anything bad — injury-wise — happen to me.

I was always interested in doing something that involved kids. I enjoyed going to Children's Hospital and things like that, in many cities.

76

Franco Harris and author Jim O'Brien served on championship committee to develop the Western Pennsylvania Sports Museum at the Heinz History Center.

Jim O'Brien

I liked being able to do nice things for my parents. Football afforded me that opportunity. As a child, we never went to a restaurant. I mean never. We never went on a vacation. I was the third oldest of nine children. We always had what we needed, and we were never without essentials, but there were no extras. It felt good to give them something back.

Coming from a situation where my father didn't have much of a formal education — he really couldn't read or write — and my mother had only an eighth grade education. Well, when it came to school, they were very strict about it. We had to show them our report card. If we got anything less than a "C" it was whipping time. I remember one time my sister had a bad report card, and my dad tore her up. Man, my dad didn't play around.

He was always there, though. He worked two jobs to make ends meet. He worked hard. He had his certain ways. When you have nine kids, I guess you've got to have rules. It's funny, but with all those kids he still controlled the total situation in the home. He controlled everything. He only said something once and you better do it.

I'd have to say that it was because of him and the way he controlled the house that none of us ever went astray in any way. There could have been opportunities when I was young, on being on that thin line when I could have done something bad, and I thought of my dad and the consequences, and I didn't do it.

I really had a happy childhood, relating to other people, other kids. My father was great with people. He didn't care about color. He knew all kinds of people. When I was three or four, we moved into this project area of Mt. Holly. I guess we were like the second black family to move into that area. Soon the street was full of families with mixed marriages, blacks with European wives, Italian and German. There was quite a bit of that.

At the funeral for my dad, I saw a lot of them. I hadn't seen some of them between the time I was five and ten. A lot of the old Italian ladies who came over with my mom were there. They were all shipped over together, and they had stayed together.

I think it helped, coming from a family like I did. I really do. My mom, she thought European. She was strict and conservative. The children always came first. They would do certain things for us.

One thing they had a dream of doing. They wanted to get out of that project area. When I was nine, my mother went out by herself, bought a piece of land. She had to go by herself. My dad couldn't go; they wouldn't have sold that land to him. It was seven years later before they had the money to build a home on that piece of land. They did it and we moved into the new house. They had accomplished that dream. Maybe that's where I got my patience.

Rocky Bleier:

"Every payday is a good payday."

Franco and I both lived in East Liberty in our early days with the Steelers. Franco didn't have a car for a time, and he used to take the bus to Three Rivers Stadium. Sometimes I'd drive over to his place and pick him up. I'm not sure, but I think he got his first car when he was named the NFL Rookie of the Year. Let's just say Franco was frugal in those first few years.

Andy has always been my advisor. I was in business with him for awhile, as part of Russell, Rea, Zappala & Bleier, a group that did bond issues out of the Roosevelt Hotel when you and I first met. Dwight White used to say that like Yogi Bear he was smarter than the average bear, and Dwight has shown he was right about that. He's been successful in business. Well, the same is certainly true of Andy. He'd been around and he knew more than most about the real world. He helped a lot of us in that respect. We trusted what he was telling us.

I have benefited from playing with and, more importantly, becoming close to Andy and Franco.

I got so much value out of playing football, plus I got paid. I've always said that every payday is a good payday and that was certainly true of all my years with the Pittsburgh Steelers.

Once you pass 60 that makes you start to think about where you've been and what you've done. I am lucky to have a great wife in Janet (Gyuriuna), and we adopted two little girls that are going to make me keep plugging away.

We have two great little girls who came from the Ukraine. Elly is 10 and Rosie is 9 and they're getting so big. They'll keep me hustling. We needed a bigger home for them so we moved to another place near us in Mt. Lebanon.

You don't always realize the impression you leave or the impact of your actions. I just got an e-mail from a Notre Dame grad. He graduated in 1976. I was a senior class fellow when I was at Notre Dame and I came back to the campus to speak. This guy tells me he was there and that he remembers it to this day. He said he got my book, and he wanted to get it autographed. So there's one person I made a positive impression with.

I wish I knew then what I know now and I would've given a better speech. It was so important to that fellow that he still remembered it.

You can't get all the details right about all the days in your life, but the football and the speaking are all part of my life. You think about that and what you've experienced.

Another guy e-mailed me and said his father played basketball with my father. He got hurt and he said my father loaned him the crutches I used when I came back from Vietnam. He wanted to know if I'd like to have those crutches now. He thought I could give them to some charity to auction off. I had no idea where those crutches were. I do know that my father never played basketball in his life. It must have been my uncle who did that. But those crutches were part of my life, too. Sometimes it's hard to separate fact from fiction with some of these stories. We were all in our early 20s when we started with the Steelers. That's all you knew at that point in your life. In truth, you didn't know crap. You were worried about yourself for the most part.

I've ended up making my living as a motivational speaker. Someone approached me and asked me if I thought I could get Franco to deliver a speech to his organization. They were willing to pay $15,000 for Franco to talk to them. He turned it down. He didn't want to do it. He said he wasn't confident about doing that sort of thing. I've heard him speak at several events and I thought he always handled himself well, just being Franco Harris, just being himself, and talking from the heart. That's all he has to do. But Franco has definite thoughts about what he will and won't do.

We used to refer to "Franco time." If he tells you he will be somewhere, he'll be there. But he'll show up on his time. He might delay you, but he won't disappoint you.

Franco is much more comfortable talking these days than he was when he was first with the Steelers. In the beginning, Franco didn't say anything. When I was a sportscaster at Channel 11, I tried to interview Franco a few times and it was never satisfactory. As a result, many in the media never talked to Franco. Now he has questions. He wants to know, like we all do, what it was all about.

Going to a funeral for Myron Cope makes some of it come back to you. He was part of all of this. You went through a lot together. I always felt privileged and honored to hang around Myron. He was always connected to certain people and he'd been around a lot of interesting people and places. I liked to listen to Myron's stories. He was fun.

We all have stories about how we got to where we are today. The road was different for all of us, more difficult for some, but we all had our ups and downs. It wasn't a straight line.

We knew we couldn't always play football and we all dealt with the uncertainty differently. We didn't need Chuck Noll to needle us about preparing for our life's work. That would come soon enough and it was, or could be, frightening.

"Our fans make Pittsburgh special.
— Rocky Bleier

Rocky Bleier often dines at Don DeBlasio's Restaurant near Rocky's residence in Virginia Manor section of Mt. Lebanon. Below, Bleier follows Ted Petersen on run against Kansas City Chiefs.

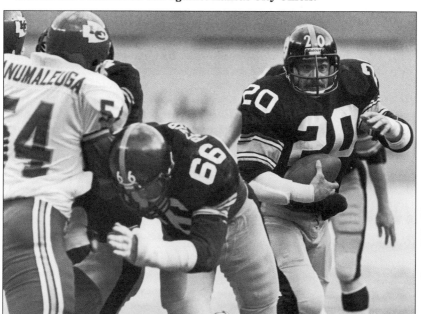

Football was part of the fabric of our lives. A game, a season, a career, a beginning, a middle and an end. When I am out talking to people, no matter what business they might be in, I tell them that we're all creating hope. I hope I can do this, I hope I can do that. No matter what you do, you are creating hope.

I had to have hope to come back after my Vietnam experience. I have never portrayed myself as a war hero; I wasn't. If my story has any meaning to anyone else it's how I worked so hard to get over the effects of the wounds I suffered in the battlefield in Vietnam.

I grew up in the backyard of the Green Bay Packers and the Lombardi years. My favorite pro football team was a championship team. I was the captain of a national championship team at Notre Dame. Not too many colleges can claim the history they have at Notre Dame. So I was well schooled in what it meant to be part of a championship program. I was lucky to get drafted by the Pittsburgh Steelers. They were patient with me and gave me a chance to get myself physically prepared to play again. Mr. Rooney was always in my corner. Chuck Noll might not have been sure about me, at first, but he certainly had my back during my stay with the Steelers.

At the funeral, I saw some of my teammates like Mel Blount and Lynn Swann, Mike Wagner, Randy Grossman, Tunch Ilkin and Craig Wolfley and, of course, Franco and Andy. They all serve as reminders of some of the best days in my life.

It also reminds you that too many of my teammates have died. You remember those funerals as well. Ray Mansfield was the first, at 56. He was the first one of our team to die. It kinda took your breath away.

We all face these things. But you didn't expect it to happen so soon. Then we lost Steve Furness. And Joe Gilliam. It hurt when you heard that Mike Webster died; he looked like he was getting his act together again. It was such a shame. He was working to get things back to where they were and he had a heart attack. Tyrone McGriff and Dan Turk were Steelers some people don't remember, but they're gone, too. We lost Theo Bell. We lost some of our coaches, Rollie Dotsch, and then Dennis Fitzgerald and Bud Carson. Then Steve Courson gets killed cutting down a tree. He tries to save his dog and the tree crushes him. Steve had worked so hard to stay alive after he had his heart problems. And now, just a month back, we lose Ernie Holmes. How could we ever forget him? Ernie had a good heart; he just had a hard time disciplining himself.

That's why I appreciate opportunities to get together with my teammates for reunions and dinners. It was nice to be invited to Myron's funeral — you had to be invited — and to see my teammates there.

Jack Lambert drew a lot of criticism for not coming to the 75th anniversary celebration. I keep in touch with Jack and I know what his issues are with the team. He makes his living doing signings and endorsements and he feels the team has not paid him properly for some of the throwback jerseys they sell, stuff like that. I understand where he's coming from and why he feels the way he does. I know Jack and he's a man of great principles.

The fans want Jack Lambert to be there. The fans want their world to be what it is. Should Jack have been there? Yes. I wish he'd have been there. He was such a big part of our success. Jack called me and he explained why he wasn't coming. He wanted me to understand his spin on the situation. He just wanted to let me know why. I know he told Dan Rooney why he wasn't coming. I think Dan has tried to square things with Jack. The image he has with the fans is not the real Jack Lambert. Jack is a very disciplined guy in his beliefs. To him, everything is black and white, and he doesn't yield on too many things. He has his own ideas of right and wrong and he doesn't waiver. I believe he has the right to make money and to be paid for his appearances and for his jersey and things like that.

Jack was my roommate. We've been through a lot together. Jack is my friend. I'm proud to say that. We're different in our approach. But I would never attempt to tell Jack what he ought to do. Hell, I'd be afraid to. You think I want him to get mad at me?

Jack wasn't very pleased when you wrote that book about him. You know how he is about such things. He'll never tell you this, but deep down I think he liked most of what you wrote. Personally, I thought it was a nice tribute to him. But I wouldn't tell that to Jack. He believes that No. 58 belongs to him.

There is only one number — 70 — that is officially retired by the Steelers. That was worn by Ernie Stautner. But there are jerseys that are not given out to players anymore. Tony Parisi, the equipment man, and now Rodgers Freyvogel, don't give out Bradshaw's No. 12, Lambert's No. 58, Ham's No. 59, Joe Greene's 75, Franco's 32. They may hold back Jerome Bettis' 36 now.

Sometimes they need to use those numbers during training camp because they have so many players then. I found out they gave them to guys they didn't think had a prayer of making the team.

The next guy to wear No. 20 after me was Dwight Stone (1987–1994). I was told they didn't think he'd make the team.

I had three different numbers during my days with the Steelers. I had No. 24 when I first went to training camp. Then I got 26 before the season (1968) started. When Preston Pearson was traded by the Colts to the Steelers in 1970 he got No. 26. When I came back from Vietnam and rejoined the team in 1971

I was given No. 20. No one had worn No. 20 the year before.
Paul Martha had worn it for six years (1964–1969).
It took awhile, but I finally realized that I was given No. 20
because they didn't think I'd make the team.

Photos by Jim O'Brien

Janet and Rocky Bleier appear at a wine tasting party at Grand Concourse.

Rocky Bleier is flanked by two members of the Pro Football Hall of Fame,
Dante Lavelli of the Cleveland Browns, and Dave Robinson of the Green Bay
Packers, at a special salute in Canton, Ohio shrine to all NFLers who served in
the military. Bleier has been involved in a program to promote visitation to the
Vietnam War "wall" memorial in Washington, D.C.

Franco and a soldier's story

Frank Haller, a friend of mine, forwards stories, jokes and you name it to his pals on his e-mail hit list. Here's a keeper that he sent me regarding Franco Harris and a soldier. I made efforts to find out who wrote the following message -- the soldier's aunt -- and the name of the soldier, but was unable to get that. So this is a story about Franco and an unknown soldier. There was a photo attached, but without identification.

It's a feel-good story about someone in sports who has never thumped his chest, but went about his work with a quiet dignity. "It ain't charity if you talk about it," Art Rooney Sr. used to say.

(Even if you're not a Steelers' fan, send it to your friends who are.)

Let me tell you about one soldier's return flight to Iraq. He saw a man walk into the bathroom at the Pittsburgh Airport and thought he recognized him. When the man came out he went over to him and said, "Excuse me, sir, but are you Franco Harris?"

The man replied, "Yes, I am," and then, being such a big Steelers' fan, the soldier asked him if he could have a pic of him. Franco was agreeable to this. After taking the pic, they talked for a few minutes and (the soldier) told him he was on his way back to Iraq. Franco acknowledged his sadness and gave him encouragement and (wishes for a) safe return.

Then they shook hands and parted on their ways. The end of the story you would think, but not so...

You see, after a while the soldier's name was announced over the loud speaker to come to the desk...which he did...Once there the lady behind the counter informed him that there was an empty seat in first class and she was going to bump him up to that seat if it was OK with him. He said he didn't care where he sat in the plane, as long as he made it to Atlanta to catch the Army plane. So she informed him that he was now going first-class to Atlanta.

He thanked her and went back to tell everyone (in his family) as he waited to board the plane. Once he was seated on the plane, he was waving out the window to his Dad and Pap. He felt a hand on his left leg. He turned to his side and there was Franco sitting in the seat next to him!!!

Needless to say, they talked all the way to Atlanta about the Steelers and then parted with Franco taking his address and giving his signed ticket stub to the soldier as validation of their trip together. This was a trip not of sadness and loneliness, but one this soldier will never forget and will talk about forever thanks to Franco Harris.

This act of kindness and generosity from this man is one that words cannot express. In my opinion, Franco Harris is 'the man of all men.' I wish I could thank him for making a soldier's lonely flight back to war one of his ultimate lifetime experiences that he will talk about forever.

Thank you, Mr. Franco Harris.

Herb Douglas
Sharing a round table with Olympians at his 85th birthday celebration

"You gotta make it happen."

March 21, 2007

Astack of sports magazines sat high on the end table next to my boyhood bed back home in Hazelwood, at the eastern end of Pittsburgh. It started with *Sport* magazine and continued with *Sports Illustrated*, and I can still see the covers of my treasure trove. I also collected bubble gum cards of football and basketball and baseball players and memorized some of the notes and statistics on the backs of them. I sorted them out and studied them and the images remain emblazoned on my brain.

Sports news was sparse in the late '50s and early '60s. You didn't get to see all the Steelers and Pirates games, or any of the Hornets, our team in the American Hockey League, on television. And television was black and white, with lots of snow. We saw the Steelers one weekend and the Baltimore Colts the next weekend. Johnny Unitas of Pittsburgh, whom the Steelers had cut without giving him an honest look, was the star quarterback of the Baltimore team.

Duquesne had the best basketball team in Pittsburgh in those days, but there was no March Madness. Pitt had a pretty decent team, but they were not in the same league as Duquesne.

There were no round-the-clock sports talk shows on radio and TV. I recall that Joe "The Screamer" Tucker had a 15-minute report around dinnertime on WWSW Radio. He was also the voice of most of the sports broadcasts in the city. Rosey Rowswell and Bob Prince did the Pirates.

I lived about five miles from Oakland where all the teams played in those days, yet it might as well have been 500 miles away. We didn't have a car and my dad didn't even know how to drive one. Less sports news was better. It left more to the imagination. Sports figures were magic figures that lived in some Wonderland far away.

There were national highlights screened between the movies and the cartoons on Saturday at the local theater.

Track & field was one of my first loves. I knew all the ace athletes from around the world and knew their stories. I even had my own track & field team when I was 12 and 13, consisting of kids who were nine to 11 from the neighborhood. I conducted track meets on Sunnyside Street where I lived, and had T-shirts with SUNNYSIDE A.C. across the chest. I built a broad-jump pit across the street from my home. I fashioned a discus from some wood from the local lumberyard. I borrowed a bowling ball—the smaller ball used for rubber-

Olympic gold medalist Mal Whitfield with his friend Herb Douglas at Herb's 80th birthday at Duquesne Club.

Herb Douglas shows his track shoes and shirt from his glory days at Pitt to Franco Harris, chairman of the championship committee for the Western Pa. Sports Museum.

Bullet Bill' Dudley   *Herb Douglas*

Photos by Jim O'Brien

Swin Cash, who came out of McKeesport High School to star for UConn's national championship women's basketball team and with the WNBA, is flanked by Pro Football Hall of Famer "Bullet Bill" Dudley, left, and Olympian Herb Douglas.

band duckpins—to use for our shot put. I bought trophies that had a gold plate—World's Greatest Athlete—from Murphy's 5 & 10. I bought them with my own money.

I started writing about our athletic activities and that's how I landed a job as the sportswriter of our hometown weekly at age 14.

If you know this you can appreciate how I felt on a Saturday evening at the outset of this month. I was the co-emcee along with WQED's Chis Moore of a dinner at the Heinz History Center and Western Pennsylvania Sports Museum in The Strip.

We were there to celebrate the 85th birthday of Herb Douglas Jr., one of my first sports heroes in Hazelwood, who won a bronze medal in the long jump in the 1948 Olympic Games at Wembley Stadium in London. He calls me at least once a month from his residence in Philadelphia. He still maintains his boyhood home in Hazelwood.

My wife Kathie and I were seated at a round table with a galaxy of Olympians. We were surrounded by greatness. Best of all they were good company. This is one of those nights I'll be muttering about some-day as I sit in a rocking chair on the porch of a nursing home.

To my left, clockwise, sat Roger Kingdom, Harrison Dillard, Donna de Varona, Edwin Moses and Dr. Charles Jenkins. All were gold medalists in Olympic Games competition. You have to be a fan of the Olympic Games to get a real appreciation for this assembly. The lone woman in that group of gold medalists, de Varona, was a great swimmer and ABC Sports analyst.

Then, too, there was Rev. Jimmy Joe Robinson at our round table. He was once a civil rights leader in this community and marched in The South with the Rev. Martin Luther King Jr.

Rev. Robinson was the first black football player to perform at Pitt in 1945, two years before Jackie Robinson broke the color barrier in major league baseball. Robinson was joined a few weeks later by Herb Douglas and Alan Carter on the Panthers' eleven.

Arnie Sowell sat nearby. He was the favorite in the 800 meters in the 1956 Olympic Games and one of the greatest track stars in Pitt history, but he finished fourth in the Games.

Consider the accomplishments of these gifted individuals:

Kingdom won the gold medal in the 110-meter hurdles in the 1984 Olympic Games in Los Angeles and the 1988 Olympic Games in Seoul, Korea. He's one of only two athletes to win 110-meter hurdles in back-to-back Olympic Games and he set Olympic records in Seoul.

Dillard won two gold medals in the 1948 Olympic Games, winning the 100 meters and the 4 x 100-meter relay. In 1952 he won gold in the 100-meter hurdles and the 4 x 100 relay. No one else in the history of the Olympic Games enjoys that distinction. He set a world record in the 100-meter hurdles and tied in the 100 meters.

De Varona won two gold medals and established 18 world records before the age of 17. She excelled in the Olympic Games in Rome in 1960. Upon retiring from competitive swimming in 1964, she became the youngest and first full-time female sportscaster in network television.

88

Olympic gold medalists Roger Kingdom, Edwin Moses and Harrison Dillard all looked great at Herb Douglas' 85th birthday celebration at Heinz History Center.

Olympic lineup, left to right, includes Roger Kingdom, Harrison Dillard, Dr. Charlie Jenkins, Herb Douglas, Edwin Moses, Donna de Varona, Steve Riddick and Arnie Sowell.

Photos by Jim O'Brien

Roger Kingdom

Edwin Moses won two gold medals and one bronze medal in the Olympic Games. He bettered the Olympic and World records in the 1976 Olympic Games in Montreal. A physicist from Morehouse College in Atlanta, he had a winning streak in the hurdles that spanned 122 outings. Dr. Charles Jenkins won a gold medal in the 1956 Olympic Games in the 400 meters and another gold medal as a member of the 4x100 meter relay team. He and his son Charles Jr. are the only father and son tandem to win Olympic gold medals in the same event. Charles Jr. won his as a member of the 4 x 100 meters relay team at the Olympic Games in Barcelona in 1992.

Arnie Sowell was the greatest track & field competitor born in Pittsburgh. He followed the great John Woodruff in the same events, 880 yards and 800 meters, and established world records in the 880 yards event. He competed in the Olympic Games in 1956, but suffered an off day and didn't medal, finishing fourth in the 800 meters.

Steve Reddick, a member of the gold medal 4 x 100 relay team in the 1976 Olympic Games, was seated elsewhere. All of them paid tribute to Douglas as a friend, mentor and counselor. He has been all of those to me as well through the years. He's been an inspiration to many. He was not only a success in sports, but he was one of the first black athletes to make the transition to the corporate world as a prized executive. He's been a great ambassador for all he represents and he's moved among giants in every respect. I recall seeing a photo of him with South African leader Nelson Mandela.

When I've complained about a problem here and there in my business, Herb Douglas scolds me and boosts me at the same time. "You can't hope it will happen," he says, "you've got to make it happen."

My sports magazines came to life when I sat at this round table at the Heinz History Center. King Arthur never kept better company at his round table. These men and women had achieved great things. This was a black tie affair so they looked so attractive and dignified.

They still walk tall and proud, yet they are humble and so down to earth, and easy to be with. They let their records speak for themselves, and they remain grateful for those like Herb Douglas who helped them achieve greatness in their Games.

Jim O'Brien

Author's wife, Kathleen Churchman O'Brien, is flanked by Olympic gold medalist hurdler Roger Kingdom and swimmer Donna de Varona.

Frank Gustine, who earned letters in three sports at Pitt, talks to Herb Douglas, who lettered in two sports at Oakland school.

Photos by Jim O'Brien

Arnie Sowell

Two of Pitt's finest, Rick Leeson and Arnie Sowell, swap stories at Varsity Letter Club's Homecoming Dinner at Alumni Hall.

Jim Render
USC coach didn't flinch
in WPIAL championship game

November 29, 2006

I have been rooting for Jim Render and his Upper St. Clair Panthers for the past 28 years. That's why I was so elated and felt so good for Render when he rallied his troops in the final minutes of a hard-fought contest to defeat Penn Hills, 18–12, to win the WPIAL Quad A title on Friday night at Heinz Field.

The Panthers were trailing 12–11 with 5:41 left to play when they mounted "the championship drive" of 59 yards. It took nine plays, capped by a torrid 10-yard run by Dane Conwell for the winning touchdown. Then Conwell intercepted a pass to seal the victory, and gain team MVP honors.

I was impressed with how confident and composed Render appeared on the sideline. "Somebody had to be," he said when I spoke to him about it on Sunday evening. "I gave myself a little pep talk on the sideline. I said, 'Don't flinch.' I felt we could do it."

I was just as impressed with the way Render embraced Neil Gordon, the Penn Hills coach, at midfield following the game. They held onto each other for a few minutes, and spoke to each other at length.

"I really felt empathy for him," related Render. "I know how tough it is to lose that game. Neil and I have enjoyed a good relationship through the years, and do each other favors, and I respect him and his program. I knew how he felt. I've been there."

This was Render's 10th appearance in the WPIAL finals in the last 18 years, and this was the fifth time his team came away with the championship trophy. This will be his fifth championship ring. He truly won one for the thumb with this one.

Render and I both came to Upper St. Clair in 1979. It was good timing. The Pirates won the World Series that year and the Steelers won their fourth Super Bowl in six years. Those were the glory days and we thought they'd never end. I have often said that since then I have been able to rely on Render and his Panthers more than my alma mater Pitt Panthers or the Pittsburgh Steelers to deliver a winner. That was certainly true last weekend.

Render and I are the same age—64—and the same size, about 5–8½, and we're usually on the same page. We compare notes from time to time when we meet at King's Family Restaurant in Upper St. Clair. That's where my wife Kathie and I found him and his wife, Pam, their son Eric, and John Miller, USC's defensive coordinator, enjoying breakfast the morning after the championship game. The Render's other son, T.J., is an assistant coach on the team.

Don Yannessa and Jim Render are two of the greatest football coaches in the history of the WPIAL.

Render had great role models while growing up in Ohio in football legends such as Paul Brown, left, and Don Shula.

I told Render that Kathie and I had gone to the Petersen Events Center on Friday night to watch Pitt defeat Florida State resoundingly in a basketball contest. We stopped on the way home for something to eat at Bado's Restaurant in Mt. Lebanon.

The WPIAL finale was on television. We borrowed two high-stools from the bar and moved them close to a television in the corner of the bar area and watched the fourth quarter. When Conwell scored the game-winner, I jumped off my seat and shouted with glee. Then I turned around and saw a lot of men, mostly from Mt. Lebanon, and apologized for the outburst. They said it was OK. They've been there, too.

I ran into Mark Gentile the next day at Ross Park Mall. He was the starting quarterback in his junior year when he led the USC Panthers (15–0) to the state title in 1990. He introduced himself by saying, "I sat near your daughter Sarah in a social studies class. She was a big help." I told him about my behavior at Bado's the night before.

"I did the same thing at a bar in the North Hills," he said. "I was so excited for Coach Render and the team. I remember him being tough but fair. He prepared us well for football games. He knows the game and he knows how to win."

Render has had his critics through the years, and there were misguided people who tried to get him fired. He never bowed to any of them. He'd grown up in Ohio, which has produced more great football coaches perhaps than any state in the country. He admired Paul Brown, Woody Hayes, Bo Schembechler, Ara Parseghian, Don Shula and Weeb Ewbank, to name a few Buckeye-born coaches. They had their critics, too. He read their books and knew what it took to be a winner.

I told Render that this only reaffirmed what I knew a long time ago, that he knew how to coach a football team. To which Render replied, "I'm sure I still have some skeptics out there."

He says he was fortunate to come to a school such as Upper St. Clair and have the kind of kids he had to work with through the years. "I always felt that if you get an Upper St. Clair kid to commit to football that he was really willing to work hard and prepare to play. I have had very few kids that have quit the program.

"If they give you a commitment they will do what you ask them to do in the off-season to condition themselves for football. That's not true at all high schools. Many of them come from success-oriented families where they won't settle for second best. Of course, I've had parents of kids who were never satisfied or happy with whatever I did. Parents usually think their kids are going to play for the Steelers some day.

"I was lucky to coach in an area like Western Pennsylvania where there were so many good coaches. I learned from the best of them. I grew up admiring guys like Woody Hayes and Ara Parseghian and an uncle of mine who coached, and I've learned from the best. I've been lucky to be able to lead the life I wanted to lead when I was in college."

Jim Render went on to direct the USC Panthers to the Quad A PIAA state title, the second such title in his career.

"Times of Greatness"
gives insight to black baseball

August 24, 2005

A wise writer named Alex Haley once said, "Whenever an old person dies it's like a library being burned down." In doing his painstaking research on the sad story of slavery from Africa to America, Haley interviewed a lot of old people to get their stories and the stories that had been passed down through generations to write his wonderful book *Roots*. That became a made-for-TV series that captured the nation's attention. I remember how my older daughter, Sarah, was captivated by the story. She watched the TV series, read Haley's book, and then read books about Jackie Robinson and Connie Hawkins, and couldn't get over how poorly those black athletes were treated in their early years of competition. It's important to remember so we don't forget those injustices and make the same mistakes again.

"Times of Greatness" is a mobile exhibit sponsored by Roadway that relates the story of the Negro Leagues and the many storied achievements of African-Americans in baseball. It's coming to Pittsburgh for a one-day stop. The Roadway van will be set up in Red Lot Six, the parking lot on General Robinson Street directly across the street from PNC Park, this Saturday, Aug. 27, from 4:30 to 7:15 p.m.

You can catch the exhibit and see the Pirates play the Cincinnati Reds. Sean Casey of Upper St. Clair and Ken Griffey Jr. of Donora are stars of the Cincy club. The exhibit includes historic photos, video, and memorabilia from the original 24 Negro League Baseball teams.

It's worth doing some research on this story. I read a book last week called *Black Diamond—The Story of the Negro Baseball Leagues*, written by Patricia C. McKissack and Frederick McKissack Jr. It's a story of courage and determination, and it's a story that all baseball fans and those interested in the history of our country ought to check out. It documents the belief held here that Pittsburgh was once considered the capital of black baseball. Two of the best teams ever were the Homestead Grays and the Pittsburgh Crawfords. They have gotten more attention in this area since the High Level Bridge in Homestead was renamed in honor of the Grays, and since the opening this year of the Western Pennsylvania Sports Museum at the Heinz History Center in The Strip district.

There aren't many people left who saw Satchel Paige pitch or Josh Gibson catch and hit prodigious home runs. They were two of the greatest and best-known stars of the Negro Baseball Leagues. They and others have been honored by inclusion in the Baseball Hall of Fame in Cooperstown, N. Y. I know I saw the Homestead Grays play at Burgwin Field, less than a mile from my home in Hazelwood, but this was after the team's greatest stars had completed their careers.

96

Sean Gibson, the great grandson of the immortal Josh Gibson, checks out model for Western Pa. sports museum with championship committee chairman Franco Harris.

One-year-old Margaret Zirwas, the author's granddaughter, sizes up Roberto Clemente statue outside PNC Park.

Joe Chiodo shows off team photo of Homestead Grays that was displayed at his Homestead restaurant and bar.

Jackie Robinson

The Negro Leagues were at their greatest level of competition before there were blacks in Major League Baseball. Cubans and Indians were permitted to play, but no Negroes, as blacks were known at the time. So some light-skinned blacks said they were Indians and Cubans so they could play. There was even an all-black team called the New York Cubans. For the record, there were no Cubans on that team.

This was before Branch Rickey would sign Jackie Robinson of the Kansas City Monarchs to a major league contract to play for the Brooklyn Dodgers in 1945. Robinson broke the color barrier in 1947. After that happened, the Cleveland Indians signed some black players as well.

One of the things I learned in reading the book was that in 1947 the Dodgers showed the world that integrated baseball was not only morally right, but it was also profitable. The integrated Dodgers and Indians reached the World Series and set all-time attendance records. So more clubs were willing to invest in black players.

When Robinson, Paige, Larry Doby, Monte Irvin, Don Newcombe and Roy Campanella came to the major leagues, it was the beginning of the end of the Negro Baseball Leagues. Young players such as Henry Aaron, Willie Mays and Ernie Banks got their first taste of big league ball in the Negro Leagues. Josh Gibson, known as "the Babe Ruth of the Negro Baseball Leagues," was too old to make the transition. He was upset because he had been bypassed and became an alcoholic and died in January of 1947. It was believed he died of a broken heart.

So many of baseball's best players have been blacks. Nowadays Latin Americans actually dominate the game. So one has to wonder what impact the ban on blacks had on baseball in those early years.

Branch Rickey moved from the Dodgers to Pittsburgh. One of the first things he did was draft a young ballplayer the Dodgers were trying to hide in their farm system, a talented young Puerto Rican named Roberto Clemente. Curt Roberts, a second baseman, was the first black to play for the Pirates, and Roman Mejias and Carlos Bernier were the first Latin players. Then came Clemente and he became a Hall of Fame baseball player. He and Honus Wagner of Carnegie are considered the greatest Pirates of them all.

Jackie Robinson, I have learned in researching the life of Clemente, had a hand in Roberto becoming a Bucco. Buzzy Bavasi, the general manager of the Dodgers, approached Robinson and asked him what he thought of the idea of bringing Clemente up to the majors to play left field for the Dodgers. The Dodgers had five blacks on their ballclub at the time. Robinson said that the Dodgers' left fielder, George "Shotgun" Shuba, while not a standout, was a popular player on the team and it might upset some of the white veterans if Clemente came up at that time. It was thought it would be a good idea to wait a year. That's how Clemente ended up playing for the Pirates. It's ironic that Jackie Robinson was involved in that occurrence.

The Pirates would be wise to take their present-day players on a field trip across the street to see this exhibition. They have it made compared to these great players of the past.

Joe Chiodo
An Italian leprechaun

Jim O'Brien

"Art Rooney cared about me."

I still have some mementos from Chiodo's Tavern, a landmark restaurant and bar in Homestead. I have two red poker chips. It says CHIODO'S TAVERN on one side and DRAFT on the other side. Someone gave them to me when I was visiting the Carnegie Library of Homestead at the outset of 2008.

"Here's a keepsake for you," said one of the library's directors. "I thought you'd like to have them."

If you were in the midst of drinking a beer at Chiodo's Tavern and a customer bought you a beer, Joe Chiodo, the owner, would carefully place one of those red chips next to your bottle or glass. It meant he owed you one. Some bars put an empty shot glass in front of you on the bar to indicate the same.

When I pick up the chips now and roll them through my fingers it reminds me of Joe Chiodo, an icon in the Pittsburgh sports arena. His tavern/restaurant was popular once upon a time with the working people of Homestead, when there were people working at U.S. Steel and Mesta Machine Company, but those internationally known and respected companies are long gone from the local landscape. College kids came from Oakland because Chiodo's had a grand assortment of beers from all over the country and, indeed, the world. They could relax there and the owner appreciated their business. They got a kick out of Joe Chiodo, and loved him and his bar. It remained popular with sports fans from everywhere.

Frankly, I could never understand the charm of the joint —and that's what it was — except for the presence of Joe Chiodo. He stood only 5 feet 4 inches tall, at best, and sometimes he looked like he was kneeling behind the bar. But he was a giant in the business. He knew how to run a restaurant and bar the way Frankie Gustine, the former Pirates' ballplayer, knew how to do it. Frankie Gustine's Bar had been a must-stop place near Forbes Field and the University of Pittsburgh campus for more than 30 years. Gustine and Chiodo knew their customers well and always made them feel welcome. A newcomer could see Chiodo's as dark and dreary and a bit worn at the edges, but as soon as they caught Chiodo in action behind the bar their impression changed. Joe lit up the place like a light tower on the shore.

In his latter years, Chiodo told people his name was pronounced Key-oh-doe. He had visited Italy and learned that was the proper way to say it. Before that, most people addressed him as Joe Cho-do. His long-time pals accused him of pulling a Tony Dorsett on them. When Dorsett first came to Pitt his name was pronounced DOOR-sit. When he became famous it became Door-SET. The emphasis on the second syllable instead of the first syllable. Joe first came to America from Italy in 1927. His father was a shoemaker, but he bought a storefront in Homestead that had been a bar and, before long, he owned a bar as well as a shoemaker shop. Joe Chiodo learned to be a cobbler, too, and worked for years at Mesta Machine Company.

My father, Dan O'Brien, and his two brothers, Rich and Robbie, worked most of their adult lives at Mesta. So did my brother, Dan, who went to Pitt on a Mesta scholarship and became the treasurer of the company. I had that bond with Joe Chiodo as well. He displayed a large sign from Mesta at the rear end of his Homestead establishment.

I probably visited Chiodo's Bar a dozen times in my life. Yes, I ate the "Mystery Sandwich" on a visit there with my wife, Kathie, but never felt the urge to try it again. Mostly, I drank I.C. Light. I went there a couple of times in the weeks before it closed. Joe always made me feel like a celebrity, but he did that with everyone. There are certain people — Art Rooney, Doc Carlson, Frankie Gustine and Baldy Regan — who always made you feel good whenever you saw them.

Before he closed the bar, Joe asked me if there was anything I wanted from his eclectic collection of sports memorabilia. There were signed bras hanging from the rafters above the bar. They had been left there by female customers who got caught up in the spirit of the place. There were football helmets and baseball bats and ball caps and all kinds of sports stuff up in the rafters, and God only knows what else. I'm sure there was dust, too, but the health inspectors were too charmed by Chiodo's hospitality to take a close look.

I requested and received a framed photo showing Babe Ruth as a coach with the Brooklyn Dodgers with Ollie Carnegie, a top-notch minor league ballplayer from Hays, just down the road from Chiodo's. I remember my father telling me about Ollie Carnegie when he worked with some of his brothers at Mesta Machine Company. Joe also gave me a framed set of football bubble gum cards. There were three cards in that frame, Marshall Goldberg of Pitt and the Chicago Cardinals; Bill McPeak of New Castle and Pitt and the Pittsburgh Steelers; Ted Marchibroda of St. Bonaventure and the Pittsburgh Steelers. I have them in my home office. Where else would you find those three football figures in the same frame?

I have lots of pictures of Joe Chiodo and his customers that I took during my visits.

There was a Campbell's Corner in the back of the bar. It was named in honor of his good friend Bill Campbell and his family. Bill Campbell came out of Homestead where he'd been a good all-around athlete and became the head football coach at Columbia University.

Campbell wasn't that successful as a coach because it was too difficult to win with Columbia's high academic standards, but he was popular with the media and much respected for his football knowledge and his leadership skills. Somehow, Bill Campbell ended up in Silicon Valley and became a multi-millionaire in the high tech industry, serving as the president and CEO of Intuit in Mountain View, California.

Campbell brought friends from Silicon Valley to the Mon Valley and he always brought them to Chiodo's for an evening in his hometown. Campbell never forgot where he came from, and was most generous in sending funds for many projects in his hometown. His father William Campbell had been the superintendent of schools in Homestead, his Uncle Neenie had been a highly successful basketball coach at McKeesport High School, and his brother Jim was a star receiver at Navy when Roger Staubach was the quarterback, and later became an assistant athletic director at the U.S. Naval Academy.

Bill Campbell was never happier than he was when he came home to Chiodo's Tavern. He invited me to be there on one occasion when he brought family and friends to Chiodo's.

"Joe Chiodo had the common touch," claimed Bill Campbell. "He knew how to relate to people better than most of the corporate types I have mixed with through the years. Joe just got it."

No one wanted to see Chiodo sell his place. "I want to retire," he said. "I am 86 years old. No one works at 86. I've been married to the same girl for 54 years and I have not had dinner with her for four months. No one lives like that unless they are separated or divorced. I am tired and I want to get out."

"Joe Chiodo took care of his friends."
— Darrell Hess

During the glory days of the Steelers in the '70s, Chiodo's gained national attention in television and magazine and newspaper reports as an example of the kind of setting where Steelers' fans faithfully gathered to talk about their favorite team, and debate all kinds of sports issues. Whenever a member of the media asked Joe Gordon, the public relations director of the Steelers, where they could find some local color as a backdrop for their stories on the Steelers he would inevitably direct them to Chiodo's. It was located on a corner of Eighth Avenue at the intersection with the Homestead Hi-Level Bridge, since renamed the Homestead Grays Bridge in honor of one of the great baseball teams from the Negro Leagues.

Gordon knew the territory well because his father had once owned a bar of his own, the Hi-Lite, in the same neighborhood. His father's name was Manny Gordon, and he'd been a good baseball player in his day.

Joe Chiodo owned and operated his tavern for 58 years, until he closed its doors for good in April 2005. "The first 20 years here," he said, "I never had a vacation."

Chiodo's gave way to a Walgreen's, a drug store chain that was fast appearing in a lot of places around Pittsburgh. We needed another chain drug store like we needed more potholes in our streets. It upset his regular patrons quite a bit, but Chiodo, then 86, was having some health issues and, frankly, he was getting tired of the hours he'd been keeping for so many years. The financial offer was a good one, too good to turn down. He said he wanted to spend more time with his wife, Florence, at their home in nearby Munhall.

I was tipped off that Chiodo's would soon be closing by Darrell Hess, a good friend from West Mifflin, who was a frequent customer and close friend of Chiodo. Hess, a retired guidance counselor at West Mifflin High School, owned a card shop in Munhall and sold promotional materials for sports entities.

Hess has been the catalyst for much civic activity in the Homestead-Munhall area. He and his wife Betty helped raise funds for the Carnegie Library of Homestead, and he runs a golf tournament for the Homestead Lions at the Duquesne Golf Club, which became the Westwood Golf Club. He has coordinated a notorious sports dinner at the Thompson Club in West Mifflin for 50 years. Sports broadcasters Bob Prince and Bill Hillgrove held forth as the master of ceremonies during its lifetime. Myron Cope was a frequent speaker at the sports dinner.

"Joe Chiodo took good care of his friends," said Hess. "Then again he considered everyone who came to Chiodo's a friend"

I used to see Joe Chiodo holding court at a front row table at the Thompson Club dinner. That pointed up his celebrity. Someone had to die in order for a ticket to become available at that annual sold-out event. I was one of the speakers and I always said something to tease Joe Chiodo, usually about his diminutive size. I'd ask him to stand up and when he did I'd repeat my request for him to stand up. Little guys get that all the time. Chiodo was a favorite with Myron Cope. I always suspected Cope liked him because they could see eye to eye when they discussed most matters. They were about the same height. Cope might have had an inch on Chiodo.

I recall seeing Al Vento in the company of Chiodo at the Thompson Run Sports Dinner. Vento owned Vento's Pizza in East Liberty and had gained even more fame as a general in Franco's Italian Army.

Chiodo was not an official member of that Italian Army, but he had served a tour of duty in the U.S. Army. Bud Ward, a close friend and a regular at the bar, said that Joe was proud to have landed on Normandy Beach three days after D-Day.

Chiodo loved to talk to people. He was an engaging guy. He was more animated than Art Rooney, and talked louder, but he had some of the same qualities. He appreciated people, whether they were sports or political celebrities or just common people. Chiodo thought he was as common as they came. He liked to put his hand on your shoulder to make sure he kept your attention when he was talking. There was a warmth about him that was appealing.

Asked by Brian O'Neill, the columnist for the *Pittsburgh Post-Gazette* if he had any parting words before he closed his place, Chiodo exclaimed, "Tell the people of Homestead, West Homestead, Munhall, Allegheny County and the world: Thank you very much. They've been great!"

An auction was held to clear out Chiodo's of all the stuff that had been accumulated through the many years. The money went to charity.

Joe Chiodo died on a Sunday night. August 25, 2007, at the age of 89. His wife chose to have a private service and interment. There was no viewing. There was no opportunity for friends to pay their respects. I thought that was strange. Joe Chiodo had been a man of the people. Later, some friends held a memorial service for him, but the general public never got a chance to say goodbye to a good man.

As a tribute to Joe Chiodo, I am reprinting a chapter I wrote on him for an earlier book, *The Chief*, which was about his dear friend, Art Rooney Sr. "Art Rooney cared about me," said Chiodo one day when he was complaining to me about the poor treatment he was getting from the current club management.

"I couldn't do that to my loyal customers." — Joe Chiodo

It was a shame that Joe Chiodo couldn't be there when he was inducted into the Italian-American Sports Hall of Fame on April 29, 2001. Chiodo, a Homestead icon whose family restaurant has drawn national media attention through the years, was ill at the time.

He had been battling the gout since, interestingly enough, St. Patrick's Day. He may have contracted it from eating corned beef and cabbage at some Irish gathering and the Gaelic fare didn't agree with his Latin lining.

The gout is a metabolic disease marked by painful inflammation of the joints. It's tough to move about on sore feet. It is caused by uric acid in the blood and can be debilitating. So Chiodo's loyal customers had not seen much of him at his landmark restaurant on Eighth Avenue at the Hi-Level Bridge (since renamed the Homestead Grays Bridge).

He would have been thrilled to be honored at the Italian-American Sports Hall of Fame's 15th annual dinner at the downtown Hilton. He was one of three men inducted. Former pro golfer Jim Masserio Jr. and bowling standout Rocco Coniglio were the other two men similarly enshrined. Chiodo had great pride in his Italian heritage, so this was significant.

Then, too, some of the top achievers in about a dozen categories were honored at the same dinner. An old friend of Chiodo's, Charles "Corky" Cost, former Pitt three-sport standout and construction magnate from Wilkinsburg, was honored as "Man of the Year." He followed Armand Dellovade, a construction magnate from Avella and one of Pitt's most loyal boosters, who had been similarly honored the previous year.

It was apparent that Chiodo wasn't doing well when he failed to appear at his front row table for the 43rd annual Thompson Run Athletic

Photos by Jim O'Brien

"That isn't junk. It's love."
—Joe Chiodo

Association's Sports Night at the West Mifflin club a week earlier. Chiodo had perfect attendance at the first 42 award dinners and was always among those to be acknowledged in the audience. Chiodo stood only 5-feet 4-inches tall, but he's a big man in the Steel Valley.

I was honored to be asked to accept the award for Chiodo by Tony Ferraro, a national director of the Italian-American Sports Hall of Fame. Ferraro has serviced Chiodo's Restaurant for years as a sales executive for the Pittsburgh Brewing Company. Ferraro's wife, Kathy, and my wife, Kathie, are friends on the medical staff at Allegheny General Hospital. At an earlier dinner, Ferraro asked me to accept an award for Joe Montana, the Hall of Fame quarterback with the San Francisco 49ers and Kansas City Chiefs who hailed from Monongahela. Standing in for Joe Chiodo and Joe Montana is not an easy task. That's a real parlay.

I had been honored as a so-called "legend" at the same dinner two years ago. Not many Irishmen are honored at these affairs, so it was real special. Maybe they found out that I grew up surrounded by Italian families on Sunnyside Street in Glenwood. Glenwood is next to Hazelwood, which is better known, not always for the best reasons. I may be guilty of being a social climber when I tell people I'm from Hazelwood.

Chiodo's award and medals are now on display, along with the magnificent sports memorabilia adorning the walls and ceiling of Chiodo's Tavern. Everyone was rooting for the grand old gentleman, 83 at the time of the dinner, to rally and get back to his bar so he could share the good news with friends and customers.

Chiodo is a little guy with a big heart, something of an Italian leprechaun — a tricky little old man in Irish folklore who, if caught, may reveal the hiding place of treasure — and a tough cookie in his heyday.

He had been a Steelers' fan from the start, and has been running bus trips to away games in Cleveland, Cincinnati, Philadelphia, Detroit, Chicago and other NFL outposts since he formed a football club when the bar opened back in 1947. At last count, he held 36 season tickets to Steelers' home games.

Chiodo once nixed the sale of his saloon when the prospective buyer insisted that the 36 Steelers tickets be part of the deal. "I couldn't do that to my loyal customers," Chiodo said.

"I felt important to them."

During the Steelers' run in the '70s when they won four Super Bowls and were honored as the NFL's Team of the Decade, Chiodo's Tavern received a great deal of attention from network and local TV, magazines, newspapers, you name it, as a retreat for loyal Steelers' fans. Pictures of favorite players, banners, newspaper clippings, helmets, trophies, even colorful bras, can be found at Chiodo's. God only knows what all is up in the rafters, maybe even some of those infamous "Mystery" sandwiches.

As for the countless bras, Joe explained, "The young ladies, they come in here and get in a mood." And another bra goes up into the rafters. Signed most times by the donor, no less.

Chiodo's Tavern was a magnet for travelers from all areas of Pittsburgh, and from the Oakland campuses, long before The Waterfront was on the planning boards. It was Joe Chiodo who made it someplace special. The college kids loved to talk to him. He had so many stories to share, and he appreciated those who frequented his place.

For the record, Joe Chiodo was born in the little town of St. Tommaso Soveria Mannelli in the Province of Catanzaro, Italy in 1917. In 1927, at the age of 10, he came to America with his mother to join his father, who was already here.

As a young boy, he learned the shoemaker trade and worked in a shop in Homestead. It was there that the Chiodo family decided to live.

At the age of 18, Chiodo attained Eagle Scout ranking. In 1941, he served in the U.S. Army, where he progressed from corporal to sergeant. He served five years and, during the Battle of Normandy, was given a field commission to lieutenant.

In 1947, he and his father, Pietro, opened the Chiodo's Tavern on 8th Avenue in Homestead. It was to become well known as a sports hangout, and was popular with the workers at nearby U.S. Steel and Mesta Machine Company, when those mills were going full blast. .

One of Joe's biggest thrills came when he was pictured on a Steelers' game ticket in 1992, the team's 60th anniversary season. He was so honored because he had been a lifetime Steelers' fan. "I felt important to them."

He has sponsored teams in golf, bowling, baseball and softball. So he was honored as a contributor in the sports world.

Joe and his wife, Florence, celebrated 50 years of marriage the previous year and they lived up on the hill in West Homestead.

"The attention was good for business."

I was coming from Clairton to Pittsburgh on a dreary night, Tuesday, June 5, 2001. I was driving along the Monongahela River from Clairton to Duquesne and past West Mifflin and Munhall before I hit Homestead. They were once all great steel towns and football towns. I had attended the funeral of my Aunt Mildred K. Clark, my mother's kid sister, that evening. Aunt Millie was 87 when she died. My mother, Mary O'Brien, was 94 and struggling toward 95. It hurt that I couldn't tell my mother that her sister had died. It wouldn't have registered.

When I spotted Chiodo's Tavern, I thought I had better stop to see if by any chance Joe might be there tending bar. I had heard he wasn't coming in much lately, since his battle with the gout, but I also thought there might not be too many opportunities to catch Chiodo in action. So I pulled into the parking lot next to his place.

There were only a few customers at the bar when I walked through the door to check it out. Business picked up later. Out of the corner of my left eye, I caught Chiodo coming down the hall, greeting me enthusiastically, the only way he ever greeted anyone who came through that door. "Jimmy, it's so good to see you!" Chiodo cried out. "I saw you through the window and it made me feel so good." He extended his left hand to shake mine, saying his right hand still hurt too much to have anyone squeezing it.

He ushered me into the dining room where he had been sitting with two good friends, Tom Lacey, a retired instructor from the art department at the University of Pittsburgh, and his wife, Eileen. Lacey, who grew up in Munhall, was a sculptor, working at Pitt with the renowned Virgil Cantini. One of Lacey's steel renderings paying testimony to Chiodo's beginnings as a shoemaker was on display in the bar next door. Lacey once taught art and coached the wrestling team, an unusual combination, at West Mifflin High School and also later served on the school board.

Chiodo called for a bottle of I.C. Light with a frosted glass for me and, after I had turned him down several times, succeeded in talking me into having a cheeseburger. It was just right, and hit the spot, as did the I.C. Light. Chiodo kept his elbows on the red and white checkered oilcloth table covering as he spoke.

There was a GUINNESS mirror directly behind Chiodo and that got him talking about a trip he made to Ireland. Then he brought out some Ireland guidebooks to show me his picture in both of them. He's pictured in a bar in Ireland drinking a glass of Guinness.

"I got better treatment in Ireland than I did in my homeland of Italy," said Chiodo. "The Irish are good people. I was disappointed the way my wife and I were treated in Italy. I'm not eager to go back."

Chiodo told me he had gone down to the UPMC Sports Complex the Steelers share with the University of Pittsburgh football program on the city's South Side. Chiodo was not happy with his seat location in the new football stadium, and was bitter about the treatment he was getting from the Steelers.

"I asked them to put me on the Steelers' side of the stadium," he explained. "I thought I might get some special consideration after all these years, with all those tickets I've had, with all those bus trips I lined up to take my customers to away games. I wanted to be on the shady side of the stadium. Hey, at 83, I can't handle staring into the sun anymore. It's hard enough to see."

Chiodo recalled the days when he'd go down to the Fort Pitt Hotel, or the Roosevelt Hotel, or Three Rivers Stadium and see the owner of the team and talk to him about his needs. Chiodo recalled how he used to bring a box of chocolate candy for each of the secretaries at the Steelers' offices.

"I don't know anyone there any more," Chiodo complained. "I couldn't get to see the people I wanted to talk to. The receptionist kept telling me this one or that one was busy, or at a meeting and couldn't be disturbed. It's not the same anymore. I went over to the Pitt side of the building, and was able to see Coach Walt Harris. He was great. He took me on a little tour of the place. He signed a miniature Pitt helmet for me. Come, let me show it to you."

Chiodo escorted me into the bar area, and proudly pointed toward the ceiling, where a shiny new blue and gold helmet hung from the rafters, right up there with the bras and the shoulder pads and you name it. What a sports museum! "That isn't junk," said Chiodo. "It's love."

He showed me his own little Hall of Fame. He had affixed the nameplates of some of his departed friends in the sports business to a counter top along the window facing 8th Avenue. The names included Art Rooney, Bob Prince and Steve Petro, who'd all been to his place.

"When my mother died — back on June 1, 1973 — some of my own neighbors did not come to the funeral," he said. "Art Rooney was at a cottage in Ligonier when he learned of my mother's death. He and Joe Carr and Jim Boston came to my mother's funeral. I was just a lowly customer of his, but he came all that way to pay his respects. That's the kind of man he was.

"When I first started buying all those tickets, Joe Carr, their ticket manager, gave me three books of season tickets for free. I got three books when they played at Forbes Field, two books for free at Pitt Stadium, and nothing for free when they moved to Three Rivers Stadium. Shouldn't I have gotten at least one at Three Rivers? Now I can't get anyone's attention about my ticket location. It's not as good as it was at Three Rivers. I had 72 people going to games on the road with me at one point. Doesn't that count for anything anymore? We'd charter a bus from the DeBolt people in Homestead and we had a great time."

My late brother Dan used to go on those trips, along with his good friends, Bob "Blue" Martin and Bob Vavro. Chiodo told me Vavro, a retired barber and barbers' union official from Hazelwood, was still handling the business books for Chiodo's football club when it came to an end. It disbanded when the Steelers moved to Heinz Field.

He said Joe Gordon, the former public relations director for the Steelers, was always good to him, and sent sportswriters and broadcasters out to see him and his bar during the glory days of the Steelers. "The attention was good for business," claimed Chiodo. "I appreciated that."

His friend had a big book on the table that I recognized. It was a book about John Adams, our second President, by David McCullough, a Pittsburgh-born writer who was educated at Pitt and Yale. McCullough won the Pulitzer Prize with his biography *Truman* a few years earlier.

That prompted another story by Chiodo. "When someone dies, I like to buy memorial books for the Carnegie Library in Homestead," he said.

"When Mrs. Rooney died, I didn't buy flowers. I sent money to St. Peter's, the Rooney's church on the North Side, for them to buy some books in her memory for the grade school there. I did the same thing when Mr. Rooney died. Flowers last a few days. Books are forever."

Many of his past patrons came to Chiodo's in the closing weeks, just to see it and experience it one more time. "Where have you been?" Chiodo usually asked them as they shook hands and exchanged pleasantries. "If you'd been around more often I might have stayed in business."

Among those in attendance at Armand Dellovade's annual "Italian Stag" party at his home in Lawrence were, left to right, Joe Chiodo, Don DeBlasio, Dan Onorato, Joe Natoli and Tony Ferraro.

Joe Chiodo joins old-time friends Aldo Bartolotta, Joe Santoni and Joe Natoli at Armand Dellovade's annual "Italian Stag" social event.

Bill Campbell
He loved and admired Joe Chiodo

*"I always felt comfortable
going home to Chiodo's."*

I always think I'm doing something right as a writer when I can get someone to smile or cry when they read my stories. It's not difficult to get Bill Campbell to do both. In the same paragraph. Or in conversation. He's got a great Irish smile, and gleaming hazel eyes that appear to turn green in bright light. He's sentimental and tears show quickly on his rosy cheeks. He's my kind of reader, my kind of guy.

Bill Campbell is an American success story, a Homestead success story, a hometown hero, indeed. He and his brother Jim were both terrific all-around sports stars and top-notch students in their schooldays in Homestead. Their father, William V. Campbell Sr., was a respected school administrator and became the superintendent of schools there. His father had dropped out of the University of Pittsburgh to enter the military service during World War II and completed his college education at Duquesne upon returning home. He worked in the mill during his college days. Their uncle, Neenie Campbell, was a highly successful and popular basketball coach across the Monongahela River at McKeesport High School.

That's why it was gratifying to see Bill honored with the Lifetime Achievement Award at the 50th Anniversary Sports Night at the Thompson Club in West Mifflin on Thursday, May 8, 2008.

"I have deep affection for this area," said Campbell in accepting the award from his friend Darrell Hess, who has coordinated the dinner from Day One. "Everything I have achieved started right here in this community. What I learned here, in regard to academics and athletics, has served me well all my life. I learned to compete here, and I learned to have compassion. I've done my best to try and pay back."

Jack Butler, a former defensive back for the Steelers and the recently retired director of the Blesto scouting service, was present for the dinner. He had been honored at the initial dinner 50 years earlier. "Bill Campbell has always been a class act," said Butler, who has made Munhall his home for many years. "I dealt with him when he was an assistant coach at Boston College and when he was at Columbia, and he always treated me well. He's never forgotten where he came from. He's one of the good guys."

I first became aware of Bill Campbell when he was the head football coach at Columbia University in the mid-70s. I was working at *The New York Post* at the time. One of my colleagues, Paul Zimmerman, had played football at Columbia and he was a big fan of Campbell. They had played on a rugby club team together. Zimmerman wrote glowing columns about Campbell even though his Lions' teams weren't that successful in Ivy League competition. Zimmerman knew a great leader when he saw one. Zimmerman has become even more famous as Dr. Z, the highly respected pro football pundit at *Sports Illustrated*.

Campbell was the captain of the 1961 Columbia football team, the only year Columbia won the Ivy League football title. He weighed just 170 pounds, but he was a two-way interior lineman who often faced opponents 20, 30 and 40 pounds heavier than he was and more than held his own. He stayed on to get a master's degree at Columbia's Teachers College while serving as an assistant coach to Aldo "Buff" Donelli, another Western Pennsylvania sports legend. Donelli, out of Bridgeville, shared coaching duties with Bert Bell with the Steelers in 1941. Donelli didn't tell many people that his record as head coach of the Steelers was 0–5. He was the coach of Duquesne University at the same time, and gave up the Steelers' post to pay more attention to his duties at Duquesne. Yes, it was a different era.

Campbell had less success in his six seasons as head coach of the Columbia team during the mid-70s. He gave up the ghost and got on with what Chuck Noll would call "his life's work."

At the Thompson Club dinner, Campbell sat on the dais next to Randy Grossman, the former Steelers' tight end from the '70s, who was honored as the recipient of the Man of Yesteryear Award. "Randy asked me how I went from football to high tech," said Campbell with a smile. "I told him to look at my record at Columbia. That'll explain it."

Campbell got out of coaching and became a big success in the business world, first at Eastman Kodak Company, then Apple Computer, Inc. He also founded Claris, a software company, and Go, a pin-based operating company. Then he served for five years as president and chief executive officer at Intuit. During a 15-year span, he was the chief executive of three high-tech companies. He's now the chairman of the board of trustees at Intuit, Inc. His office is in Palo Alto, near Stanford University and about a ten-minute drive from the corporate headquarters of Intuit at Mountain View. "When you're the chairman it's best not to be looking over the shoulder of the president," explained Campbell. He is known as 'Coach' in Silicon Valley.

He has a dedicated table in a Palo Alto pub called the Old Pro, and there's a plaque that reads "Coach's Corner" in his honor. He's been known to keep late hours there, a holdover from his Homestead days perhaps. At Chiodo's, I recall seeing a sign that read "CAMPBELL'S CORNER" in the back on the left side.

I talked at length to Campbell over the telephone on Wednesday, March 19, 2008. His secretary, Debbie Brookfield, told me to call at 4:30 p.m. that day. Campbell was in such an upbeat mood. I realized why he was in such good spirits when I read the business section of the newspaper the next day and saw that one of Intuit's software products, Turbotax, had reported a 16 percent rise in sales over the previous year's first quarter. Turbotax is a respected personal finance software. According to *The Wall Street Journal* report, Intuit had sold 12.5 million units of Turbotax as of March 15.

Lifetime Achievement Award recipient Bill Campbell Jr. is flanked by former Pitt football standout Dave Jancisin, left, and dinner chairman Darrell Hess at West Mifflin's Thompson Club Sports Night.

The late Jim Campbell, one of the best all-around athletes to hail from Homestead, gets warm embrace from Joe Bugel of Munhall, the former NFL coach, who was honored in his hometown.

Campbell was 67 at the time and serving as the chairman of the board for Intuit, a high tech company that employed 8,200 in what is known as Silicon Valley. He was talking to me from his office.

Mountain View, by the way, is about an hour's drive south of San Francisco. Intuit provides business and financial management solutions for small and medium-sized businesses, financial institutions and accounting professionals in the U.S. and internationally.

They offer Quicken, an accounting software, as well as Turbotax, among other products. Since he arrived at Intuit in 1994, revenues have soared from $200 million to $2 billion.

Campbell is on the board of trustees at Columbia. In 2000, he was presented with the Alexander Hamilton Award for distinguished service and accomplishment by his alma mater. A contingent of bagpipers and drummers from the New York Police Department's Emerald Society surprised Campbell and added to the festive occasion. His son, Billy, was graduated from Columbia in 2004. Bill and his wife, Roberta —they met at Columbia—also have a daughter, Maggie, who is a high school student. Speaking about his wife, Campbell mentioned that she was the first woman dean at Columbia. "She's the smart one in the family," he said.

My friend Darrell Hess, who is the catalyst for so much community activity in the Steel Valley, was the first to tell me about all the good things Bill Campbell did for the schools in his hometown. Hess oversees a William V. Campbell Scholarship Dinner for student athletes from Steel Valley High and West Mifflin High, where Hess once worked as a guidance counselor. Hess often calls on Campbell to finance his community projects. "Andrew Carnegie's spirit to create good things in the communities where he had steel mills is still alive in Bill Campbell's generosity," said Hess.

Campbell personally funded and directed the reconstruction of Campbell Field, named for his father; the technology program at Steel Valley High School; the establishment of the James Campbell Gymnasium; the renovation of the athletic Training and Exercise Room at Carnegie Library of Homestead, and many other civic and athletic functions in the Steel Valley. Steelers quarterback Charlie Batch was present at the Sports Night Dinner. He has been helping out in many ways to better the lives of children in his home area, and he wants to build some dwellings and shops in the community, and has spoken to Campbell about assisting him in his mission.

I once served as a pinch-hitter for Bill Campbell at the Steel Valley scholar-athlete banquet. I met Bill's mother, Virginia, at the dinner. Bill had been in a biking accident—shades of Ben Roethlisberger—and couldn't make it. I brought a young man from my neighborhood with me to observe what I was doing. That was Doug Miller. He was a high school student and had expressed an interest to get into my business so I had him tag along with me to sports-related events. I gave him a game plan and he played it out to perfection and then some. I've always enjoyed mentoring young men and women, so I can appreciate what Campbell has achieved with his largesse.

114

Bill Campbell and Joe Chiodo are kings of the mountain when Campbell brought his son, Bill, and good friends from California to his hometown of Homestead.

Bill Campbell Jr. shows off aerial view of renovated stadium at Steel Valley High that is named in honor of his father.

Photos by Jim O'Brien

Joe Chiodo and Bill Campbell enjoy reunion in front of replica of old streetcar.

During our respective days at Pitt, I set up Miller with an internship with the New York Jets. He stayed on for 17 years in the Jets' publicity offices, and was now in his second year as the senior public relations director of the New Orleans Saints.

Darrell Hess speaks glowingly of Bill Campbell and Joe Chiodo.

"Bill and Joe Chiodo were a great team," said Hess. "Joe Chiodo knew how to treat his customers. He was like Frankie Gustine in that regard. He made everyone feel at home. Bill Campbell never forgot where he came from. He was so proud of his family and where he got his start, and he's done so much to pay back to the children and grandchildren of people who helped him along the way. I'm privileged to have known Joe Chiodo—I loved going to his place and talking to him and Bud Ward—my cousin and great friend—and the regulars at the bar —and I'm lucky to have Bill Campbell on my support team."

Hess had organized a dinner a year or so earlier to pay tribute to Bill's brother, Jim. He had been a star receiver for the Navy football team when Roger Staubach was the quarterback for the Midshipmen. "Jim caught eight or nine passes when they beat Pitt in 1963," his brother recalled. "Navy played in the Cotton Bowl that year and Pitt (9–1) didn't go to a bowl game." Jim became ill and the dinner to honor him had to be cancelled. He died on March 8, 2006. Bill had such admiration and love for his brother, who later served as an assistant athletic director at the Academy in Annapolis. "I have a picture of him in my sports bar," said Bill Campbell.

Joe Chiodo always called him Billy and was quick to point out a photo of him that hung proudly alongside photos of the Pittsburgh Pirates, Pittsburgh Steelers, Homestead Grays and other local luminaries.

It's interesting to note that he is also called "Ballsy" by those who know him well. As Charles Butler pointed out in a profile in the *Columbia College Today* magazine, "it's not exactly the kind of name you'd expect for a guy who has been compared to such luminary businessmen as Jack Welch and Bill Gates. This is the sort of prominent fellow who hangs around with the likes of Steve Jobs and other Silicon Valley legends."

So Butler was surprised to end up interviewing Campbell at Chiodo's, his favorite hangout back home in Homestead. When Chiodo showed his visitor Campbell's photo, he said, "This is Billy Campbell, the young man from our hometown who gave so much to his hometown."

Talk to Betty Esper, the mayor of Homestead who goes by the nickname Bo, and hear her brag about Billy Campbell. He has sent her $1,000 check so there could be a Christmas parade in Homestead, a $20,000 check to put computers in police cars, and other checks to support other local projects.

"Billy always told me, 'There is never a time you can't call me,' and this was before he was so well known. I remember a time I called him and we got to talking about Homestead, and I remember at one point he got all choked up—because he misses home, he's still a hometown boy—and he said, "You know, Bo, one of these days when I'm able to, I'm going to do something for my hometown.'

"And he has certainly done it. He has never forgotten his roots. If everyone was Billy Campbell in these small towns and gave back, it would be a better world, for sure."

Chiodo was closing up shop in Homestead in 2006, giving way to a Walgreen's, and the news was like hearing of the death of a loved one to Bill Campbell. "Oh, young Campbell, he was always a likeable fellow," said Chiodo. "When he was young, he worked as a pin boy at a bowling alley for my brother and his uncle. He was always a hustler."

Bill Campbell:

I'll tell you how I became so close to Joe Chiodo, and why he meant so much to me. I'm a really young guy and my Uncle Johnny Dauria—my mother's brother—and Sam Chiodo—Joe's brother—owned and operated the Arcadian Lanes on Eighth Avenue in Homestead. I went down there to work as a pinsetter and, after awhile, I got to be the counter boy.

That was my start in business and learning how to deal with customers and solving problems. I think they had ten or twelve lanes with rubber-band duckpins. Later, they added a few more lanes with tenpins. I worked there all the time I was in high school, and then they got automatic pin-setting equipment. I worked there in the winter and on weekends year-round. They taught me how to look after things.

I got to know Joe Chiodo because he came around to see his brother Sam. Joe took a liking to me, and I adored the guy. I was bigger than he was, but I looked up to him.

When I came home from college, I'd hook up with Tom Stanton and the McDonald Brothers and my brother Jim and my dad and we'd go to Chiodo's. That was a big deal for my dad. He was the superintendent at Homestead High and the only places he usually went to were the Thompson Club and the Duquesne Golf Club because he didn't want to get hassled about something that was going on at the high school. He was very conscientious about not drinking in public.

Chiodo's would get crowded around 4 p.m. We'd be drinking with all the steelworkers. The guys would come there from the nearby U.S. Steel and from Mesta Machine Company in West Homestead. Joe used to work at Mesta. We'd sit there all night until the guys would be coming in off the 4-to-12 or 3-to-11 shift, and have a few beers before they went home.

We'd play shuffleboard—when it was working—and have a great time. I'd come back through the years. When I was at Apple and now at Intuit, I'd come back home and I liked bringing some of my friends in the business. I wanted to show them a good time. Joe had all those tickets to the Steelers' games

117

and organized those bus trips for the guys to Steelers' games on the road. Then the Steelers won all those Super Bowls in the '70s and newspaper guys from all over the country would come to town and they'd be directed to check out Chiodo's. It was thought to be the best example of a hangout for Steelers' fans. I'd see Joe and he'd gleam. "Bill, I've been discovered," he'd say. He was great with my friends. He was great with everybody. Why'd I keep coming back? Well, it's like 'Cheers'—that show that took place in that bar in Boston. You want to go where everybody knows your name.

Joe used to tell stories. Our family and his went back a long way. When Joe first came to this country from Italy my mother translated for him and looked after him. She took good care of him. I get a little teary talking about that. His father, Sam Chiodo, had a shoe repair shop at 9th and Amity. Joe was my family. When I left to go to college I missed the men in my hometown. Whenever I'd come home, I'd go to Chiodo's. It was always a good place I could take my dad. It was the most exciting thing in the world, something we could do together.

There was a fellow named Dr. Pat Crecine who was a provost at Carnegie Mellon University. When I was at Apple we worked on some projects with people at CMU. He was known as the father of academic computing for what he did at CMU. He went on to become the president of Georgia Tech. Now he's back at CMU as a visiting professor. He loved to go to Chiodo's. We spent all kinds of time at Chiodo's. It caught on with the college crowd. Joe put in all those imported beers, and the kids from CMU and Pitt and Duquesne started coming to his place. He was great with the college kids.

My Uncle Neenie—you remember him as the basketball coach at McKeesport High School—used to go there. When his team played at Homestead, the kids would holler out, "Let's have a weenie for Neenie!" When Chick Davies was the Homestead coach they would holler at him similarly when he took his team to McKeesport. They'd holler out, 'Let's have a dick for Chick!" Chick Davies was my English teacher at Homestead High.

So I kept going to Chiodo's. Joe always treated me so well. I had the greatest respect and admiration for the man. He'd give us some homemade red wine when we'd go to his home.

I have been a loyal Homestead guy, a Steel Valley guy. I've helped in many ways, where I could. I helped out at the Carnegie Library of Homestead. We gave them several million to put computers into the classrooms. One of my classmates, Bobby Wargo, is on the school board and I've gotten money to them through his efforts. Joe calls me and tells me they've got a coach at Steel Valley—a nice young man, says Joe—and he needs video equipment. So I sent a check for $20,000 to take care of that. I helped the boys' sports programs and then I talked to my wife and she thought I should do the same for the young women's programs. I'm also friendly with Joe Ducar—he owns Duke's Upper Deck Café on Eighth Avenue just across from where Chiodo's was located—and I've worked with him to help out there. Joe was the president of the school board. I've become much more involved with them. We fixed up the football field. We refurbished the place and put in artificial turf. We put in lighting and it's dedicated to my dad.

I don't worry about it. I know the money will be well spent. I like what Charlie Batch is doing at Steel Valley. He also grew up in Homestead and he's doing a lot of good things for the kids in the community. Being a Steeler gets the right kind of attention, and he's got some great plans for building homes and apartments in his hometown. He's a wonderful guy and I salute all he's done.

I've been keeping up with the Terrelle Pryor story. I am glad he's going to Ohio State. A good friend of mine, Joe Daniel, is the quarterback coach there and helped recruit Pryor out of Jeannette. Joe and I were both assistant coaches at Boston College way back when. He was the receivers coach and I was the linebackers coach. I'll be keeping a close eye on the Buckeyes to see how they do. They're getting some great players out of western Pennsylvania.

Jim O'Brien

Bill Campbell Jr. accepts Lifetime Achievement Award at 50th annual Sports night at Thompson Club in West Mifflin.

Bill Mazeroski
Baseball's reluctant hero

The last half of the ninth inning...And Ralph Terry, of course, on the mound, will be facing Mazeroski...Here's a ball one, too high, now to Mazeroski...Now the Yankees have tied the game in the top of the ninth inning...Well, a little while ago when we mentioned that this one, in typical fashion, was going right down to the wire, little did we know... Art Ditmar throws. Here's a swing and high fly ball going deep to left... it may do it! Back to the wall goes Berra. It is over the fence! Home run! The Pirates win! (Continuous cheering without comment for 35 seconds.) Ladies and gentlemen...Mazeroski has hit a one-nothing pitch over the left field fence at Forbes Field to win the 1960 World Series for the Pittsburgh Pirates by a score of 10-nothing. Once again, that final score: the Pittsburgh Pirates, the 1960 World Series Champions, defeat the New York Yankees, the Pirates 10 and the Yankees 9. It is all over in one of the most dramatic finishes on (sic) history. Bill Mazeroski has hit his second World Series home run over the left field barrier, 406 feet away, and the Pirates are the 1960 World Champions of baseball."

**—Broadcast call by Chuck Thompson
at 3:36 p.m. on October 13, 1960**

Bill Mazeroski was sitting in a rocking chair in the dimly-lit family room of his home in Greensburg, Pennsylvania. Mazeroski was rocking back and forth and smiling like a Cheshire cat as he listened to a tape recording of Chuck Thompson's call of Maz's famous home run.

Mazeroski's wife, Milene, sat silently in a chair nearby. Bill chortled every now and then, positively purring, whenever Thompson made a mistake in his commentary, like having Art Ditmar instead of Ralph Terry throwing that fateful pitch (Ditmar was warming up in the bullpen), or the final score (10-nothing) the first time around. Mazeroski memorized the script long ago. His eyebrows shot up knowingly each time Thompson said something wrong, and Maz seemed to be talking under his breath.

"He sounded more excited than I was," said Mazeroski, smiling at his own line, remembering how he had run around the bases waving his ballcap and carrying on like a kid in a playground.

When Thompson said the crowd was 36,683, Mazeroski smiled once more and said mockingly, "And I've talked to every one of them!" And probably another hundred thousand or so who believe they were there that afternoon.

Mazeroski continued to smile as he listened to what he quickly recognized as a re-created post-game interview with broadcaster Bob Prince. "Bill, how's it feel to be the hero of the World Series?" Prince asks on the tape I was playing for Mazeroski's amusement. That's not the way it went. In truth, at the time, Prince had no idea how the 1960

This is path Bill Mazeroski used to walk from his boyhood home.

A three-mile stretch of Route 7 that passes through Rayland, Tiltonsville and Yorkville is dedicated to hometown hero.

Bill Mazeroski relaxes after a golf outing at Dick Groat's Champion Lakes Golf Course.

Maz enjoys cigar while he demonstrates how he held his glove when he played second base for the Bucs.

World Series had ended. He left the broadcast booth early so he could get to the clubhouse immediately after the game to do interviews with the winning team. Prince had brushed off Mazeroski, the first player to come his way in a crazy clubhouse at Forbes Field following the game. Mazeroski never had much to say.

Mazeroski remembered it differently.

"I didn't think I remembered him talking to me like that after the game," he said. "I was pushed toward Prince, and he asked me a few questions. He said, 'How's it feel to be on a world championship team?' I always wondered why he didn't ask me about the home run. I asked him a year later, 'Did you want Dick Stuart to hit the home run or me?' (Stuart was on deck when Mazeroski hit his home run, and often said he was planning to hit the home run to be the game's hero.) The truth is that, at the time, he didn't know who hit it."

I had borrowed my daughter Rebecca's portable tape player and brought it with me when I visited the Mazeroskis at their home on Saturday morning, November 21, 1992. Doug Hoerth, then of WTAE Radio, had been thoughtful enough to send me a tape recording of the seventh game of the 1960 World Series after learning of my book project. Hoerth was a big fan of Bob Prince.

I would play that same tape when I visited the homes of Harvey Haddix in Springfield and Rocky Nelson in Portsmouth, respectively, in central and the southern tip of Ohio.

I thought that playing the tape would be a good way to set the mood for my Mazeroski interview. It worked. It lit up Maz and set the tone for two-and-a-half hours of pleasant and insightful conversation. He remains the only man to ever end a seven-game World Series with a walk-off home run.

"I wish somebody else would do it," said Mazeroski. "Maybe they'd be more outgoing and they could explain it better."

(On October 23, 1993, Joe Carter of the Toronto Blue Jays became only the second man in baseball history to end the World Series with a home run. His three-run homer in the bottom of the ninth inning off Mitch Williams gave the Blue Jays an 8–6 win in Game 6 and their second straight World Championship.)

I remember that Bill and Milene and their dog Muttley were all sitting on the front porch of their home on a dreary day when it was cool and there was a light rainfall. They were sitting there wearing sweaters. They said they wanted to make sure I didn't drive by and miss their home. I had been there once before to interview Bill for a *Sport* magazine piece during his playing days with the Pirates.

That tells you something about the Mazeroskis. When I mentioned to Milene that I remembered the white doilies she had stretched across the tops of the couches and chairs in the family room, she smiled demurely. "I'm sure it's the same furniture from your last visit, too," admitted Milene. That also tells you something about the Mazeroskis. There's never been any pretense with the Mazeroskis.

I also remembered that the two of them retreated to Schenley Park right after the game, and stood in a clearing where they could see the skyline of Downtown Pittsburgh. "No one was in the park," recalled Maz. "There weren't even any squirrels. I think they went all Downtown to join in the celebration."

I thought Mazeroski did just fine. He would break into tears and not be able to read his acceptance speech years later when he was finally inducted into the Baseball Hall of Fame in Cooperstown, New York. That was fine, too. Those of us who were there to see him get his due will never forget Mazeroski's special moments at the induction ceremony. It was so Maz. He has never shared his unspoken script with the public.

"He's so damn real," Steve Blass has said admiringly of Maz.

It was his humble, unassuming manner that made Maz such a popular and enduring hero. I recall enjoying a beer with him one afternoon after a charity golf outing at the Duquesne Golf Club (now Westwood Golf Club) when I told him, "I am always excited to be in your company." He stared at me quizzically and asked, "Why?" And I responded, "Because of who you are and, more importantly, because of the way you are."

Maz could never understand why fans fussed over him.

He was the starting second baseman for the Pirates from 1957 through 1970, and there was none like him. "He became the most proficient second baseman the Pirates or possibly anyone else ever had," wrote Roy McHugh in *The Pittsburgh Press*.

In recent years, I've traveled to the neck of the woods where Mazeroski grew up in the most modest of circumstances. His house is no longer there. They were dynamiting for coal with warning signs posted everywhere the last time I was there. His dad had been a coal miner. He was also a promising ballplayer. But his foot was badly injured in a coal mine accident and his baseball career came to an abrupt halt. He was a heavy drinker, a heavy smoker, a quiet man. Maz was close to his mom, a heavy-set woman who thought the sun set on her son.

Maz spent a lot of time with his grandparents. I've run into boyhood friends and former grade school and high school classmates of Maz. They all talk about how quiet and unassuming he was. They say his sister was even quieter. They say he used to come out of school at lunchtime and go fishing in the nearby Ohio River. His nickname then was "Catfish."

Maz is usually reluctant to reflect on his boyhood or his home. Bill was born in the hospital in Wheeling, West Virginia. "My mother went across the bridge to the hospital in Wheeling, and then she went back home to Ohio," said Maz.

"It was a little place called Witch Hazel. It was near Adena, Ohio. It's back in the hills between Steubenville and Wheeling. We didn't have electricity. We had outhouses. We didn't have a refrigerator. We just didn't have much where I came from. I dug my uncle's outhouse for my first (baseball) glove. And you go down pretty deep when you dig an outhouse. We got the glove for me as a reward for my work. It might have been one of those three-finger gloves."

The stretch of Route 7 nearest his boyhood home is now called Bill Mazeroski Highway. It's a three-mile stretch that runs by Rayland, Tiltonsville and Yorkville. Bill owned a golf course in Rayland and a bar that was called Bills' Ribs that he owned with Bill DelVecchio, a local real estate broker. It's the same stretch of highway where former Pirates' pitcher Bob Moose of Export, Pennsylvania lost his life when he went off the road in his automobile. It was determined that Moose was drunk when he was driving that night. He died in Martins Ferry on October 9, 1976 -- after a party to celebrate his 29th birthday.

I learned that Maz once hit a home run in the final inning to deal Phil Niekro of Blaine, Oho, near Martins Ferry, his only setback as a pitcher in their respective high school days. Niekro is now immortalized in the Baseball Hall of Fame. Doug Huff of the *Wheeling News-Register* related those two items to me after I had written a book called *MAZ And the '60 Bucs*. I wish I had known that information when I was writing the book, but it's that way with all the books I've written. I always learn some stories later that I would liked to have included in the original text.

Maz once told me, "I can remember walking down dirt roads and picking up a broom stick and hitting stones and pretending to be Babe Ruth and winning a World Series."

I thought about his telling remark as I retraced his steps on those same gravel stone paths near his boyhood home on July 1, 2005. I picked up some of those stones, but didn't have a stick to swat at them.

"As a kid, you always dream of hitting the home run to win the World Series," said Mazeroski. "It just happened to come true for me. A day doesn't go by during baseball season that someone doesn't come up and mention the home run to me. At least, it seems that way. I never thought that home run would stay with me the rest of my life."

Maz leads a simple, untarnished, almost philosophical life. "I look for the easy way to do things," he once said during his playing days. He hasn't changed. He lives in solitude for the most part, picking his spots when he wants to tune in to the real world. "I am just myself…the same person I have always been," he assures you.

The Pirates hired him to be a training camp instructor when the team went to Bradenton for spring training in 2008. When one of the present-day Pirates spotted him sitting on a stool alongside a fence at one of the playing fields, he pointed him out to a teammate. "Look," he said, "there's The Legend."

Willie Stargell
A Star That Still Shines

"He respected everybody."
—Dave Giusti

W illie Stargell, one of the most popular athletes in the history of Pittsburgh, died the morning of April 9, 2001—Opening Day for the Pirates at the brand new PNC Park. Stargell had been suffering from kidney failure for years before he died at New Hanover Regional Medical Center in Wilmington, North Carolina, where he had been residing. There was so much irony to the timing of his passing.

A 12-foot bronze statue in Stargell's likeness had been unveiled on the Federal Street sidewalk outside PNC Park just two days earlier. Stargell had been unable to attend because of his illness, but it was hoped they could hold an official celebration with him present later in the summer. There was hope his health would improve.

He was only 61 when he died. Once the strongest of men in Pittsburgh, he had withered to a mere shadow of himself in his last months in Wilmington. His second wife, Margaret, had been a popular political leader in Wilmington for many years, and that's how Stargell ended up there.

I had spent time with Stargell on many occasions, and interviewed him from time to time. It was always time well spent. I remember sitting next to him on the dais at a sports banquet in Greensburg back in the early '80s. He was nervous about speaking in public like that. I felt confident in such circumstances, but can remember how nervous I was when I played in a media baseball game before a Pirates' game at Forbes Field one evening. I was playing second base, but no one would have mistaken me for Bill Mazeroski. They do now, believe it or not, when I'm out signing books, but not that night at Forbes Field.

I had upset Stargell early in both of our professional careers. I wrote a front-page headline story about him having a clubhouse fight with Roberto Clemente in Pittsburgh Weekly Sports, an irreverent tabloid newspaper that Beano Cook and I published from 1963 through 1968. Beano had given me the scoop he'd gotten from an usher at Forbes Field. "This will make us," Beano boasted at the time. It turned out that the actual fight had involved two other black ballplayers, Donn Clendenon and Maury Wills. I realize now that having an usher named "Big Bob" as your best source doesn't merit a banner headline in a tabloid newspaper, especially one that was already operating on a shoestring budget.

One of our subscribers was an attorney for Clemente and Stargell. We were sued for $1 million in damages in Clemente's case, and $750,000, for some unexplained reason, in Stargell's situation. I was a little nervous, and I am sure my intended bride, Kathleen Churchman, was having second thoughts about getting mixed up with me as well.

I was scratching to come up with $25 for a tuxedo for our scheduled wedding.

The case was later dismissed. There had been no malice on our part, simply stupidity. Young writers make mistakes, too.

Clemente was killed in an airplane crash on New Year's Eve, 1972, and we never had a chance to kiss and make up. Stargell and I patched up our differences once we got to know each other better. He always had an I-told-you-so smile for me in the years after that fiasco. Stargell was too nice a man to hold a grudge.

I was thinking about all those things as I drove to PNC Park on Opening Day. I was looking forward to seeing the new baseball park -- one of the most beautiful ballparks in America, they say -- and to seeing Stargell's statue. Like most Pittsburghers, though, I had a heavy heart. It hurt to see Stargell after he'd become ill, when he was taking dialysis treatments regularly, and it hurt to hear on the radio that morning that he had died.

"Now, every opening day at PNC Park, everybody will know this is Willie Stargell's day," said Chuck Tanner, Stargell's manager with the Pirates from 1977 through 1982. "He's up there, proud to know the Pirates are opening today."

Tanner would offer a similar version of that same remark later on at a memorial service at St. Mary's Catholic Church in downtown Pittsburgh. I recall that the church was packed and Stargell fans surrounded the church that day.

I had written a story about Stargell on assignment from Jim Lacchimia, the editor of Gameday, *the Pirates' ballpark program. As I approached PNC Park on Opening Day, I was wondering how that story would strike everyone now. It's reprinted here, with some revisions and additions.*

I had attended a press conference at the Pirates' offices to show off a small replica of the statue of Stargell. Stargell and his wife, Margaret, had come from Wilmington, North Carolina for the press conference. It was easy to see that Stargell was sick. He looked scared. There was a haunted look in his eyes. He had lost a lot of weight. No one in Pittsburgh had any idea that day that Stargell's stay on earth would soon come to an end.

From *Gameday*, September, 2001

All is in place now at PNC Park and there is a statue paying tribute to Pirates Hall of Famer Willie Stargell. It stands on a sidewalk outside the left field stands. It will be out there in the area around the ballpark with statues honoring Honus Wagner and Roberto Clemente. Wagner's statue was first erected when the Pirates were playing at Forbes Field in Oakland and Clemente's came into being when the Bucs were playing at Three Rivers Stadium. They were moved to PNC Park.

The statue of Clemente was unveiled in 1994, the summer when the Pirates hosted the Major League Baseball All-Star Game. I took my daughter Sarah with me for the ceremonies. I introduced her prior to

Grieving fans brought flowers to lay at pedestal of Willie Stargell statue outside PNC Park when he died on Opening Day of 2001.

Willie Stargell and his wife, Margaret, marvel at model version of statue to be created by sculptor Susan Wagner in his honor.

Photos by Jim O'Brien

Stargell is flanked by Pirates' owner Kevin McClatchy and former teammate Steve Blass at press conference to reveal model version of Stargell statue.

the unveiling of Clemente's statue to Phil Dorsey, Roberto's best friend during his days in Pittsburgh. We had second-row seats, right behind many of the former Pirates who had been invited to attend and club officials who presided over the ceremonies. Pirates' broadcaster Lanny Frattare was the master of ceremonies. Stargell played many years in the shadow of The Great Roberto, but he was one of his biggest fans and admirers. Clemente had been his mentor in so many ways.

Stargell started out at Forbes Field back in the summer of 1963, walloped some wondrous home runs there and at Three Rivers Stadium, and hopes to be able to enjoy watching the Pirates perform in their new playpen on the city's North Shore for a long time. Stargell hit seven of the 18 home runs that cleared the right field stands at Forbes Field, starting with Babe Ruth's final home run (No. 714) on May 25, 1935.

Stargell, who turned 61 this March, has been challenged the past eight years by a serious kidney ailment, but is optimistic—his optimism has always served him in good stead—that he will be around for the excitement to come. He wants to continue to pass along tips on how to play the game of baseball and, more important perhaps, the game of life. Stargell understood his role on and off the field better than most, and passed out gold stars to all that followed his lead.

He was the patriarch of the Pirates' "We Are Fam-i-lee" team that won the World Series in 1979. He distributed his cherished Stargell stars for extra effort to teammates who proudly attached them to their ballcaps.

Forbes Field and Three Rivers Stadium are no longer visible, except in photographs, artists' renderings and the minds of baseball and sports mavens, so it's impossible to point out the distant places where Willie's monstrous home runs landed. But those people fortunate enough to have witnessed what Willie did in Pittsburgh for 21 mostly splendid seasons will be obligated to share their stories with the young or newcomers to the city.

Anyone who met this man will see more in the statue than might at first meet the eye. They will see a warm smile, and they will see Stargell in motion, like the mannequins that move in department store windows, coming out of that fixed left-handed batting stance, and whirling that huge bat until he becomes a windmill. Can you feel the breeze? It's the way we will always remember Willie Stargell, whipping that bat around and around as he stared out at the opposing pitcher.

That swing was something else.

Dick Groat, another popular former Pirates' star, the National League's MVP during that World Series-winning season of 1960, didn't know Stargell that well. But he remembers seeing Stargell at spring training in 1962, Groat's last season with his hometown team before Joe L. Brown traded him to the St. Louis Cardinals. Groat was at his home in Swissvale and getting ready to go to New York with the University of Pittsburgh men's basketball team for the Big East Tournament in March—he's the analyst on Pitt basketball radio broadcasts—when he took time out to speak about Stargell.

128

"I remember going up to Joe Brown," said Groat, "and asking him, 'Where'd you get this kid from? He's got the best swing I've ever seen in this camp.' He was a natural. They sent him back to the minors that year, but he came up late that season. That swing served him in good stead for a long time."

Stargell became a baseball legend, while earning the love and respect of the people of Pittsburgh. He was inducted into the Baseball Hall of Fame in Cooperstown in the Class of 1988. His No. 8 had been retired by the Pirates in 1982.

Wilver Dornel Stargell was born on March 6, 1940 in Earlsboro, Oklahoma of African-American and Seminole Indian descent. His family later moved to Oakland, California, where he grew up. Many great athletes, including Bill Russell and Tommy Davis, grew up in Oakland, California. Then Stargell made his mark in the Oakland section of Pittsburgh, where many great athletes grew up, such as Danny Marino and Bruno Sammartino and Frank Thomas. When Stargell played for the Pirates, he lived in a home in South Oakland owned by Marino's grandmother, and played catch at Frazier Field (now Danny Marino Field) with young Marino.

Stargell was a big man, at 6–4, 235 pounds. He had round shoulders and big hands and a big heart.

Stargell was sitting in his office at Three Rivers Stadium on January 3, 1994, talking about the plans to have a statue of his dear friend and mentor Roberto Clemente unveiled that summer. What he said back then is relevant now in providing insight into the significance of his own statue.

"I am glad they are having a statue in his honor," said Stargell, "and that they are showing the kids how Clemente played the game, with such grace. He was like poetry in motion. It will be a legend living on.

"This renewal of interest in Clemente and what he was all about is good. It could help some kids. I know he'd like that an awful lot. After so many years, it brings a very special man back into our lives. Let that memory, that river, continue to flow. I'm all for it."

Stargell was always a thoughtful, eloquent spokesperson for the Pirates and for baseball at large. His statue will be shaped by the same artist who did the Clemente creation and who does the Hall of Fame plaques that are displayed at the sport's shrine in Cooperstown, New York. Susan Wagner, who lives in the city's Friendship section, flanked by East Liberty and Garfield, has the prized assignment. It's not just in her hands, however, to shape the Stargell story.

When Stargell saw a model statue back in September, he said, "Awesome!" I was there for the press conference. Steve Blass served as emcee.

Blass wore one of Stargell's gold stars that he used to dole out to his teammates on the left lapel of his blazer. "I've kept those stars," said Blass. "They're like having gold bars."

Stargell sat directly behind Blass that September afternoon. Seeing Stargell, with hollowed-out worried looking eyes, and his skin

129

taut against his jawline, and his dark hair combed differently from what I remembered, was difficult to deal with that day. He didn't look good, and it was obvious he was really ill. You knew he was in trouble. Stargell looked scared that day. He was never scared when he was playing for the Pirates.

He dealt with difficult days. It wasn't easy being a black ball-player when he first came up, but he was always a smooth talker and a smooth thinker, and he knew how to deal with such challenges. He had problems with women—there were times when he was too popular for his own good—but that didn't make him unique in Major League Baseball. Tom Johnson, a Pittsburgh attorney who was a part owner of the Pirates, always got Stargell out of his legal scrapes, quietly and out of court and out of the public spotlight.

"Awesome!"

That word also sums up Stargell's statistics during his Pirates' career. He is the all-time Pirates leader in home runs (475) and runs-batted-in (1,540). He was the World Series MVP in 1979 and the co-MVP of the National League that year, sharing the award with Keith Hernandez of the Cardinals. Just as Clemente used the 1971 World Series to showcase his considerable skills, Stargell, who did not perform up to snuff in that earlier series, came through in grand style in the 1979 World Series. Stargell was an All-Star Game selection seven times.

In 1979, when he was 38, Stargell hit 32 home runs to lead the Bucs to a National League championship that wasn't nailed down until the final day of the season. Stargell then drilled two home runs, drove in six runs and batted .455 in three NL championship series games as the Pirates swept the Cincinnati Reds.

In a seven-game World Series with the Baltimore Orioles, Stargell posted the best all-around numbers with a .400 batting average, three home runs and seven RBIs. His home run in the seventh game—in which he went 4-for-5—decided the Series. He was the oldest player to win the World Series MVP award.

It's up to all that have known and loved Stargell to tell the stories to those who will stare up at the statue.

Among those equal to the task would be his former manager, Chuck Tanner, and teammates and friends such as Steve Blass, Dave Giusti, Manny Sanguillen and Kent Tekulve, who have remained in Pittsburgh and will be frequent visitors to PNC Park.

Tanner has been challenged himself by health issues the past year, and required chemotherapy treatments to deal with prostate cancer. Tanner's upbeat attitude that was the basis for his ballplaying and managing success in the big leagues remains intact. So does his admiration for Stargell, the main catalyst for the Bucs' success when they won the World Series in 1979. If the Bucs were, indeed, a Fam-i-lee in those days, dancing to the popular disco song by Sister Sledge, it was because of Stargell's sunshine attitude and leadership. That's when Stargell was known as "Pops," a term of respect and endearment, and was the big man in the Pirates' picture.

"His attitude in the clubhouse inspired everyone," said Tanner. "He was a great leader. It was an honor to manage a player like Willie Stargell."

One of his teammates, Phil Garner, who went on to manage in the major leagues, learned a lot from Tanner and Stargell. Speaking of Stargell, he said, "I never saw him get mad. I can't do that. But it helps. I feel myself trying to emulate him."

No one had a closer look at Stargell over an extended period than Giusti, who won "Fireman of the Year" honors when his 31 saves led the league in 1971. "I had the locker next to his in the clubhouse for seven years," said Giusti, who remains active in Pirates' Alumni activities, and frequently joins former teammates at Pirates' home games. Nellie Briles, who looked after the alumni activities, said he could always count on Giusti to show up. His managers through the years felt the same way.

"Willie Stargell is one of the greatest power hitters in baseball history," said Giusti. "He was a very patient, emotional player. His extent of arguing a call was giving the umpire a quick stare. Then he'd get back to the business of hitting the baseball. He was a friend of all the umpires. I think he got a lot of calls in his favor that way.

"He was a gentle man and a gentleman. I never saw him too excited or too disappointed. There were no extreme highs and lows with him. He was good at maintaining an even keel, and it helped the rest of us. He was very stable. He was there for those who sought his advice, but he never offered advice on his own. Someone had to solicit it.

"He was a lot of fun. He was good to my dad, also Dave Giusti, and he'd kid with him, tell him how great I was. He was always picking hairs out of my chest. He was jealous. He didn't have any hair on his chest. You remember crazy stuff like that.

"One of his great attributes was that he took you for what you were. He was as good with the fringe players or the rookies as he was with the stars and veterans. He respected everybody.

"I admired Roberto Clemente and I admired Willie Stargell. Both had a very good knowledge of the game, and both handled themselves well. There was the way they appreciated hitting and what was involved. There was the way they appreciated defense. They paid attention to the details of the game.

"Willie didn't say much. He could go 0-for-4 against a pitcher one time and hit two home runs off him the next time. He'd think about what he needed to do, what the guy was doing against him in his pitch selection. He was a thinking man's ballplayer.

"Regardless of whether you were a teammate or an opposing player, Willie respected you. When I was pitching for the Houston Astros, I knocked him down a few times with inside pitches. I hit him this one time. I can remember Dock Ellis screaming at me from the dugout when I did it. But Willie just walked down to first base, without a word. We talked about that when I came over to the Pirates. Willie understood what I needed to do. We had some fun talking about it. You couldn't let him just dig in there at the plate. He'd pull you right out of the park. I don't remember him talking negatively about pitchers or other people. He always maintained an even keel.

"He always made you feel confident. He and Clemente could talk to you on a very personal level. They wanted to know how you were feeling, not just how you were playing. They wanted to know how your family was doing. They'd pick you up, help you when you were hurting."

Blass, no doubt, will share stories about Stargell, as well as recollections of Clemente, during Pirates' broadcasts on radio and TV this year in his role as an analyst and color man. "I always thought I was lucky to be in major league baseball, and to wear a Pirates' uniform," said Blass. "I thought I was fortunate to play with and to get to know individuals like Clemente and Stargell, and so many of my teammates. I was lucky to get to know Pirates who had played before me, like Bill Mazeroski and Bill Virdon and Bob Friend, fellows like that. It's been one great fraternity, and I feel blessed to have been all the places I've been with those guys. If you looked and listened carefully, you could learn a lot from someone like Willie Stargell."

Tekulve, who lives in the same Upper St. Clair community as Blass and Giusti, gushes when he speaks of Stargell. "He was always good to me; he didn't know any other way to treat people," said Tekulve. "A relief pitcher always appreciates a power-hitter behind him who can end a game with one swing in the late going. Stargell was such a man. But I'll remember him most fondly for the fun he created in the clubhouse, and how good it felt to have him award you one of those gold stars he was always passing out."

Manny Sanguillen, an outstanding catcher in Pirates' history who has set high standards for the likes of Jason Kendall, remembers Stargell and Clemente with special fondness. "I tell people that Willie was my friend," said Sanguillen, who lives in Green Tree, when I caught him not far from his home at Atria's Restaurant & Tavern in Mt. Lebanon. "He was so warm, and he was always trying to help me. I loved being around that man. He made you feel good. He made you feel important. He was always after me to stay the same, to believe in myself. He told me I was the best catcher in the league. He always told me that."

Dave Parker, who succeeded Stargell as the Pirates' big man, once called Stargell "my baseball father." Unlike Parker, who lost many of his fans when he got implicated in drug usage scandals, Stargell managed to maintain his popularity with Pittsburghers.

Kevin McClatchy, the Pirates' managing general partner, likes what he's seen of the model for what will be a larger-than-life 12-foot bronze statue of Stargell. "He looks like he's ready to knock the stuffing out of the ball," commented McClatchy at the press conference. "He was always a class act."

McClatchy does his homework, whether he's checking out Stargell's statistics, or those of Bill Mazeroski, when he spearheaded a Pirates' promotional campaign to boost Bill's candidacy for the Baseball Hall of Fame. McClatchy may be a newcomer to the city from

Willie Stargell earned a few stars himself in his latter years with the Pirates.

Stargell leaps high to celebrate Bucs' victory.

Jim O'Brien

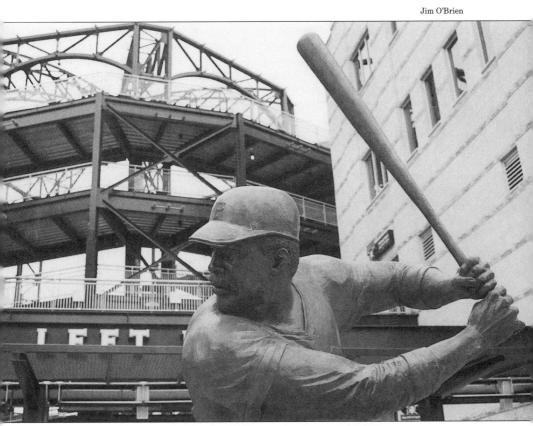

Stargell statue attracts many admirers at PNC Park.

Sacramento, California, but he genuinely cares about the Pirates' history and tradition.

"They're terrific, they're amazing," McClatchy said of Stargell's stats. "But I think that only tells a small part of the story. Willie Stargell is one of the greatest Pirates to ever put on a uniform, and he's one of the classiest people I've ever had the pleasure of meeting."

It was McClatchy who hired Stargell as a special assistant to Pirates' general manager Cam Bonifay. Stargell's involvement has been limited in recent years because of his health problems. "If you had asked me how was my health in July, I'd probably have said it's not the time to talk about it," said Stargell. "But I'm happy to say that I've been given a green light to travel. I'm getting stronger. They said my destiny is up to me."

When Willie Stargell speaks people have always listened. They had to. He has always had a compelling voice. He and Joe Greene of the Steelers were the most philosophical and fascinating sports figures in Pittsburgh during the '70s when the town came to be known nationally as "The City of Champions."

They were both large men who made sense. Stargell was 6–3, 235 pounds. He was born in Oklahoma and came out of the housing projects of Oakland, California to a ballpark in the Oakland section of Pittsburgh to begin a wonderful whirl through the major leagues. He now calls Wilmington, North Carolina, his home base.

I've been to Wilmington with my wife Kathie on two occasions. I learned while there, thanks to some plaques on a wall of a building that Wilmington was the hometown of such sports Hall of Famers as basketball's Michael Jordan, football's Sonny Jurgensen and Roman Gabriel and tennis titan Althea Gibson, as well as newsman David Brinkley and entertainers such as the Charlie Daniels Band.

Wilver Dornell Stargell was something special all right. He offered us many words of wisdom and showed us the way.

"We're only playing out there," he once said. "If we had to concentrate so damned hard that we can't have any fun, we may as well put on a suit, sit in an office, and give dictation to some secretary. That's how a business should be run.

"It wasn't always this way. But you must sit back and evaluate what are the important things. Do you dwell on things that tear you down? Baseball is a tremendous challenge and it damn sure ain't easy. But everybody has a choice. You decide what kind of life you want to live. Is it going to be a miserable life or a happy life? I don't want to go to bed at night disliking anyone, or walking around grumpy as hell. What I try to do is adopt an attitude when I'm getting ready for a game.

"I tell myself, 'This is going to be the best day I've ever had in baseball...and the most enjoyable.' I try to put nothing but positive thoughts in my mind. We do want to have fun. We only have a few years in the game. There's so much to learn, so much to enjoy. You can't be tied up in knots and play baseball. When the umpire hollers, 'Play

134

ball!' He says 'Play Ball!' That means fun. He doesn't holler, 'Work ball!' Remember that.

"It's talent that gets a player here and mentality that keeps him here. You come into the game without ulcers. It's important to leave the game without ulcers. Each game should be cherished as the highlight of one's life. When I first got to the big leagues, I struck out seven times in a doubleheader in St. Louis. People clapped. The rest booed. It really hurt. I went back to my hotel room and cried. I kept asking myself, 'Is this what I want to do with my life?' I decided that I would have to put up with the action and the reaction. I was OK the next day."

In time, Stargell became the 17th player elected to the Baseball Hall of Fame in his first year of eligibility, being inducted in 1988.

In the mind's eye, it's easy to see Stargell swinging his bat as he waited for the right pitch. He was a lefty all the way. He'd rock back and forth, and swing that heavy bat in a circular motion before, in his own words, "launching myself" into the ball. He was one of the top sluggers in the game. He could sky the ball the way Mark McGwire of the St. Louis Cardinals and Sammy Sosa of the Chicago Cubs have been doing in more recent summers.

Stargell credits Clemente as being his greatest influence when he came along, but he looks back to his beginnings with the Pirates and knows the immense pride he had in just being in the same uniform and same clubhouse as many of the players he had heard about when he was a teenager.

"The Pirates won the World Series in 1960, two years before I came up," Stargell told me during a long interview session in his office at Three Rivers Stadium, where photos of Clemente were framed on the wall, along with other ballplayers Stargell admired.

"You are talking about guys I had admired so much. There were guys who really impressed me, like Smoky Burgess, Dick Stuart with his flamboyant ways, the astonishing hands of Maz, the smart and solid way that Dick Groat played shortstop, the military personality of Dick Hoak, and the gem of a manager in Danny Murtaugh. Guys like Ducky Schofield, who could fill in everywhere, and all the pitchers, Bob Friend, Vernon Law, ElRoy Face, Harvey Haddix, Vinegar Bend Mizell, Joe Gibbon, guys like that.

"It was a real treat to be with them. I was proud to be in the Pirates organization. I was desperate to be like them. They were definitely an inspiring force in my life. They let me look up to them when I did come up, and not one of them treated me anything less than I could have dreamed about."

Once the Willie Stargell statue is in place, others with similar dreams will be able to look up to him.

* * *

Wilver Stargell

135

Remembering Pops

A memorial service to celebrate the life of Willie Stargell was held at midday on April 17, 2001 at St. Mary of Mercy Church in downtown Pittsburgh. It had turned cold over the weekend and it was 39 degrees. It felt colder that afternoon.

I was sitting in the midst of the gathering of several hundred mourners and fans of Willie Stargell. The Pirates' party filled the first few pews. The theme of the program was "Remembering Pops."

Kevin McClatchy, the front-office boss of the Pirates back then, said he had gotten to know and appreciate Willie Stargell in recent years while he was employed in an ambassadorial role with the team. He noted that Willie knew he was ill, but that he made it to April 9— Opening Day for the Pirates.

He said, "Willie, we love you very much and we will miss you."

The Rev. Thomas Smith, from the Monumental Baptist Church, looked heavenward when he spoke, saying, "Thank you for sending Pops our way." He said that Stargell had been "called to a better place."

Bishop Donald Wuerl, representing the Catholic Diocese of Pittsburgh, was present as well. He said, "We bring our memories and our prayers and express our affection for him. We offer words of praise to a good man. May the memories remain as we comfort one another."

Chuck Tanner, Steve Blass and Al Oliver all offered remarks for their departed pal. The hymn that was sung was "On Eagle's Wings," a song written by Michael Joncas.

Rev. James Simons spoke of Stargell's dedication. "We would learn from his example." He added that baseball was, after all, "a game that is ultimately about coming home. He is now safe at home."

Al Oliver was overcome by his emotions, and hesitated from time to time, as he offered his thoughts. But he came across like the preacher he prides himself to be. "Willie Stargell was, indeed, a part of my life in so many ways. Wilver, as I always called him, and he called me Chief. Pittsburgh, in the 70s, was always someplace special. He fit in so well with the city of Pittsburgh," said Oliver.

"When Wilver was inducted into the Hall of Fame in 1988, I called him and congratulated him. I said, 'Will, you got it. Roberto, he got it. I was the one who got left out going to the Hall of Fame.

"Willie Stargell brought the Pirates together. The torch was passed to him by the great Roberto Clemente. He brought us all together. It didn't matter if you were African-American, Latin or white, all that mattered was winning.

"Willie Stargell was a winner, in every aspect of the word. He taught me a lot of things that my father taught me. He made Pittsburgh a completed puzzle. Wilver and Pittsburgh were someplace special."

Steve Blass was next and he was emotionally moved as well. Speaking of Stargell, Blass said, "His memories have been with me this week. I shared Willie Stargell stories with Joe Morgan at the airport in Wilmington, where Willie had been living in recent years.

"Willie had corns on top of his toes. Tony Perez would signal for a pickoff play, and Tony would get the ball and whack Stargell on his toes. It was the closest we ever saw Willie Stargell looking like Fred Astaire.

"He had a passion for people. I met Willie for the first time in 1961 in Jacksonville, Florida. A bus would take the black players to a special section of town where they were housed. They had separate housing and this was 1961!

"He told me once, 'I haven't changed, but people act different because of what I've accomplished than they used to.' When Roberto died, I went to Willie. When I wasn't sure what to do, I'd go to Willie. He always knew what to do. I don't know what to do now, and I can't talk to Willie to get the answer.

"Willie got us to the World Series in 1971 and he struggled, oh how he struggled in that Series. He came back in 1979 and, boy, did he come back. We're all a little bit better because Willie Stargell was and always will be a Bucco."

Rev. David Taylor of St. Charles Lwanga Church said God "taught us to forgive, to forget and to love, and Willie Stargell followed his example. With the spirit of Willie, when we work together that there is a reward."

Chuck Tanner, who had managed Stargell, said, "I'm sure Willie saw it all on Opening Day." Looking to the ceiling, Tanner said, "You will always be remembered on Opening Day."

Reflecting on Stargell, Tanner said, "He had the heart of a lion. He could relate to everybody. He could do so many things that other people couldn't do. He was so humble about his ability. He had fun and he was funny. He helped me so much. He's the one who started We Are Fam-a-lee. He was like a shepherd with a flock of sheep. He passed out stars to the players as if they were his students. Willie, I'm hoping to meet you again some day."

The closing hymn was "Amazing Grace."

Stargell had once spoken of coming through the Fort Pitt Tunnel and seeing Pittsburgh for the first time and how it opened its arms to him. "It was the most impressive sight I've ever seen," he said of that first sighting of the Golden Triangle.

"I knew I had found a home."

* * *

The Pirates paid a special tribute to "Pops" at the team-sponsored "Fantasy Camp" in Bradenton, Florida in February of 2008. Whenever the participants did something special in the games at the Pirates' training complex they were given stars to stick to their ballcaps, the kind that Stargell used to pass out to his teammates. "I got one for volunteering to play catcher on our team," said Rich Corson, who grew up in Scott Township and now lives in Bluffton, South Carolina. "No one else wanted to do it. I could hardly walk when the week was over."

137

Aaron Smith
Signs on for neglected kids

"I slept with a baseball bat under my pillow."

October 11, 2006

I saw Aaron Smith signing autographs at a fund-raising luncheon earlier this month and I had to smile. Smith was one of several Steelers, past and present, who was lending his support for a fund-raising luncheon to benefit Holy Family Institute at the Heinz Field East Club Lounge.

Holy Family Institute looks after children who are neglected or abused. It's been a pet project for many years of the Rooney family that owns the Steelers. This was the 14th annual Arthur J. Rooney Sr. Courage House Luncheon. Greta Rooney, the wife of Steelers' president Art Rooney II, chairs the event.

Smith knows just what it's like for many of the children who benefit from the programs and support offered by Holy Family Institute. A few weeks earlier, Smith appeared at a fund-raising event for the Auberle Foundation in McKeesport, which looks after the same kind of challenged children. Smith is the starting defensive end for the Steelers, and one of the stalwarts of the squad.

I would later see him participating along with other Steelers, including Ike Taylor and Charlie Batch, at a fund-raising affair for Every Child, Inc., at Dave & Buster's at The Waterfront in Homestead. Every Child, Inc. is an East Liberty-based organization that assists hard-to-place children to find foster and adoptive homes.

Smith has a passion for helping such institutions and the kids they care for. "We lived in a trailer park," Smith said, sitting with me in a one-on-one session at the cafeteria at the Steelers' complex at the UPMC Sports campus. He told me some stories that raised the hair on the back of my neck because they were so candid and revealing. "We were the family that got the Christmas turkeys, the government cheese, welfare coupons. Things were often tough."

I have spoken to many Steelers about some of the challenges they encountered as kids. It's the theme in my book, *Steeler Stuff*. Such stories are a passion of mine. I am interested in knowing where pro athletes come from, what their family life was like, and how they got from there to here. How did they succeed? Who helped them along the way? I have always been more interested in these stories, about these people who play sports, than I was in the games themselves.

When I was in high school, I loved to read books about athletes who had overcome one kind of adversity or another to succeed. Now I write those kind of stories.

Alan Faneca, for instance, found out he had epilepsy when he was 14. Kendall Simmons has to poke himself with needles every day to deal with his diabetes. Troy Polamalu had to move from his parents' home to relatives' home in another state as a child because he was getting into serious trouble in the mean streets of Los Angeles.

Aaron Smith had a father who stood 6–4, and weighed about 250 pounds, and was having a tough time dealing with diabetes. It turned him into a menacing and difficult dad. He was a mean drunk and Aaron and the family feared him.

None of the Steelers have stories as horrific as Aaron Smith's story. "I can't remember when my father wasn't swearing at us. I thought it was the American way," said Smith, now in his eighth NFL season.

Smith has a long, often stoic face, like one of those carved stone faces on Easter Island. As a kid, his face was even longer because he was often sad. His home was hardly a haven. In truth, it was a dangerous place.

"I was 12 when my mother divorced my dad," said Smith as a starter for his compelling story. "I remember that my mom called my oldest brother, David, and had him get all the firearms out of the house before she told my dad what she was doing. She was worried about what he might do. He scared all of us.

"When I was eight, nine and ten, I was so angry with my father. I told him every night I loved him because I was afraid he'd kill us, and I thought maybe he'd spare me if I told him I loved him. I slept with a baseball bat in my bed in case I had to protect myself.

"My dad's name was Harold Smith. He died when I was 16. He had a heart attack and died in bed. He died alone. I saw him four to six months before he died. I went to my grandmother's house for some family function, and he was there. He stood up to hug me, and I walked right past him. Talk about guilt. I thought about that a long time after he died."

Aaron and his wife, Jaimie, live year-round in Pittsburgh with their three young children. This summer, Aaron's mother moved in with them to help out with her grandchildren.

"It's good to have her here," said Smith. "She's been a big help, and I just want to help her have a better life. She didn't deserve the life we led in that trailer camp out in Colorado. Things are fine now. I think anyone who has ever accomplished anything had to overcome some kind of adversity"

I thought I was hearing a confession instead of conducting an interview when I spoke with Smith. I couldn't believe how candid he was, how trusting with his heartfelt disclosure. I'm not sure I'd have shared such stories with anyone. My dad drank too much and smoked too much, and he was not home as much as he should have been. But he loved us and he was never in my face. He didn't hit anyone in our home. He had a good sense of humor. I realized how lucky I was by comparison to Smith's experience.

When I later ran into Smith when he was out supporting one of the charity fund-raisers close to his heart, he came over to say hello. I extended my hand to shake his, but he brushed that aside. "Hey, give me a hug," he said with a bright smile. "Hugs are good." I could not have agreed more with Smith's observation.

I thought about that hug later. Maybe Aaron Smith appreciates anybody who likes him and anybody he truly can trust.

Steelers' defensive end Aaron Smith speaks to teammate during drills at summer training camp at St. Vincent College in Latrobe.

Dick Groat
Pride of Swissvale
loves Senior Days

This was written before the University of Pittsburgh basketball team became only the second team in Big East history to play four straight days and win the league's tournament title, upsetting Georgetown in the championship game in late March, 2008. They would go on to defeat Oral Roberts in the first round of the NCAA Tournament before dropping a disappointing game to Michigan State in the second round.

March 13, 2008

The 2007–2008 college basketball season has been a great one for Dick Groat. His Pitt Panthers posted their seventh straight 20-victory season and seem a good bet to be invited to the NCAA men's basketball championship tournament, and Groat enjoyed several personal tributes along the way.

Groat, who grew up and still resides in Swissvale, is best known in Pittsburgh as an outstanding shortstop for the Pirates, teaming with second baseman Bill Mazeroski for one of the all-time best double play combinations in Major League Baseball. Groat led the National League in batting in 1960 with a .325 average and was named the league's MVP while leading the Pirates to a World Series championship season.

He had a fine 14-year big-league career, playing for the Pirates, Cardinals, Phillies and Giants from 1952 to 1967, interrupted by a military stint. He batted .317 one summer in St. Louis. His career batting average was .286. That would make you a lot of money these days.

But Groat was a great basketball player, too. He was a first-team All-American at Duke in 1952 and was named the College Basketball Player of the Year. He is the only player ever to lead the nation in scoring and assists. He was a second team choice the year before. He was also an All-American baseball player as a shortstop for an outstanding Duke nine. He played one season (1952–53) with the NBA's Fort Wayne Pistons, averaging nearly 12 points per game, before Branch Rickey, the Pirates' general manager, made him give it up because he feared that Groat would get worn down playing two pro sports. Paul Birch was his coach at Fort Wayne. Birch would later coach at Rankin High School.

Back on Nov. 18, twelve days before his 77th birthday, Groat was inducted into the charter class of the newly created College Basketball Hall of Fame in Kansas City, Missouri. On Dec. 20, when Pitt played Duke at Madison Square Garden, Groat was given a standing ovation by 18,000 fans when his Hall of Fame selection was announced to the crowd during a timeout. The Panthers went on to defeat Duke with a buzzer-beating 3-point shot by Levance Fields.

141

That night was special to Groat in so many ways. "I live and die with the Pitt basketball team," he proudly says. "Duke's my alma mater, but I'm one of Pitt's biggest fans now. I root for Duke every other game they play. I've been a Pitt man my whole life. This goes back to when I was 5 years old. My only association with Duke now is with Mike Krzyzewski and some of his assistants. I will forever be indebted to Billy Hillgrove for getting me involved with Pitt basketball. It's been a fun run."

When Groat got the call that he had been chosen for the charter class of the College Basketball Hall of Fame he was overcome with joy. "I always thought I was a better basketball player than a baseball player," said Groat. "I had tears in my eyes when they called me. It's the greatest honor I've ever received. As great as the two World Series were and the batting title, to be recognized in the sport you felt you played the best is special.

"I was not a Hall of Fame baseball player. That's for superstars. Mazeroski and Clemente were superstars. I was honored just to be nominated for the Baseball Hall of Fame."

Groat was also introduced and recognized for his College Basketball Hall of Fame induction during the 2007–2008 season at one of the home games at the Petersen Events Center, and drew a long and warm applause from Pitt's fans.

Groat was also invited back to Duke on Saturday, February 9, when the Blue Devils were entertaining Boston College in an ACC contest, to be recognized at halftime for his Hall of Fame induction. His jersey has long been retired at Duke, and a replica remains on display in Cameron Indoor Stadium.

He has been honored on more than one occasion at the annual Sports Night dinner at the Thompson Club in West Mifflin.

On February 23 of this year, after Jeannette's Terrell Pryor put up some unbelievable numbers in the WPIAL's Class AA championship game against Beaver Falls—39 points, 24 rebounds, 10 blocked shots, six assists—his jubilant coach, Jim Nesser, proclaimed, "What can I say? He's the greatest athlete in the history of the state of Pennsylvania."

Maybe, coach, but not yet. Think about what Dick Groat accomplished. And he wasn't a bad golfer either. Groat continues to own and operate the Champion Lakes Golf Club in Bolivar, Pennsylvania, not far from Ligonier. Tell Terrelle Pryor about Groat and some of the guys from these parts who've had great sports careers to keep things in their proper perspective. I've seen Pryor play and he is impressive. Let's say he has great potential.

Here's a list, and it's not a complete one, to check out during study period, of some of the greatest athletes ever to perform in Pennsylvania schools:

Jim Thorpe, Pistol Pete Maravich, Arnold Palmer, Wilt Chamberlain, Joe Namath, Dan Marino, Marc Bulger, Dick Allen, Christy Matthewson, Stan Musial, Arnold Galiffa, Johnny Unitas, Norm Van Lier, Reggie Jackson, Josh Gibson, Bill Tilden, George Blanda, Earl "The Pearl" Monroe, Roy Campanella, Art Rooney, Chuck

Jeannette's Terrelle Pryor is honored as the high school male athlete of the year at 2008 Dapper Dan Dinner & Sports Auction.

Michael Dradzinski

Jeannette's Terrelle Pryor

Photos by Jim O'Brien

Jeannette basketball coach Jim Nesser, at right, guided his team to WPIAL and PIAA Class A championships in 2008.

Bednarik, Jack Twyman, Frank Thomas, Terry Hanratty, Tom Gola, Johnny Lujack, Armon Gilliam, Jack Ham, Pete Duranko, Maurice Lucas, Maurice Stokes, Jim Kelly and Honus Wagner.

Groat gets worked up while analyzing the action alongside Bill Hillgrove on Pitt's basketball radio broadcast team. This is Hillgrove's 39th consecutive year doing this, and Groat has been with him for 29 of those years. "It's my good fortune to work with the best play-by-play announcer in the country," says a partial pal. Groat and Hillgrove both refer to each other as "roomie" and "my best friend."

Groat gets choked up every year on Senior Day (so do I), as it's difficult to see the Pitt players in their last game on campus. "Billy and I both got all teared up," Groat told Ronald Ramon, one of those seniors, during a post-game radio interview after Pitt defeated DePaul. Groat is old enough to be a grandfather to the present-day players, so it's understandable that he often addresses them as "young man" and "son" when he is talking to them.

"It's been fantastic," said Groat, when I talked to him about his experience this season. "I had no idea a lot of these tributes were coming my way. I have always told people I was a better basketball player than a baseball player. So it's nice to be recognized so many years after playing.

"I think our coach, Jamie Dixon, and the Duke coach, Mike Krzyzewski, may have teamed up long-distance to arrange the tribute at Madison Square Garden. And when Jamie came all the way to Kansas City for my Hall of Fame induction that meant a lot to me. It sure did.

"My association with Pitt all these years has been fantastic," Groat continued. "Basketball's always been my first love and I'm grateful to Pitt that they've kept me on doing the radio broadcasts. Traveling with the Pitt basketball team and Bill Hillgrove is something I truly love.

"It's kept me young. I live and die with these basketball games. The fans never seem satisfied, but these last seven years have been the golden era of Pitt basketball. Ben Howland and Jamie Dixon have done things that were never done here.

"It took me awhile to accept their basketball philosophy, I must admit. They stress defense, and I was always an offense-oriented guy. They've lost something recently from the way they usually play. They've been completely out of sync. But I liked the way they played their final home game against DePaul. That may have been their finest team effort of the season."

Groat was looking ahead to the Big East Basketball Tournament at Madison Square Garden and to the NCAA Tournament. "I'm hoping they can win four more games so the seniors will be part of 100 wins in their four-year careers," he said.

Groat has become a great ambassador for Pitt and Duke basketball. He promotes Pitt wherever he goes. I've heard Groat speak at many sports luncheons and dinners and he always speaks glowingly about the Panthers. At the same time, he says he never considered going to Pitt when he was a senior at Swissvale High.

Dick Groat, at left, hosts his former Pirates' teammates at his highly-regarded public golf course in Bolivar, including Bob Friend, El Roy Face and Bill Mazeroski.

Photos by Jim O'Brien

Dick Groat relaxes at corner table at Applebee's Neighborhood Bar & Grill at Edgewood Town Center near his home.

"I played ball in the summer with some of the Pitt guys," explained Groat, "and they told me to stay away from Pitt. I liked to run and shoot. Their coach, Doc Carlson, is in the Basketball Hall of Fame, but he played a style of basketball that wouldn't have suited me. He played a highly disciplined figure-8 offense. They ran a weave and waited for the best possible shot. It was too slow for my game. It worked for them most of the time, but it wouldn't have worked for me. I went to Duke because they had a first-class baseball program under Jack Coombs, who had played for the Philadelphia Athletics, and a fine basketball coach in Jerry Jerard."

One of Groat's big fans is Armand Dellovade, a long-time Pitt booster who owns a sheet-metal construction business in Canonsburg. Groat's 1960 World Series ring had been stolen from his golf club, and when Dellovade heard about that he decided to replace it. He called Groat's youngest daughter, Allison Groat DeStefano, the general manager of the golf club, to get her dad's ring size and swore her to secrecy. "I think Groat belongs in the Baseball Hall of Fame," declared Dellovade that day.

"I think I know Dick pretty well," said Bill Hillgrove, who served as the master of ceremonies at that celebration, "and he was moved by this. He didn't expect this."

When I was covering pro basketball back in the '70s for *The New York Post* and *The Sporting News*, I met many NBA old-timers who still raved about Groat's scoring ability. He was right up there with Bob Cousy and Bob Davies and Dickie McGuire, according to the likes of Red Auerbach, Red Holzman and Marty Blake.

"I was a better basketball player than a baseball player," said Groat. "Baseball was a bigger game then. It was truly America's pastime."

There were times when he had second thoughts about his decision to pick baseball over basketball. "There were many nights in 1955 and '56 when I walked the streets in Cincinnati and St. Louis late at night thinking I had made a mistake," Groat said. "Then in 1957, I batted .315."

When Dick Groat was inducted into the WPIAL Hall of Fame on June 20, 2008, he said, "To quote (former Pitt and NFL standout player and coach and Aliquippa High graduate) Mike Ditka, 'If I had my life to live over again, had my choice of growing up and playing my sports in California or North Carolina or Florida ... no matter how great the weather is, I would choose once again to play my sports in Western Pennsylvania. It's the greatest area in the whole wide world.'"

Dick Groat's No. 10 jersey is retired at his alma mater.

Groat was College Player of the Year at Duke in 1951-52 when he led nation in scoring and assists.

Some of Pittsburgh's all-time best basketball players, from left to right, are Dick Groat, Brian Generalovich, Connie Hawkins, Ed Fleming and Dr. Don Hennon. They were honored at a Curbstone Coaches luncheon in 1981 at the Allegheny Club at Three Rivers Stadium.

Groat turned out to be one of the best shortstops of his era. He was the 1960 National League Most Valuable Player. He won the NL batting title with a .325 average and helped the Pirates beat the Yankees in seven games to capture the World Series. He was a five-time All-Star selection and won another World Series title with the St. Louis Cardinals in 1964 after the Pirates traded him. He has never forgiven Joe L. Brown, the Pirates' GM at the time, for trading him away, even though he concedes he loved playing in St. Louis.

Groat is a good example of an athlete who did not possess great speed, but had quickness. He couldn't cover as much ground as some shortstops in baseball, but he was smarter than most, studied the opposing hitters, and positioned himself to be able to make the plays.

He also has a life-long habit of cupping his hand around his mouth while he's talking to someone. "It's as if he doesn't want a batter to read his lips," says one of his former teammates. Groat is still in the game, still competing.

Groat had great pride; he still does. He remains one of the most competitive people I have ever met. I often wonder why his teeth aren't ground down to dust. Bill Soffa, an engineering professor at Pitt and more recently Virginia, was a fine basketball player out of Duquesne who set scoring records at Carnegie Tech.

"Groat and some of the other Pirates would come over to our gym and play with us," recalled Soffa. "I'd go one-on-one with Groat, and he was tougher than anyone I ever guarded. He gave me no slack. He was out to beat me, every time up the floor. It helped me get ready for our team's games."

Anyone who ever under-rated Groat's ability remains on his mind. He doesn't forget who didn't think he was good enough to play pro ball. He's been known to curse at the sound of their names. I know at least three I am reluctant to mention in his company, so I don't. Sometimes I introduce a new name that brings out the worst in Groat.

One day, a few years back, I joined Groat and Hillgrove and Pitt basketball coach Ben Howland at a table during a Pitt press conference at the Petersen Events Center. I need to provide some background so you can appreciate this story.

I had just read a story in the *Post-Gazette* that morning that a former Pirates' pitcher Mace Brown had died. I felt bad because I had gotten to know Mace Brown while working on my books. He had been a rookie in the Pirates' dugout the day Babe Ruth hit three home runs in his final appearance at Forbes Field on May 25, 1935. Ruth was playing for the Boston Braves of the National League in his last go-round.

After hitting his third home run, Ruth came into the Pirates' dugout and sat down next to Mace Brown. "Boy, that last one felt good," said Ruth. It was only the seventh inning, but Ruth went to the visitors' clubhouse after that home run—his 735th—and retired from baseball altogether only a week later.

I had visited Mace Brown in his home in Greensboro, North Carolina on three occasions, and I treasure those meetings. Brown had been a scout for the Boston Red Sox into his seventies, and shared

Bill Hillgrove and Dick Groat team up to do Pitt basketball radio broadcasts.

Dick Groat was a great admirer of teammate Roberto Clemente.

Roberto Clemente

great stories. There were pictures of Ted Williams, Carl Yastrzemski, Tony Conigliaro and Joe Cronin and Bobby Doerr in his den, and he could tell tales about all of them. He was a grand old man, a baseball man through and through, and I enjoyed the time I spent with him.

He had been the goat of the game when the Pirates blew a chance to win the National League pennant in 1938. Brown had been good enough to pitch in the All-Star Game that season and finished with a 15–8 record, his all-time best. But he gave up a home run to Gabby Hartnett of the Cubs in Chicago. He had thrown two strikes with his first two pitches before surrendering the gopher ball. It was getting late in Chicago—the ballpark didn't have lights—and they were about to call the game. It was referred to as a "home run in the glomin." The Pirates were leading the NL race by seven games on September 1, and had started to add seating at Forbes Field for the anticipated World Series, but that game in Chicago led to other losses and they failed to win the pennant.

When Brown died, the *Post-Gazette* headline read "Pitcher Who Cost Pirates Pennant Dies." I thought about Bill Buckner, who once allowed a ground ball to roll between his legs in a World Series game in Boston that led to the undoing of his team. Someone wrote that the ball "rolled between his legs and into the first paragraph of his obituary."

So I said to Groat, "Did you see that Mace Brown died?"

"To hell with Mace Brown!" Groat roared.

I was caught off guard. I'm glad I wasn't sipping hot coffee. "Where'd that come from?" I asked Groat.

"Mace Brown was a Red Sox scout and he said I'd never make it as a big league shortstop," Groat explained. "I never had any use for him."

That's all that mattered to Dick Groat. Mace Brown missed the boat on Dick Groat's baseball ability. Mace Brown and Joe L. Brown could both go to hell, as far as Groat was concerned. They were first cousins in Dick Groat's grading book. The fire still burns.

"That's my buddy for you," said Bill Hillgrove with a grin when I recounted this exchange to him a few years later. "Dick doesn't forget slights. He keeps a list."

* * *

My buddy Bill Priatko passed along an interesting story about Dick Groat that points up a more sentimental and softer side of Groat. Priatko, who played sports at North Braddock Scott High, at Pitt and with the Steelers, and his son, Danny, attend a basketball game at Duke each year as guests of Coach Mike Krzyzewski. Mike and Danny are both alumni of the U.S. Military Academy. Priatko checks the Duke basketball Internet web site from time to time and came up with this gem:

On Senior Night, Feb. 29, 1952, Groat scored a school record 48 points in leading Duke to a 94–64 victory over North Carolina. He had set a record when he scored 46 points earlier in the season in a victory over George Washington.

Dick's dad, Martin, traveled to Duke to see his son play his final game at Cameron Indoor Stadium. Mr. Groat stumbled over a curb and fell in the parking lot and hurt his knee. He was taken to the Duke Medical Center to be checked out. Duke held up the start of the game for ten minutes so Dick's dad could get back and see the entire game. That, of course, was before ESPN and Dick Vitale and all the games like that being on national television. They wouldn't hold up the game today.

Groat was pulled from the game with 15 seconds remaining and received a standing ovation from the Duke crowd.

Dick Groat didn't mention this story, but it might be one of the reasons he gets choked up on "Senior Day." When I related this story to him, Groat corrected some numbers—it always amazes me how athletes and coaches can recall the details of their heydays—and said, "You might be right about that."

Michael Dradzinski

Dick Groat has a great personal affection for Pitt's basketball coach Jamie Dixon who traveled to Kansas City to attend Groat's induction into the newly-formed College Basketball Hall of Fame during the 2007-2008 season.

> *"My association with Pitt all these years has been fantastic."*
> **—Dick Groat**

Terry Hammons Jr.
Talks about Mike Tomlin, his former college teammate

January 31, 2007

A friend and former teammate of Mike Tomlin offered a strong endorsement for the Steelers' new head football coach. Terry Hammons Jr., who grew up in Upper St. Clair and starred as a wide receiver for Jim Render's Panthers before graduating in 1991, knows Tomlin well. They were together for four years at William & Mary College, and were the starting receivers for winning teams at the 1-AA collegiate playing level.

Much has been made of the fact that Tomlin is the first black head coach of the Steelers, but Hammons believes Tomlin has what it takes to be successful. Then, too, the timing couldn't be better. Both coaches in this year's Super Bowl—Tony Dungy of the Indianapolis Colts and Lovie Smith of the Chicago Bears—also happen to be black. This is a first for the Super Bowl; another barrier is broken.

Tomlin was a year ahead of Hammons at William & Mary and both were red-shirted their freshman years. So they were teammates over a four-year span and bonded easily. Hammons succeeded Tomlin as team captain after Tomlin graduated. "It's unusual for wide receivers to be captains," Terry told me in a telephone conversation soon after Tomlin was hired by the Steelers, "unless you're Hines Ward or someone like that."

Hammons is a corporate attorney living near Allentown in the southeastern end of Pennsylvania

Reflecting back on their days together on the picturesque Williamsburg campus, Hammons said, "Mike was just a natural leader. I first met him when I went there on a recruiting visit in February of 1991. When I came there in the fall we became fast friends. We played the same position. He looked after me, took me under his wings, showed me the ropes.

"You weren't allowed to have a car during your first year, and he'd pick me up in his car after study hall. He lived just ten miles away in Newport News, and he'd take me to his home on special occasions like Thanksgiving. He comes from a great family.

"He was pretty much a leader even though he was a young guy. Mike is a very outgoing guy, very charismatic. I sort of looked up to him. He's smart and he has a brilliant football mind. We all figured Mike would play on Sundays. He was the prototypical wide receiver— 6–3, 200 pounds, a 4.45 in the 40, a 40–inch vertical leap—and he had tryouts with the 49ers and Browns but he didn't stick. But he found a way to make it in the National Football League. He sure did.

Mike Tomlin and his wife Kiya at Mel Blount's Celebrity Roast Dinner at Hilton.

Terry Hammons and Mike Tomlin in their William & Mary days.

Terry Hammons and Dr. Sarah O'Brien were inducted into the Upper St. Clair Academic Hall of Fame during 2007 football season.

"I talked to Mike on the phone before his second interview in Pittsburgh, and I can't remember him being more excited since we were getting ready to play Virginia when we were at William & Mary."

Hammons was a year ahead of our daughter Sarah at Upper St. Clair so I was well aware of him, his kid brother Barrett, and their parents, Anita and Terry Sr. Hammons played with Doug Whaley at USC. Whaley was a few years older. Whaley went to Pitt where he started as a defensive back and earned Big East and Academic All-America honors. I watched them both when they played for the Panthers, as I have season tickets for Upper St. Clair High School football games.

Whaley is now in his 10th season as the Steelers' pro scouting director. He spent one year as a broker on Wall Street before getting into pro football.

Young Hammons went from William & Mary to the highly competitive Georgetown Law School, where his father was proud to tell me he graduated cum laude. Get the picture? He and my daughter were inducted into the Academic Hall of Fame for the Class of 2007 at Upper St. Clair High School.

The Upper St. Clair football and basketball teams usually have one or two black students on the team and they are invariably star performers, both on and off the field. Dane Conwell was this year's star on the school football team. He was the star performer on their state championship football team. These kids have led the way. They are exceptional, and not because of the tone of their skin. They stand out in all the best ways.

Hammons has no doubt his friend Mike Tomlin, just 34 years old —the same as Bill Cowher when he became coach of the Steelers—will do the same. "He was made for this job," said Hammons.

I first learned of the Hammons-Tomlin connection when I accompanied Jim Render and his son J.T. to a sports banquet honoring high school football coaches that was held in Ambridge two weeks ago. Render was honored for coaching USC to the state Quad A title.

A week later, my wife Kathie and I ran into Anita and Terry Hammons Sr. outside the Petersen Events Center prior to Pitt's victory over St. John's. They told us they had moved from Upper St. Clair several years ago back to their hometown of Clairton to be closer to family and friends and their church. "We're glad we lived in Upper St. Clair when we did," said Anita. "Our kids got a fine education and we made a lot of friends there."

Her husband shares their son's excitement about Mike Tomlin becoming the head coach of the Steelers.

"I spent time with Mike on several occasions when we went to William & Mary to visit Terry," said Terry Sr. "He was somebody who impressed you right away, by the way he carried himself. I remember he was a very confident individual, very respectful, and just pleasant company. The Steelers have got themselves a good man."

Mike Tomlin
Left his mark at William & Mary

Steelers' head coach Mike Tomlin returned to his alma mater, The College of William & Mary, on May 11, 2008, to deliver the commencement address. He did the same at St. Vincent College in Latrobe, where the Steelers conduct their annual summer training camp.

Retired U.S. Supreme Court Justice Sandra Day O'Connor delivered the welcoming remarks at The College of William & Mary commencement. So Tomlin was keeping impressive company on the college campus where he once starred as a wide receiver for the football team. Tomlin received an honorary doctorate of humane letters at the ceremony. Anybody who's talked to Tomlin would know he'd be proud of that honor.

June 27, 2007

Williamsburg is about 400 miles from Pittsburgh. It's an idyllic community in the scenic southeast end of Virginia. The College of William & Mary, one of the most beautiful campuses in the country, is located there. It's near Jamestown and Yorktown, which played a big part in the early settlement of America.

It's a great place to visit if you want to learn a lot about early American history. My wife Kathie and I traveled there last week with our friends Sharon and Alex Pociask for a seven-day stay at the Powhattan Plantation. It was warm, in the high 90s most of the week. You can also learn a little more about Mike Tomlin, the new coach of the Pittsburgh Steelers, while in Williamsburg.

Tomlin captained the Tribe football team in 1994. He was an outstanding receiver and a first-rate student. He was the kind of student-athlete Jimmye Laycock continues to look for, as he approaches his 28th season as the head football coach at his alma mater. He's had 23 winning teams.

William & Mary is where Phi Beta Kappa was founded. It's a national fraternity for outstanding students.

"We want someone who will become integrated into the student body," allows Laycock. "He has to be coming here for more than to play football. We look for someone who wants to get a quality education, get his degree and be a member of a championship football team."

Mike Tomlin, from nearby Hampton, was such a young man. "We're proud of what he's accomplished," said Laycock, "and not completely surprised." The average SAT score for the incoming freshman class was 1344 a year ago.

They are building an $11 million football complex alongside Zable Stadium and it will be named in honor of Laycock. The seating capacity at the campus stadium is just over 12,000, but they've had crowds as big as 19,000 for a contest with North Carolina and over 18,000 for a game with rival Richmond. They play in the Atlantic 10 Conference. The big game this year will be at Virginia Tech.

I was surprised to learn that they don't plan a special page or two in the next football guide to call attention to Mike Tomlin becoming the first African-American coach in the Steelers' 75-year history.

"We've had a lot of special people come through here," said Pete Clawson, the assistant athletic director for sports information. Clawson is a Pitt grad, class of 1995, and worked as a student intern in the sports information department at Pitt with sports publicist Sam Sciullo of Castle Shannon. Lou Creekmur, 1949, is in the Pro Football Hall of Fame. I witnessed his induction in Canton in 1996.

Thomas Jefferson was in the class of 1762 at William & Mary. That's a tough act to follow. Students could be seen doing archaeological digs on the William & Mary campus, as well as at Jamestown—celebrating its 400th anniversary—and Yorktown. It's easier to dig up information on Captain John Smith and Pocahontas than it is Mike Tomlin. There were just two feature stories on him in his thin file. They were positive and pointed up his terrific attributes.

His coach at William & Mary remembered Mike Tomlin, that's for sure. Laycock recalled Tomlin as an outstanding wide receiver and a real student of the game. He recalled a touchdown catch Tomlin made at the University of Massachusetts field. "It was in the back of the end zone—real acrobatic—and it was as great a catch as I've seen in football," said his proud coach.

Tomlin is trying to get the Steelers to improve their practice habits, pointing out each of their missteps in a daily report, but it turns out that Tomlin wasn't the best practice player, either, in his William & Mary days. "I have to work on my concentration," he conceded back then, "because I'm not exactly what you would call a practice player. I've come to realize that it carries over to game day."

Some, like teammate wide receiver Terry Hammons of Upper St. Clair, thought Tomlin would be good enough for the NFL, but he didn't make the grade after a couple of tryouts. Laycock also spoke well of Hammons, now an attorney, and his coach at USC, Jim Render, "We plan to recruit more up that way," said Laycock, "now that Mike's coaching the Steelers. Render runs a fine program."

Tomlin thought about coaching, perhaps on a college level, when he was at William & Mary, watching game films.

"The more I look into it, the more I want to get into coaching," said Tomlin during his senior season. "I find myself not only focusing on what I'm supposed to do, but studying schemes and techniques of other teams. I can't even enjoy the game that much, from a spectator's point of view, because I start to analyze things. Football is something I really love and being around it in some capacity—while getting paid—would be great."

"It is what it is."
— **Mike Tomlin**

Author Jim O'Brien visits Jimmye Laycock, William & Mary's football coach, during visit to historic Williamsburg.

Photos by Alex Pociask

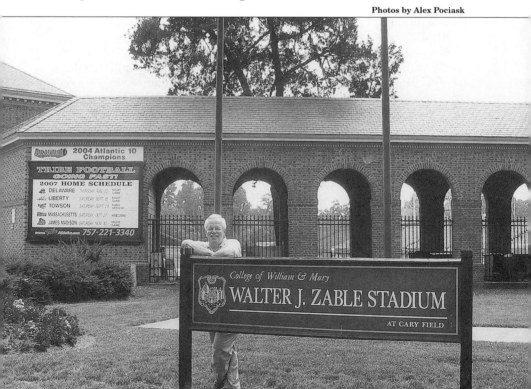

O'Brien had a chance to check out the Walter J. Zable Stadium where Mike Tomlin once starred as a receiver under Coach Jimmye Laycock.

Life is strange sometimes. I went to Williamsburg for a vacation. But I can be idle and relaxed for only so long. Soon after Alex and Sharon Pociask had invited my wife Kathie and me to join them to enjoy their time share at Powhattan Plantation in Williamsburg, I started thinking that The College of William & Mary was located there, and that maybe I could visit the school and speak to some people who remembered Mike Tomlin.

I called the sports information office and was prepared to explain who I was and what I wanted while I was in the neighborhood. Pete Clawson, the assistant athletic director for sports information, answered his phone.

"Are you the Jim O'Brien who writes the sports books in Pittsburgh?" he asked soon after saying hello.

I told him I was, indeed, that Jim O'Brien. When I asked him about Mike Tomlin, he said, "I know more about you than I do about Mike Tomlin."

He told me he'd arrange for me to see Coach Jimmie Laycock when he would come into the office later that morning. When I called back later, Clawson said I could see Laycock for about 15 minutes. "He's a busy man," claimed Clawson. I wondered about that. I'd gotten more time with coaches from a lot bigger programs than William & Mary, but I said that was fine.

I felt that once Laycock and I started talking, he'd be comfortable with a longer stay. And that's exactly what happened. We talked for at least a half-hour, and he was terrific. He never gave me the impression he was pressed for time, and he never glanced at his wristwatch when I was talking to him.

I saw student guides taking prospective students and their parents on tours of the campus, and I mentioned Mike Tomlin to them. "You might want to tell them that one of your alumni is now the head coach of the Pittsburgh Steelers," I suggested, remembering my own days of leading students on tours of the University of Pittsburgh campus. "He's the first black coach in the 75-year history of the franchise, and he's a William & Mary grad."

None of them knew about Mike Tomlin. A receptionist in one building did write a note about it, after I mentioned Mike Tomlin and his accomplishment to her. Maybe she was just being polite and showing me that she was listening.

I think I was more excited about Mike Tomlin than any of the students or people who worked at William & Mary. When I was visiting the campus bookstore, I bought a black and gold jersey with William & Mary in script across the front. I thought I'd give it to Mike Tomlin when I next saw him, sort of a welcome-to-Pittsburgh gift. I wanted him to know that I didn't plan to be part of the media mob. As always, I would set myself apart from the pack. I'd be coming at him from a different slant, looking for different stories.

I've always thought you end up getting better stories when folks aren't afraid of you, when they can trust you. Grantland Rice played golf and cards and drank with the likes of Babe Ruth, Ty Cobb, Jack

Dempsey and Bobby Jones. I'm sure he ignored some of their missteps, but in the end he had to have better stories because he kept company with the sports greats of his day. I'd read a collection of his stories— *The Tumult and the Shouting*—that had been given to me during my student days at Pitt by the late Doc Carlson. He was the head of the student health services, but he'd been the basketball coach at Pitt once upon a time. He was in the charter class, along with Uniontown's Charley "Chipper" Hyatt, in the Basketball Hall of Fame in Springfield, Massachusetts.

Carlson wanted me to be a positive writer like Grantland Rice and not a negative writer—or muckraker—like Westbrook Pegler. I think he thought I was too critical and too much of a know-it-all as a student writer at Pitt. But that's the way college students are; they think they already know everything.

I learned a lot of positive stuff about Mike Tomlin in talking to his old college coach. Laycock was laid-back as he sat behind his desk, but I could tell by the way he talked that the fire was still burning in his belly. He was about winning at William & Mary, and winning the way that would gain approval by the school administrators. He wanted to get more Mike Tomlin-like prospects, young people who could handle the demanding academic curricula at the highly rated school, play terrific football and stay out of trouble.

I remembered that a William & Mary player had graced the cover of *Street & Smith's College Football Magazine* way back (1950) in my grade school days. I had seen it framed on the wall at the offices of *Street & Smith's,* where I was the founding editor of its Basketball magazine back in 1970. That same cover, featuring "Flyin' Jack" Cloud, a menacing looking fullback, was on display in the hall outside Coach Laycock's office. There were pictures of some of the school's other fine players.

Buster Ramsey played on the William & Mary football team and he came to Pittsburgh from Detroit as a member of Buddy Parker's staff from 1962 to 1964. Another former William & Mary player, George Hughes, was a guard for the Steelers (1950–1954) and I'd met him at a Steelers' reunion at Robert Morris University about five years earlier.

He was the Steelers' third-round draft choice in 1950, following Lynn Chandnois, a great running back from Michigan State, and Ernie Stautner, a defensive end and linebacker from Syracuse. Chandnois still holds some Steelers' records for kick returns, and Stautner's No. 70 is the only Steelers' jersey to be officially retired. Stautner is a member of the Pro Football Hall of Fame.

The Steelers also drafted Penn State running back Fran Rogel (8th round) and Pitt's defensive back and punter Carl DePasqua (29th round) that same season. DePasqua would later coach the Steelers, as an assistant to Chuck Noll in 1968, and become head coach at Pitt a year later.

Rogel was the first Steeler I ever met, with my father Dan O'Brien at the bar at Frankie Gustine's Restaurant in Oakland. By the way, the Steelers also drafted a player named Tomlinson from Kansas that year.

Laycock had 23 winning seasons at William & Mary, and it wasn't easy. "It's hard to get kids in here," allowed Laycock in our conversation. "They don't let in anyone just because he can play football. I want players to understand what playing here is all about.

"We want you to get a quality education and want to compete for a championship in football. There's no ifs, ands or buts that promise that it will be easy. Ever so often, I have to get them in my office and say, 'Don't you remember what we talked about?' This is fun and games football—we're not on the top level in NCAA competition—but we want you to be serious about being at this school. We write out the commitment we have in mind for them.

"It's not all football here. We want them to be a part of the student life. We don't have athletic dorms here. We've had good people here. I succeeded Lou Holtz as the football coach here and Holtz succeeded Marv Levy. They're both in a lot of Halls of Fame.

"I coached one year in high school before I got into college coaching. I felt like I was farther along. Being a very good coach is demanding in many ways. We've had success here. We won 11 games in 2004 and we graduated all the seniors. That's what we are looking for.

"Mike Tomlin is a strong individual. Coming out of high school down here in Hampton, he was a bright young man. He had a real upside to him as far as football was concerned. I thought he was very consistent. He was very enthusiastic about the way he appreciated football. He paid attention and he soaked it all up.

"He had a quality about him that was contagious. His enthusiasm spread among others. We had a really good quarterback when he was here, and Mike and Terry Hammons benefited from that. Mike was very much involved in the game, the way a quarterback might be. He made suggestions . He was never a problem. He was a good receiver for us. He and Terry talked a lot. They did their own kind of trash talking, but it never went over the top.

"His dad died when he was young, but his step-dad was a good man, and close to Mike. Mike's mother was a great mother. They came to the games. They went to Maryland to see us play there.

"I think he'll be a good coach for the Steelers. I think he'll be a good fit there. I'm happy for Mike. This is a great opportunity for him. The Steelers seem to be a class organization. They must have been real impressed with him to give him this job at his young age. I'm just very proud of him.

"He's a great representative of William & Mary College and I'm sure he'll do well. In meeting Mike, you're going to be inspired. He called me when he got the job. Before he made any move he always called me. When he was talking with the Steelers, he called me. Before he went to Minnesota, he called me. I told him, 'Is this something you want? If you do, then go for it.' He doesn't need me to hold his hand. He's ready for this assignment. I'm always here if he wants to talk to me, not that I have all the answers or anything. But he can talk to me;

he knows I'm on his side, and will support him in every way. He told me, 'You keep my head on straight.' I'm glad he sees me in that respect. I'll always be his coach.

"I got to know Chuck Noll a little. He lived here for a few years in retirement. We went to the same church—St. Bede's Catholic Church—and that's how I met him. The priest there introduced us. That's how I got to know him and Marianne. I talked a little football with him. Why not? He was not real outgoing. He was very 'old school' in many ways."

I told him I had seen a sign on the highway for St. Bede's, just outside the Powhattan Plantation resort where we were staying. I later drove back to see the church. I knew that Chuck and Marianne Noll attended church faithfully during their stay in Pittsburgh.

As I spoke with Laycock, construction had already started on a new football facility adjoining the stadium. It would be named in Laycock's honor. "We want to keep our program on a first-class level," said Laycock.

William & Mary's long time coach Jimmye Laycock is still a big fan of Mike Tomlin.

Ben Roethlisberger
Boosts Mike Tomlin
at William & Mary camp

July 4, 2007

en Roethlisberger went from Pittsburgh to Williamsburg last week. He was one of the headliners at the 2007 Colonial All Pro Football Camp at The College of William & Mary. Roethlisberger was performing on the same field at Zable Stadium where his new coach, Mike Tomlin, had starred as a wide receiver for the Tribe 13 years earlier.

Big Ben was on Tomlin's turf, and heard some stories about Tomlin from Jimmye Laycock, who has been the head coach at William & Mary for 28 years and remains an admirer. Tomlin was an archetype of the true-student athlete Laycock likes to recruit to this idyllic college campus in a history-rich community in Virginia. Now that he's got some more background on his boss, Big Ben will be able to appreciate Coach Tomlin more than ever.

Larry Fitzgerald, the former Pitt receiver now starring with the Arizona Cardinals, was the featured speaker last Monday and Big Ben took his turn on Tuesday. (This was before Ben signed an eight-year contract for $125 million and Fitzgerald signed one for four years and $40 million.)

Michael Vick of Virginia Tech and the Atlanta Falcons was scheduled to be the main attraction, but he cancelled his appearance because of the bad publicity surrounding his alleged involvement in dog fighting at a home he owns in Virginia. (This was before Vick was sent to prison for his crime.)

I was in Williamsburg and visited with Coach Laycock a week earlier. I had no idea that two great football players with Pittsburgh connections would be coming a week later. Imagine what a great passing combination Roethlisberger and Fitzgerald could form. Both are classy individuals as well.

The week I was there coincided with a convention that drew owners of Model T Fords from the '30s. There were over 400 of them on the streets and highways and parking lots around Williamsburg. They were real gems. They were on display at The College of William & Mary when I was there.

The Model T Fords gave way on the local roads toward the end of the week when a convention of Harley Davidson enthusiasts came to town. There must have been a thousand motorcycles in Williamsburg that weekend for another convention.

When he saw them, Big Ben must have thought he had died and gone to heaven. That almost happened to him just over a year earlier. It was on June 12, 2006 that Big Ben was injured in a motorcycle-car

Photos by George Gojkovich

Ben Roethlisberger

collision on his way to work at the Steelers' South Side training complex. "This is the day last year," Big Ben said when he reported for a workout on that date this year, "I almost lost my life."

Big Ben says he's now riding a 10-speed bike. When he got to Williamsburg, the sports media there wanted to know if he was still riding a motorcycle and whether or not he was wearing a protective helmet when doing so. Roethlisberger had no desire to talk about that. He feigned deafness, drawing smiles from his audience.

Roethlisberger was also reluctant to dwell much on the Steelers' disappointing 8-8 record and their failure to make the playoffs that year. That was history, as far as he was concerned, and not the sort that attracts so many visitors to Williamsburg and nearby Jamestown and Yorktown.

Since he was at William & Mary, Roethlisberger was eager to say nice things about Mike Tomlin. Tomlin hails from nearby Newport News, near Vick's hometown of Hampton. In doing so, Big Ben was accused by some as being critical of Bill Cowher, his former coach. That wasn't his intent, trust me. When Tony Blair addressed the British Parliament last week he said the British soldiers in Iraq were the best and the bravest, but this was not meant to reflect on American soldiers being second best. Blair, one of our best allies as world leaders go, was playing to his audience. That's what Roethlisberger was doing as well.

"I think Coach Tomlin is a good change for us," remarked Roethlisberger. "People always worry that change is bad. I think that Coach Tomlin is a good guy. He's really going to work hard. He's got a lot of enthusiasm, a lot of excitement and that's good for us."

Asked to compare Tomlin to Cowher, Roethlisberger responded with a smile. "He seems to be more fun. He seems to smile a lot more than Coach Cowher did. Obviously, Coach had the reputation of being 'The Chin' and 'The Frown,' and the scary guy all the time.

"But, what I like best, and what a lot of guys do, is that he's around. You see him with the offense, you see him with the quarterbacks, and you see him with the tight ends. You see him with everybody, and not just the defense. And I think that's important to see."

That's an honest and accurate assessment. It's no knock on Cowher. Hey, he and Big Ben combined to win a Super Bowl less than two years ago. They were a winning team.

"Our fans want us to win the Super Bowl every year," said Roethlisberger. "Last year wasn't a complete failure. It's not like we didn't win any games. It's the expectation of Steeler fans. In my book, it's unsatisfactory for me because I want to be the best and I, obviously, want to win another Super Bowl."

164

Luke and Mike
Taking the town by storm

August 22, 2007

I like Luke. That's Luke as in Luke Ravenstahl, the boy mayor of Pittsburgh. Those of us who live in the suburbs still have a stake in the city of Pittsburgh, so he's our mayor too.

If I were managing his campaign for the upcoming election where he has no real opposition to continue as mayor I'd make up a lot of tin badges and buttons that proclaimed I LIKE LUKE. As in I LIKE IKE.

It worked for Gen. Dwight D. Eisenhower when he was running for president of these United States. It will work for Luke Ravenstahl as well. What's not to like about Luke Ravenstahl?

Luke is learning on the job to be the mayor of our fair city. Hey, he's only 26 years old! He thinks the glory days of the Steelers were when Bill Cowher led them to the Super Bowl victory in Detroit two years back. He wasn't even born when the Steelers won the fourth of six Super Bowls back at the outset of 1980.

David Letterman likes Luke, but our local TV celebs are continually finding fault with Luke's activities. Jon Delano, Kevin Miller and Marty Griffin, to name a few of our diligent naysayers, are always bashing our boy mayor about one thing or another.

They really got on him for being the guest of UPMC in a celebrity golf outing at the Laurel Valley Country Club. That was a mistake. He should have been a celebrity participant and he shouldn't be the guest of any company or organization at any of these charity-related affairs. He says he recognizes that now.

He likes to golf and he likes to mix with the great sports celebrities who come here, whether it's Tiger Woods or Mario Lemieux or Ben Roethlisberger. Who can blame him? After all, he's 26 and a bona fide sports fan even before he succeeded the late Bob O'Connor as mayor.

I knew both Bob O'Connor and Dick Caliguiri well. They came out of Greenfield and Squirrel Hill and Taylor Allderdice and they were street smart and had a feel for the people of Pittsburgh and became fine mayors. I saw O'Connor at several of Lemieux's celebrity golf outings at The Club at Nevillewood, and he was known to steal away from the office for a round of golf at the city's Schenley Park Golf Course. Why do you think they renamed it in his honor?

I saw O'Connor on many occasions on the sideline in the VIP seats at Pitt basketball games. Caliguiri played golf on occasion at Churchill Country Club. Being the mayor is like being a sportswriter. It gets you a free pass to a lot of places around town. The job has its perks.

Luke is the face of Pittsburgh these days, and it's a good face. It's a fresh face, clean-cut. No earrings are evident, no tattoos, just brushburns from getting roughed up by the local media so much. He looks like an altar boy, an acolyte, and he can lead Pittsburgh in a positive

Tomlin talks to Pitt football coach Dave Wannstedt.

Mike Tomlin talks to Jeff Reed and Jeff's mom, Pam Reed, at UPMC Sports Complex indoor field.

Photos by Jim O'Brien

The calm before the storm . . . Pittsburgh Mayor Luke Ravenstahl watches Steelers practice at South Side indoor facility just before a bad storm struck the city, forcing an early departure to look after problems.

direction. It's a changing Downtown and he could be our mayor for another 30 years, unless he becomes governor along the way.

The mayor and I had similar plans on a recent Thursday. We were going to travel to Latrobe to look in on the Steelers at one of their summer training sessions. Heavy rains washed out their morning workout. More of the same was predicted for the afternoon.

So Mike Tomlin switched the second session to the team's South Side complex. I was in North Versailles when I made a U-turn to attend the practice. I caught a Pitt practice afterward. No sooner did I arrive at the indoor complex than I saw Mayor Ravenstahl coming through the door and joining us spectators on the sideline. I'd rather see him on the sideline watching practice than Lawrence Timmons, the team's multi-million-dollar bonus baby and No. 1 draft choice, who's been a spectator at too many sessions.

I had a chance to chat with the mayor. He's a Democrat and I'm a Republican but I'm a supporter of his, as I was of Caliguiri and O'Connor. I recommended a good book for Luke to look up. It's called *Leadership*, and it's by former New York mayor Rudy Giuliani. Rudy writes about his experiences of being mayor of The Big Apple and how there was no guidebook for him to study when he got the job.

"I see myself as an ambassador for Pittsburgh," said Luke Ravenstahl. "I'm proud to be the mayor of this city, and I want to lead it in a positive direction. People are always going to be critical."

When I mentioned to him that I was pleased to see the progress being made in the way of new venues and new restaurants in Downtown Pittsburgh, Ravenstahl replied, "We are bringing Downtown Pittsburgh back to life. I think it really once again allows Pittsburghers to see that what previously had been a dream is now becoming a reality."

About 15 minutes later a severe storm, with tornado-like winds, struck the fair city of Pittsburgh. The lights went out in the building. Luke started getting calls on his cell phone. Trees were falling down and basements around town were flooding. He had to get back to work. It's a good thing he wasn't out in Latrobe. He was whisked away by his aides. I figured there'd be hell to pay when the media learned that Luke was at a Steelers' football practice when Pittsburgh was in the midst of a terrible storm. As if Luke could have halted the storm.

The mayor is expected to be everywhere at one time. Everyone wants his attention. He couldn't have held up the trees and—unlike the Dutch boy who stuck his finger in the hole in the dike—Luke couldn't have stopped the floodwaters. But, as expected, he caught hell for being at a Steelers' practice. Let's cut Luke a break. He's younger than both of my daughters. Luke has to learn on the job. He's young and enthusiastic, and he likes to play golf and watch the Steelers practice, and shake hands with famous people. How does that make him different from most of the movers and shakers about town? O'Connor and Caliguiri grew into their roles, and so will Cool Hand Luke.

My wife Kathie and my buddy Bill Priatko both called me on my cellphone to inform me of the change in the Steelers' practice venue that day. Those two, and two other friends of mine, are the only ones who have my cell phone number. I use a cell phone only when necessary.

It's funny how you make a U-turn in your car and head home when you hear that the Steelers' practice has been shifted from St. Vincent College to the UPMC Sports Complex on the city's South Side, and a wonderful afternoon awaits you somehow. At first, I thought I'd just go home.

Then, as I drove westward, following familiar routes, I thought I'd stop midway at the UPMC Sports Complex and catch some part of the practice session. I had no idea how well things would turn out. It turned out to be a difficult day for most Pittsburghers, but a great day for me. Life is funny that way. I've had my share of difficult days.

Everyone seemed especially warm and friendly that afternoon when I entered the indoor practice facility. At first, I mixed with the media, catching up with a few I hadn't seen in a while. I ended up seeing and chatting briefly with the Mayor of Pittsburgh, and the head coaches of the Steelers and the Pitt football team. That's quite a trifecta.

Luke Ravenstahl is 26, Mike Tomlin is 35 and Dave Wannstedt is 55 and I was nearing my 65th birthday. I liked it better when the mayor and the football coaches were all much older than I was. Bring back Jock Sutherland, Buddy Parker, Davey Lawrence, Joe Barr and Pete Flaherty.

I'd been to a Steelers' alumni golf outing the week before and embraced two old friends. Lou "Bimbo" Cecconi was a backfield coach at Pitt during my student days in the early '60s and had been a terrific three-sport athlete himself. Paul Uram was the conditioning coach for Chuck Noll's four Super Bowl championship teams. Cecconi had come out of Donora High to star at Pitt. Uram was a gymnastics coach in Butler.

I'd always been too small to take sports seriously as a participant, but I was now aware that as I held Cecconi and then Uram in my arms that I was bigger than they were. It was a strange turnaround.

When I was at the Steelers' practice, two of the assistant coaches who were holdovers from Bill Cowher's staff came over to the sideline to say hello. One was John Mitchell, the Steelers' defensive line coach. He had been the first black to play for Bear Bryant at Alabama. He had just been promoted by Mike Tomlin to be the Steelers' associate head coach. I congratulated him on his promotion. Then Dick LeBeau came by and patted me on the back. LeBeau is one of the nicest coaches I have ever met. He's the defensive coordinator of the Steelers. He was an outstanding defensive back for the Detroit Lions when I first became aware of who was who in the National Football League back in the '50s. He'd been a teammate of Joe Schmidt and Bobby Layne with the Lions.

I also liked LeBeau because he was older than I was. He would be turning 70 the first week in September. I liked it better when the coaches were older than I was. They don't come with any more class

Former Pitt basketball standout and UPMC exec Curtis Aiken chats with good friend Mayor Luke Ravenstahl at 2008 Dapper Dan Dinner & Sports Auction.

Jim O'Brien

Mike Tomlin and Mayor Luke Ravenstahl were both guests of Curtis Aiken at courtside seats at Pitt basketball game. Tomlin has become a big fan of all the Pittsburgh sports teams. Bob Anderson, the Pitt band director, is at far left.

than Mitchell and LeBeau. Tomlin will benefit from their company and counsel.

I saw a few scenes that stay with me, and reinforce my earliest feelings about Mike Tomlin. He is different from Chuck Noll and he is different from Bill Cowher. Tomlin was talking to team president Art Rooney II at midfield when I greeted him and shook his hand. I told him of my recent trip to Williamsburg, and how I had visited and interviewed his old coach, Jimmye Lacock, at William & Mary. Tomlin was easy to talk to.

Cowher, like his boss, Dan Rooney, was never easy to talk to. Tomlin is an attractive figure in so many ways.

Jeff Reed approached Coach Tomlin and introduced him to his mother and sister. Reed has an interesting family and he has good bloodlines. His father, Morris, played basketball at Wichita State, and his mother, Pam, was a cheerleader at Wichita State. Jeff's sister, Kristen, played professional soccer.

"I'll bet you're proud of your son," Tomlin told Jeff's mother, putting an arm on her shoulder. She nodded in agreement with an accompanying great big smile. I wondered how Cowher would have handled that meeting.

Jeff asked the coach if they could get some pictures with him, and he posed with Pam and Jeff while Kristen took the pictures. Kristen got into one of the pictures herself.

Then Tomlin joined his family on the sideline. His wife Kiya is petite. He embraced her and then their two boys, Dino and Mason, and then he picked up his little girl, Harlyn Quinn. It was obvious she is close to his heart. He kissed Harlyn Quinn a couple of times on her cheek. It was a good scene. I had used all my film and was wishing I had another roll of film with me. Damn it. Of course, I had seen Cowher do the same on many occasions with his wife and their three daughters.

I thought to myself that this Tomlin is an all right guy and he's going to take this town by storm. I thought that, in time, he would be more popular than Cowher, especially during difficult times. All coaches are popular when they are winning. Cowher once owned Pittsburgh. He could do no wrong.

Tomlin has a presence about him. He is clear and concise in his communication, much like Noll. I had been impressed with him from the first interview I saw on television, by what I read of his remarks relating to several situations. I liked where he was coming from. Cowher would be a tough act to follow because he was a winning coach and continued the high standards established by Noll.

Pro football researcher John Bennett says that 13 Steelers who played on one of the team's first four Super Bowl champions have died before they reached the age of 60. They are Ray Mansfield, Steve Furness, Steve Courson, Dwight White, Ernie Holmes, Jim Clack, Ray Oldham, Jim Wolf, Joe Gilliam, Mike Webster, Ron Shanklin, Theo Bell and Dave Brown.

Sam Davis
The missing guard
on Steelers' All-Time team

"Sam was a real team leader."
— **Andy Russell**

November 8, 2007

Ican still see Sam Davis. He was bright-eyed and all smiles as he stood in front of his new store at South Hills Village. It was called "Only Happiness," and it was a card and gift shop, full of toys and trinkets, inexpensive stuff.

He was proud and optimistic, expressing positive thoughts, as always, that all would go well. That was in the summer of 1983.

The last time I saw Sam Davis he was signing autographs in a vacated store area at Century III Mall in West Mifflin. He was there with Joe Greene, L.C. Greenwood, Dwight White and Ernie Holmes, the front four of the Steelers' vaunted Steeler Curtain defense of the '70s.

Sam's wife, Tamara Davis, who married him two years after he opened "Only Happiness," had brought him to the mall. She is his third wife, and has remained loyal to him. Sam needed some assistance from two young men as he signed his name to photos of him in his heyday with the Steelers. That was on April 19, 2004.

This was a different Sam Davis. He was dulled and slow of speech, much like Muhammad Ali these days. He had come to Century III mall from a modest personal care home in McKeesport. He has been living there the past ten years or so. I spoke to him once as he visited a convenience store nearby to get some candy.

He is popular with people in the neighborhood, including the school crossing guard, and a familiar sight on the streets. He likes to get out and take a walk now and then.

It was reported by the Pittsburgh media that Sam Davis was badly injured in a fall in his home in Gibsonia back on Sept. 9, 1991. His wife Tamara found him at the bottom of the stairs in his basement when she returned home.

None of the Steelers who knew Sam, and saw him recovering at Allegheny General Hospital soon after, believed that story. John Banaszak, who lives in McMurray, and Mel Blount, who operates a home for wayward teenage boys in Taylorstown, both told me they thought Davis was assaulted by thugs.

When "Only Happiness" went out of business, Davis started a construction business. It's believed he borrowed money from the wrong kind of people, and paid the price and then some when he couldn't make good on his payment schedule. Blount said Davis had deep bruises all over his body, and thought some thugs had taken baseball bats to him to teach him a lesson.

Sam Davis was once one of the great success stories of the Steelers. He signed as a free agent out of little Allen University in South Carolina before the 1967 season. He was one of five players who survived the transition from Bill Austin to Chuck Noll as the head coach of the Steelers to play in Super Bowls.

"Sam was a remarkable athlete and a real team leader," said Andy Russell, who resides in Nevillewood, and also survived the switch in coaches along with Rocky Bleier, Ray Mansfield and Bobby Walden.

"Sam played for our Steelers' basketball team, and he didn't play like you'd expect a football lineman to play. He could run and jump with anyone. When we played those great defensive lines of the Dallas Cowboys their guys just disappeared in front of Sam and Larry Brown, who played tackle next to him. Sam and Larry never got the credit they deserved because we had so many other great players."

Sam was the starting guard on four Steelers' teams that won Super Bowls. He played for 13 seasons until 1979. He was a wise man, a pleasant man. I often went to him seeking insights into the other Steelers. They respected him and called him "Tight Man" because he had it all together. He worked as a sales representative for over two years with the H.J. Heinz Co., starting in 1981. He wore No. 57 and was a perfect fit for Heinz and its 57 varieties of food offerings.

Sam Davis was born on the 4th of July in 1944. He's 64 years old. The Steelers hosted a dinner at the David L. Lawrence Convention Center this past Sunday night to celebrate their 75th season. They introduced their All-Time Team and their Legends Team (pre-70s) at the dinner and again at halftime of their nationally televised game with the Baltimore Ravens on Monday night at Heinz Field.

There are 33 players on their All-Time Team, but for some strange reason there is only one guard. That's Alan Faneca, a perennial Pro Bowl choice on the current club. Sam Davis deserved to be on that team as the other guard. Art Rooney II, the team president, conceded last week that Davis probably should have been on the All-Time team. Maybe they didn't want to put the spotlight on Sam Davis in his diminished condition.

There were other omissions. Players such as "Bullet Bill" Dudley, John Henry Johnson and Bobby Layne, who are in the Pro Football Hall of Fame, should have been on the Steelers' All-Time Team. Frank Varrichione, a tackle on the "Legends" team, should have been on it, too. Punter Pat Brady, defensive back Mike Wagner and linebacker Levon Kirkland, receiver Louie Lipps and kick returner Lynn Chandnois would have made some sense as selections as well.

Every team should have a coach and there was none better than Chuck Noll, who coached those four Super Bowl title teams that included Sam Davis in their lineup. It was difficult to see Chuck Noll requiring a cane to get around the field when he was recently introduced at a halftime ceremony at Heinz Field. I thought the Steelers should have provided a golf cart for him and his wife Marianne to transport them that day. Maybe Noll was too proud to accept such an offer.

I run into Tamara and her teenage daughters from time to time at the malls, and ask about Sam. They are beautiful women and they have stayed faithful to him in difficult times.

Anyone who knows the Steelers' history knows that Sam Davis remains one of their all-time best ballplayers and ambassadors.

Jim O'Brien

Sam Davis stops to talk to McKeesport High School students during one of his daily strolls in neighborhood near nursing home where he resides.

In his heydey, Sam Davis (57) is seen with teammates Joe Greene (75) and Jack Lambert (58). Davis was a natural as sales rep for H.J. Heinz Co.

Johnny Unitas
A kid couldn't have a better hero than Johnny U.

September 19, 2002

I felt a strange sadness on September 11, like one feels a few days after a family funeral. I wasn't sure what to do on the first anniversary of the terrorists' attack on America, another infamous day we shall never forget. None of us will ever forget the sight of the World Trade Towers collapsing into a dust pile. I picked up a new car that day and it's a reminder of that horrific event.

Then, as if things weren't bad enough, the news came that Johnny Unitas had died. He suffered a heart attack while doing rehabilitation following surgery and died at age 69. Unitas, who had grown up and played schoolboy football in Pittsburgh, starred for the Baltimore Colts in the '50s and '60s and was regarded as one of the greatest quarterbacks in pro football history. He was my boyhood hero.

We'll never forget that John Unitas died on September 11, one year after the terrorist attack on America. Talk about timing. It was like Willie Stargell dying the same day the Pirates opened PNC Park.

Frank DeFord, one of the most famous sportswriters in America, grew up in Baltimore. Unitas was his hero, too. DeFord, whom I met during my days of working in New York, said in a television interview the next day, "The death of Johnny Unitas is like the official end of my boyhood." Indeed.

When I played sandlot football in the late '50s, I wore No. 19, high-top black shoes and a crewcut, just like Johnny Unitas. I practiced throwing the ball just past my right ear with a downward thrust on the follow-through. Like a pitcher putting some spin on a baseball. It was a thrill to play on some of the same sandlot fields here where Unitas had played for the Bloomfield Rams for $6 a game after the Steelers cut him from their squad during the 1955 training camp. I still think of Unitas when I pass those fields. There is one under the Bloomfield Bridge where he practiced, and there is another at Arsenal Middle School in Lawrenceville where he played.

My friend Tom Averell was successful in getting the city fathers to erect a sign honoring Unitas and his roots on Butler Street, alongside the Arsenal Field where Unitas once played sandlot ball.

I was a reserve quarterback on the Hazelwood Steelers when we played a team from Polish Hill in a midget football league game at Arsenal Field. The field was only 90 yards long and it had no grass and was covered with oil to keep the dust down. The refs would move the ball back ten yards after you crossed midfield to make up for the difference in the length of the field. It was near the end of the game and our coach, Bill Fleming, who worked at the Baltimore & Ohio Railroad, told me to just fall on the ball three times to preserve a victory. He

didn't want our starting quarterback, Rick Reagan, to get hurt when the game was already decided.

I remember thinking when I went in that Johnny Unitas was never told to fall on the ball three straight times. So I plunged forward each time hoping to gain a yard or so, to do something positive. The other team had big linemen, I remember, big Polish kids, and I don't know if I gained much yardage anyway. I know I didn't fumble the ball, which was the most important task. Rick Reagan was too old to play for our team the next year and I got to play quarterback. If I hadn't been so small, near-sighted and slow of foot I might have been another Johnny Unitas. I was the quarterback, I think, because I could remember the plays. I also played center and linebacker. Dale Dodrill, the Steelers' linebacker, was also one of my favorites.

Johnny Unitas was the embodiment of the children's tale about "The Little Engine That Could." He was deficient size-wise and school-wise when he came out of St. Justin's High School, a Catholic Class "B" School in the city's West End, and he was passed over by Pitt and Notre Dame even before the Steelers said he couldn't cut the mustard in the National Football League. He ended up at the University of Louisville. He led the Colts to two NFL championships and was the star in the 1958 sudden death overtime victory against the New York Giants that was billed as "the greatest football game" in history. He was seen on TV a lot in Pittsburgh because the Steelers and Colts had some kind of contract with the Dumont Network to televise their games in this area. The Colts as well as the Steelers were our teams, and the Colts were a lot better than the Steelers in those days.

I spoke over the telephone with Unitas, at age 67, in late November of 2000. One day I came home and one of the messages on my telephone went like this: "Jim O'Brien, this is John Unitas in Baltimore. You called and said you wanted to speak to me." I received return phone calls from Unitas, Mike Ditka and Dan Marino in an eight-day period. It doesn't get much better than that.

The message from Unitas sounded like a voice from heaven. I told my wife, Kathie, to keep it on the message system the remainder of the month. I wanted to hear it again from time to time. I wish I still had it. Sports heroes don't come any better or bigger than those three for anyone who grew up in Pittsburgh.

One of his teammates was once asked what it was like to be in the huddle with Unitas and he said, "It's like being in a huddle with God."

"I never doubted my ability," Unitas told me over the telephone in that interview. "I knew I could play the game."

His father, who delivered coal, died when John was four. John was raised by his mother. She cleaned floors in downtown office buildings, worked in a bakery, and later went to business school to become a bookkeeper. "I learned more from her than any football coach," he said, "not about the game but about life, about being tough, about hanging in there. She was a tough, tough lady. She died about seven or eight years ago in a nursing home in McMurray.

"My sister, Shirley Green, lives in Bethel Park. I see her once a year. I have a brother, Leonard, who lives in Jacksonville. My other sister is Millicent, who lives in Gettysburg. I have a cousin, Joe Unitas, who played semi-pro football in Pittsburgh (Valley Ironmen). He has a photo studio in McMurray. I have a cousin, Bill Unitas, who lives in Gibsonia."

His sister, Shirley, also credits their mother for making a difference. "We all got our work ethic from her. They don't make them like her anymore. John never complained; he just went to work. I think we got that from our mother," she said.

John Steadman, a sportswriter in Baltimore, told me once at Three Rivers Stadium, that you could sum up the success of Unitas in two words: "Beyond intimidation."

Told that, Unitas said, "I never let stuff bother me. Just growing up the way I did in the street, or working at home. If you had a problem you looked it in the eye and resolved it. We did what we had to do in order to get along. We didn't panic."

I found myself pretending to throw a football like Unitas the other day.

Recommended Reading: *Johnny U* by Tom Callahan, Crown Books. This is a great read for anyone who was a fan of Johnny Unitas.

Harry Homa

John Unitas visits with Steelers' quarterback Terry Bradshaw in home team's locker room at Three Rivers Stadium.

Lynn Chandnois
Still a Steelers star

October 17, 2007

I walked into a restaurant in Peters Township and into my boyhood bedroom at the same time. If this sounds like the start of a C.S. Lewis tale about the Kingdom of Narnia, well, it's just as incredible.

A man looked my way and mouthed a hello as my wife Kathie and I were being seated at the Sesame Inn on Route 19 in McMurray. This was on a Sunday night earlier this month.

I said hello, but didn't recognize the man at first. His face looked familiar but, like mine, it was a little different from when we last met nearly five years ago. I thought he was a former football player, perhaps a Steeler, but I wasn't sure.

During dinner I kept looking at him across the room. I overheard some comments made at his table. He was twice addressed as Lynn. I knew for certain he wasn't Lynn Swann. I felt confident that it was Lynn Chandnois, one of my favorite Steelers when I was a kid.

He stood up, still a tall man with broad shoulders. I approached him from behind and tapped him on his shoulder. "Are you Lynn Chandnois, the greatest kick-off returner in Steelers' history?" I asked.

"Are you O'Brien, the writer? " he came back. I smiled and nodded. We embraced. His wife, Paulette, got out of the booth and I got another hug.

Kathie and I had first met them in 1982, 25 years earlier, when the Steelers were celebrating their 50th season. I'd seen them a few times since then. They were in town this time as part of the Steelers' 75th season celebration. He is 82 now and I'm 65. (Chandnois turned 83 on Feb. 24, 2008).

Chandnois had represented the Steelers of the '50s in a coin flip ceremony before the Steelers' impressive 21–0 victory over the Seattle Seahawks. Donora's Rudy Andabaker, who was also a former head football coach at Bethel Park High School, Jim "Popcorn" Brandt and George Hughes, joined him.

I still have a red autograph book containing "Popcorn" Brandt's signature from when he attended a sports banquet at my grade school in Hazelwood back in the '50s.

When I was covering the Steelers in 1982, one of their former running backs, Jerry Nuzum, invited Kathie and me to dinner at the Pittsburgh Athletic Association. At our table were former Steelers' stars "Bullet Bill" Dudley, Fran Rogel, Lynn Chandnois and Joe Gasparella.

It was such a special night. These men meant a lot to me. I first became aware of such Steelers in 1951 when I was nine years old and helping my older brother Dan deliver the *Pittsburgh Post-Gazette* newspaper six mornings a week.

STEELERS

Lynn Chandnois
HALFBACK · PITTSBURGH STEELERS

I collected bubble gum cards with pictures and biographical sketches and statistics of such Steelers as Chandnois, Rogel, Jim Finks, Bobby Gage, Bill McPeak, Dale Dodrill, Ernie Stautner, Jack Butler, Ray Mathews and Pat Brady. They were black and white cards and I wrapped a rubber band around them to keep them intact. I kept them in a closet and I'd take them out and spread them out on my blanket from time to time, and memorize the images and the information.

Chandnois still holds kickoff return records in the Steelers' media guide. He averaged 29.6 yards a return, the best in team history, and seven yards better than Rod Woodson's average. Only Gale Sayers has a higher lifetime NFL kick-off return average. Yet *Sports Illustrated* selected Woodson as the Steelers' greatest kickoff return man on their 75th anniversary all-time team. Chandnois earned All-American honors as a senior at what was then called Michigan State College.

Here's some interesting background on Chandnois culled from his entry in Wikipedia, the free Internet encyclopedia:

After both of his parents died, Lynn, who was born in Michigan's Upper Peninsula, moved to Flint to live with an aunt and go to school. At Flint Central High, he earned all-state honors in both football and basketball. After graduating in 1944, he joined the Naval Air Corps and served for two years.

He entered Michigan State when he came out of the military service. He was a halfback, a defensive back and kick returner. He was a four-year football standout and played basketball one season. He ranks first in career interceptions (20) and interception yardage (384) and was the team's MVP in 1948, and an All-American in 1949. He was Michigan's Outstanding Amateur Athlete in 1950.

Chandnois, a 6–2, 195–pound two-way back, was the Steelers' No. 1 draft choice in 1950, just ahead of Stautner and Hughes. He was the eighth player picked in the draft. He would play seven seasons (1950–1956) with the Steelers. He was the NFL Player of the Year in 1952.

Chandnois was the star in the Steelers' 63–7 victory over the New York Giants in a game played on a snowy, frigid day in late November of 1952 at Forbes Field.

It was the highest scoring game in Steelers' history and the worst setback in Giants' history. The Giants' coach, Steve Owen, had just come out with a book about his much-ballyhooed "Umbrella Defense."

"They should have delayed that," Chandnois recalled during our reunion at the Sesame Inn when I reminded him of that afternoon.

The Giants had such a regard for their defense that they chose to kick off even though they won the coin flip. Chandnois returned the kick 97 yards for a touchdown. One of his teammates was offside and the Giants kicked off again. This time Chandnois returned the kick 91 yards for a touchdown. He ran another touchdown in from five yards out.

"You can get trapped in your own greatness."
—Frank Gifford
New York Giants

Hughes, who came out of William & Mary College — the same school that produced the Steelers' current coach, Mike Tomlin — led the way with a key block.

The Steelers sidelined the Giants' top two quarterbacks with injuries that day. Tom Landry, a top defensive back, took over at quarterback for the visitors and tossed a touchdown pass to avoid a shutout.

A year later, the Giants elected to kick off again to open a game with the Steelers and Chandnois ran it back for a touchdown. He also returned a kickoff 93 yards for a touchdown against the Philadelphia Eagles at Shibe Park in Philadelphia. He still holds the Steelers' record for most kickoff returns for touchdowns with three to his credit. In truth, he did it four times, but that one that was called back against the Giants doesn't count.

Art Rooney, who owned the Shamrock Stables horse farm in Maryland as well as the Steelers, was quoted as saying, "If my horses would go that fast I'd be a wealthy man."

Chandnois was quite a success story, a real Horatio Alger rags-to-riches tale. He never forgot where he came from, because he continues to live in Flint. He remains a hometown hero.

He originally signed with the Cleveland Browns of the old AFC, just before that league was merged into the NFL. His contract was voided because of the merger and he ended up, much to his dismay at first, with the Pittsburgh Steelers.

Who could blame him for being disappointed? Paul Brown had one of the best pro teams in the nation in Cleveland at that time. They would prove to be one of the best in the NFL as well, and a team clearly superior to the Steelers for a long stretch.

Chandnois was a star for the Steelers. He was named to the All-Pro team in 1952. He was named the Player of the Year by the Washington (D.C.) Football Club. He was the first Steeler to be so honored since Bill Dudley won the award in 1946.

It's important to know the history of the Steelers. They weren't a very good team when Chandnois played for them. But they were still our Steelers. They were still special to us. I played for a midget football team in my hometown called the Hazelwood Steelers. I didn't get to go to the Steelers' games back then. I read about them in the newspapers and saw them occasionally on television. They lived in another world, a fantasyland.

What were the odds back then, living in the modest milltown of Hazelwood, at the eastern end of Pittsburgh, that someday I would come to meet and know these Steelers of my youth? The Steelers recently released a pre-70s "Legends Team" as part of their 75th season celebration.

I met and interviewed every one of the Legends except for a defensive back named Howard Hartley (1949–52). Seeing Lynn Chandnois made me feel like I was ten again.

Chandnois told me he didn't feel like a kid again. "All those bumps and bruises add up," he said. "They never go away. I've had both of my knees replaced. It was bone-on-bone on my right knee before the operation. I'd rather replace them than endure that constant pain. I can still play golf, and I still do some consulting work for Jessop Steel in Washington (Pa.), though they're operating under a different name now. Dick Groat and I both worked for that company."

* * *

There is a story within a story relating to Lynn Chandnois and his wife, Paulette. When I first met them in 1982, Lynn's wife was named Bernice and Paulette was then married to Jerry Nuzum.

Nuzum had been a running back for the Steelers from 1948 to 1951, and a teammate and close friend of Lynn Chandnois. While playing for the Steelers, Nuzum lived in a home in Hazelwood, where I grew up. People in Hazelwood would boast about Nuzum living among us. I was nine years old and delivering the morning newspaper, the *Post-Gazette*, when Nuzum played his final season with the Steelers in 1951. Nuzum had an automobile dealership in Wilkinsburg when I was in high school. By the time I was covering the Steelers for *The Pittsburgh Press*, from 1979 to 1983, he had a Chevrolet dealership in Uniontown. He took a liking to me and kept in touch.

He invited my wife Kathleen and me to join him and some of his former teammates from the '40s and '50s when the Steelers had their 50 Seasons celebration in 1982. He later gave me a photo of his wife Paulette. "Put this in your car," he said, "and check it out when you're driving. It'll make you smile."

I told this story to Paulette on the telephone a week after we bumped into each other during the 2007 season. She explained what happened. Lynn Chandnois and his wife Bernice split up first and then she and Jerry were divorced. The four of them had been great friends. So she and Lynn got together and they were married.

"Jerry was a good guy and so generous," said Paulette, "but we just grew apart. I remember that he once offered to give a black and gold Corvette to Chuck Noll and Noll turned down the offer."

I related this story to Dick Hoak, who had been on Noll's coaching staff, and he remembered it well. "I told Chuck that if he didn't want the car he could give it to me," said Hoak.

I also remember that Jerry Nuzum had been implicated in a murder case back in Las Cruces, New Mexico where he'd gone to college. In that respect, he is one of only four NFL players to this day who were ever charged in murder cases. Ray Lewis of the Baltimore Ravens was also charged with conspiracy to kill — for a murder in Atlanta during Super Bowl XXXIV — but he was never brought to trial. No one will ever forget that O.J. Simpson was arrested for the murder of his wife Nicole and her friend Ron Goldman. That was a well-publicized case that had high TV ratings. The Carolina Panthers' Rae Carruth was accused of orchestrating the drive-by shooting of his pregnant girl friend.

> *Fifty percent of NFL players get divorced within a year after retiring as players, according to an NFL Players Association study.*

Lynn and Bernice Chandnois joins 50th Season Celebration with Franco Harris at David L. Lawrence Convention Center.

Paulette and Lynn Chandnois are at home in Flint, Michigan.

In 2001, he was found guilty of conspiring to kill her. At age 34, he is still serving time in prison. He is the only NFL player to end up in prison over a murder.

Nuzum, a native of Clovis, New Mexico, died in 1997. Just before his death, he was interviewed for a documentary that was done by Santa Fe filmmakers called "The Silence of Cricket Coogler: A Political Murder and Cover-Up."

Ovida "Cricket" Coogler was an 18-year-old woman who was murdered in March or April of 1949. According to a news release from the New Mexico State University library, "Cricket had been a barfly since she was 14. She and Nuzum had been bar-hopping on the night in question, but she left him. She was last seen on Thursday, March 31, 1949 when she entered an official state car on Main Street in downtown Las Cruces at 3 a.m. Her body was found 17 days later in a shallow grave south of Las Cruces. Jerry Nuzum, a former Aggie, was arrested for the murder, jailed for a few days and then released by a judge for lack of evidence before the case went to a jury. It was reported that Jerry Nuzum had been "falsely accused." Then some political officials in the community came under scrutiny, but no one was ever convicted of the crime. It remains in the "Cold Case" files in Las Cruces.

Students at New Mexico State University were so enraged by Nuzum's arrest that they submitted a petition to the governor requesting a grand jury to investigate the Coogler murder case. The grand jury was convened but they were never able to indict anyone for Coogler's murder. It remains to this day an unsolved murder case.

I wasn't sure how to bring up this story in my telephone conversation with Paulette Chandnois, but she beat me to the punch. Talking about her first husband, Jerry Nuzum, she said, "We were divorced in 1991. We had been married for 13 years. He didn't want it, but I had to move. We weren't getting along. And you know that Jerry had that problem with that girl that disappeared in New Mexico. So it got scary for me. I moved to Mt. Lebanon after my divorce. That's where I'm from. You know Art Rooney really went to bat for Jerry when he got into that trouble down in New Mexico. He went down and spoke on his behalf to the police officials there."

I asked her how she and Lynn got together.

"Lynn was still doing some consulting for Jessop Steel in Washington, Pa. — he started working for them when he played for the Steelers — and we started dating," she said. "When he came to town he'd stay at the Holiday Inn across from South Hills Village. We'd have dinner at the Living Room. We finally got together. We were married July 18, 1993, so we've been married for 15 years now.

"He and Bernice had been married for 26 years. He loved her the way I had loved Jerry. Heck, I loved Bernice, too. We spent a lot of time together. She was so much fun. She left him a note and said, 'I've left you for another man.' Bernice ran off with a man she worked with. Lynn still looked good. He stayed in good shape. You know Lynn is the height of Narcissism, so he didn't take too well to anyone leaving him for another man. You never forget the good times. I felt badly when Jerry died. There was a long spell where he was good to me."

The Chandnois-Nuzum pairings pointed up another episode in my sportswriting career.

It reminded me of when I was covering the New York Yankees in 1972 and 1973 and how two of the team's pitchers, Mike Kekich and Fritz Peterson, swapped wives. The tabloid newspapers in New York had a field day with that story.

Once after Kekich pitched and won a game at Detroit, I asked him about his marital swap and how things were going. Yankees' manager Ralph Houk overheard our conversation and he hollered at me in the visitors' clubhouse. He dressed me down real good for asking Mike about his marital situation, screaming at me in front of all the players.

The next day, he asked me to come into his office before the game. Houk apologized to me for his outburst. "You chewed me out in front of all the players," I said, "and now you're apologizing to me when no one's around."

Jim O'Brien

Jerry Nuzum talks to Hebrew school students who attended Steelers' summer training camp session at St. Vincent College.

Tony Dungy
His last day as a player for the Steelers

"He's a wonderful human being."
— **Myrd Milowicki**

A *Steelers' fan and a loyal reader of my books sent me a yellowed copy of the sports section of the Wednesday, August 22, 1979 edition of The Pittsburgh Press. There were two stories of mine at the top of the front page. One was about Matt Bahr making the Steelers' squad as their place-kicker at the expense of popular Roy Gerela. The other was a column about Tony Dungy's last day as a player for the Steelers. He had been traded to the San Francisco 49ers during the Steelers' training camp at St. Vincent College. I was struck by how my characterization of Dungy back then was still valid 28 years later. Dungy had managed to remain true to himself and to his basic ideals.*

Dungy had gained a great deal of attention in recent seasons because of his success as the head coach of the Tampa Bay Buccaneers and the Indianapolis Colts. Some critics had thought he was too mild-mannered and soft in his approach to ever really be successful and win it all but he had proven them wrong when his Colts defeated the Chicago Bears to win the Super Bowl in February of 2007. Much was made in the media of the fact that the two coaches, Dungy and Lovie Smith, were the first black coaches to get their teams to the Super Bowl. Dungy said it was more of a story that two devout Christians had done it.

Dungy had stood out among the Steelers as a good man, a spiritual sort who was a good role model for anyone. It was disturbing news when Dungy's 18-year-old son James committed suicide during the 2005 season. It didn't add up. What went wrong? Could Tony Dungy bounce back from this tragedy in his family? Where would he find the strength to persevere?

I had an opportunity to talk to Tony Dungy at the Mel Blount Youth Home Celebrity Roast on Friday, April 4, 2008 at the Pittsburgh Hilton Hotel. He was as gracious as ever, and mingled well with everyone. I told him that I had found an article I'd written on him when he was traded by the Steelers. "All the impressions I had about you then are still valid today," I said. "You've remained the real deal." He just grinned broadly and responded, "I remember that article."

A check of other stories that appeared on the same page of the newspaper showed one with a Baltimore dateline, about how former Steelers' quarterback Joe Gilliam had been beaten up by two teenage brothers in a drug-related dispute. A column by sports editor Pat Livingston was about how Jackie Sherrill had coached the Pitt Panthers to 28 victories in three years, more than Pop Warner or Jock Sutherland, two other legendary Pitt coaches. (Sherrill went on to win 33 in three years.) The San Francisco Giants beat the Pirates, 6–1, at Three Rivers Stadium.

Jim O'Brien

Colts' coach Tony Dungy autographs football at Mel Blount Celebrity Dinner at Downtown Hilton on April 4, 2008.

Tony Dungy on Discipline:

"Discipline is the key. Discipline is not yelling at people. It's getting people to do what they're supposed to do all the time."

A rather special Steeler

August 22, 1979
Reprinted from The Pittsburgh Press

LATROBE — There were tears for Tony Dungy, and begrudging acknowledgment that Roy Gerela had done some good things for the Steelers during his long stay with them.

Three women from nearby Greensburg with several children in their company, stood outside Bonaventure Hall yesterday afternoon, waiting to say goodbye to Tony Dungy, a rather special Steeler.

The tears were swelling the eyes of Myrd Milowicki, among the most fervent of Steeler fans. Camp followers will know her as the woman with the white car who has Steelers' insignias, cartoon characters, booster messages, and player autographs all over it.

"Tony is such a beautiful person," she said. "He's religious, he doesn't drink or smoke. He's a wonderful human being."

The word spread fast yesterday that Dungy had been traded to the San Francisco 49ers for an undisclosed draft choice, and that Gerela had been put on waivers as the Steelers cut their roster to 50 players.

Myrd Milowicki, and her sidekick, Marci Matenkosky, helped spread the word. Milowicki called their good friend, Mary Ellen Tiberio, on the telephone in the lobby of one of the campus buildings. (Remember, there were no cell phones in those days.)

She reached Tiberio at Latrobe General Hospital, where she'd gone to check on the progress of her recently born child. The baby was sleeping, and all was well, so Tiberio came to the Steelers' training camp to say goodbye to Tony Dungy.

Get the picture? Yes, these are fervent fans.

While they were waiting at the front door of the dorm where the Steelers have been staying the last six weeks, they caught sight of Gerela going out the back door and down a path toward the parking lot. "There goes Roy," someone observed. To which a young boy in the party responded by saying, "I'm glad to see Gerela going."

A few minutes later, two men emerged from the dorm, walking toward the practice field where the Steelers were working out. They were Art Rooney Jr., a club V.P. responsible for the scouting department, and Bill Nunn Jr., the assistant player personnel director and the summer camp coordinator.

Nunn noted the presence of the Steeler regulars, and asked, "What's wrong? I thought you'd be glad."

"It's Tony we're sad about," Myrd Milowicki replied.

"Oh, right," said Nunn, not missing a beat. "I was thinking about the other guy. I knew you weren't a fan of his."

"That's sad, too," said Milowicki. "You can't forget the good times."

"I don't," said Nunn.

188

* * *

The women pointed to a field below where Dungy had appeared in May to represent the Steelers at the local Special Olympics.

"He was supposed to make a token appearance," recalled Milowicki, "but he stayed for all the events. He didn't just give out medals, either. He talked to the kids, and he hugged the kids who won the wheelchair race, and he communicated with all those handicapped kids. They loved him.

"He went into the city that night and did a commercial for some benefit; he was very involved with Willie Stargell and Sickle Cell Anemia. He'd bought a home here and he was a Pittsburgher. He was from Jackson, Michigan — we met his parents...lovely people— but he became a part of this community. He worked for Mellon Bank in the off-season. And now he's gone."

Dungy's teammates were hugging him in the hallway of the dorm the way he'd hugged those handicapped kids at the Special Olympics. Dungy had been among the Steelers who held regular Bible study meetings and spiritual sessions. There were over 25 who participated in such meetings.

Mike Kruczek and Rocky Bleier embraced him first, then J.T. Thomas. Ray Oldham took him aside to say something to him. Oldham had been traded to the Steelers from the Baltimore Colts and knew something about what that felt like. Fred Anderson wagged his head in disbelief. Mel Blount hugged Dungy, then shook his hand, and looked him in the eyes and said, "They'll play you out there. Go get 'em and God bless you!"

The task of telling Dungy he'd been traded was left to defensive coach Woody Widenhofer. "I've known him since junior high," said Widenhofer. "I recruited him to the University of Minnesota and I brought him here. It's hard, but he'll be a starter or the fifth defensive back at the corner. J.T. can play all the positions back there, and Woody (rookie Dwayne Woodruff) can play the corner."

"Woody's played well in games," interjected defensive backfield coach Dick Walker. "We'll all miss Tony. He's a special guy."

* * *

Dungy will miss the Steelers, too. They were special to him. Both he and Gerela thanked Chuck Noll for providing them with the opportunity to play for the Steelers. Gerela had been claimed on waivers in 1971 and Dungy was the only free agent to make the squad in 1977.

"I think it will be a good opportunity for me," Dungy said of the trade to the 49ers. "I thanked Coach Noll for the chance to play. Nobody else would give me the chance to play.

"It's a business. Everything's done for the good of the team."

Raising Kane to know
he's not the greatest

February 28, 2008

JACK TWYMAN

There's a domino effect in sports these days, with the worst behavior of the pros spilling over into the college and prep and pee wee ranks. After Schenley beat Brashear to win the City League's basketball championship at the Palumbo Center last week, Schenley's star player, Deandre Kane claimed Pittsburgh's basketball world belonged to him. "I had to show people what I was about," he said after the 6–4 senior guard led Schenley to a 72–63 victory over Brashear. "I hear about (Jeannette's) Terrelle Pryor and Jonathan Baldwin of Aliquippa and Brian Walsh at Moon, but I want people to know about Deandre Kane. I'm the real deal and this is my city."

Someone ought to tell Deandre he might be telling people more than he wants them to know about Deandre Kane. Someone ought to tell him to just shut up. Deandre Kane, like so many of today's self-centered athletes, could use a history lesson.

He needs to learn about Jack Twyman and Maurice Stokes and Maurice Lucas. They all played high school basketball in Pittsburgh and they went on to great professional careers. Twyman and Stokes are both in the Basketball Hall of Fame in Springfield, Mass. He needs to know about Chuck Cooper of Westinghouse High and Duquesne University, the first black player drafted by an NBA team — by the Boston Celtics in 1950.

Kane has a way to go before he achieves such heights in his chosen sport. He's not the first schoolboy athlete to thump his chest and proclaim his greatness, so I won't come down too hard on him. There are a lot of bad role models for young men these days in the world of sports.

Kane had declared a year ago that he was going to Duquesne University, but he has since changed his mind. He says he might be more interested in going to Pitt and being reunited with his former teammate DeJuan Blair. But Pitt doesn't have a scholarship available at this time to offer Kane. Jamie Dixon has already allotted more scholarships than allowed under NCAA rules and that means someone from the present squad will have to leave early to make room for a new recruit. Steve Pederson, the athletic director, should frown upon such practices because it can create an environment wherein a coach pushes a kid to leave the program. Kane quit the Schenley High School basketball team as a freshman because he didn't like the coach's practice of having freshmen carry equipment bags for the seniors. If I had been the basketball coach at Schenley, I'd have told Kane he could come back to the team as a sophomore, but that he would still have to carry the equipment bags of the seniors. That would be our deal.

CHUCK COOPER
First black to be drafted by an NBA team

MAURICE LUCAS
From Schenley to NBA stardom

Jim O'Brien

Jack Twyman (27), left, and Maurice Stokes (12), right, are two of Pittsburgh's top pro basketball players who are featured in display at Western Pennsylvania Sports Museum at the Heinz History Center in Pittsburgh.

Jack Twyman, now a retired millionaire businessman in Cincinnati, would smile about that, and maybe wag his head, too.

Jack Twyman is a good story and it's a story that has stood the test of time. It's a parable, an adaptation of the Good Samaritan story in the Bible. Twyman has been successful on several fronts: sports, television, business, family, community, church, you name it. He was driven to succeed, but he always took time out to look after others. That's the real charm of Jack Twyman.

He comes from Pittsburgh, but he has spent most of his adult life in Cincinnati. Most of us have heard how Michael Jordan was cut the first time he tried out for his high school basketball team in Wilmington, N.C. He came back and made the most of his second opportunity.

Well, Twyman was even more persistent in that regard. Twyman was cut from the squad three straight seasons before he made the team as a senior at Central Catholic High School. He served as the team manager for two of those years and carried everybody's bags and performed a lot of thankless tasks to help the team. It set the tone and an attitude that served him well the rest of his life.

Today, most kids who get cut never come back the next season to try out again. At some suburban schools, they come back the next day with their parents and the family attorney and threaten to sue the school for an unjustifiable act.

Twyman made all-state his senior year. He left the city in 1951 to go to the University of Cincinnati. He went on to become the first All-American basketball player at Cincinnati as a senior. He was there just before Oscar Robertson.

Twyman, a 6–6 forward, was the second-round draft choice of the Rochester Royals of the NBA when there were only eight teams in the league. He starred for the Royals, who relocated to Cincinnati, for 11 seasons, averaging 18.3 points and playing in six NBA All-Star Games. He finished second in the NBA in scoring one season, just behind Bob Pettit, and second another season behind rookie Wilt Chamberlain.

"I would've been the first player in the NBA to ever average more than 30 a game," said Twyman, "except that Wilt comes along as a rookie to steal the spotlight from me." Twyman gained attention and praise for his dedication to looking after teammate Maurice Stokes, another Pittsburgh-born NBA All-Star, for 12 long years when Stokes was stricken with encephalitis in 1958. The crippling brain disease left Stokes an invalid in a wheelchair.

Both Pitt and Duquesne had passed on taking Stokes to play on their basketball teams. Instead, he went to St. Francis of Loretto and put that school on the national sports map.

Twyman has long been involved in civic activity and has been a big fund-raiser for many charities in his community. Yet he never claimed that Pittsburgh or Cincinnati was his city. He knew better.

Baseball at PNC Park
Take me out to the ballgame
...any day of the week

July 6, 2006

I can honestly say I was there. It's a moment in Pirates' history I won't soon forget. It was a perfect afternoon for baseball. The Pirates were playing a heavily favored opponent in a high-scoring contest. The score was tied going into the bottom of the ninth inning.

An infielder was the leadoff hitter for the Pirates. The first pitch was a ball. The count was 1-and-0. The batter hit the next pitch high and deep and the crowd roared as it realized the ball would clear the left field wall. No, this isn't about Bill Mazeroski's mighty home run that beat the New York Yankees, 10–9, in the seventh and deciding game of the 1960 World Series at Forbes Field. I was one of the few Pittsburghers who wasn't present at the ballpark that day, if you believe everybody who tells you they were there.

This was last Thursday, June 29, at PNC Park. The Pirates rallied to whip the White Sox of Chicago, the same White Sox that won the World Series at the end of last season. Freddie Sanchez struck the mighty blow this time as the Pirates pulled out a wonderful, 7–6 victory. Freddie Sanchez was the man of the hour.

The win ended a modern-day club record 13-game losing streak and the Pirates mobbed one another as if they had just won a World Series. It was such a relief, to finally win a game. There was joy among most of the fans at PNC Park, if not the ones who were rooting for the White Sox.

It was one of those magic moments for a baseball fan. You never know what day or night they might occur. I had been at PNC Park two nights earlier when the Pirates lost, 4–2, to the same White Sox. There were nearly 25,000 fans at the park that night and they were into the game from start to finish. The fans that go to games at PNC Park have not given up on their team. The fans who complain about the Pirates the most are ones who have never stepped foot in PNC Park.

I have been to ten games so far this season. I was there Sunday afternoon when the Pirates lost to the Detroit Tigers, one of the best teams in baseball this season, by 9-8. The Pirates still had a chance of winning when they came to bat in the bottom of the ninth inning. It was good theater.

The Pirates have lost most of the games I've seen them play this season. It's been a difficult summer so far for the team and its followers. They've lost more than 20 games by one run. They've lost because they're not quite good enough to win yet.

I don't know why they haven't won more games. They've got some good young players on this team. Anyone who goes to PNC Park looking for the Pirates to win is going to be disappointed more often than not. It's better to go to see a major-league baseball game. If the Pirates win it's a bonus. "You're still seeing the greatest baseball players in the world," says Joe Gordon, one of the guys I sit with at most of the games. This Friday, July 7, city officials and baseball fans are going to have a Forbes Field Wall Celebration at the site of Forbes Field in Oakland. An official historical marker is going to be unveiled. What remains of the wall at Forbes Field is going to be properly preserved to call attention to one of this city's most beloved ballparks and sports venues. It's the start of a weeklong schedule of activities around the All-Star Game. Kids wearing replica uniforms of the Pirates and the Homestead Grays will play games at Mazeroski Field near the wall.

It's unlikely that baseball fans will gather in the future on June 29 to celebrate Freddy Sanchez's home run that ended the disastrous losing streak, but it's still an event to be cherished. It was special. Sanchez has been one of the bright lights in a difficult season for the Pirates. I tell people that shortstop Jack Wilson makes some plays that Honus Wagner and Dick Groat never made. Jose Castillo makes some plays at second base that even Maz never made. Wilson and Castillo are a special double-play combination. They also commit some boners that are unbelievable for such skilled infielders.

PNC Park is a better ballpark than Forbes Field in its finest hour though Schenley Park provided a special backdrop. The Pirates provide great entertainment if not always good baseball at PNC Park. Pittsburgh will be the focal point of the baseball world next week. But it shouldn't be the end of the baseball season in Pittsburgh. Life isn't about winning all the time. More often there are losses. The Pirates need fans more than ever if they are to turn things around.

George Gojkovich

Pirates' Jason Bay has been one of the favorites at PNC Park.

Majestic party ship sails by PNC Park on Allegheny River. Jim O'Brien

Freddie Sanchez led National League in batting in 2007 season. George Gojkovich

Arnold Galiffa
One of Donora's finest

"A leader of men and a truly nice guy."
— **Tribute at West Point**

Anold Galiffa was one of the greatest athletes ever to come out of Western Pennsylvania. Galiffa grew up and first gained attention as an athlete in Donora, a milltown along the Monongahela River about 28 miles southeast of Pittsburgh.

In its best days, when the steel wire and zinc mills were busy round the clock, Donora could count 13,600 citizens in its boundaries, yet it produced more top-notch athletes than almost any community in the country. Oakland, California, for instance, which is so much larger, indeed a bona fide city, can claim many great athletes as hometown heroes, but few can outdo Donora. People in Donora believe their town was "The City of Champions" before Pittsburgh laid claim to that distinction in the late '70s. There were billboards on highways proclaiming Donora as "the original City of Champions." Donora definitely had more than its share of great ones.

The list starts with Stan "The Man" Musial, "Deacon Dan" Towler, Ken Griffey and Bernie Galiffa, the nephew of Arnold Galiffa. There were so many more who played at Pitt, such as Lou "Bimbo" Cecconi and Rudy Andabaker, Bob and Mickey Rosborough, and so many others who matriculated at colleges in the area and across the country.

Ken Griffey's son, Ken Griffey Jr., is a future Baseball Hall of Famer. Ken Griffey Jr.'s grandfather, Buddy Griffey, was a terrific four-sport athlete in his day in Donora. He was limited by his short stature.

In the U.S. Military Academy archives, there is an article about one of the school's favorite sons. It begins like this: "Arnold Anthony Galiffa was a gifted athlete, a leader of men and a truly nice guy."

Baseball's legendary Branch Rickey once said Stan Musial was "the most liked player in baseball." Most of Donora's star athletes merited similar accolades. To hear people praise them, they were all nice guys. That's the way they were raised and were expected to behave.

There was one that misbehaved. That was Roscoe Ross. He was in the same backfield at Donora High School as Galiffa, Towler and Cecconi. Some say he was the best of them all, but he ran afoul of the law and aborted a great athletic career. Roscoe's sister, the lovely Loretta Manus, is one of the nicest people you would ever want to meet, and she has helped steer so many youngsters in Donora down the proper path with her guidance efforts at the Mon Valley YMCA. Her son, Charles "Yogi" Jones, excelled on and off the field as a football player and coach at Pitt.

In its day, Donora was a thriving multi-ethnic area consisting of Italians, Eastern Europeans and African-Americans that turned out steel, zinc and world-class athletes. The Depression and management chicanery took care of the steel industry. A thermal inversion—the dirty smog stayed low in the valley for weeks in October, 1948—killed 20 people, sickened 6,000 and finished off the Donora Zinc Works. That's when they started to clean the air in the Mon Valley.

Yet Donora is still there. It's fallen on hard times—a quarter of the population lives below the poverty level—but there are still many well-kept homes, many of them painted white or with white paneling, and it remains a proud community. I have appeared and spoken at the Donora Public Library and met many good people there. There are still ethnic clubs on every corner, but they have a hard time attracting new members or staying alive.

"It might have been the Iron City beer," —Joe Montana

When I stood at the highest spot in Donora and looked out on the land and homes around me I couldn't help but wonder what it was that led to Donora developing so many star performers. When Joe Montana, who grew up about 15 minutes away in Monongahela, was asked why so many great quarterbacks came from Western Pennsylvania when he was inducted into the Pro Football Hall of Fame, he said, "It might have been something in the water. Maybe it was in the Iron City beer." The sky over Donora during my visit was clear as can be, like the sky one sees on a normal day in North Carolina, and you could see forever.

Art Galiffa, a brother of Arnold Galiffa, had a good theory. "The athletes around here wanted something," he said. "They needed something. You could get a jersey, a sweater, a banquet at the end of the season. You were going to get to take a shower, and that was a big deal. If I played basketball I got to take a shower. That was something. You walked to school and you walked home. If you had a sweater or jacket with Donora on it that was a big deal."

Arnold Anthony Galiffa doesn't get mentioned much these days during sports talk show discussions about the greatest athletes from the area, but he deserves consideration. Sports fans would be wiser if they learned more about this man who was respected for his actions on and off the playing fields and gym floors.

Galiffa was a gifted athlete and a well-mannered young man when he first made his mark in Donora. He came from a good family and he represented it well in every way. Those who talked about him then, and now, always say, "And he was a great man, too."

He not only distinguished himself in sports, but he would also become successful in business as well as an engineer and executive at U.S. Steel Corporation.

He died at age 51 of colon cancer on September 5, 1978 in Glenview, Illinois. He was brought home to be buried at the Mon Valley Memorial Cemetery in Donora.

He deserves more recognition these days. He won 12 varsity letters at Donora High School, lettering all four years in football, basketball and track & field. Donora didn't have a baseball team, but Arnold was one of the best on the local sandlots. He was all-state in football and basketball. He quarterbacked Donora's undefeated 1945 football team, still regarded as the greatest team in WPIAL history.

He went to West Point to play for Col. Earl Blaik, following in the footsteps of Doc Blanchard and Glenn Davis, who both won the Heisman Trophy as the outstanding college football player in the land (1945 and 1946, respectively). That's when Army and Notre Dame, also stocked with Western Pennsylvania talent, ruled the college football world. Blaik often said his 1945 Army team was his very best. The Blanchard and Davis duo was featured on the cover of *Time* magazine.

At Army, Galiffa gained national attention as he earned 11 varsity letters in football, basketball and baseball. Freshmen could not compete in varsity football back then, or he would have won 12 letters there as well. His achievement was bettered by only one Academy graduate and equaled by only one other.

As a quarterback, who succeeded first-rate Arnold Tucker at Army, Galiffa was named to five All-America teams in 1949. He was fourth in the Heisman Trophy balloting won that year by Leon Hart, the giant end from Notre Dame and Turtle Creek High School. Notre Dame had wanted Galiffa and he nearly went there—at two different junctures. He would have succeeded Johnny Lujack of Connellsville as the quarterback at South Bend, and he and Hart would have been some pass-and-catch combination.

Galiffa appeared on the cover of *Life* magazine when that was one of the most prestigious magazines in the country. He played in the East-West game in San Francisco in 1950, and was drafted by the New York Giants. Galiffa was not a great professional athlete, which is one of the reasons he is not as well remembered as some other standouts from Western Pennsylvania.

He played one year with the Giants, where former Army assistant Vince Lombardi was the backfield coach, another with the San Francisco 49ers, and two more years in the Canadian Football League. He was plagued with injuries all four years.

In 1951, 90 cadets, including 37 football players, were dismissed from the military academy for cheating on exams. One of them was Earl Blaik's son, a promising quarterback named Bob Blaik.

Arnold Galiffa had married his high school sweetheart, Peggy Perdock, soon after he graduated in June 1950. Bimbo Cecconi was the best man at their wedding ceremony. As Galiffa's roommates knew too well, he had a habit of humming "Peg Of My Heart." The honeymoon was cut short because Galiffa and so many in the Class of 1950 went to the war in Korea.

He was a platoon leader in the 3rd Infantry Division and received a Bronze Star. He gained more notoriety when he hurled a grenade 75 yards and on target in combat. After completing his tour on the line, Galiffa was reassigned to Tokyo as aide-de-camp to Generals Matthew

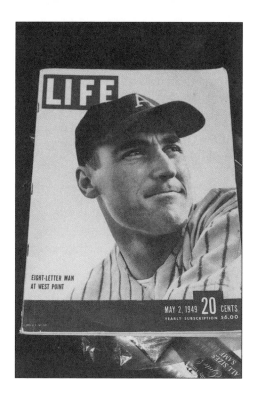

Arnold Galiffa

Photos by Jim O'Brien

Arnold Galiffa's only remaining brother, Art, shows off the album about his brother's achievements at his home in Donora.

Ridgway and Mark Clark while they were supreme commanders. He was close to General Ridgway and Arnold's brother, Art Galiffa, said that the retired military leader cried when he learned that Arnold had died.

After his tour of duty, Arnold and Peggy returned to Pennsylvania in 1955. For the next 23 years, he worked for United States Steel and became an executive there. One of his tasks, in his later years, was to supervise the demolition of the whole plant in Donora. The land that was left along the Monongahela River was donated to Donora and it became an industrial park. The street there, from one end of town to the other, is named Galiffa Drive in his honor. Peggy, who had been living in Florida, died soon after I had visited the Galiffa home in Donora.

"He had ability like Musial and Griffey."
—Rudy Andabaker

I traveled to Donora on January 25, 2007 to visit Art Galiffa, then 86, the only surviving brother in the family. I was accompanied by Bill Priatko, a dear friend who lives in North Huntingdon, but goes to church every Sunday in Donora. He is a member of St. Nicholas Orthodox Church, and I have spent time in the company of its leader, Father Igor Soroka. Father Igor has been at the church since he was ordained in 1960 and that's been his only parish. Priatko knows the streets of Donora well. Better yet, Arnold Galiffa was a boyhood idol. Priatko remains a big fan of Arnold Galiffa and feels he merits more recognition.

Priatko played football at North Braddock Scott and Pitt in the '50s, and saw duty in the uniforms of the Cleveland Browns, Pittsburgh Steelers and Green Bay Packers, and has a great appreciation for athletes. He's still promoting Arnold Galiffa as possibly the area's greatest athlete. The WPIAL, for instance, started a Hall of Fame in 2007, but to date had limited honorees to former athletes, coaches and administrators who were still living with the exception of Farrell basketball coach Eddie McCluskey. If that Hall of Fame is to have any legitimacy it has to include the likes of Galiffa and Towler, Musial, John Lujack, John Woodruff, Leon Hart and so many other sports stars.

In March 1990, Arnold Anthony Galiffa was inducted into the Pittsburgh chapter of the Italian-American Sports Hall of Fame. On September 27, 2007, on the eve of Army's home game with Temple, Galiffa was inducted into the West Point Hall of Fame. Bill and Danny Priatko, a West Point grad, and Bill's best friend, Rudy Celigoi of North Huntingdon, were present for the ceremony.

Art Galiffa was a great host and brought out scrapbooks about his brother Arnold, and showed me family photos that were proudly displayed throughout his home on Allen Street, near the peak of Donora. (The scrapbook, by the way, was a work of art and had been kept with great care by Albert Kovalik of Donora.) The former high school, now called the Donora Elementary Center, sits at the top of the hill nearby.

There was snow in the streets of Donora that day, but it was warm in the two-story pale gray shingled home of Art Galiffa.

Priatko and I visited the school. Dr. Karen Pokabla, who was then the principal but is now the assistant superintendent, took us on a brief tour. I have since heard the school might be named in honor of Stan Musial. I walked through its halls and spent some time in its gymnasium. It's an old-fashioned bandbox. I walked across its wooden floors, thinking about the games that had been played there with rival schools in the Valley, thinking about how many great players had performed on that floor. I walked across what was Legion Field when Galiffa played for the Dragons. That was also the nickname of my high school, Taylor Allderdice. The field is now called Russell Field in honor of one of the school's great football coaches, Jimmy Russell. There are still ghosts there. Some people like to walk the battlefields of Gettysburg, Antietam and Valley Forge; I like to walk the battlefields of Pittsburgh and the Mon Valley and Beaver Valley.

Joe Montana played on that field and that gym in Donora the first year of Ringgold High School before a new building was erected for the jointure of Donora and Monongahela and other smaller school districts in the region. Musial, Towler, Griffey, Cecconi and Andabaker all played there. Andabaker, still going strong, came to visit us when we were sitting in the family room at Art Galiffa's home and reflecting on his brother's distinguished career.

"Arnold had the kind of all-around athletic ability of Musial and Griffey," said Andabaker, who played for the Pittsburgh Steelers in 1952 and 1954 and coached football at Donora and Bethel Park in later years. "He was a true leader. We didn't have a midget football program in Donora, but Arnold got us together and we practiced in an alley under streetlights. We tore up cardboard boxes from the local grocery and used them for shoulderpads. He was in charge. I always looked up to him."

I called Art Galiffa on the telephone to check some facts with him on March 21, 2008. By coincidence, I caught him on his 87th birthday.

"I can't believe I'm 87," he said in a boisterous manner. "I'm so damn old. I have good days and bad days."

His wife Mary was being cared for at the Mon Valley Center. She had been residing there the past nine years. "She used to drive a truck for me," said Art, ruefully. "Now she can't do nothing."

Art Galiffa owned a popular pizza restaurant in Donora for many years. He was in the business at the beginning when pizzas were often called "those Italian tomato pies." Art recalls that "you couldn't give them away at the beginning. It took a while for them to catch on." His son, Barry, operates a pizza and hoagie business out of an immaculately clean garage in the rear of Art Galiffa's home. Operating rooms at hospitals aren't any more antiseptic. Galiffa's Pizza now prepares pizzas and hoagies for schools and fund-raisers. Barry and his wife Judy and friends tend to the tasks. The business is doing well. I met Bernie Galiffa's mother and dad, Olga and Mike, as they helped prepare the pizzas and hoagies. Two old-timers, Joe Amendola and Flavio Barbarosa, sat nearby, just hanging out.

Priatko and I were only too pleased to sample some of the offerings. They were terrific, hot from the small oven, and hit the spot.

"I remember a doctor once asked me," said Art Galiffa, telling one of his favorite stories, "what I did for a living. He said, 'You've got a brother who was an All-American football player who's a big shot at U.S. Steel, a brother who's in the CIA and a sister who's with the World Bank. Where do you fit in?'

"And I told him, 'I've got a Cadillac at the curb outside, I own a home in Florida … and I have been making pizza all my life. I make the best damn pizza in the Mon Valley."

Art Galiffa laughed at his own story. He said his getaway place was a mile from the ocean in Dania, Florida, not far from Fort Lauderdale. "I gave it to my kids," Art added.

He also mentioned that he and his brother Frank went to see their brother Arnold play in a basketball game against Navy in Arnold's freshman, or plebe, year at Army. "Arnold had a big game and Army won," recalled Art. "Afterward, however, Arnold said he didn't like all the hazing plebes had to endure at Army. He was thinking of transferring to Notre Dame.

"Our brother Frank was the oldest, and a big fellow himself, and he told Arnold, 'You're not going anywhere. Not many people of our nationality get to go to Army. It's an honor. So you're staying. I'll kick your ass if you think about leaving Army.' And Frank was big enough to stand behind his words. He wasn't to be messed with. So Arnold stayed and he never talked about leaving again. Frank was like the petrone of our family; he was the boss. He'd kick our ass if we got out of line."

Then Art Galiffa had another good story to share. "I remember we went to Philadelphia to see Arnold play against Navy in their big game that ended the season. There were over 100,000 filling the stadium. We sat on the fifty-yard line, two rows behind President Truman during the first half on the Army side of the stadium. President Truman had to go to the other side for the second half so he wouldn't show any special favor to either school. That was a big thrill for our family.

"I'm proud to call Donora my home. We have Irish, Polish—Musial was Polish—Russian, Italian, African-American, even Spanish here. We're all mixed. There was a time when downtown Donora was real busy. Everyone went downtown on Saturday. It was the only place you could go. All the stores were busy.

"We had lots of social clubs. We had the Elks, Eagles, Russian Club and Croatian Club. And there was a Polish Falcons Club. That's where Stan Musial used to go." Musial's father, Lukasz Musial, grew up in the Polish village of Mojstava in the province of Galicia and came to America in 1910, landing at Ellis Island.

John Juback, a friend and loyal reader of my books, lives in Donora and likes to talk about the town and its athletic heritage. He collects all kinds of Musial memorabilia, and has shown me his pictures and

Stan "The Man" Musial was rated by Branch Rickey as "the most liked player in baseball." Musial was inducted into the Baseball Hall of Fame in 1969. He would be 88 on Nov. 21, 2008.

Bernie Galiffa, the nephew of Arnold Galiffa, was an outstanding quarterback at West Virginia University. He returned from Wilmington, N.C. to witness Hall of Fame ceremonies at Ringgold High.

Photos by Jim O'Brien

Fred Cox, Joe Montana and Ken Griffey Sr. were inducted into the 2007 Class, along with Stan Musial, for the Hall of Fame at Ringgold High School.

trading cards and souvenirs. John Juback knows Art Galiffa and he followed the career of Arnold Galiffa.

Art Galiffa offered some background on his family history:

"My dad owned a big garden and we grew a lot of our own food. We had lots of tomatoes, and that's what we used when we got into the pizza business. We never went hungry. Our store was called Galiffa's Dairy Bar. It was on Fifth Street.

"My dad and mom raised six boys and two girls. I'm the only boy left, and one girl is left. That's my sister, Jean Greene, and she's 90. I was the sixth one and we all went to Donora High School. We played ball at Legion Field. It's still there, only now they call it Russell Field. To me, it's still Legion Field.

"My dad's name was Nazareno. They called him 'Naz' and 'Nat.' My mother was Maggiora or Margaret. My dad came over from Italy in 1914. My dad was a real big guy. He had a real big mustache. I had an Uncle Jack who never got married and he helped out in the garden. I think we had a thousand tomato plants at one time. We lived out of that garden.

"My dad worked at American Steel Wire, but they laid everyone off. He became a janitor at the high school, and he worked there when Arnold was a student there. It was tough surviving in those days, but we did it. Everyone had a place at the table. You ate whatever was put before you on the table.

"When I joined the Marines, everyone said I was going to get disciplined. Hell, I was disciplined to begin with at home. There was an Italian church, St. Phillip's, in Donora, but we went to the Polish church, St. Mary's on Second Street. There was lots of discipline in our lives, lots of discipline. None of us was ever a problem to our parents. When we'd come home from school, our mom or dad would say, 'How'd you do?' None of us got into trouble; none of us went to jail.

"Arnold was big. He was 6–2, 175 pounds when he was in high school. He put on some more weight when he got to Army. He got up to 190 then. He never talked back to anybody. He had a quiet demeanor about him. He was serious. He was genuine.

"We loved to watch him play. We couldn't get enough of it, no matter what part of the country he was playing in. He's in the College Football Hall of Fame, you know."

At one time, Arnold Galiffa was going to school and working an eight-hour shift at the mill in Donora. He was getting by on four hours of sleep. He was playing baseball and competing on the track team. "I had to quit the mill," said Galiffa at the time, "when I passed out running the half-mile one afternoon."

Art Galiffa seemed pleased when I told him I had seen his brother's display at the College Football Hall of Fame in South Bend, Indiana, near the Notre Dame campus. I paid particular interest while there to checking out the displays paying tribute to Pitt's Marshall Goldberg and Notre Dame's Leon Hart and Johnny Lujack. Pitt's Tony Dorsett is portrayed on the sign in front of the building.

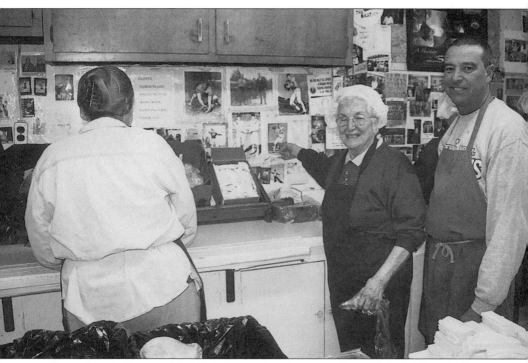

Barry Galiffa, the son of Art Galiffa, oversees the operation of Galiffa Pizza, and gets help in preparing packages by his aunt, Olga Galiffa. She is the mother of Bernie Galiffa.

Arnold Galiffa was a cadet at the U.S. Military Academy when he married his high school sweetheart Peggy Perdock with family in attendance at the ceremony.

"My brother was really something," said Art Galiffa. "And he belongs in that kind of company. When he was a kid, he always had some kind of ball in his hand. He was just a natural player. They called Arnold "The Pope," but some people thought that was inappropriate. My brother Roman was a good athlete, too, but he was the kind of guy who didn't give a damn. He played ball with Stan Musial. He went to Morris Harvey and then he went to Pitt, but he didn't get along with the coach, Walt Milligan, because he wasn't seeing much action.

"My sister Jean was with the World Bank. My brother Warren Galiffa was in the CIA for 30 years."

Just then, Art's granddaughter Dana Galiffa, entered the house, and asked if he needed anything. Her mom and dad were working in the garage out back, getting another shipment of pizzas and hoagies ready to send to Thomas Jefferson High School and Brownsville High School. Dana had started for four seasons on the soccer team at California (Pa.) University, and was now serving as an assistant coach while continuing her studies. She was a substitute teacher at Ringgold High School and was working on her master's degree in education. Dana, now 24, has since earned her master's degree and is still at Ringgold.

DANA GALIFFA

She appeared polite, personable and well mannered. And beautiful. "She's a Galiffa all the way," said her proud grandfather.

"I'm very proud of that name," declared Dana Galiffa.

* * *

I called Barry Galiffa on his cell phone on May 22, 2008. He was at his dad's bedside when I called. Art Galiffa was in the Mon Valley Hospital, having some tests and procedures, because he was suffering from congestive heart failure. His son Barry said his dad had been having some difficult days since his 87th birthday, but that he was a battler and he expected him to bounce back.

"He's so excited that you came to the house and that you are writing about my Uncle Arnold," said Barry Galiffa. "He can't wait for the book to come out."

I told him to tell his dad I would personally deliver the book to him in September, at the start of the next football season.

Lou "Bimbo" Cecconi
Still praising "The Pope"

"Arnold Galiffa was a great role model."

Lou "Bimbo" Cecconi still checks out his boyhood neighborhood in Donora on occasion. He drives from his home in Pleasant Hills back to his heydays in Donora. He has so many good memories from that time. His boyhood home is just a block away from what was once Donora High School and is now the Donora Elementary Center.

To Bimbo, the sand-colored brick building will always be Donora High and the home of the mighty Dragons. Jimmy Russell Field will always be Legion Field. The bandbox gym is more precious than the Petersen Events Center in Oakland. He grew up in Donora, just 28 miles south of Pittsburgh along the Monongahela River, when it had its own high school. That was before it was merged with Monongahela High into the Ringgold School District.

The dark-eyed Cecconi—his eyes are hooded like a raccoon's—is still a familiar figure and a popular person in the Mon Valley. He was a three-sport star and coach at the University of Pittsburgh at three different spans, and a teacher and administrator for 20-some years at Steel Valley High School in Munhall.

He can point to a block on the other side of the school in Donora where his teammate "Deacon Dan" Towler lived. They could both walk to school in five minutes—"Three minutes," corrects Cecconi. The school was at the corner of Fourth Street and Waddell Avenue, and was the highest point in Donora. On a clear day—and there weren't many of those when the mills were going full blast—you could see forever.

They were teammates in the same backfield when Donora High won back-to-back WPIAL titles in 1944 and 1945. That 1945 football team was named the best-ever in the history of the WPIAL at its Hall of Fame dinner in the summer of 2008. They were also teammates on the basketball team in 1945 that also won a WPIAL title. They were the first school to accomplish such a feat. "We lost out to Homestead in the semi-finals our senior year," recalled Cecconi, "and they went on to win the WPIAL and state title."

Cecconi checked out a dusty scrapbook he keeps in his basement after I talked to him about those days. It had clippings from *The Pittsburgh Press*, the *Post-Gazette*, the *Sun-Telegraph* and the *Donora Eagle*. "They're all yellow now and the pages are cracking," said Cecconi. "I must be getting old."

I toured Donora with my buddy Bill Priatko a year earlier. Priatko remained a big fan of Arnold Galiffa. He regards him as one of the greatest all-around athletes to come out of Western Pennsylvania. Priatko was at West Point during the 2007 football season when Galiffa was inducted posthumously into the Army Sports Hall of Fame the day before the Cadets beat Temple.

Donora's achievements were recalled in many stories relating to Jeannette High School winning WPIAL and PIAA titles in football and basketball during the 2007–2008 school session.

Terrelle Pryor, the star of the Jeannette football and basketball teams and the *Parade* magazine prep football player of the year, and Cecconi were both in the same ballroom at the 2008 Dapper Dan Dinner & Sports Auction at the David L. Lawrence Convention Center on Tuesday, April 1. I bumped into Bimbo before the dinner began and introduced him to my friends and neighbors, Danny and Ken Codeluppi. Ken had also accompanied me to the Italian-American Sports Hall of Fame Dinner earlier in the week and he couldn't get enough of Italian-American heroes.

"Deacon Dan" Towler was the fullback on that Donora championship team, still regarded as the greatest high school football team in Western Pennsylvania history. They were ranked second in the nation to a Texas prep team led by Bobby Layne and Doak Walker, both future Hall of Fame performers. Roscoe Ross was the other halfback in the Dragons' backfield. Ross was thought to be the best player on the Donora team, but he got into trouble with the law and blew his chances for college stardom. Arnold Galiffa was the quarterback. He was all-state in football and basketball.

"I was the backup quarterback," said Cecconi. "Donora was pretty special in sports in those days. We had a Cardinal in Stan Musial, a Pope in Arnold Galiffa, a Deacon in Dan Tower and a peon in Bimbo Cecconi."

Galiffa and Cecconi were Roman Catholics, in the truest sense, and shared many common bonds.

"We were not only undefeated in 1945, but our defense was unscored upon," interjected Cecconi during our conversation. "The only touchdown scored against us came when Layne Aaron of Altoona High School—he went on to play at Duke—stole the ball from Deacon near our goal line and ran it in for a touchdown."

I asked him more questions about Arnold Galiffa. Cecconi had great recall. Who else would remember Layne Aaron?

"I was a year behind Arnold in school, but we were best friends," said Cecconi. "I hung around with Arnold all the time. I tagged after him. I was his best man when he got married.

"Arnold was the first sports icon in my life. He was an all-around athlete, a great individual and a real role model who came

208

Lou "Bimbo" Cecconi

Arnold Galiffa as he appeared in 1945 when he played basketball for Donora High School and wore the black and orange uniforms.

Jim O'Brien

2008 Dapper Dan Dinner lineup, left to right, are Danny and Ken Codeluppi, Tony Ferraro, Lou "Bimbo" Cecconi and Jim Duratz, as they appeared at sports auction at David L. Lawrence Convention Center.

out of Donora. I was 5–8, 160 pounds as a senior, and he was 6-2, 190 pounds when he went to Army. Because of his stature, I always looked up to him in more ways than one. He had great athletic and academic ability. He was also a great student. He was a leader and I followed him around.

"I was his best friend. He didn't smoke or drink. He won 11 letters at Donora and at Army. He was on the track and field team at Donora. He wasn't especially fast, but he threw the javelin and shot put. He had large hands, and he was stronger than the rest of us. I played basketball for Doc Carlson at Pitt. When we played basketball at Army once I stayed overnight with Arnold in his room at the Academy."

Galiffa died at 51 from colon cancer. "A doctor once told me, 'Your friend would still be around if he'd taken the test.' He said that because two of Arnold's brothers also died of colon cancer," recalled Cecconi, "and Arnold should have been checked for that. It ran in the family."

Cecconi was 79 when we spoke and he would turn 80 on October 13, 2008. "Can you believe that?" asked Cecconi. He still looks good and gets out with some of his long-time buddies to play golf on good days at South Park. He is still bright-eyed and good company. There was a time when he looked so young for his years it was thought he made a pact with the devil. Now there's gray in that once-so-black hair. He was an assistant coach to John Michelosen during my four-year stint (1960-1964) as a student and the sports editor of *The Pitt News*. He was in his early 30s back then. I remember his salary was $7,500 and Michelosen was making $17,000. "I had to take a cut when I came from coaching and teaching at Sharpsburg High School," recalled Cecconi.

He was a backfield coach with Michelosen from 1958 to 1965, then went to Indiana State in Terre Haute for a few years before returning to Pitt as an assistant to Carl DePasqua from 1969 to 1972. I visited Cecconi and his dear friend Bill Kaliden, a great student athlete from Homestead High who had coached with Cecconi at Pitt, during their days at the Terre Haute campus. "We were there before they ever heard of Larry Bird," said Cecconi. Or Tunch Ilkin, for that matter.

Reflecting on his final days at Pitt with his pal Carl DePasqua, Cecconi said, "We were fired on a Sunday in November, and I went to work on Monday—the next day—as a substitute teacher at Steel Valley High School. Hey, I had five kids. I had to have a job. I was a pre-dental student at Pitt with some science background so I ended up teaching biology at Steel Valley. I became an assistant principal and activities director there. I came in right after George Novak left for Woodland Hills. Jack Giran was the football coach and athletic director at Steel Valley and he won two WPIAL football titles while I was there. Bill Cherpak, who's become one

Lou "Bimbo" Cecconi joins Dick Hoak and Frank Cignetti in coaches confab at a monthly meeting of the Westmoreland Athletic Club at Mr. P's Restaurant in Greensburg.

Photos by Jim O'Brien

Dick "Little Mo" Modzelewski of Natrona Heights and "Deacon Dan" Towler of Donora were inductees into the western chapter of the Pennsylvania Sports Hall of Fame.

of the best coaches in the WPIAL (at Thomas Jefferson High), was a player on those teams."

Donora produced so many outstanding athletes during Cecconi's schooldays there. Among those who came to play at Pitt back then was lineman Rudy Andabaker, who later played for the Steelers. Other Dragons to play at Pitt were Nick DeRosa and Tony Romantino. They were small in stature, but tough cookies. Cecconi still gets together with those guys to attend sports events. Cecconi recalled that Bill Doziski, Bill Samer, Andy Lelik and Gabe Dombrowski all came from Donora to Pitt to play football around that same time.

The Panthers were 6-3 in Cecconi's last two seasons at Pitt under Mike Milligan. They beat Penn State and West Virginia twice, but were crushed and shut out by Notre Dame (40–0) and Ohio State (41–0) his junior season. Cecconi earned four varsity letters in football and basketball (freshmen were eligible for varsity play at the time as a result of so many men serving in the military service when he first entered Pitt) and one letter in baseball. Not bad for a little guy from Donora.

When I was working at Pitt in the mid-80s, my boss was Dr. Ed Bozik, who came from Donora and had been a classmate of Cecconi's in high school. Dr. Bozik invited Bimbo to accompany our Pitt party to New York to attend the College Football Foundation's Hall of Fame awards dinner at the Waldorf-Astoria Hotel, one of New York's poshest hotels. I recall that many former Heisman Trophy winners, including Leon Hart of Turtle Creek and Johnny Lujack of Connellsville, who both starred at Notre Dame, were present for the dinner.

So was Yale's Jay Berwanger, the first Heisman Trophy winner. Ohio State's Woody Hayes was the featured speaker and just about called for World War III and received a standing ovation from the conservative crowd.

Dr. Bozik asked me, at the last minute, if I minded sharing my hotel room with Bimbo Cecconi. I could hardly decline Dr. Bozik's request, but I was hoping that no one would tell my wife that I was sharing a room with a Bimbo in New York.

Rudy Andabaker, Tony Romantino, Nick DeRosa and "Bimbo" Cecconi were all Donora products who played at Pitt in the '40s.

Andy McGraw
Remembers Art Rooney well

"He was such a humble guy."

December 12, 2007

Jim O'Brien

Andy McGraw and I agree about many things. We believe in our hearts that we will always be Pittsburgh guys, Pitt men and admirers of the late Art Rooney Sr. McGraw and I were students at Pitt at the same time—the early to mid-60s—and we've shared a lot of common personal experiences. He played soccer for four years at Pitt and was the punter for the Panthers' football team in his fifth year on the Oakland campus. He was out of high school for several years before he came to Pitt.

I was a goalie for the freshman soccer team and the sports editor of *The Pitt News* during most of McGraw's tenure there. Leo Bemis, the soccer coach, pulled me out of a phys ed class where he taught a session on soccer to play for his freshman squad. I had never played soccer before I went to college. I wanted to be a sports writer, though, and became the sports editor of the campus paper as a sophomore, and that was a demanding task that didn't allow time for soccer.

I enjoyed a reunion with McGraw earlier this month when we met at Rudy Zupancic's Giant Eagle market in Bridgeville, Pennsylvania, about four or five miles from my home. McGraw grew up in nearby South Fayette and has lived there all his life. He got into politics after he left Pitt, and was a state legislator for ten years from 1967 through 1977. "He could have been governor he was such a popular guy," said my buddy Baldo Iorio of Heidelberg, who remembers McGraw with great gusto. McGraw, at 69, remains a handsome man. No matter what he wears, and everything is always coordinated just so, he looks terrific. His once-so-dark hair has gray edges, but his smile, even after a morning session at the dentist, is still straight out of Hollywood. Like Tyrone Power. McGraw is gregarious and loves to talk. So am I, so a conversation between us is like playing bumper-pool.

He remembers meeting Art Rooney, the founder of the Steelers, at an intra-squad scrimmage in Jeannette or Latrobe back in the late '60s. "My son, Andy, was about 12 at the time," said McGraw. "He got to shake hands with Mr. Rooney that day. We were in this press box that was like a chicken coop on stilts.

"That was during the summer. Just before Christmas, a UPS truck comes to our home in South Fayette. There's a box addressed to Andy McGraw Jr. It contained an official NFL football signed by many of the Steelers. There was a beautiful letter from Mr. Rooney. As best I can remember, he told Andy how nice it was to meet him, and how he was glad he took such an interest in sports and the Steelers, and to keep it up. Can you believe that?"

I can, of course, because I was the benefactor of similar kindness by Mr. Rooney. I've written a book about him called *The Chief*, but I continue to hear stories about him that I wish were in that book. Other people talk with pride about meeting Art Rooney and shaking his hand, and how personable and accommodating he was. It was a big event in their lives. "Everyone has an Art Rooney story, I know," said McGraw.

He shared another story about how he and his brothers, Pete and Tom, who lived in Denver, were given tickets for a Steelers' game in Denver. "He asked me how many tickets I needed," said McGraw. "I asked him how big a crowd of Steelers' fans he wanted in the stadium. I think he got me a half dozen tickets.

"As if that weren't enough, Mr. Rooney asked me how I was getting back home," recalled McGraw. "He told me I was welcome to accompany the Steelers on their charter flight. He said, 'Bring your bag to the front desk and I'll make sure it gets on our bus. We leave right after the game on the road, so be ready to go.' Can you imagine that? He was such a humble guy. I know he didn't personally put my bag on the bus, but just to tell me what I needed to do points up how concerned he was that nothing went wrong."

McGraw and I were reflecting on the Pitt-West Virginia football game that ended the 2007 schedule for both teams. We agreed that we both started out wanting West Virginia to win because they had a chance to accomplish something great: the Mountaineers could be national champions. Pitt was going nowhere. It was good for this area and it was good for the Big East, we convinced ourselves.

I told him that I had listened to a sports talk show the morning of the game and that Joe Starkey and Beano Cook commented that any Pitt fan or alumnus that rooted for West Virginia in this game was an idiot. We smiled about that. "It wasn't long after the game started," said McGraw, "that I changed my mind and started pulling for Pitt. They were playing so hard and you had to root for them."

I said I had a similar experience. My wife Kathie asked me during the game, "How come you're so quiet?" I said I was having inner turmoil. "I have to root for Dave Wannstedt and I have to root for Pitt," I said. McGraw and I said we felt sorry for Rich Rodriguez and West Virginia because we liked the WVU coach and his team had played so well all season. Unlike some fans at Pitt and West Virginia and Penn State, we don't hate the opposing schools or teams.

"It was one of the greatest upsets I have ever witnessed," said McGraw. "Geez, I remember the year I punted at Pitt was John Michelosen's last season as the coach. I admired that man so much. We went 3–7 that year and beat Penn State at home in the final game.

"Pitt had posted a 9–1 record two years earlier, and didn't get to go to a bowl game. They held out for a big bowl game and the Penn State game was postponed because of the death of President John F. Kennedy. They ended up not going to a bowl game. He got fired following that 3–7 record. I wondered about that. How could John Michelosen have forgotten so much about football in two years that he deserved to be fired? So many memories…You make me think of my Pitt days, and that was a great time in our lives."

Memory of "an older gentleman"

Author Jim O'Brien received an e-mail from George Bertha of York, Pa. on June 25, 2008 that goes well with Andy McGraw's memories of the special treatment he received from Art Rooney Sr., the founder of the Pittsburgh Steelers.

Dear Mr. O'Brien:

I just finished reading the copy of *The Chief* that you were gracious enough to sign for me at the "Parade of Champions" at the Heinz History Center last weekend. It was hard for me to put down. Some of the anecdotes made me laugh, some brought a tear to my eye. I never knew that The Chief was responsible for Dick Stockton hooking on with CBS-TV (I used to watch him do the sports on KDKA many years ago) and that Bill Hillgrove was from Garfield! I lived there on the corner of N. Mathilda and Rosetta Sts. when I was a kid.

I have my own story about Mr. Rooney that I related to Art Rooney Jr. at the same show (at the Heinz History Center) and he loved it! Here it is, maybe you can pass it on:

When I was about 10 or 11 years old my brother and I used to shine shoes for spending money and usually we went to see the Pirates when Three Rivers was first in use.

One night, I had to go to the game solo; my brother got grounded or something and I was crossing the Fort Duquesne Bridge and I got rolled by a bunch of kids. They took my money, but they left me with my game ticket.

Well, I went to the game, and really didn't have a good time considering what had happened to me. After the game was over, I was wandering around the North Side wondering how I'd get home. I was crying and this "older gentleman" came up to me and asked me what was wrong and I told him what had happened.

He told me that he'd take me to the bus stop and pay my fare. Well, we got to the bus stop and the bus came. I got on and he paid the fare and said something to the bus driver and I was on my way. Sometime later, I saw a picture of Mr. Rooney in *The Pittsburgh Press* and I almost fell over. The "older gentleman" who helped me was the man in the newspaper picture! Wow! And as I read your book, I see that he did things like that for almost anybody. I also told Art Rooney Jr. that his dad was a "great man." I know he appreciated it.

Keep up the good work,
George Bertha
York, Pa.

Recommended reading: *Ruanaidh: The Story of Art Rooney and His Clan*, by Art Rooney Jr. with Roy McHugh. That's Gaelic and pronounced Ru-ah-nee. Two quotes of Art Rooney Sr. stand out:

"I wish I had been nicer to people."
"Never allow anyone to mistake kindness for weakness."

Tom O'Malley Jr.
He manages Steelers on the court

"I was the original T.O."

April 4, 2007

A busy man, Tom O'Malley Jr. sells insurance by day and moonlights as the manager of the Pittsburgh Steelers' basketball team. He's so busy with both endeavors he hasn't had time to get married—those Irish guys are notorious for taking their time—so he remains, at 52, one of the most eligible bachelors in town. He does have a steady girlfriend.

Gerry "Moon" Mullins, a guard in the Steelers' glory days of the '70s who works out of Bridgeville, once tabbed him "T.O." and it stuck. "I was the original T.O.," O'Malley boasts. And he's a sharp contrast to the other T.O., the recalcitrant Terrell Owens of the Dallas Cowboys.

O'Malley oversees the Bob Purkey Insurance Agency on Brightwood Road in Bethel Park, so he didn't have far to travel, a little more than a mile, on this Thursday evening, March 29, 2007, when he had the Steelers booked for a basketball game at Bethel Park High School.

That's better than Bentleyville and Brownsville, two earlier road-stops for the Steelers. He had scheduled about 60 games for the Steelers.

O'Malley started helping Baldy Regan run the Steelers' off-season basketball team in 1970 when he was 14 years old. Regan, who was known as "the Mayor of the North Side," was famous for taking note of anyone's career successes by bellowing, "Only in America," whenever he spotted them in a crowd.

O'Malley's dad sold advertising for *The Pittsburgh Press* for 45 years and had people skills that ran on the other side of the tracks from Regan's "Bowery Boys" routine. O'Malley's dad was so proud of being the mayor of Castle Shannon (1983–2000) and of his Irish heritage. Young O'Malley took his cues from his dad and Regan, and picked up some diplomatic ways from Bob Purkey, once a terrific pitcher who came out of Mt. Washington to star for the Pittsburgh Pirates and Cincinnati Reds. Now the older O'Malley and Regan have died and Purkey and his wife Joanie were residing at Sunrise Assisted Living of Upper St. Clair (before they died a month apart soon after I wrote this story.) Those men had a gift for making you feel good about yourself when they said hello.

"I had three great mentors," said Tom Jr. when we talked to him at halftime of the Steelers vs. Bethel Park All-Stars contest. "I learned from each of them. Baldy bent the rules a little bit when it came to business, whereas my dad was a straight arrow all the way. I learned how to do it right from him. Bob Purkey is such a gentleman. He had

Zeb Jansante, the principal at Bethel Park High School, and his dad, former Steelers' star receiver Val Jansante, participated in ceremonies relating to Steelers' basketball game in Blackhawks' gymnasium.

Tom O'Malley Jr. manages the Steelers' basketball team that includes, left to right, Rod Rutherford, Louis Lipps, Ricardo Colclough, Lee Mays, Brad Kiesel, Ben Roethlisberger and Chris Hoke as they appeared for game at Mt. Lebanon High School.

been a great athlete, but he was so down-to-earth in the way he dealt with people. I knew Art Rooney Sr., the owner of the Steelers, and I watched him when I was growing up. I saw how he spoke to people. I always tried to treat people the way I wanted to be treated, or even better than I wanted to be treated. Baldy was strict with his kids and me, and made sure we all said 'Yes, sir' and 'No, sir.' He was big on pleasantries, stuff like that.

"I learned to always be polite. Try to do the right thing. Treat people properly. I go back even farther with Baldy than basketball. I helped out in the press box at Pitt Stadium when the Steelers played there in the '60s. I worked with Baldy and Bernie Stein and Mike Kearns. We ran off the stats and play-by-play sheets on those old dirty mimeograph machines. When I'd ask if we'd be back the next year, Bernie Stein always said, 'You never know. I'm still trying to make the team.' He thought you should never take anything for granted. You better do it right every week and you might get invited back the following week to do it again."

Now it's O'Malley who oversees the operation in the press box at Heinz Field to provide stats and play-by-play sheets for the media. One of Baldy's best friends, Paul Tomasovich, helps him. Tomasovich was once a home run hitting terror on the national slow-pitch softball circuit. Indeed, he was called "the Babe Ruth of slow-pitch softball" the same way that Josh Gibson was called "the Babe Ruth of Negro League Baseball."

The Steelers like to play basketball for kicks and to stay in shape during the off-season. They pick up some mad money by doing so, getting a share of the gate, and most of the receipts go for some worthy cause embraced by the promoters of the games. "We help a lot of schools raise money for special causes," said O'Malley.

When they have played at Mt. Lebanon High School in recent seasons, some of the proceeds went to Amy's Army, a group of volunteers working hard to find a donor for Lebo student Amy Katz, who needs a bone marrow transplant in her bout with leukemia.

The Steelers play all sorts of men and women with varying skill levels as far as basketball is concerned. Sometimes teachers or coaches and local police officers and firemen get carried away with their competitive fervor. They want to show up the Steelers. When they get over-zealous, the Steelers respond by playing a little more physical and flashing their speed and quickness with full-court press defenses.

It's fun to watch the Steelers playing basketball. It reminds you of what great athletes they are, and that they could've been standouts in other sports as well. Several of the players who were at Bethel Park that night were defensive backs. They included Troy Polamalu, Deshea Townsend, Anthony Smith and Ricardo Colclough.

They are so quick and they fly high to steal passes. Watching Polamalu pressing young high-school-age guards, pursuing them from one side of the court to the other in a frenzy, is worth the price of admission. Polamalu puts up an occasional three-point shot and is pretty accurate. They give each other high fives when they hit those long shots.

The Steelers win ninety percent of the time, or better, so O'Malley may have a record that rates inclusion in the Basketball Hall of Fame. Only there are no records. "We forget the score once we leave the building," says O'Malley, "but there's no doubt when the outcome is in jeopardy my guys pick up their game. They don't like to lose no matter what they're playing."

O'Malley is never sure who will show up for any of the games. The fringe players, the ones who make the least money, are the most reliable performers. Brett Keisel, the defensive end, was one of his best basketball players, but he had hurt his knee and wasn't available for the ballgame at Bethel Park.

Ben Roethlisberger plays every now and then and it's a real bonus for the game promoter when he comes. He draws the longest lines for autograph seekers at halftime. Some times O'Malley must call former players such as Louis Lipps and Edmund Nelsen and Brian Hinkle to fill out the roster. He likes to have at least seven or eight Steelers so he can give everyone a break.

Hines Ward had played in previous seasons but hadn't played yet during the 2007 schedule. Santonio Holmes, Chris Hoke, Charlie Batch, Nate Washington, Anthony Smith and Deshea Townsend had played, and Max Starks had said he planned on playing.

O'Malley says he has three rules he imparts to his players. "Protect yourself at all times. We don't want anyone getting injured. Sign autographs at halftime for anybody who asks for one. Have fun."

O'Malley books the games anywhere in the tri-state area where they can draw a crowd.

"It's a chance for the fans to get to see them up close," added O'Malley. "The tickets don't cost that much. They get to see the guys without their helmets and equipment, and they get to collect autographs and door prizes. It's a fun night out for the family."

The Steelers, led by Polamalu, and Bryant McFadden, rallied in the final quarter to beat Bethel Park, 79–77. Bethel Park was led by 6–9 alumnus Armon Gilliam, a 14-year-veteran of the NBA. "We only lost about two games out of 55 last year," said O'Malley, who may be keeping score after all. "Our guys don't like to lose."

O'Malley was driving his convertible around the South Hills when the sun was so bright at the arrival of spring. So he got some sunburn on his bald head and looked more like Hall of Fame basketball coach Red Auerbach, except for the beard, than ever before.

* * *

I sat on the Steelers' bench for the game at Bethel Park High School between Tom O'Malley and Val Jansante. Jansante was a star receiver for the Steelers in their early years and led the team in pass catches five straight seasons (1946–1950). It was a record Hines Ward had broken only a year earlier when Ward led the Steelers in receiving for the sixth straight season. Jansante had played his college ball at Duquesne University and was one of Art Rooney's all-time favorites.

Jansante would turn 87 on September 27, 2007. His son, Zeb, is the principal at Bethel Park High School. I had first met Zeb when I spoke at Quaker Valley High School when he was the principal there. He later served as principal at Mt. Lebanon High School. Zeb had his father introduced to the crowd at the Steelers' game at Bethel Park High School. The current Steelers seemed impressed when they learned of his achievements with the Steelers.

As a kid, I had Val Jansante's bubble gum card. I always loved his name. It sounded good, like Bobby Gage, Jimmy Finks, Pat Brady, Jack Butler, Elbie Nickel, Dale Dodrill, Joe Geri, Jerry Nuzum, Jerry Shipkey, Bill Walsh and Johnny "Zero Clement." They sounded like football players. People who consider themselves staunch Steelers' fans should be familiar with these names and their stories and their place in Pittsburgh sports history. Jansante played two seasons under Jock Sutherland and four more under Sutherland's protégé John Michelosen before he was traded to the Green Bay Packers. He retired after one season with the Packers and returned home to Bentleyville where he grew up and where he still remains.

I know Val Jansante for another reason, and I always remind him about it. He was the head football coach when I went to Central Catholic High School in the fall of 1956. I was one of the smallest students in the school, but I had started as a halfback at St. Stephen's Grade School in Hazelwood and I had the temerity to try out for the Vikings' football team.

Jansante knew a future sportswriter when he saw one. He cut me the first day. All I did was run around the outskirts of the football field behind the castle-like building that was Central Catholic High School in Oakland. I cut myself midway through my sophomore season and transferred to Taylor Allderdice High School in Squirrel Hill. I didn't make the football team there either. I passed up the chance to be the Dragons' third-string quarterback in favor of a Friday and Saturday job as a copyboy at *The Pittsburgh Press*.

Jansante was surrounded by his grandchildren when he entered the gym this evening at Bethel Park High School. He had a cane which he used now and then. When he was announced, I held his left arm to steady him as he rose from his seat. I wondered what he was thinking as he stood during the playing of the National Anthem, standing at the back of the line of current Steelers. He looked proud to be in their ranks. I wanted to tell each of the Steelers Val Jansante's story.

Val Jansante

Steve Blass and Dave Giusti
Rain delays remind us
of better days at ballpark

October 11, 2007

A rain delay at a Pirates' game at PNC Park offers an opportunity to reflect on better days in the team's history. During such delays the Pirates entertain the fans with different offerings on the huge video screen on the scoreboard in left field at PNC Park. I sat through three rain delays during this past season.

I was there on Opening Day and Closing Day this year and for about a dozen more Pirates' games in between. The Pirates finished with a 68–94 record. It was the 15th straight season they finished with a losing record. This year they finished last in the Central Division with the worst record in the National League. Only Tampa Bay had a worse record in Major League Baseball.

So the rain delays were a bit of a respite. One of them lasted two-and-a-half hours and it was worth the wait because the Pirates won an exciting contest. One of them was different because it never rained and yet the game started a half-hour later than scheduled.

During these delays they usually show a Bugs Bunny cartoon or the famous Bud Abbott and Lou Costello comic routine "Who's On First?" I always thought this was a short piece, but the one the Pirates show seems as long as "The Ten Commandments" or "The Longest Day." Sometimes they show a music group performing.

More often than not they show highlights from the Pirates' winning efforts in the World Series in 1960, 1971 and 1979. They provide reminders for the older fans of better days at the ballpark in Pittsburgh, and a history lesson for younger fans that have never experienced such exciting times with the hometown baseball team. They remind us of the excitement we're missing by not being part of the playoffs at this time of the year.

On one of those days I had breakfast with my friend Ron Temple at Eat'n Park Restaurant at South Hills Village. While we were eating, Steve Blass stopped by to say hello. He was there with his wife Karen. They live only a mile away in Upper St. Clair. It's the house he bought when he became a Bucco back in the early '60s.

"I've had the same house, the same team and the same wife all my adult life," boasts Blass.

About fifteen minutes later, Dave Giusti came by our table with two of his grandchildren. Giusti and his wife Ginny live in the same neighborhood as Blass. He also stopped to say hello and introduced the kids.

I also bump into Giusti on occasion at Atria's Restaurant & Tavern in Mt. Lebanon. His signed photo is on the wall in the bar area.

Jim Leyland, Lanny Frattare, Blass and Chuck Tanner all have autographed photos that appear on the walls at Atria's.

Later that day, I saw Blass and Giusti on the Jumbotron at PNC Park. They were pitching in the 1971 World Series.

When I saw them later on, at a Pirates Alumni Golf Outing at South Hills Country Club, where they are both members, I asked them what it's like when they see those images on the screen at PNC Park.

"That's not me up there on the screen," observed Blass. "It's somebody else wearing my number and my uniform. But I do sneak a peek every so often. It's a reminder of a good time in my life. I still like to look at it."

Pirates' broadcaster Greg Brown overheard my conversation with Blass. "He still enjoys those highlights," said Brown. "Who wouldn't?"

Blass pitched two complete games in that 1971 World Series, beating the Baltimore Orioles, 5–1, in the third game, and 2–1 in the seventh and deciding game. Nobody pitches complete games anymore, let alone in the World Series. He remembers Bill Mazeroski complimenting him after that seventh game, saying "That's a real big-league pitching performance. It's not easy to pitch with a one-run lead."

Later, I had an opportunity to watch that seventh game of the 1971 World Series on ESPN Classics. Blass had to pitch an outstanding game that day because Mike Cuellar of the Orioles was outstanding as well. It's always great to watch a game like that which featured Frank Robinson and Brooks Robinson and Boog Powell of the Orioles, and, of course, the great Roberto Clemente (he had a home run to give the Bucs an early 1–0 lead in that last game), Dick Groat and Bill Mazeroski.

During rain delays at PNC Park, they have shown Mazeroski so many times hitting his home run to win the 1960 World Series that Ron Necciai said he would surpass Henry Aaron for career home runs. "He'll pass Aaron before Bonds does," joked Necciai.

Blass has been a frequent speaker at the annual Sports Night at the Thompson Club in West Mifflin, and has played in the Homestead Lions' Club Golf Outing at Westwood Golf Club. He's a funny guy. Bucs' broadcaster Lanny Frattare says Blass may be one of the most popular Pirates in team history.

Giusti pitched in three of those World Series games against the Orioles, getting a save in the fourth game. He won the Fireman of the Year Award given by *The Sporting News* as the best relief pitcher in baseball that year. El Roy Face, the most famous relief pitcher in Pirates' history, gave him the award in a pre-game ceremony. "It's nice to have people stop you in the street and say they saw you pitch, or offer a compliment," said Giusti. "You don't need that, but it's nice."

Kent Tekulve, another great Pirates' relief pitcher and now an advance scout for the team, also lives in Upper St. Clair with his wife Linda. I saw him at the Pirates' golf outing at South Hills Country Club in July. He is often shown on that scoreboard at PNC Park pitching in the 1979 World Series. "I've seen that so often, I guess I take it for granted," said Tekulve. "Steve and I took those films out to so many

When it rains it pours at PNC Park. Fans pass the time watching Maz hit the home run again . . . and again . . . to win the 1960 World Series.

Photos by Jim O'Brien

Barry Bonds is on all the TV monitors in press box at PNC Park as he was approaching Henry Aaron's career home run record.

bars on behalf of Frank Fuhrer's beer distributing company that I saw it in my sleep. But it's all new to the young fans."

I didn't know it at the time, but Giusti had all the guys sign a "get well" card for Nellie King that day, and he delivered it to King at Mercy Hospital where he was a patient. So they can be thoughtful guys, too.

I saw some other familiar Pirates that day at South Hills Country Club. They included George Medich. I had covered him in New York when he was with the Yankees. It was also good to see Jim Sadowski, who had a short stay with the Pirates, but treasures his membership in their alumni ranks as much or more than any of the better known Pirates. Medich and Sadowski both grew up on Pittsburgh's sandlots. I shake their hands, exchange some comments, and think to myself how I know their stories and their achievements, and still enjoy their company.

Blass, Giusti and Tekulve are all in their 60s now. We see them so often I sometimes think we take them for granted. I also attended alumni golf outings this past summer of the Penguins at Valley Brook Country Club in McMurray and the Steelers at Diamond Run in the North Hills. People pay good money for good causes to play a round of golf with these guys. I know their personal stories and their glories, and think about them as they pass. It's always good to see them. Pittsburgh has a rich history in sports accomplishment. We've been spoiled.

We think we're always going to win, that we should always be the City of Champions. To my way of thinking, we still hold that title, for reasons beyond the sports world and the giant video screens at PNC Park or Heinz Field.

Dave Parker, Dock Ellis and Dave Giusti get together at Pirates' reunion at PNC Park.

Grant Jackson and Steve Blass both came through in big way in World Series win by Bucs.

George Gojkovich

Tony Dorsett
Still brings hope to Hopewell and McGuire Home

"I can. I can. I can."

"I can!" Tony Dorsett said those two little words three times in succession as he delivered his acceptance speech on the front steps of the Pro Football Hall of Fame. "I can! I can! I can!"

He urged us to repeat those words whenever we felt challenged or overwhelmed, whenever we thought something was too much, more than we could do, when perhaps someone told us we weren't equal to a task.

It helps, it really does.

When those damn deadlines are pressing, and you feel like you've just squeezed your head into an undersized football helmet, it helps.

I can. I can. I can.

They are words that might prove helpful to Dave Wannstedt and the present-day Pitt football team in its mission to return the Panthers to the ranks of the proudest programs in the country.

Tony Dorsett showed us the way. His success story has always been an inspirational one. He was too small when he first showed up for practice at Hopewell High School, near his home in Aliquippa. He wasn't tall enough, he didn't weigh enough. No one, not even back then, ever questioned his speed. He was always fast enough. He had heart and he had a gleam in his eye. They even called him "Hawk" because he could see everything. He had great vision.

He put stones in his pockets when he weighed in, and there was just something about his manner, his attitude, the way he walked, that appealed to the late Butch Ross, his football coach at Hopewell High. Ross died late in 2007 and, to the end, Ross loved to relate stories about what Tony Dorsett did during his days at Hopewell High.

Even though Tony had a sensational high school career, some thought he'd be too small to play big-time football at Pitt. Even though he had a sensational college career at Pitt, some thought he'd be too small to be successful in the National Football League.

I've stood alongside Tony Dorsett on several occasions, often at Armand Dellovade's tailgate parties outside stadiums where Pitt was playing, and always found myself staring at Dorsett. He was no taller than I am—at 5–8½—but he has always been so sculpted, so athletic looking, handsome and ready to roll again. He's a real life story of the Little Engine That Could.

Dorsett fooled all his doubters. He took the ball, feinted this way and that, left everyone else stumbling in his path, and zigged here and zagged there, and put up numbers like no other runner had before—on every level. Bill Hillgrove, the Voice of the Panthers and the Steelers on radio broadcasts, loves to tell stories about the thrills he experienced calling the action when Dorsett had the ball, and how much he has gained personal satisfaction from Dorsett's successes in life. "It was an honor to do his games," says Hillgrove. "I felt the same way about Danny Marino and many of those guys from that era. I still feel privileged to do the Pitt and Steelers games."

At Pitt, Dorsett led the nation in rushing his senior season with 1,948 yards in 11 games. In four seasons, he averaged 141.4 yards rushing per game, and 153.8 yards all-purpose per game. He topped the nation's runners with 21 TDs his senior season, and scored 55 TDs altogether, returning seven kickoffs for scores. He averaged 177.1 yards as a senior when he led Pitt to an 11–0 regular season record and a national championship. He won the Heisman Trophy in that 1976 season. The Dallas Cowboys traded up to get the second pick in the 1976 draft so they could get Dorsett.

That's why he was saying those two little words over and over again at the Pro Football Hall of Fame ceremonies at Canton, Ohio back on July 30, 1994. I can. I can. I can. Tony Dorsett never doubted himself. He knew he could.

Tony Dorsett
HOF

I'm prejudiced, I know, but I thought Tony Dorsett stole the show at the Pro Football Hall of Fame in the summer of 1994. The Class of '94 was a considerable one, including Minnesota Vikings coach Bud Grant, Cleveland Browns running back Leroy Kelly, St. Louis Cardinals tight end Jackie Smith, San Francisco 49ers defensive back Jimmy Johnson and Dallas Cowboys defensive lineman Randy White.

Several of them tugged at your heart-strings with some of the remarks they offered, but none of them was quite as prepared and as effective as Dorsett, who turned the podium into a pulpit and delivered an old-fashioned Baptist sermon. He was 40 years old—hard to believe—and he had aged well. (It's harder to believe he's now 54.)

Many of the former football players walk awkwardly, or wobble like penguins, wherever they go these days, but Dorsett looked as sure-footed and strong as ever. He looked great in his bright gold HOF blazer.

Anybody who wears a Pitt ring, cares about the Blue and Gold, or is employed by the University had to feel proud if they were present for all the weekend's activities at Canton. I went there every summer, for a long span, with my pals Bill Priatko and Rudy Celigoi, to see all the old pros at the Hall of Fame Weekend. It was a rite of summer. It was always especially exciting when a former Steelers player or someone with Western Pennsylvania roots was among those inducted into the sport's pantheon.

The late Hopewell High School football coach Butch Ross loved to reminisce about his days with Tony Dorsett.

Danny Rains and Tony Dorsett were a backfield duo at Hopewell High and now team up at annual fund-raising golf outing for McGuire Home.

At a dinner the night before, for instance, when they introduced all the inductees and past Hall of Famers who were present, I felt a rush when a U.S. Air Force band played "Hail to Pitt" as Dorsett was ushered across a stage by a local pageant queen. I thought Priatko, who grew up in North Braddock admiring local hero Fran Rogel and played football at Pitt and with the Steelers in the '50s, would burst with pride.

"This is great," opined Priatko.

The school fight song never sounded better, but it may have been the setting. There were laser lights and all sorts of special effects accompanying the visuals at the Civic Center in Canton. Multi-screened images of Dorsett in action for the Dallas Cowboys came at you from every direction. Super stuff.

Then, too, I had images of my own. I was working in New York at *The New York Post* when Dorsett was doing his thing at Pitt. I remembered a game when I accompanied several old Pitt classmates from Manhattan to the U. S. Military Academy at West Point, and we saw Dorsett personally destroy the once-proud Army football team with a 200-yards-plus rushing effort. I remembered sitting a few rows behind his parents, Wes and Myrtle Dorsett, and how proud they were.

I remembered a dark night at Three Rivers Stadium, the night after Thanksgiving 1976, when I was with old schoolmates once more to see Dorsett lead the Panthers to a big victory over Penn State in the regular season finale. Pitt would go on to beat Georgia in the Sugar Bowl to complete a 12–0 season and win the national championship.

What sweet memories.

I can. I can. I can.

Dorsett was keeping good company in Canton. It's become an annual pilgrimage for me because I feel like a kid again, meeting and socializing with the stars of my youth. It's like having your childhood bubble gum card collection come to life. In addition to the inductees I mentioned earlier, the different events were attended by the likes of Dick "Night Train" Lane, Marion Motley, Pete Pihos, Frank Gifford, Dante Lavelli, Arnie Weinmeister, John Henry Johnson, Ray Nitschke, Bob St. Clair, Lou Groza and Doug Atkins.

There were also some I covered during my days at *The Miami News, The New York Post* and *The Pittsburgh Press* such as Earl Campbell, Tom Landry, Don Shula, Ernie Stautner, Bart Starr and Willie Brown. It's well worth the 110-mile easy-motoring trip from Pittsburgh to see these great players up close.

When Dorsett spoke the next day, so clearly, with a well-thought-out message, a heartfelt offering, I remembered seeing a tape of him being interviewed when he was a student at Pitt, and I thought about the progress he had made, the polish he had picked up along the way while playing professional football, and being exposed to situations that demanded he keep sharpening his skills and his speaking methods.

Tony Dorsett never forgot where he came from, and paid tribute to his parents and relatives and friends from his early days, but it was quite evident that he had indeed, come a long way from Aliquippa.

Tony Dorsett had some of his best days against Notre Dame. In 1973 game seen here, he rushed for 209 yards against Fighting Irish.

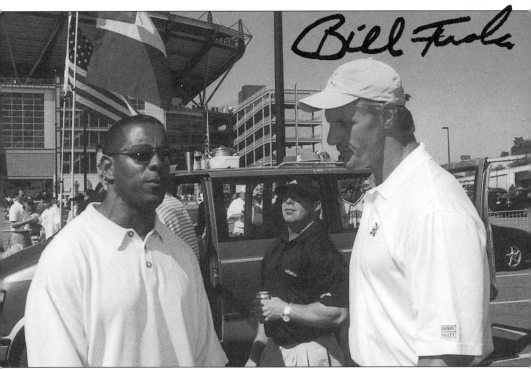

Tony Dorsett and Bill Fralic both had their jerseys retired at Pitt. They get to see each other at Armand Dellovade's tailgate picnics outside Heinz Field on North Shore.

"It's been a long journey for me to get back here," Dorsett said in his talk. "From Alquippa to Dallas and now Canton. It's been a journey that's been filled with hope and been filled with heart."

Dorsett has not forgotten where it all began. He gets back to his home area annually to lend his presence, and that of many of his former teammates, to a golf outing to raise funds for the McGuire Home. He teams up with Danny Rains to recruit the celebrity participants and corporate sponsors. Rains once ran in the same backfield with Dorsett at Hopewell High School and they have remained close friends. Rains went on to play linebacker at the University of Cincinnati—he's in the Athletic Hall of Fame at UC with another Pittsburgher, basketball star Jack Twyman of Central Catholic—and with the Chicago Bears. He was on Mike Ditka's team that won Super Bowl XX.

I can. I can. I can.

No other single player ever had the impact on a college football program as Dorsett did at Pitt. The team was 1–10 the year before he and Johnny Majors took over the program. Foge Fazio took Majors and his top assistant, Jackie Sherrill, to Dorsett's home to meet him and his parents. Majors had to shout at his assistants and tell them to cool it when they were reacting excitely to Dorsett's performance in the Big 33 Game in Hershey. That's when Majors really knew he had something special among his first recruits at Pitt.

Pitt won six games and went to a bowl game in Dorsett's first season. Majors was named the national Coach of the Year.

"Tony was one of the greatest college and pro football players ever," said Majors, when asked about his contribution to his success during his first stay at Pitt. "He's the only player ever to win a college championship, a pro championship, the Heisman Trophy and be inducted into the Hall of Fame for both pro and college football."

Dorsett joined Joe Schmidt and Mike Ditka as former Pitt players honored as inductees at the Pro Football Hall of Fame. His name can be mentioned along with other legendary figures at Pitt such as Pop Warner, Dr. Jock Sutherland, Marshall Goldberg, Hugh Green and Danny Marino, and Dorsett may have been the most spectacular of them all during his student days on the Oakland campus.

The only Pitt man to have had a greater impact during his Pitt stay was Dr. Jonas Salk, who discovered the anti-polio vaccine in a lab across the street from Pitt Stadium (now the Petersen Events Center) back in the mid-50s. Pitt should erect statues to Dr. Salk and Tony Dorsett somewhere on the upper campus.

Anyone tackling such an ambitious project should keep Tony Dorsett's mantra in mind: I can. I can. I can.

"Most of us are much more acquainted with losing than we are with winning."
—Charles Schulz
"Peanuts" **cartoonist**

Don Yannessa
Still standing on a corner in Aliquippa

"I like to travel first-class."

May 4, 2007

I have to smile when I consider Don Yannessa. When I picture him, he has a smile on his handsome swarthy face, more of a smirk really. Like he knows something you don't know. Like the cat that just swallowed the canary. He was 67 years old when we did a one-on-one interview in the summer of 2007, but there's still a lot of schoolboy in Don Yannessa, like he's still dressed for a Friday night dance at his hometown of Aliquippa or during his college days at New Mexico State University in Las Cruces.

Not too many kids from Aliquippa ever make it to Las Cruces. In those days, most of the kids came out of high school and went directly to work for the rest of their lives in the steel mills that lined the Ohio River. Tony Dorsett's dad, Wes, worked in those mills. Mike Ditka's dad, also named Mike, worked at the Aliquippa & Southern Railroad (A&SRR). The men looked forward to watching Friday night football. It was something to get excited about. That was in a different era. They're not making steel in those mills any more. The jobs and many of the people have gone away.

Yannessa is a proud man who checks himself out in the mirror each morning and makes sure his hair, still so solid black for his age somehow, is parted just so. There is still a lot of Fonz or Fonzarelli (from the popular TV sitcom "Happy Days") in Don Yannessa. I can imagine Yannessa winking while approving his own image.

I visited him at Baldwin High School on Wednesday, February 21, 2007. He was 66 at the time. He showed up wearing a long black leather coat—like the outriders wore—black slacks and a purple turtleneck jersey tight on his still firm and athletic-looking body. He was serving, at $280 a day, as the interim athletic director at Baldwin High, where he had previously coached the football team and looked after the athletic program. He had been retired for just over four years from full-time work, and he was looking forward to his fifth year as the football coach at Ambridge High School.

He was a bit late for our scheduled appointment. "He's not here," a custodian told me as I entered the building. "His car's not out here in the parking lot."

I guessed by the tone of the "his car" comment that his car had to be a Cadillac. It turned out to be a shiny black Cadillac, of course. Yannessa leases a new one every two or three years, I am told.

Yannessa has always made a good buck in a profession where everyone else wasn't doing quite so well. He had moved up to Center Township a long time ago, and had a nice home there. His wife Elaine was an administrative secretary for Conrail for over 40 years and was now retired. He and Elaine had been married for 41 years. They had no children. His players had always filled that void.

Two things caught my eye as I drove onto the campus at Baldwin High School that morning. Teachers were on strike in the Baldwin-Whitehall School District and were waving signs at passing motorists as they stood on busy Rte. 51. One of the professionally painted signs a teacher hoisted high said it was the FIRST STRIKE IN 32 YEARS. Another neatly printed sign announced that they had been working 235 DAYS WITHOUT A CONTRACT.

High on the hill, there were temporary fences set up to allow construction workers space to do a major renovation on the school. I later learned that the school was in the midst of a $65 million high school renovation project. The building was starting to look a lot like Upper St. Clair High School in my neighborhood. I learned that the same construction outfit was working on the Baldwin project. Baldwin had one of the highest school tax rates among the 42 suburban school districts in Allegheny County, it was reported in the *Post-Gazette* the following day. Voters in Upper St. Clair had turned down the idea of building a new school, so they simply built a new school in front of the old school and attached them. I refer to USC as the University of St. Clair, but I like what they've done even if the annual tax bill can cause heartburn. The school serves as an outstanding centerpiece for the community.

Only the seniors were in class that day at Baldwin High, and they were being taught by members of the administration so they would qualify to graduate on schedule. Yannessa introduced me to the principal, Todd Keroskin, and the two assistant principals, Dan Castagna and Keith Konyk. I also met Yannessa's administrative assistant, Mrs. Cindy Leaf. She was his right arm when he was the full-time athletic director at Baldwin.

I spoke with Yannessa and Leaf on Don's last day at Baldwin— Friday, May 4, 2007—and gained some more insights. He had been part of a selection group that hired Bennie Sortino as the athletic director and Dan Polante as the football coach. The basketball coach continued to be Kyle DeGregorio. I had worked with his father, Joe DeGregorio, for four years at Pitt, and had the highest respect for him as a coach, teacher and team player. "Do you have to be Italian to work here?" I asked Leaf. "I'm Irish," she said. "I'm a Kelly."

Yannessa had a knee replacement in December, 2006, but he was still walking tall as we toured the school hallways. "I'm doing all right," he said, flashing that signature smile my way.

Appearances have always been important to Don Yannessa. He went first-class, long before he could afford it. He is a winner in so many ways. He dresses like a winner. He looks like a winner, even when he doesn't always win. He wears more rings than the Steelers of the '70s. He's been a winner at Aliquippa, Baldwin and Ambridge, and he's always improved the programs and their appearance. He dressed up the schools and their facilities so they were first-class. He painted everything purple at Baldwin High, and made people proud to wear

Don Yannessa stands guard at Ambridge High School.

Foge Fazio, Jim Render, John Majors and Don Yannessa enjoy a party at home of Armand Dellovade, as attorney Bob Taylor, a Pitt and Ambridge fan, looks on in background.

the school colors. He interjected "Fighting" into the school's nickname and the Baldwin sports teams became The Fighting Highlanders.

After Don departed from the building, I spoke with his administrative assistant some more, and offered my views about her boss, just to check out their appropriateness.

"I worked with him for ten years altogether," said Cindy Leaf. "When he came back here five months ago he picked up where he left off. It was like he had never been away. He's a wonderful man. He's a true leader, and fun to work with. When he enters a room, he commands respect, and he offers respect. I'll miss him. He's a good guy, a wonderful man in so many ways.

"He plays the part, but down deep he's really a down-to-earth person. He's fun to be around. He's loyal to his coaches, co-workers and the school administration. He appreciates family. He adores his wife and you can tell they truly enjoy each other. Your impression of him is right on. You've got him pegged perfectly."

Yannessa is a great salesman and he's always rallied strong support from businessmen in whatever community he has worked. He's always developed a good following.

"I know Don a little bit from being at banquets and golf outings with him," said Jim Rooker, the former pitcher and broadcaster for the Pittsburgh Pirates who owns Rook's Saloon on 4th Street in Ambridge. "When I heard he was coming to Ambridge as the football coach I thought it was going to be like the savior coming to town. I heard so many positive things about him from so many people.

"I never knew him coming here was going to have such an impact on my restaurant business. He comes to my place with his coaches from time to time. Fans come before and after the home games. I was so happy. Hey, he's way up here in the coaching fraternity. He's in the coaches' Hall of Fame, isn't he? He talks the talk and walks the walk. He does what he says he's going to do. I was all charged up. I told our Chamber of Commerce to get him into our community parade. We needed some excitement around here. He's been a blessing in Ambridge."

Rooker, now 64, lives in Jacksonville, Florida and returns once a month to check on business at his restaurant. Rook's Saloon has some great sports pictures on all the walls. I've been there on several occasions and enjoyed the company of local attorney Bob Taylor, a former Pitt football player. Rook's Saloon reminds me of Frankie Gustine's Restaurant, operated for over 35 years by a former Pirates' infielder, just a block away from Forbes Field in Oakland.

Taylor, age 62, has been an attorney in Ambridge for 37 years. He shares offices on Merchant Street with Andrew M. Hladio, his partner the past 18 years. Taylor was a lineman who lettered for the Pitt football team in 1966. "My claim to fame is that I was the backup to Marty Schottenheimer," Taylor tells you.

"Don Yannessa brought a lot of spirit and confidence to our town. That aura he had has helped out a lot of the players. He helped a lot of them get scholarships. He knows the great players will get scholarships to Pitt and Penn State and places like that. He personally contacts the small colleges and sells his players. He's been a positive image for the whole team. He's been a real plus for Ambridge."

Randy Cosgrove, a long-time publicist, school official and the public address announcer for Steelers' games at Heinz Field, is a big booster of Yannessa.

"I use the old Syd Thrift line," said Cosgrove, the athletic director at Ambridge, referring to the former Pirates general manager. "It ain't easy resurrecting the dead, but Yannessa did it." Cosgrove, in his ninth year as athletic director after three years at North Hills, first approached Yannessa about coming to Ambridge. They met at The Ground Round Restaurant in Moon Township to discuss the possibility. "It's an absolute pleasure to work with him. It's a joy because of his positive outlook and the positive impact he has on his players," continued Cosgrove. "We have kids who come here and haven't had breakfast at home in the morning. They know he cares about them."

The Steelers may be kings as far as sports in Pittsburgh are concerned, but high school football remains the bedrock upon which the game's popularity was first built in the region.

"Being on the high school football team was a big deal when I was growing up," said Yannessa. "Everybody I knew played on the football team and went to college. It was a way to get someplace. The Steelers weren't as big a deal in those days. The Pitt Panthers were the team, not the Steelers. This whole corner of Pennsylvania was pulling for the Panthers. Now, there's no doubt about it, this is Steeler Country."

Ambridge had a rich tradition as far as football went, sending eight of its young men on to the National Football League. The most successful was the latest to join the pro ranks, Mike Lucci. He was preceded by his coach during his Pitt days, John Michelosen, as well as Ted Greb, Len Syza, Harry and Ed Ulinski, Leo Nobile and Bud Gaona. Yannessa reminds his players of their predecessors to inspire them.

Kenny Miller has served Yannessa for 24 years as his equipment manager, first at Aliquippa, then at Baldwin and now at Ambridge. He was a student in the English class taught by Yannessa at Aliquippa High. Asked what he learned from Don in those days, Miller says, "I learned how to answer the telephone properly."

I first met Yannessa back in 1980 when I was a sportswriter at *The Pittsburgh Press*, and I talked *The Press* management and the movers-and-shakers at the Pittsburgh Brewing Company into reviving the Curbstone Coaches. It was a series of luncheon programs that featured football coaches on every level in the Pittsburgh area. I had attended it faithfully during my schooldays at Pitt in the early '60s. I was surprised to learn, when I returned home after a year in Miami and nine years in New York in the '70s, that the luncheon series had ceased to function during the '70s. That was the same span when Pittsburgh became known as "The City of Champions" for all its sports successes. What poor timing, I thought. It had been originally held on a weekly basis in the fall at the Roosevelt Hotel.

Art Rooney Sr. was a regular attendee in those days, leaving his offices in the hotel lobby to join fellow sports enthusiasts in a dining hall one floor above. Chester L. Smith, the sports editor of *The Press*, was the emcee, and the powers-that-be included Emil Narick, Jim Daniel, Tommy Davies and Art and Vee Toner of Pittsburgh sports fame.

"Make sure it's always over by the advertised 1:30 time," Rooney repeatedly advised. "Those guys have got to be back in their offices as promised. If they get hell from their boss they won't come back."

Bill Smith and Dan McCann of Iron City fame went for the idea right away. McCann has coordinated the event ever since, and found the financing from the brewery to keep it going. Bob Prince and I shared emcee duties for the first four years of the revival.

The luncheons were held each month in the fall at the Allegheny Club at Three Rivers Stadium. In recent years they were held at The Riverside complex in The Strip District and the luncheon series has been renamed Coaches Corner. By either name, Don Yannessa has always been one of the star guest speakers.

There is a pecking order at the luncheon program. The high school coaches speak first, followed by the college coaches and the featured speaker is always a player or coach from the Pittsburgh Steelers, past and present. There have been Hall of Fame caliber people on the program on every competitive level through the years. No matter who was on the program, however, when Don Yannessa appeared he was always the star.

Some coaches who could compete with him on the football field felt out of their league at the lectern with him on the same program. Some envied him; some resented his big-time act. "He's a good speaker," offered his wife Diane. "He likes the mike."

He out-dressed everyone else on the dais, and he out-talked them as well. He always appeared more confident, classier and more comical. He told better stories. There was something about his style that commanded attention. He always traveled with a bigger entourage than every other coach, so the audience was filled with his fans, always eager to laugh and to clap enthusiastically when he completed his skit.

We both like to share stories about Mike Ditka. Yannessa was a year behind Ditka at Aliquippa High School. I was a freshman at Pitt, back in 1960, when Ditka was a senior there. We agree that Ditka was the greatest competitor and the quintessential athlete at our respective schools. We both measure everyone else by how they compare to Ditka. No one else quite measures up to Ditka.

No one in the high school coaching ranks of Western Pennsylvania quite measures up to Don Yannessa. There are coaches who have compiled better records, like my friends Chuck Klausing and Jim Render, for instance, but none of them walks the walk or talks the talk quite like Don Yannessa. He's a tough act to follow.

He told me that Press Maravich, the father of Pete Maravich, was his basketball coach at Aliquippa High School. "He came to our school from Baldwin, believe it or not, and he was at our school from 1954 to 1956," said Yannessa. "He was my gym coach, but we never saw him. He'd roll a ball out on the floor and retreat to his office. He left to become an assistant at North Carolina State. Then he went to Clemson as the head coach and came back to N.C. State as the head coach. Then he went to LSU and then Appalachian State. He was a trip. He had that crew-cut hair and he was a no-nonsense guy."

Yannessa was a consultant and made a cameo appearance back in 1983 in the 20th Century Fox movie "All the Right Moves," starring a young Tom Cruise as the quarterback of a high school team in Johnstown, Pa., who was looking to football as a way out of a struggling steel town. Yannessa proudly tells you he still gets residuals from that dual role. That movie still shows up on TV every now and then. Or you can watch a video tape of it in Yannessa's game room. It gained Yannessa the nickname of "Hollywood Don."

Yannessa enjoyed his greatest success at his alma mater during his 35 years as a head coach in the WPIAL. During his 17 years at Aliquippa, he won four AAA championships. He moved to Baldwin as the coach and athletic director in 1989 and remained for 14 years. He had two winning seasons and two playoff appearances in his first two seasons at Baldwin. He turned the program around, but he couldn't get over the top. He was the head coach in the Big 33 game in 1999.

When Yannessa became the coach in 1972 at Aliquippa the football team was playing its home games on Saturday afternoon before 400 to 500 loyal fans, mostly family of the players. He turned Carl A. Aschman Stadium, named for his coach at Aliquippa, into "The Pit," judged the toughest place to play in a poll of coaches by Mike White of the *Post-Gazette* in1998.

"When I took over," recalled Yannessa, "they hadn't played a football game on Friday night in five years." The following year, Yannessa convinced school officials to let him play one Friday night game. He picked the one with perennial power Butler High, coached by Art Bernardi, then ranked No. 1 in the state. Aliquippa prevailed 9-0 before a big crowd. "In 1974, they told me I could play all my home games on Friday night," said a smug Yannessa. The Indians (Aliquippa was the name of an Indian queen) drew large and enthusiastic crowds on a consistent basis after that.

When H.G. Bissinger of *The Philadelphia Inquirer* was looking for a school to feature in a 1990 book that became the award-winning "Friday Night Lights," he considered Aliquippa. He would settle on Permian High School in Odessa, Texas as the setting for his revealing inside look at a high-powered high school football program. The book became a movie and more recently a TV series. "I might still be getting residuals on that as well if he'd have picked Aliquippa," says Yannessa.

By the early 1980s, Yannessa had fireworks at home games at Aschman Stadium. "I think the first time we had the Indian come out on the horse was for a playoff game against Keystone Oaks in 1983," Yannessa said. "It snowed a lot and the horse slipped and almost fell. We almost had to shoot him in the middle of the field. But when the Indian came out and threw a flaming spear into the turf it always sparked the crowd. That Indian, by the way, is called Chief Aliquippa."

In the next few years, Yannessa had parachuters land on the field before some games. "People used to be afraid to come to Aliquippa games, "Yannessa said. "We wanted to make it a show."

Then only the visiting teams were afraid to come to Aliquippa. There was an intimidation factor. The visiting team's locker room was a dungeon, and the visitors had to back their bus down a steep hill to get near that locker room. "That thing's a real dungeon," Yannessa says almost proudly. "That goes back to when Roosevelt was in office. You go in there and expect to see guys like Bela Lugosi and Boris Karloff from those horror films."

Mike Zmijanac, a former Yannessa assistant who lives in Mt. Lebanon, became the head coach at Aliquippa, and he kept the fireworks, the horse and flaming spear, and the winning tradition intact. He's turned out championship teams in football and basketball. Aliquippa has turned out some great athletes, many who've made it to the NFL.

Yannessa's name is in the list of the Top Ten WPIAL coaches in a poll conducted by the *Tribune-Review* in 2006. The list, in order, included Chuck Klausing of Braddock and Pitcairn, Lindy Lauro of New Castle, Jim Render of Upper St. Clair, Pete Antimarino of Gateway, Jack McCurry of North Hills, Art Bernardi of Butler, Larry Bruno of Monaca and Beaver Falls, Art Walker, Sr. of Mt. Lebanon and Shady Side Academy, Yannessa and George Novak of Steel Valley and Woodland Hills.

For the past 39 years, there has been an Italian Football Coaches Dinner held in Ambridge. It was started by Joe Zerilla, a coach and official in his heyday, and has been maintained since Zerilla's death by his nephew, Gus Mittiga, a salesman at John Seretti Chevrolet, Inc. in Moon Township. It was always held in the hall at Christ the King Catholic Church before Yannessa came to coach at Ambridge. Now the dinner is held at the Jevy's/Franzee's Banquet Hall in midtown. It's an improvement.

I attended the 39th annual dinner there in the company of Jim Render, who was being feted for winning the AAAA and PIAA football championships. This was in January of 2007. Lauro, Bruno, Bernardi, Pat Tarquinio of Beaver and Hopewell, Joe Hamilton of Blackhawk, Carl Florie of Ellwood City and Riverside, were seated at the same table. I was impressed by the caliber of the coaches in attendance. I had last attended the dinner 24 years earlier in the company of Foge Fazio, the head coach at Pitt at the time.

Render and Hamilton both said they married Italians to gain admission to this select circle of coaches. "I married Pamela Jo Churico so I could come here," kidded Render. Legends such as Lauro, Bruno and Bernardi were all in their 80s. I thought I had better talk to these guys while they were still around. What football glories they have witnessed in their time. They are so much a part of Western Pennsylvania's rich football heritage. It wasn't long afterward that Bruno was in the hospital out in Aliquippa for several health issues.

238

DON YANNESSA
Enjoyed Joe Paterno's book,
The Lion in Autumn

Photos by Jim O'Brien

2007 Italian Football Coaches Dinner in Ambridge attracted the likes of legendary coaches, left to right, Larry Bruno of Beaver Falls, Lindy Lauro of New Castle, Joe Hamilton of Blackhawk, Karl Florie of Ellwood City, Art Bernardi of Butler, Pat Tarquinio of Hopewell and Jim Render of Upper St. Clair.

Yannessa has been inducted into the Western Chapter of the Pennsylvania Sports Hall of Fame, the Pennsylvania High School Coaches Hall of Fame, the Pittsburgh Chapter of the Italian-American Sports Hall of Fame, the Beaver County Sports Hall of Fame and the New Mexico State University Hall of Fame.

Yannessa had already spent time at Ambridge High before reporting to Baldwin the day of my visit. Yannessa told me that he and his wife Elaine had just picked up their tickets for a Rod Stewart concert. Yannessa and Stewart were soul brothers.

* * *

I had an opportunity to visit the new Ambridge High School, which is next to the old school, on Thursday, January 17, 2008. The new gym is impressive and so is the weight room and the Mike Lucci Locker Room. Some of Lucci's awards and memorabilia and signed footballs are in a display case in the middle of the garnet and gray room. Randy Cosgrove took Bob Taylor and Jerry Morrow and me on a tour. We had a chance to check out the football field and Cosgrove showed us where new seating and a new press box would be erected. Things looked in order for Don Yannessa's seventh and perhaps final season at Ambridge High.

Don Yannessa:

"Now that you're a Hollywood movie star, I hope you won't forget us."
—Joe Paterno, 1983

When I was a senior at Aliquippa High in 1957, we used to spend two weeks at Raccoon Creek State Park at a training camp. The field was in bad shape and we lived in cabins. We ate our meals in a big cabin. A woman came in from Burgettstown and cooked us three meals a day. I remember Joe Paterno coming there and staying for five days. He was an assistant to Rip Engle at Penn State. He wanted Mike Ditka in the worst way, and Ditka had said he was going to Penn State. There were no written commitments, or national letters of intent, in those days. A kid could change his mind at the last moment.

Notre Dame and Pitt were after Mike, too. Paterno was 28 and still single at the time. Ditka had already graduated and he was going to play in the Jaycees All-Star Game at Forbes Field. So he worked out with us to get ready for that game. He came in one night with Mike Lucci of Ambridge and they turned our beds over around midnight and caused a ruckus. They really tormented us, but it was all in good fun. Ditka could get away with it because he was Coach Aschman's boy.

Paterno was buddying up with our coach, Carl Aschman. Paterno didn't get Ditka and he held it against Aliquippa for a long time. He never came back to Aliquippa to recruit a kid until 26 years later. Paterno is like that. He came from Brooklyn, I think, but his Italian heritage is part Sicilian and part Calabrase. Those are the two most hard-headed segments of the population in Italy. Some Pitt people in Aliquippa got to Ditka and convinced him to come to Pitt. They promised him he'd get into Dental School. Can you imagine Mike Ditka as a dentist?

When I was involved in that movie "All The Right Moves" in 1983, I received a card from Paterno. He wrote, "Now that you're a Hollywood movie star, I hope you won't forget us."

I saw Paterno at the Pete Dimperio Coaches Clinic in Green Tree that same year, 1983. I had a kid named Marcus Henderson, a strong safety. I told Joe this kid wanted to go to Penn State. I told Joe it was about time he returned to Aliquippa. I told him he had a vendetta. He said, "I don't have a vendetta." I told him, "You tell that to a Polish guy; don't tell it to an Italian."

So he came to Aliquippa and he signed Henderson. He was on the varsity all four years—he didn't red-shirt—and he started for two seasons. He was on their national championship team and started when they beat Miami in the Fiesta Bowl.

When Joe finally came back to Aliquippa, he came in a private airplane that landed at a private strip just off the regular runways at Greater Pittsburgh Airport. He went to the Serbian Club in Aliquippa. My uncle handed him an envelope with $500 in it to pay him for his appearance. He said, "I came here for Don." And I told Joe, "Hey, you came here for Marcus Henderson." He then went to the Quippin Club, a club frequented by black people. He spent nearly an hour at both places and mixed with everybody. He works a room like nobody's business. He buys drinks in the bars and they loved him. He was great with my assistants and support staff. They loved him. They were impressed by the way he talked to me like we were old friends. He invited us all to attend Penn State's spring practice.

When we went, he invited us over to his house. It was a modest home near the stadium. I'm sure he could have a palace at Penn State if he wanted one. He introduced us to his wife, Sue. She did some student teaching once upon a time at Baldwin. Joe was telling one story after another. He was drinking bourbon and he had some good wine for us.

Aliquippa has always been important to me. I was actually born in Ambridge in 1940, and I lived there till I was eight. So I started to school in Ambridge, but we moved to Aliquippa and it was Aliquippa all the way after that.

241

There were 18,000 people employed at J&L Steel along a seven-mile stretch of the river,—13,000 blue collar and 5,000 white collar workers—and there were 30,000 people living in Aliquippa. It was a vibrant community. We had great recreational facilities. We had everything. It was a great place to grow up. Nearby, things were just as well for Hopewell, Conway, Monaca and West Aliquippa. When that industry dried up it devastated Beaver County. Now there are 9,000 people in Aliquippa, less than a third as many as there were in the heyday of the steel business.

I worked in the mill during the summer of 1959. My uncles were in the union there and they got me in. I'll tell you it was a scary place. There were four and eight ton coils being carried overhead by magnets. If they came loose, you had better not be under them when they fell.

You could get maimed or killed there. There were rats the size of cats. My dad fell from a crane there and got hurt. He could have been killed. There was a pretty good athlete name Jughead Walker who fell into a pot of molten steel and just evaporated. The mills were a dirty, dangerous place. I was there for five or six weeks and I was happy when the workers went on strike. I was happy to get the hell out of there. I worked harder when I got back to New Mexico State. I knew I wanted to work someplace other than the mills.

People get romantic and wax nostalgic about missing the mills in the Ohio Valley. No one who worked in those places misses them. They might have liked the money they were making, but not the labor. It was demanding and dangerous.

No one ever asked me if I wanted to be a doctor or a teacher. Everyone wanted to know if I was going to play football. Back in the '40s, '50s and '60s, most of the boys wanted to play big-time football. This area had one of the richest traditions for football in the entire country.

I was a tackle on the football team at Aliquippa from 1955 through 1957 and I graduated with the class of 1958. In Ditka's junior year, my sophomore year, we won all eight games on our regular season schedule and we beat Mt. Lebanon, 14–13, at Pitt Stadium to win the WPIAL title for the 1955 season. The following year we were a big favorite to repeat as champions. In those days, you couldn't lose a game or you were out of consideration for the playoffs. In the third game, we got beat by Duke Weigle's team at McKeesport. That broke an 11-game winning streak for us. That was it! We were knocked out of the championship run.

They had an old stadium in McKeesport. We had to climb through a big window to get into the visitors' locker room. Ditka is so upset. He's going around punching lockers. He's taking a fit. He's yelling and he's crying. Ditka's our captain and several guys took their cue from him. The next time I look around, everyone is pounding the metal lockers, screaming and crying. Our coach, Carl Aschman, is upset with this behavior. Only Ditka can get away with that stuff. Aschman went around the locker room and got the attention of several players and told each of them, "You're not playing next week." He didn't say anything to Ditka about what he was doing. We were 5–4 that year. We lost 28–12 at Duquesne. We ended up taking a real ass-kicking to Ambridge. We lost 53–13. Mike Lucci was a senior on that Ambridge team. Lucci, by the way, cares about what our Ambridge team is doing now. He lives in Bloomfield Hills now. He's got a big place in Boca Raton, Florida. He was a vice-president with Bally's Fitness Centers. He was seriously challenged by cancer, but he received treatment at Sloan-Kettering Hospital in New York. He's still strong as a bull. He went to Pitt for a few years and got into some trouble on the campus and transferred to Tennessee. He was an All-American at Tennessee and a great player after that for the Detroit Lions.

When I was at Aliquippa, Mike Ditka did a lot for us to help us raise money. He headlined an annual golf outing for our boosters. He said, "Don, whatever I can do for you, just let me know." And he kept his word. We held our fund-raising golf outing at the Beaver Lakes Country Club. We were one of the first to have such an outing. Now there's a million of them.

In the spring of 1987, after Ditka's Bears won the Super Bowl, Mike asked me how I was doing financially. I told him that my wife and I were both working and that we never had any kids. "Do you need any money personally," Ditka asked me. "Let me know if you need it. I'm giving money to so many people right now. You might as well get some of it." I said, "I don't ask for money." When I told my wife I had turned down Ditka's offer, she said, "Are you crazy?"

That shows you how down-to-earth Mike Ditka is. He figured a coach from his old school might be able to use a few bucks. He wanted to help someone from his hometown. He's like that. I like that. We were able to buy all kinds of stuff for our football program at Aliquippa because of the money Mike helped us raise.

Someone asked Mike what kind of golfer I was. Mike told the guy I was a terrible golfer and that I had an ugly golf bag. He had a custom-made golf bag with his name on it. He told me that if I won a championship he'd get one for me. We beat New Castle 26–14 in the title game the next year and, sure enough, Mike sent me a custom-made golf bag. It was red and black and it had to cost a thousand dollars or more.

I've met a lot of great football coaches from this area and many of them have helped me through the years. Those guys you saw at the Italian football coaches dinner are among the best in the business. They are great human beings. They all have different personalities and idiosyncrasies, but they are all good people. They were all big winners. When I got the job at Aliquippa, I went to all those great coaches and asked them how they did what they did. I learned a lot from them. I picked their brains pretty good. I was the new kid on the block and everybody had something to offer.

They kicked my ass early in my coaching career, but I caught up. There were a lot of football coaches out there who were real assholes. They weren't good for the kids and they weren't good for football. The guys I went to for help were giants in the business and they weren't afraid to help me improve my program. Those guys, like Lindy Lauro and Art Bernardi and Larry Bruno, ought to have a monument built honoring them like Mt. Rushmore.

Jim Render does a great job at Upper St. Clair. They have established a great football tradition at Upper St. Clair. They have it at Mt. Lebanon. We never were able to do that at Baldwin. Woodland Hills is relatively new, but they have a football tradition already under George Novak. There was some tradition in some of the schools that were part of that merger. I always said Baldwin was an enigma wrapped in a mystery. Dave Wannstedt played there, and they had some good players, but they never won it all. I never did either, but it wasn't because I didn't work hard or try to deliver a championship team. I'm proud of what I did wherever I worked.

"A good coach can be worth his weight in gold."

I spoke to Don Yannessa on another occasion, on Wednesday, June 27, when he was one of the celebrities playing in the annual Homestead Lions Golf Outing at Westwood Golf Club in West Mifflin. Former Pirates Bob Friend, Bill Mazeroski, Don Schwall and El Roy Face played with foursomes as well that day, as did Dick Hoak, the former star running back and coach of the Steelers.

Two young men from Aliquippa had been shot during the previous six months. One of them, a star football player at Rochester High, had been killed. Rochester football coach Gene Matsook, whom I had met at a coaches' dinner in Ambridge the previous winter, said it was one of his most difficult days when he received a telephone call informing him that his star running back, Tyler Wade-Epps, had been shot and killed at a project in Aliquippa where he lived. The other young athlete, Herb Pope, a star basketball player at Aliquippa High School, recovered from his gunshot wounds in a separate shooting incident. It painted a poor picture of what was going down in Aliquippa these days.

I had stopped at a Wendy's in Aliquippa one morning a few months earlier when I was en route to visiting Larry Bruno, the former football coach at Monaca and Beaver Falls, who had been Joe Namath's high school coach and had introduced him at his Pro Football Hall of Fame induction in Canton. I got a kick out of listening in on a conversation among older men having their coffees. They were swapping stories about Aliquippa legend Mike Ditka.

One told a story about how Ditka had gotten mad at his brother for misplaying a fly ball in the outfield in a baseball game, and then chased him all the way home. It sounded like something Ditka might have done. Ditka was a source of pride to these men. Some of the more recent athletes were not, though the school continued to send players to the pro ranks.

"The biggest problem today," ventured Yannessa, "is that there's no support at home. "Pope's old man spent more time in prison than he did at home. It's ugly what goes on these days.

"I was there 17 years as a coach. I played there as a high school student. I never realized how much pressure there is to succeed there than I realized later on. They fired four guys before I got the job as head coach. They had been 12-and-51 in the years before I took over.

"I didn't realize before I became the coach how tough it could be. You get a lot of that. The athletes are there. They have a great track team and they don't even have a place to practice or compete. They practice in the parking lot. Now they get to do it at Hopewell High on occasion.

"There's a lot of pressure to succeed in sports at Alliquippa. I wish there was as much pressure to succeed academically and socially. I think a kid's got to know that his coach is going to be there for him whenever he makes a mistake. A good coach is worth his weight in gold. He can be as good as any clergy or any parent.

"Hey, whenever the crowd stops roaring, none of that shit matters. It's what you do after high school that counts. When I was there most of the starters got some kind of scholarship or another and it was our way to get to college and make something of ourselves. Any of us who worked in the mills during the summer months knew that's not what we wanted to do the rest of our lives.

"The guys didn't forget where they came from. Mike Ditka helped me so much in raising money when I was at Aliquippa, and now Mike Lucci is doing the same for us at Ambridge. They both live the good life, but they help any way they can back home.

"My wife and I never had any kids, but we've had a great marriage. The secret to a good marriage is this ... you start out with passion and, as it goes on, you'd better become best friends.

"My dad believed in discipline. He made us earn our spending money. He'd say, 'You want a quarter for what? What did you do to earn it?' You know the saying about how the older you get the smarter your father gets? Well, that's certainly true in my case. He passed away at age 76, but he left me in good stead.

"I like to go to Vegas on occasion, but my cap is $1,000. I work too hard to throw money away. I was 40 years in education before I retired as a teacher, and my wife worked just as long in the railroad business.

We've worked hard to get where we are. We have a nice home and we have a nice life. I've built two nice homes and I drive nice cars. I hope to keep it that way."

Photos by Jim O'Brien

MIKE LUCCI

Ambridge High School athletic director Randy Cosgrove shows off locker room memorabilia donated by Mike Lucci, the outstanding former NFL star of the Detroit Lions.

Staff Sgt. Patrick Kutschbach
His family said Pat was proud to serve

"It is foolish to mourn the men who died.
Rather, we should thank God that such men lived."
—General George S. Patton, sent to me
by Debbie Huffner, Pat's mother

November 28, 2007

A siren sounded somewhere in the distance. Flashing red lights could be seen through a long line of trees as an ambulance or Emergency Medical Service van streaked down a road to my left. Otherwise the scene at Bethel Cemetery was quiet and still. The leaves were still on most of the trees, later than usual in mid-November, I thought. The trees were a tapestry of yellow, brown, orange, burgundy and amber. The sky was a Pittsburgh signature sky, steel gray, with the sun peeking in now and then as a tease. Two workmen passed nearby in a truck, toting a ditch-digging machine on a trailer behind them. Their work was done for the day. The driver tooted the horn and they both waved to me.

Charles Gibson, 46, of Bethel Park, and Don Rader, 49, of South Park had put the finishing touches on the grave of Staff Sergeant Patrick Kutschbach and gone home. I'd seen a woman walking two small salt-and-pepper terriers, and a young man jogging on the same path, but now I was alone in the cemetery. It was just after 4 p.m. School buses were shooting past, taking boys and girls home to their parents.

There were many small U.S. flags staked near the tombstones of many of the graves on this grassy knoll. They had been planted there the previous Monday, which was Veterans Day. There was no breeze, so the flags were limp against the sticks. There was a chill in the air. It was getting dark. I remembered how I used to run past Calvary Cemetery where Hazelwood meets Greenfield and Squirrel Hill in my teen years because it was a bit spooky.

I checked out the grave stones at Bethel Cemetery. I was surprised by how many of the men had served in some branch of the Armed Forces, in so many different wars. Some from World War I, some from World War II, some in Korea and Vietnam. I knew there were soldiers in the older part of the cemetery from the Civil War. On this day, the scene reminded me of Flanders Fields. I was sent to the U.S. Army Hometown News Center in Kansas City and to Fort Greely, Alaska for my two-year stint, and was fortunate not to have to go to Vietnam. I even got an "early out" to go to graduate school at the University of Pittsburgh, to major in English Literature. I'm glad now that I was in the Army.

I was drawn to Bethel Cemetery after reading the obituary of Staff Sgt. Patrick F. Kutschbach. My wife and I read the obits every morning, but this one tugged at my heart. Pat had left behind his wife Ginger and their one-year-old son Bastian. Pat had been an all-state volleyball player as a senior in 2000 at Montour High School in Kennedy and later coached the team at his alma mater. I didn't know him, but he was the kind of kid I liked to write about.

He had attended elementary school at St. Louise de Marillac in Upper St. Clair, and that was close to our home.

He was a Green Beret and was serving with a special forces unit in Afghanistan when a vehicle in which he was riding was struck by a direct rocket-propelled grenade and small arms fire while on a military action. He died, at age 25, from wounds suffered in Tagab, Afghanistan, a long way from home.

I was speaking at a luncheon at Mr. P's Restaurant in Greensburg during the burial at 1:30 p.m. I told my buddy Bill Priatko about Staff Sgt. Patrick Kutschbach and he read the obituary as well. Priatko told me how thankful he was that his son, David, had survived three different military assignments in the Mideast. He was now a Lt. Colonel in command of an Army battalion at Fort Benning, Ga. "I worried about him and prayed every day that he'd be safe," said his father.

There was a passage at the bottom of the obit for Staff Sgt. Kutschbach in which his family expressed his great pride in what he was doing. ""Patrick felt privileged," it read, "to be an American and was proud to serve and defend his country."

As he lay dying, he expressed a desire to be buried with his boyhood friend Russell A. Kurtz, an Army sergeant who was killed in Iraq, on Feb. 11 of this year. Kurtz was 23. There was a green rectangle, an instant-grass patch, outlining Kurtz's gravesite at Bethel Cemetery. There were five small U.S. flags staked into the ground about his tombstone.

"My step-daughter, Mandy Sherman, went to school with the Kurtz kid," said Gibson, the gravedigger. "This hits home."

Gibson had mud-streaked goggles half-way back on his orange and brown hunter's hat. He said his father founded a company in 1958 to dig graves and did so for as many as 22 cemeteries at one time. "I started going with him to help when I was 8, and I've been at it ever since," Gibson said. "This was my second today, but it's different than when you're burying someone who's lived a full life and a young man like this."

Many Pittsburghers were sad this particular Monday because their beloved Steelers had managed to lose a football game to the lowly New York Jets the day before, but Bethel Cemetery held a real reason to feel sad. There are stories on so many stones in a graveyard.

I noted the names of some of the veterans buried in nearby graves. There was John Park Martin, who served in the Army in World War I; Carl M. Cooley, in the Army Air Corps in World War II; B. Boyd Thomas, an Army private in World War II; Thomas J. Goodwin, in the Navy in World War II; Melvin Dean Paul, in the Navy in World War II; Elmer

Photos above provided by Debbie Huffner

Staff Sgt. Patrick Kutschbach and wife Ginger show off 1-year-old son Bastian at home and on vacation in Paris. His father David Kutschbach and wife, Debbie Huffner, flank Patrick at his graduation ceremonies at Fort Bragg, N.C. on St. Patrick's Day, 2006. Below, the burial scene at Bethel Park Cemetery.

Jim O'Brien

H. Hoft, in the Army in World War I. But, judging from their birth and death dates, they all came home from their respective tours of duty.

I remembered that I had read a story by Jimmy Breslin, one of my favorite writers, after the assassination of President John F. Kennedy. Breslin had interviewed the man who dug JFK's grave. "It's the last thing anyone is going to do for him on earth," said the proud grave-digger, "and I wanted to do it right."

I thought of that as I saw Gibson and Rader rearranging the floral bouquets that had been brought to the cemetery. They stepped back to make sure it looked right, and adjusted it once more. The floral arrangements had red, white and blue ribbons, and there were red roses, lilac violets, white and orange carnations, white baby breath, and an assortment of flowers I can't identify by name.

Gibson and Rader groomed the mound of fresh dirt. There'd been some light rain and it was damp and held firm. It will soon sink and flatten out to the level of the surrounding graves. "You should have been here at 1:30," reported Rader. "There were so many people here. They just kept walking in. Every police officer in Bethel Park must have been here."

"They were concerned there might be some protests against the war," interjected Gibson. "None of that happened, thank God."

Staff Sgt. Kutschbach is buried in one of the few plots that was available near his friend, Sgt. Kurtz. Sgt. Kutschbach is buried amid the family plots of families named Reisch, Bramwell, Johnson and Potter.

One of the tombstones in the Bramwell plot caught my eye. It was for Laura Elizabeth Brammel, who died on Nov. 10 of 2000. She was only 15. The tombstone message read: "Our Daughter—Beautiful Wonderful and Perfect In Every Way."

Thanksgiving and Christmas were coming soon, I thought, and my daughters, Sarah and Rebecca, would be coming home, Sarah for Thanksgiving and Rebecca for Christmas. I was looking forward to seeing them in their respective rooms again. Any parent can appreciate that; you know the feeling.

There was a mention in the obituary for Staff Sgt. Kutschbach that asked, in lieu of flowers, that donations could be made to a school tuition savings account for year-old Bastian Kutschbach. I asked my wife Kathie to send a check for $25 as a Thanksgiving gesture from our family to his family, thanking him for his service to our country. I loved the note she wrote. "I've been living with you long enough to know the right message," she said with a smile.

I would urge you to consider a Christmas gift to this fund. Make the checks payable to Fidelity, and mail to Gina Nicastro, All-State Insurance Company, 52 Sharpsville Ave., Sharon, PA 16146. It seems like the right thing to do.

> **"Like Yogi Bear used to say, I'm smarter than the average bear."**
> **— Dwight White**

Billy "Ace" Adams
My first sports hero

Billy "Ace" Adams, a terrific all-around athlete who quarterbacked the J.J. Doyles of Hazelwood, one of the outstanding sandlot football teams in Greater Pittsburgh back in the '50s, was inducted into the Minor League Football Hall of Fame on June 7, 2008. The ceremony took place at the Western Pennsylvania Sports Museum at the Heinz History Center in Pittsburgh. Major Harris, a former quarterback at Brashear High School and West Virginia University, was in the same induction class. Tom Averell, who looks after the legacies of the great players who performed in minor league competition, presented the award to Adams whose family was present for the ceremony. Adams, age 79, called me in advance to thank me for my support for his induction. I was pleased to have played a minor part in his just recognition. It completed the cycle for my lifetime of admiration for "Ace" Adams.

July 12, 2000

I bumped into my boyhood sports hero last week and we had a good time reminiscing. What I learned only reinforced my feeling that I had picked a good person to look up to as a young child. His name, believe it or not, is Billy "Ace" Adams. It's a name right out of the sports books I read as a youth, those inspirational fictional tales told by the likes of John R. Tunis and Clair Bee, among others.

"Ace" Adams excelled at all sports. There wasn't anything he couldn't do. He was a scholastic and sandlot sports star. He gained his nickname at age 14.

He never made it to the big leagues or made big money with his sports skills, but he remains a good model, as I discovered in our conversations over a four-day stretch. So many sports stars today disappoint us with their behavior, but Adams remains an admirable figure.

Forbes Field and Pitt Stadium were only four miles from our hometown, but we didn't get to go there often. The Pirates and Steelers were seldom on TV. So pro sports stars lived in another world, a magic kingdom. We tended to identify more with our sandlot stars. We could see them up close, shag flies in the outfield during pre-game warm-ups, or catch passes from them on the sidelines. They were a big deal.

Kids today have no such experiences. It was great to be out on the field when the lights were on.

Adams was in attendance at the West Penn & National Collegiate Clay Court Tennis Championships at the Martin L. Tressel Tennis Center in Mt. Lebanon. He didn't start playing tennis until he was 37 years old, but he has been a U. S. Tennis Assn.-certified pro instructor the past 25 years.

He has given tennis lessons on courts in Upper St. Clair, at Hidden Valley Tennis Club in McMurray, Washington Plaza, South Park and Monroeville.

No one played tennis in our hometown of Hazelwood. There was never a net to be found on the only public tennis court in the community.

Adams was the quarterback of our local sandlot football team, one of the best in Pittsburgh. The team was called the J.J. Doyles. They played their home games at Burgwin Field. That's where I first saw him in action and came to admire him.

He starred in soccer, baseball, basketball, hockey and diving. During his Taylor Allderdice High School days, he was the City League diving champion and finished runner-up in the PIAA competition. He would later play squash, golf and tennis. I continually hear from people about how Adams assisted them somehow to learn how to play this game or that game, or simply extended some random act of kindness on their behalf. That's the Ace Adams I've known all my life. He looked after people from the beginning. It's just his nature.

He was offered a scholarship to attend the University of Miami to play football, but he had gotten married and had to go to work.

Things were different then. It was the mid-40s. Today, Adams would have better channeled his athletic abilities, concentrating on fewer sports. He'd have lifted weights and would've been directed to go to college.

He ended up going to Carnegie Tech—as it was called then—to play football and basketball at the age of 27. He stayed two years, plus some night school, which was twice as long as most athletes from our hometown lasted in college or in the minor leagues before they'd return home to work in the mills. Billy Adams wasn't called "Ace" for his academic acumen. Tech was too tough for him in that respect.

My friend Bob Milie was the backfield coach at Carnegie Tech when Adams was a student there. He and Earl Birdy, who was a swimming coach and physical education instructor, speak fondly of Adams. Milie came out of East Liberty and Birdy out of Hazelwood and both are the best guys you'd want to know, so it's fitting that they admire Adams.

The quarterback at CMU who is still best remembered is the late Howard Harpster, who led Carnegie Tech in its finest days back in the '30s when they beat Notre Dame at Forbes Field. That's when Pitt, Tech and Duquesne all played football on the highest college level. One year they all played in major bowl games, and Tech was in the Orange Bowl. Dick Swanson, Harpster's son-in-law and a major Pitt fan who lives on Mt. Washington, loves to talk about the late Howard Harpster and his heroics. There is a walkway under the stands that leads to the football field at CMU that is named in honor of Howard Harpster. So he's still a big man on campus.

Adams got into sales, working for several companies. He was good at it. People liked Adams. He was an affable soul, with a constant smile on that lantern jaw, an easy conversationalist with an unassuming manner about him.

He was popular. That was pointed up by the number of passersby who offered greetings and a kind word or two at the West Penn Tennis Tournament. Rege McDonough, a plumber from Mt. Lebanon who plays a pretty fair game of tennis himself, spoke of Adam's ability and smarts on the tennis courts. "People like to play with him," said McDonough.

Adams was 71 when we spoke at the West Penn event. How can that be possible? I was 14 when he was 28 and in his second season as the quarterback at Carnegie Tech, and getting some ink in the Pittsburgh newspapers. He was always bow-legged, but now he has balky knees, too, which remind him of his age.

I learned last week that he never smoked or drank—his dad, like mine, did enough of both to teach him that wasn't such a smart idea. He's been married to Lenore Heilmann for 51 years. He's lived in Brentwood for 40 years, yet when anyone asks him where he's from he always says Hazelwood.

He was boasting about his grandkids and what they were doing in sports. One of them is Michael Dugan, a 16-year-old hockey player from Mt. Lebanon. It sounded as if each of them was a chip off the old block. I sometimes bump into Tom Adams, a son of "Ace" Adams, who lives in Butler. He likes to tell people that I was his first baseball coach, and that I saw his father play sports when I was a young sportswriter. It was an honor in both cases.

Jim O'Brien

Backs John Mamajek and Billy "Ace" Adams, both members of the Western Pennsylvania Minor Football League Hall of Fame, flank their coach John Howard of J.J. Doyles fame.

Bob Friend
Reflects on Baseball All-Star Game

July 11, 2007

A good reputation is hard to come by and it requires life-long maintenance to remain intact. Bob Friend, now age 76, is held in the highest regard by those who know him.

Friend was one of the finest pitchers in Pirates' history. He was known for never missing a turn, going to the mound every fourth or fifth day and doing his best for the Bucs. He was the ace of the staff, along with Vernon Law, back in the '50s and '60s.

Steve Blass and Lanny Frattare were talking about Friend during a recent Pirates' radio broadcast. They mentioned that he pitched 163 complete games, a statistic that today's pitchers will never approach. His record of 161 complete games with the Pirates is still a team record, and he had two more complete games in his final season spent in New York, divided between playing for the Mets and the Yankees. How many can say they played for both of those teams in the same season?

Today, it's considered "a quality start" if the pitcher lasts six innings. Friend says he never missed a start in his 16 years as a Pirate. He averaged nearly 32 starts a season.

He won 197 games, 191 as a Pirate. That's more than any Pirates' pitcher in the past 75 years. His 22 victories in a season (1958) have not been equaled since then. One wonders what he would have accomplished if he had pitched for a better team.

Blass said he was fortunate when he broke in to have Friend as a roommate and mentor. "That's when you had a roommate," offered Blass. "He showed me the ropes, told me what to do, how to pitch, where to go, where to eat, how to behave. He really helped me. His wife Pat helped my wife Karen get established. They gave us some furniture."

After all these years, Blass still can be counted upon to mention Friend in the friendliest of terms during summer baseball broadcasts.

Nowadays Friend is still a reliable fellow, still looking after others and helping where he can. He shows up at least once a week this time of year at one of the hundreds of charity-related golf outings held in this area, and travels the country with invitations to participate in similar outings. They know Friend will show up and be friendly with his foursome, something some celebrities neglect to do.

Through the years, I have found Friend to be one of the most approachable athletes I've met. I can call him on the telephone to check with him on something from the Pirates' past. He never acts like you've interrupted something. His wife Pat is just as polite and easy to talk to.

I learned a valuable lesson from Bob Friend a few years back. His son, Bobby Jr., a fine golfer, relayed the lesson to me that he had learned from his father. He said "My father is the best man I've ever known." He also said that his father told him that when you make a commitment you have to keep it, and you can't change your mind when a better or more inviting offer comes along. "That's right," the elder Friend said when I reminded him of what his son had said to me. "You have to be good for your word."

(Friend's words came to mind when I was scheduled to speak at a dinner one night in Coraopolis. The weather was bad. It had been snowing all day and I don't like driving on bad roads. I wanted to stay home. But I went. I had given the sponsors my word. When I got there, I learned that several of the speakers had called to say they weren't coming. When I got home that night, safely, I was glad I went. But the drive home was scary. I blamed Bob Friend for putting me in danger.)

Two weeks ago, I found Friend and several of his former teammates, such as Bill Mazeroski, El Roy Face and Don Schwall, at the Homestead Lions annual outing that Darrell Hess coordinates at Westwood Golf Club in West Mifflin. This past Monday Friend was one of the early arrivals at Frattare's annual golf outing for Family Links at the St. Clair Country Club. That organization used to be known as the Family & Child Guidance Center in Banksville.

Blass and Kent Tekulve of Upper St. Clair, along with Pirates manager Jim Tracy, were among the celebrities for the Family Links outing. Frattare's wife, Christine, helped coordinate the event.

Friend and his wife, the former Pat Koval of Houston, Pa. who was a nurse for the Pirates' team physician, Dr. Joseph Feingold, are a great couple. They were planning to go to New York this weekend to help honor his former teammate, Ralph Kiner, the long-time announcer for the New York Mets. "We were honored to be invited," said Bob Friend. By coincidence, the Friends were married in New York following a Pirates' game there with the Giants.

Pat urged Bob to tell me a story about one of his three All-Star Game appearances. He pitched in the 1956, 1958 and 1960 All-Star Games.

I asked Bob to repeat his story when I rode with him in a golf cart for a few holes at St. Clair Country Club this past Monday, the day before the Major League All-Star Game in San Francisco.

Friend was the starting and winning pitcher in the 1956 All-Star Game at Griffith Stadium in Washington, D.C.

He gave up three hits, struck out three batters, and gave up no runs in the All-Star Game stint. He struck out Mickey Mantle and Yogi Berra of the New York Yankees and Ted Williams of the Boston Red Sox.

"I struck out Ted Williams with the bases loaded for my last out," recalled Friend. "I have a photographic memory of everything I did in baseball. The count was three-and-two and I threw him a curve inside. It was a hard curve. He swung and missed. I can see it like it was yesterday."

Pat had prompted him to add to that anecdote. "Tell him the story," urged Pat, "about when you and our son Bobby bumped into Ted Williams at the airport in Atlanta."

Bob smiled and continued. "Bobby and I were walking through the airport about 15 years after that All-Star Game and I spotted Williams and went up to him. I said, 'Hi, Ted, I'm Bob Friend; it's nice to see you. This is my son, Bobby.'

"And Williams looked at me, and said, 'I remember you. You know, I never thought you'd curve me.' Bobby just stood there with his mouth open. He couldn't believe what he'd just heard Williams say."

"You remember pitches like that?" I asked.

"I'd remember it because it was Ted Williams," said Bob. "That was my last out in the All-Star Game that year."

The All-Star Game was a bigger deal then. The National League and American League players only competed against each other in the All-Star Game and World Series in those days. The game was more important.

"It was a great honor to be on the All-Star team," said Friend. "We took it quite seriously. I was twice invited by Walter Alston of the Dodgers to be on the team. It meant you were one of the best in the game. There were some great pitchers back then, like Robin Roberts and Warren Spahn, and it was nice to be on the same playing field with the best."

Bob Friend of Pirates and Billy Pierce of Chicago White Sox were starting pitchers in 1956 Baseball All-Star Game at Griffith Stadium in Washington D.C. Friend struck out Ted Williams with the bases loaded.

Jack Riley
An awesome afternoon in the life of Riley

October 4, 2007

Jim O'Brien

J ack Riley just kept repeating himself. "This is awesome!" he'd say. "This is amazing! I can't believe this!" Riley was sitting in a front row seat in a private suite along the first base line at PNC Park to see the Pirates play the Arizona Diamondbacks last Thursday afternoon. Riley wasn't reflecting on the play of any of the Pirates or D'Backs, but rather his surroundings.

He couldn't get over PNC Park. The Pirates completed their seventh season at PNC Park on the city's North Shore last Sunday, but this was the first time Riley had attended a game there.

Riley, age 88, was the original general manager of the Pittsburgh Penguins and put the team together back in 1967. That's 40 years ago. I remember that well because I married Kathleen Churchman the summer before the Penguins played their first season at the Civic Arena, now known as the Mellon Arena.

Riley remains one of the good guys in Pittsburgh sports. He has always been easy to see, easy to talk to, and never thought he was a big deal. When State Senator Jack McGregor and Peter Block and a group of investors put together an NHL team they were smart to hire Riley to run the hockey side of things.

Riley did two stints as the team's GM under four different owners in those difficult, often frustrating early years in the National Hockey League. He has resided in the same home in Scott Township since he first signed on with the original owners back in 1966. He's been a popular and familiar figure on the Pittsburgh sports scene ever since.

He still plays a fair game of golf. "I used to be able to shoot in the '80s, but I can't do that anymore," related Riley. "I just play at golf now. I'm not very good at it anymore." I saw him in August, 2007 at the Penguins' Annual Alumni Golf Outing at the Valley Brook Country Club in McMurray. I know he gets out on occasion, so I was stunned to learn that he'd never attended a game at PNC Park. (He never misses a Penguins' home game.)

I have friends and neighbors who have never been there either. It made me wonder how many Pittsburghers who profess to be sports fans have never seen a game at PNC Park, Heinz Field, Pitt's Peterson Events Center or Mellon Arena for that matter. Riley follows sports on TV and radio and in the newspapers, yet this was his first day at PNC Park. "This is awesome, this is amazing!" he'd say to the next person he spoke to in the suite. "I can't believe this!"

He was a guest of Joe Gordon, best known as the former public relations director of the Steelers. Gordon served the Penguins in a similar capacity, as well as the Pittsburgh Hornets and even the Pittsburgh Rens of the old American Basketball League before that. Bill Heufelder, who covered the early Penguins for *The Pittsburgh Press*, sat next to Riley. Gordon took Riley on a tour of PNC Park.

"I can't believe this ballpark; it may the best in baseball," observed Riley when he returned. "I can't imagine what the new arena for the Penguins will look like."

Pittsburgh's L.D. Astorino Architects and HOK Sport of Kansas City designed PNC Park. There's 2.2 acres of Kentucky bluegrass and that caught Riley's eyes. "It reminds me of the first time I went into a big-time baseball park back in Toronto," said Riley. "And that was 70 years ago. Seeing all that green grass, and the white lines. I'll never forget that. This brings my boyhood back to mind."

Maple Leaf Stadium in Toronto was owned by Jack Kent Cooke, who would later own the Los Angeles Lakers of the NBA and the Los Angeles Kings of the NHL, and would be one of the promoters of the first Ali-Frazier heavyweight championship fights—billed as "The Fight of the Century"—at New York's Madison Square Garden.

King decided it would be a good idea to put a hockey franchise in Los Angeles when he learned that there were 350,000 Canadians living in the greater metropolitan area. When his team didn't draw well, at first, King commented, "I think those Canadians came here because they hated hockey." I remember entering the Toronto Maple Leaf Gardens once, back in the late '60s in the company of Riley, and having him point out all the famous hockey players pictured on the wall. There were players pictured such as Syl Apps Sr., Charlie Conacher, King Clancy, Tim Horton, Red Kelly, Johnny Bower and Turk Broda. I remember that all the male fans in the best seats near the ice wore business suits to the game at that time.

I remember on that same visit to Toronto that one day I was about to enter the Royal York Hotel, and I spotted jazz legend Erroll Garner exiting the hotel. I stopped him and introduced myself. "I'm Jim O'Brien, a newspaperman from Pittsburgh," I said. He smiled and shook my hand warmly.

"Can I ask you a question?" I said.

He smiled and simply nodded.

"How do you account for the fact that so many great jazz musicians," I began, "such as you, Dakota Stanton, Lena Horne, Earl 'Fatha' Hines, Mary Lou Williams, Ahmad Jamal, George Benson and Billy Eckstine and others, all came out of Pittsburgh?"

He bowed his head—his hair was shiny black—and he stroked that dark goatee of his a moment, and looked up at me bemused. "Maybe because we were all born there," he said.

I was expecting something a little deeper, more philosophical perhaps, but when I think about Garner's remark now I have to smile and appreciate its wisdom.

"Pittsburgh is where I had fun."
—Syl Apps Jr.
Penguins Hall of Fame

Mario Lemieux and Jack Riley were inducted into the Penguins' Hall of Fame with Craig Patrick, left, and Paul Steigerwald, as presenters for the ceremonies in February, 2000.

Penguins Alumni Golf Outing in 2007 brought together, first row left to right: Duane Rupp, Pierre Larouche, Denis Herron, Mario Lemieux, Bryan Trottier, Eddie Johnston and Jack Riley. Second row: Ken Sawyer, Eddie Gilbert, Dave Hansen, Pierre Leroux, Warren Young, Randy Hillier and Dave Morehouse. Third row: J.S. Aubin, Dennis Owchar, Kenny Wregget, Phil Bourque, Mike Yeo and Kim Clackson.

Riley remembered the Royal York as well. "It was the best hotel in Toronto at that time," he recalled.

You don't forget meeting the great ones. I related to Riley how I remembered meeting the great Maurice "The Rocket" Richard and Jean Beliveau in the press room at The Forum in Montreal when I was covering the Islanders for *The New York Post*. Richard was one of Riley's hockey heroes, and he admired Beliveau as well. "Rocket was the best I ever saw from the blue line in," remarked Riley. "He was absolutely obsessed with scoring goals."

He had seen a lot of hockey greats in his time, more than any other Pittsburgher, I'd bet. Riley estimates he has attended, as a player, coach, scout and front-office official and retired fan over 4,000 hockey games. Yet this was his first Pirates' game at PNC Park. It had to be special.

Riley has seen it all in his 40 years in Pittsburgh. I tested him and he remembered that the first Penguin was goalie Les Binkley, signed from the Cleveland Barons the year before the Penguins started playing. Riley recalled that Joe Daley was the first Penguin picked in the goalie draft that preceded the regular expansion draft. The NHL had expanded from six teams to twelve in one swoop for the 1967–68 season. The Pittsburgh Pipers with Connie Hawkins were formed that same season. Winger Earl Ingarfield of the New York Rangers was the first player chosen by the Penguins. They later got a steal in Andy Bathgate of the Rangers.

"Our entire payroll that first year for 20 players was $315,000," said Riley. "The lowest player in the NHL makes that much today." Riley was paid $25,000 and Red Sullivan, the coach, was paid $17,000 that year. By comparison, my wife Kathie was paid $7,000 that year as a social worker at Presbyterian University Hospital.

"The Penguins got lucky when Mario Lemieux came along, and then they won the lottery again when they got Sidney Crosby," said Riley. "Everyone wants to compare Crosby with Lemieux and Wayne Gretzky, but he's different.

"They might have been more clever, but he's stronger in the corners and along the boards. He's got legs like oak trees. He's a very competitive kid. I can only compare him to Bobby Orr. He played defense and led the league in scoring. I've talked to Sid and I'm impressed with his maturity. He always does and says the right thing. He never says the wrong thing. Like Lemieux and Gretzky, he's not selfish and he cares about the other players. He cares about the game and its history. He's a bit of Bobby Orr, a bit of Mario Lemieux and a bit of Wayne Gretzky.

"I told Crosby about Bobby Orr. I still think he was the greatest hockey player of them all. He revolutionized the game, a defenseman who could lead his team in scoring. Bobby would stop the puck at one end and then lead the charge up the ice. He was a defenseman who led the league in scoring two years in a row.

"Lemieux and Gretzky were better scorers than Crosby. They were great passers, both of them. Crosby is a little different. He wins

Back in early '70s, Coach Red Kelly, center, and GM Jack Riley are flanked by County Commissioners, left to right, Tom Foerster, Leonard Staisey and Dr. William Hunt on Penguins Day in Pittsburgh

Jack Riley congratulates Syl Apps Jr. and Dave Burrows for being inducted into the Penguins' Hall of Fame in April, 1995.

battles along the boards and he looks after himself well. He doesn't need a bodyguard out there.

"Mario was here when we won two Stanley Cups. He and Gretzky were a couple of seconds ahead of everyone else in their thinking. They were anticipating passing and shooting before they did it. It's hard for anyone to touch them.

"Crosby comes to play. He's won a scoring title and he's won the Hart Trophy as the most valuable player in the league. The best is ahead of him if he stays healthy. I think Crosby and Pittsburgh are a good match. He likes it here. He's a bigger deal in Canada and does more commercials there, but I think he can lead a more normal existence here. Everyone knows him in Canada. They knew him before the NHL draft. They all wanted him, but Pittsburgh won the lottery and got him. I think the team can go a long way with him at the lead.

"He stays in good condition during the off-season. You couldn't hope for more. He reminds me of Orr because he's so gung-ho. I don't know who's the greatest. I can name a couple of hockey players who were pretty outstanding. When I first got involved in hockey, I was talking to Bob Davis, a coach of the Hornets. I asked him who was the greatest he ever saw. He said Howie Morenz of the Montreal Canadians. Now he came along before me, but they say he was the speediest hockey player on ice in his day. They say he could fly.

"There are more players in the NHL today and they're better conditioned. You go into a clubhouse today and you see all the exercise and weight machines. Our guys would come into camp with bellies from the summer. The season was shorter and they had more time to get out of shape. Overall, the players today are better. I don't know if the competition is as intense. There were some real rivalries built up when you played only five other teams all winter.

"I think Ovechkin with the Washington Senators is probably a super hockey player. He wants to score goals. He goes after that puck and wants to put it in the nets. That Russian team in the next Winter Olympics (2010) is going to be special.

"I've talked to Crosby on a couple of occasions. I introduced myself and he was genuinely interested in what I had to say. He wasn't like some guys today who say hello and goodbye in the same sentence. He asked about the old days. I can't find anything to knock this kid. He's a good kid and a wonderful hockey player. I told him about some of the good ones we had here that he may not have heard about, such as Syl Apps, Jean Pronovost and Pierre Larouche. I think Michel Briere was going to be a good one, too, but he got killed young in an auto accident. Les Binkley was one of our best as a goaltender. He had six shutouts in our first season in the NHL.

"They're very fortunate to have gotten the great players they've had. Don't forget Jaromir Jagr, too. They've picked up some good players. That (Evgeni) Malkin kid is a different type of hockey player than Crosby, but he's going to be one of the best, too. It's hard for me to think that they can't get to the Stanley Cup finals. They've got a great young goalie in (Marc-Andre) Fleury. He was well coached as a goalie by Gilles Melloche. The new guy (Marian) Hossa is one of the strongest and fastest skaters they've got. He looks like a guy who can be as good as he wants to be. Then you've got (Jordan) Staal and that (Ryan) Malone is playing excellent hockey. I think Ray Shero will do a great job as general manager. He comes from a hockey family, and he knows the game and what it takes to put a championship team on the ice. His dad did it in Philadelphia with the Flyers a few times.

"They were lucky to get someone like Sidney. He's something special. It was like winning the million-dollar lottery. He asked me if I ever saw 'Rocket' Richard play. And I did. He was a great one. He scored 50 goals in a 50-game season when there were only six teams. Each team had six defensemen, so he was playing against the 30 best defensemen night after night. Now there are about 180 to 190 defensemen in the National Hockey League. There were only 90 players in the NHL back then. Now there are 600.

"Back then, when there were only six teams, each city had a trainer or an equipment man who was the backup goalie, and that was for either side. Can you imagine one team's trainer playing goalkeeper for the visiting team? That's the way it was. Baz Bastien was a great goalkeeper for the Hornets here, but he couldn't get an opportunity to play in the NHL. Then he lost an eye in a training camp accident while he was here, and that cost him his playing career. There's a lot of good hockey history here. The Penguins picked up some other terrific young players at the same time they came by Crosby. I don't think they'll win the Stanley Cup this season, but they can go a long way in the playoffs. They're on their way to the top. They say they lack experience, but sometimes experience breeds laziness. I think there is so much promise with this club. Hey, I see where a cup of beer here costs $6.50! I could get a case of beer at that price when I was a young man. I haven't been in any of the new buildings in the NHL, but I have a feeling the Penguins will get it right, and have one of the best, just like this ballpark."

Jim O'Brien

Jack Riley dons classic Penguins jacket from the team's first season. The colors then were dark blue, light blue and white. Red Sullivan, the coach at the time, has the only other jacket like this one. They were produced by the Pittsburgh Sports Shop. "Mine's in pristine shape," boasts Riley. "I've not worn mine. Red says his is worn to shreds."

Thumbnail sketches on some of the players Jack Riley refers to when comparing the Penguins' Sidney Crosby to some of the great ones of the past:

HOWIE MORENZ—He was known for having great speed and a hard shot. "His shot was just like a bullet," recalled King Clancy of the legendary center who starred for the Montreal Canadiens, Chicago Black Hawks and New York Rangers from 1923 to 1937. He won two scoring crowns and was named the league's most valuable player three times. He broke his leg in five places when he jammed into the boards in an NHL game and, while recovering in a hospital, died at the age of 34 from blood clots. His funeral was unlike any seen before in Canada. On March 11, 1937, Howie Morenz's body lay in state at center ice in the Montreal Forum and a reported 50,000 mourners passed his casket, and an estimated 250,000 people lined the route of his funeral procession.

MAURICE "THE ROCKET" RICHARD—He was a folk hero in French Canada. He was one of the toughest and greatest goal-scorers in NHL history. "I had the same kind of determination from the time I was a boy of 7 or 8," he once said. He was a hometown hero, born in Montreal in August of 1921. He spent his entire career with the club from 1942 to 1960. Richard's record of 50 goals in 50 games, set during the 1944-45 season, stood until Mike Bossy of the New York Islanders equaled his achievement in 1981. Richard was the ultimate clutch player and was best known for his performances in the Stanley Cup playoffs. There was one game, against the Maple Leafs, in which he was named the first, second and third star of the game. "I wanted to win all the time," he said. "I wanted to score goals; that's all I wanted to do."

WAYNE GRETZKY—He set 61 scoring records before he retired from the NHL at the end of the 1998-1999 season. He had great natural gifts, but he was also a hard worker as well as an outstanding ambassador for the league. He was much more comfortable in the spotlight than Mario Lemieux, for instance. He dominated the NHL, most notably with his 92-goal, 120-assist 1981-1982 campaign, and his 52-goal, 163-assist 1985-1986 season. He led Edmonton to four Stanley Cups. "Kids grow up dreaming about holding up the Stanley Cup," he once said. "That dream fuels you in the playoffs. I couldn't beat people with my strength. My eyes and my mind have to do most of the work." His trade to the LA Kings was considered a national tragedy in Canada, but it helped popularize the sport in America. After a short year in St. Louis, he went to New York and played with the Rangers where he was a Broadway star. He was an All-Star 15 times and won the Ross Trophy ten times and the Hart Trophy nine times.

MARIO LEMIEUX—He scored on the first shift of his first NHL game with his first shot on net. No other player ever made a more auspicious debut. The Pittsburgh Penguins rejected all sorts of trade offers to pick Lemieux first in the 1984 entry draft. "Super Mario" dethroned Gretzky as the league's scoring champion with 168 points in the 1987-88 season and led the Penguins to consecutive Stanley Cup titles. He won another scoring title in 1991–92 season, but was admired even more for what he did the following season. He was diagnosed with Hodgkin's disease and underwent two months of grueling radiation treatment before rejoining the Penguins. He retired once after the 1996-97 season, but came out of retirement in 2000 when the team's financial future was in jeopardy and pumped new life into the franchise before retiring for good after the 2003–2004 season. He's known for twice saving professional hockey in Pittsburgh, as a player and as an owner. He opened his home to newcomer Sidney Crosby when he came to Pittsburgh, and provided him with a comfortable place to reside while far from his home in Nova Scotia.

BOBBY ORR—He revolutionized the game of professional hockey with his offensive-minded play as a stout defenseman with the NHL's Boston Bruins (1966-78). He set offensive records, twice winning the Art Ross Trophy as the NHL's leading scorer and finishing runner-up to teammate Phil Esposito three times. In the 1970–71 season, Orr set the high mark for assists and total points by a defenseman, with 37 goals and 102 assists, a record that still stands. He won the Norris Trophy eight consecutive years. He led the Boston Bruins to two Stanley Cup titles. He had bad knees that limited his career to less than ten years. He was finished at the age of 30. "Losing Bobby Orr," said Gordie Howe, another great player, "was the biggest blow the NHL has ever suffered."

Jim O'Brien

Young fans flock to Mario Lemieux's Celebrity Golf Tournament at The Club at Nevillewood.

"I consider myself a Pittsburgher. This is my town."
— **Mario Lemieux**
Summer of '99

Bill Baierl
Pitt's Mr. Basketball

"His was a lifetime of generosity."
—Chancellor Mark Nordenberg,

University of Pittsburgh Chancellor Mark Nordenberg and two of the school's most loyal sons, Bill Baierl and Tom Bigley, were walking down a street in Atlanta. Nordenberg found a penny on the sidewalk and picked it up. "A lucky penny," he announced.

"Mark, that won't bring you any luck," came back Baierl, "unless you give it to someone."

That remark remained with Nordenberg. He thought about it when Pitt completed a wildly successful capital campaign drive, and when he was the featured eulogist at the memorial service for Bill Baierl when the Pittsburgh auto mogul died a few weeks later on April 14, 2007. The service took place on April 19.

"Bill was the greatest," said Nordenberg. "He was a great businessman. His most basic gift was to the community. His commitment to giving back was extraordinary. His was a lifetime of generosity."

Rev. E. David Streets, the pastor of the Ingomar United Methodist Church where the viewing and the memorial service were held, asked everyone in the church who had directly benefited from Baierl's generosity to stand up. Nearly eighty percent of those in attendance rose in unison. I was one of them. It was like a revival meeting. The reflections on Baierl and remembrances of things he had said were inspirational.

Nordenberg, Baierl and Bigley were in Atlanta to attend the NCAA Basketball Final Four Tournament. They had done some sightseeing while there. Bigley told me they had visited the Ebenezer Baptist Church, where Dr. Martin Luther King Jr. had preached and served as pastor. They were walking near their hotel when Chancellor Nordenberg found the penny. Bill Baierl was known as "Mr. Basketball" at Pitt. He had grown up on the city's North Side, graduated from Allegheny High School, and came to Pitt and played basketball, as a reserve forward, for Doc Carlson's teams, lettering in 1949 and 1950.

He had majored in education and hoped to get a position as a teacher and do some coaching. He couldn't find an opening. So he went to work in 1954 with his cousin, Bob Baierl, at a Chevrolet dealership that the family had just opened in Ambridge. The rest is history.

The dealership was relocated to Wexford, where it thrived. Today, Baierl Automotive includes nine different dealerships in the North Hills, and employs over 450 people. Lee Baierl, the second cousin of Bill Baierl, has succeeded him as president of Baierl Chevrolet Inc., and Baierl Automotive. Lee has been in the business since 1980 and he often accompanied his father and his cousin in their travels so he knows the Baierl legacy well. I first met Lee Baierl when he was about 12 or 13 and his "Uncle Bill," as he called his older cousin in those days,

Bill Baierl, Lee Baierl and Jim O'Brien get together at Pitt social at home of Linda and Frank Gustine Jr.

Father Francis Fagini of St. Augustine in Lawrenceville joins Jack McGinley Jr. and Jack McGinley Sr. for lunch at Del's in Bloomfield. Jack Sr. owned the Wilson-McGinley Beer Distributing Co. in Lawrenceville. The McGinleys own 20 percent of the Steelers.

used to bring him to Pitt sports events. I remember sharing a box of popcorn with him at the Pitt Field House. He was called "Butch" back then.

I met Bill's dad, also Bill but often referred to as "Uncle Ben," and Bill's brother, Ralph. They both worked in the family business. Ralph Baierl had been a lineman for Maryland's national championship football team in 1953 under Jim Tatum. Eddie Vereb, from my hometown of Hazelwood and Central Catholic High School, was an All-American halfback on that Terrapins' team. Ralph's wife, Nancy Baierl, did some decorating in our home in Upper St. Clair.

Bill Baierl was known for being a big guy with a big heart, yet it was his heart that failed him. He had been challenged for several years with heart problems. I was aware of the serious state of his health challenges. At one of our last meetings, he told me his doctor said he couldn't do anything more to mend his ailing heart. Even so, it was difficult to accept the news of his death. He was one of those larger-than-life figures. It didn't seem right that he had died, not at 78. He didn't look 78. He had always brightened every room he entered. He had the big smile, the gleam in his eye, the hardy handshake. He was always so positive, so optimistic. He married late in life, but came up with a winner in Carole Smith, a legal secretary when they first met.

"All of us were shocked when Mr. Baierl died," said Anna Eichler, his long-time secretary and receptionist.

He had recently lost two of his dearest friends, Tom Carmody, a basketball coach and business school administrator, and Tom "Maniac" McDonough, a retired insurance salesman whom he frequently lunched with and who had been one of his regulars in his Big East entourage. So Bill knew his turn would come.

Bill Baierl had celebrated his 78th birthday on March 26, 2007. It had been the best of months for Bill Baierl. Nobody loved March Madness any more than Bill Baierl, and that's because it had basketball and more basketball, plus his birthday. He had gone to New York for the Big East Basketball Tournament at Madison Square Garden with his wife, Carole, and his best friends, as he did every year. Tom Maloney, the former basketball coach at North Hills High School, was another of Bill's buddies who went to the Big East Tournament with him every year.

Baierl was there from March 8–11. He saw Pitt beat Marquette and Louisville before succumbing to Georgetown in the semi-final round.

Then he went to Buffalo to follow Pitt in the first and second rounds of the NCAA Basketball Tournament. The Panthers beat Wright State and Virginia Commonwealth. He went to San Jose, California, where Pitt was defeated 64–56 by UCLA, coached by Ben Howland who had previously resurrected Pitt's basketball program before turning it over to his top assistant, Jamie Dixon.

Howland made a one-day trip from Los Angeles to attend Baierl's funeral service. Dixon was sitting in front of the Ingomar United Methodist Church as well. Three former Pitt basketball players were pallbearers. Charles Smith, Billy Knight and Frank Gustine had remained close to Bill Baierl through the years. He had helped them all.

Agnus Berenato, the Pitt women's basketball coach, and Carol Sprague, the senior associate athletic director, had brought the women's basketball team in a bus to both a viewing session and to the memorial service a day later. That's the kind of regard and respect they had for Bill Baierl.

"When you think of Pitt's favorite people," Chancellor Nordenberg said during the service, "Bill Baierl is near the top of the list. He's one of the region's best-known and respected businessmen. His name is synonymous with Pitt athletics."

There is a Baierl Athletic Center with exercise and conditioning equipment that athletes and students alike utilize at the Petersen Events Center. He endowed several scholarships at his alma mater. He was one of the first movers and shakers in the athletic department's "Wheels of Support" program. He not only provided automobiles for coaches and administrators, but he talked other automobile dealers into doing the same to support the program. He was on the board of the former North Side Bank.

He was one of my first angels. Beano Cook, the sports information director at Pitt, and I started *Pittsburgh Weekly Sports*, a tabloid devoted to the city's sports scene in 1963, my senior year at Pitt. We kept it going on a shoestring budget for four-and-a-half years. Baierl Chevrolet ("The Little Profit Dealer") and Frankie Gustine's Restaurant in Oakland were our first and most loyal advertisers. Frank Haller of BBD&O got us a regular ad from Vern Staley Dodge.

"I bought the last car I owned at Baierl," boasted Beano Cook when I called him in late May, 2007 for his reflections on Bill Baierl. Cook has a large bank account, mind you, but he doesn't tap it too often. "It was a 1963 Corvair. I paid $1800 for it. I leased a car from him for two years later on. But if I ever bought another car I would've bought it from Baierl. He was a great guy."

The high price of gasoline doesn't concern Cook, who lives in a downtown apartment and is able to secure a ride when he requires one.

Baierl and Frank Gustine Jr., a son of the former popular Pirates' infielder who owned the landmark restaurant on the Pitt campus for over 30 years, have been patrons of my book writing and publishing efforts from the start in 1979. Baierl helped the younger Gustine get started in the commercial real estate business. Tom Bigley and Mark Nordenberg have supported my efforts as well.

Bill Baierl came to the wedding reception at the Croatian Club in Duquesne when Kathleen Churchman and I were married on August 12, 1967. Baierl had been to a top-drawer wedding reception in Beverly Hills the week before. He said they served roasted duck under glass. I'm sure we had some kind of chicken and a buffet meal at the Croatian Club. Looking up at Kathie and me when we stopped at his table, Baierl said, "The food here was better. This was more fun."

Bill Baierl was ever the booster. He kissed the bride and he gave her a kiss on the cheek every time he saw her in the following years. I was one of his loyal customers. There was a time when both of my daughters came to visit our home that there were four cars in my driveway that had been purchased at Baierl Automotive.

He held an annual Christmas party for his staff and friends, and he gave out copies of my books as presents. Now Lee Baierl plans to do the same. I am grateful for the continuance of the Baierl support.

"If you can sell yourself you can sell anything."
—Bill Baierl

We all learned a lot from Bill Baierl. In more recent years, I often was his guest for lunch at Carmody's Restaurant or Atria's Restaurant & Tavern in Wexford. I would invite him, but he always insisted on picking up the tab. So many people would stop at the table to say hello to Bill Baierl. He'd provided the seed money to build a new YMCA in the North Hills. Development Officer Rosemary Mendel considered Baierl her best ally. He sent a lot of checks to the local schools. He gave millions to Pitt. People knew business was never a one-way street with Bill Baierl. He opposed the demolition of Pitt Stadium, and helped fund a protest movement, but never balked about the plans publicly. He thought he had a deal completed to have his family's name on the new basketball facility but that didn't happen. He was disappointed,but he still continued to give major gifts to Pitt.

John Wesley, who founded the Methodist Church, had said, "Do all the good you can," and Bill Baierl believed in that principle.

Chancellor Nordenberg recalled the Bill Baierl had once told him, "If you can sell yourself you can sell anything." That is so true.

I knew that Bill Baierl also stood behind every car that came off his lot. If there was a problem he'd fix it and fast.

Anyone who attended Bill Baierl's funeral service that bright afternoon had to feel as if he or she was at a revival meeting.

John Guest, the rector and senior pastor at Christ Church at Grove Farm and a close friend of Bill Baierl, also spoke that day. He mentioned that Bill Baierl had suffered some setbacks in his life. "He recognized the importance of humility and serving others," offered Rev. Guest. He cautioned those in attendance not to feel bad about Baierl's death. He said, "When you die you will be more alive than ever."

I hope that is true. Bill Baierl was not my only benefactor who died in 2007 and 2008. Several of my most loyal patrons passed away as well. Jack McGinley, who along with his sister, Rita, owned 20 percent of the Pittsburgh Steelers, also died. He was always so kind and generous and humble. I had an opportunity to speak to him over the telephone the week before he died and to thank him once again for caring and sharing. "Stop up and have a glass of wine with us," he'd say when he'd see me before Steelers' games at Three Rivers Stadium.

Mel Bassi, an attorney and chief executive of Charleroi Federal Savings, died. I am so glad that when I was in Charleroi for a book-signing appearance I had stopped and visited with him at his office for a half-hour in 2007. A week later, Bassi sent me the most beautiful letter, telling me why I could count on him to support my writing and publishing efforts. He died a few months later.

Mayor Bob O'Connor died since I wrote my last book. We had grown up in neighboring communities and both graduated from Taylor Allderdice High School, so we had some common bonds. When he was the president of City Council, he was responsible for my having a day of recognition before City Council and receiving an honorary key to the city.

Steve Previs purchased books from me every year since the start. A retired insurance salesman and the father of Steve Previs, who starred in basketball at the University of North Carolina, he's had some serious health issues in recent years. As I was working on this book, I learned from his son, John Previs, that his dad was now in residence at an assisted-living facility, the Baptist Home in Castle Shannon. I've met few people more positive than Steve Previs. He passed out pencils with erasers at both ends.

Losing so many friends who supported my efforts gave me great pause for thought and reflection. We all need angels in our life. No one really gets anything accomplished alone. My wife Kathie has helped me to stay the course while others have provided financial support to sustain my book-writing efforts.

I have been fortunate to know men and women who want to promote Pittsburgh in a positive way. It hurt when Myron Cope died. He had been a mentor and a role model for anyone interested in journalism. I've done my best to be a mentor for young men and women who are interested in the media. I've passed along what I learned from others when I was a young man. This book is about Pittsburgh as I see it. I still feel like I'm playing hooky every day. I've met a lot of interesting people and have stories to share about them in this book.

Mel Bassi of Charleroi, Aldo Bartolotta of Monongahela and Rudy Andabaker of Donora dine at The Back Porch Restaurant in Speers.

Praying for Mayor O'Connor
and other friends

July 19, 2006

A college classmate of mine told me that his roommate at Pitt, and a colleague of ours in our days on *The Pitt News*, had gotten a worrisome report from his physician. The doctor had seen something on an x-ray he didn't like and wanted to do further tests.

Stan Stein, an attorney in downtown Pittsburgh, had shared this news with me while I was doing a booksigning in the lobby of Oxford Centre on Friday, July 7 (2006) as part of activities surrounding the All-Star Baseball Game.

An hour or so earlier, a woman approached me and asked me if I remembered her. I asked for some clues. Turned out I hadn't seen her since I was 14 or 15 years old, and I didn't know her well then. That sort of thing happens to me frequently. She is the cousin of a man I grew up with in Hazelwood. He and I lived five doors from each other on the shady side of Sunnyside Street. She told me he had been hospitalized and had to go back for further medical attention.

This man, who now lives in South Fayette, had been one of my best friends when we were kids. He'd been in my wedding party. I had visited him in St. Clair Hospital a few years earlier when he was having some heart problems.

I also learned that a dear friend, Sally O'Leary, who had been a stalwart in the Pirates' publicity department for 34 years, had suffered the loss of her sister Kathie back in May. I missed that news item. I also got late word that a man in our neighborhood who belonged to our church had died at age 87.

So many losses and worrisome situations. I try to be positive in my approach to writing stories, and do my best to always put on a happy face, but this was too much troubling news at once. I mentioned this to my wife Kathie when we awoke on Saturday morning. Then our daughter Sarah called and asked if we had heard about Mayor O'Connor's setback. We had missed the news on TV and radio the night before.

The latest we knew Mayor O'Connor had ulcers and flu-like symptoms. Sarah informed us that he had a rare form of cancer that was invading his brain and spine. This was really serious. Mayor O'Connor was in trouble. Newscasters spoke about how vibrant he was for his age. He's only 61. I'm 63 and I'll be 64 next month.

No sooner had Pittsburghers stopped praying for Ben Roethlisberger, who'd been badly injured in a motorcycle accident, than it turned its attention to praying for Mayor O'Connor. No matter what political party you might favor you ought to have a soft spot in your heart for Mayor O'Connor. He's a good guy and he's gotten off to a great start as the mayor of our greatly challenged city.

dick caliguiri

He and Big Ben both rode in open vehicles in a parade back in February to salute the Steelers' Super Bowl XL victory. Mayor O'Connor said you couldn't beat riding in a parade in Pittsburgh like that. Both Big Ben and Bob O'Connor were on top of the world. Neither had any idea of the life-threatening events that lay ahead.

Life is like that. You just never know. We all hurt for both of them and, at the same time, it makes us feel more vulnerable. No one is free of difficulty or challenges.

When I was sitting in the lobby of Oxford Centre that Friday afternoon I could see a statue of the late Mayor Dick Caliguiri across the street in front of the City-County Building on Grant Street. When I was 14 and the sports editor of *The Hazelwood Envoy,* I used to visit Dick Caliguiri and get bowling scores off him when he was looking after his father's bowling alley on Second Avenue. He and Bob O'Connor both grew up in Greenfield and, like me, they are Taylor Allderdice High School graduates. Mayor Caliguiri died in office back in 1988 of a rare disease. During the All-Star Week, we were also shown TV images of the statues of Roberto Clemente and Willie Stargell. I knew them both. It's unsettling when people you knew become statues.

Roberto Clemente at PNC Park

Photos by Jim O'Brien

Mayor Richard Caliguiri at City-County Building

Larry Bruno
Joe Namath's high school coach

"Don't get old."

Larry Bruno was lying in bed, looking worried. His eyes looked like the pupils were dilated, like ebony marbles surrounded by white ovals. His bed was one of those adjustable models, bent at the top to prop him up. The dark hair that remained was damp and matted to his head. There was sweat on the bald area on top and it glistened under the recessed lighting overhead. Nurses and attendants came and went and tried to make him more comfortable, fluffing a pillow or moving his frail body up a little in the bed.

Even so, Larry Bruno looked like he had just awakened from a bad dream. Larry Bruno had been one of the toughest guys on the block as a young man, an athlete who feared no one. Now he feared his own image in the bathroom mirror.

Bruno might not have known what he had for breakfast, but he knew something was seriously wrong with him. He was suffering from dementia and had memory lapses. He had a condition called neuropathy; he didn't have much feeling in his feet or legs. He had breathing-assistance apparatus jutting from his nostrils. No wonder he looked worried.

"Don't get old," Bruno advised me after a brief greeting and a slight smile. He was wearing a pale blue hospital gown, one of those god-awful gowns that look like they had been washed paper-thin on rocks in the nearby Raccoon Creek. That creek runs through the golf club — Shadow Lakes Country Club that used to be Beaver Lakes County Club — that can be seen from the hospital windows above.

This was Wednesday, March 28, 2007, a cool, dank day, with temperatures in the 40s. Bruno was 85 years old. Bruno had been rehabilitating from several ailments in the second bed of Room 347 at Aliquippa Community Hospital. The man in the next bed knew about Larry Bruno and had seen his Beaver Falls teams play Aliquippa on many occasions.

There were Easter decorations and GO STEELERS signs on display in the hallways of the hospital. It was an effort to lend some cheer to the place.

It's a hospital that was having financial problems and was an endangered species, just like Larry Bruno. It was nearly closed down a half-year later, but was rescued by a health service chain that took over the operation of the facility. It was a hospital that had known better days and happier scenes. It's a hospital where Pistol Pete Maravich and Tony Dorsett were born within seven years of one another, June 22, 1947 and April 7, 1954, respectively. It's a hospital where three brothers — the Zernich brothers, Steve, Wally and Mickey — went to Pitt and played basketball and became medical doctors and came back

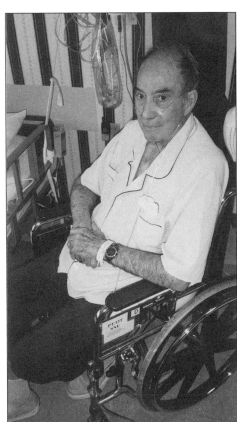

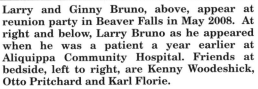

Larry and Ginny Bruno, above, appear at reunion party in Beaver Falls in May 2008. At right and below, Larry Bruno as he appeared when he was a patient a year earlier at Aliquippa Community Hospital. Friends at bedside, left to right, are Kenny Woodeshick, Otto Pritchard and Karl Florie.

home to look after the health needs of the people in their neighborhood. That was back in the '40s and '50s. There was a time when Pitt had four future physicians on their starting basketball team — three doctors and a dentist — and six altogether on the squad. That will never happen again.

Beaver County has turned out more than its share of famous sports figures, but none was more popular than Larry Bruno. He was heralded as "the Vince Lombardi" of Western Pennsylvania high school football.

He was Joe Namath's coach at Beaver Falls High School when the team won the WPIAL football championship in 1960. Namath held Bruno in such regard that when the New York Jets' quarterback was inducted into the Pro Football Hall of Fame on Saturday, August 3, 1985 he had Bruno introduce him to the crowd at the Canton, Ohio sports shrine.

Namath never forgot where he came from, and what an important role Bruno played in his life. Namath came from a broken home and benefited from Bruno's benevolent backing. "He knows football," noted Namath on one visit to Beaver Falls when he was with the Jets. "He works hard. He knows how to handle people."

Asked about the number of great athletes from Western Pennsylvania, Namath had more to say.

"They got great soil for growing stars in my home area," Namath once remarked. "It's great football country. It's the home or more All-Americans per square mile, I'll bet, than any other section of the country."

Asked to explain why so many great quarterbacks came out of Western Pennsylvania, Monongahela's Joe Montana remarked, "There must be something in the water. Maybe it's the Iron City beer."

It's a line that Mike Ditka and Pitt's Dave Wannstedt have repeated through the years. "Sportswriters always said I grew up in a coal-mining town," noted Namath, "but Beaver Falls was a mill town. We didn't have any coal mines."

Bruno was familiar with all these great players. He had matched wits with most of them, at one time or another. He knew them well. Or at least he used to. So many of those images are now blurred, hard to retrieve from the memory bank in the mind of Larry Bruno.

"The Coach has good days and not-so-good days," offered his friend, Karl Florie, a well-respected former head football coach at Ellwood City and Riverside, when I asked him about setting up a visit. Florie was a frequent visitor to the hospital and kept in touch on a daily basis with Bruno, even when he went to Florida for a brief vacation. They were best friends.

Florie ended up with some health problems of his own within a year of accompanying me to visit his friend Larry Bruno at Aliquippa Community Hospital. "Larry is doing a lot better than when you saw him last," offered Florie, "and I'm worse than when you saw me. I've got to keep doing some exercises, use my muscles more. That's what I need."

During our visit, Florie helped Bruno get out of bed and into a wheelchair so he could talk to us at eye-level.

"You got more out of him that I thought you would," offered Florie when we left the hospital and went to a nearby bar for a few beers. "The coach was pretty good today. Your timing was perfect. It's a shame you didn't know him at his best. He's been quite a guy."

Bruno and Florie were among the legendary figures who shared the same round table at the annual Italian Football Coaches Dinner in Ambridge a few months earlier. They were seated with Art Bernardi of Butler, Lindy Lauro of New Castle and Pat Tarquinio of Beaver and Hopewell. Joe Hamilton of Blackhawk (his wife is of Italian heritage) was also at the table. Hamilton was a head coach for 43 years and was the winningest coach in Beaver County history, so the Italians were happy to have him break bread with them. Two regulars, Don Yannessa of Ambridge and Pete Antamarino of Gateway, were not present that particular night. Yannessa had a knee replacement that month and wasn't getting around so well. And he was younger and in better shape than any of those other guys. I thought that I better not wait too long to get in touch with these guys to get their stories.

"He was my mentor.
He was like my big brother."
— Karl Florie

Bette Davis, the movie actress, once said, "It takes courage to get old." I know this book has too many stories about sports figures that have gotten old and ill and some that have died. It's the other end of the spectrum from the sports successes of their younger years. It's, as Paul Harvey liked to say in his radio broadcasts, the rest of the story. It might be sobering stuff for the likes of Sidney Crosby, Jordan Staal and Max Talbot, or Freddie Sanchez, Willie Parker or Max Starks. But old people simply have more life experiences, more stories to share. When someone feels like their days may be numbered they are more reflective about their lives.

I didn't know Florie that well, but I was told I should contact him if I wanted to see Larry Bruno. Florie was 68 and retired from coaching when I met him. Florie is a big fan of Larry Bruno. "He was the best, and there were the rest," Florie offered in assessing the coaching fraternity of that era. Florie served as an assistant to Bruno at Beaver Falls in 1967. In 1973, Florie became the head football coach at Riverside High School. He later coached at Ellwood City. He was a coach and athletic director for over 40 years.

"He was my mentor," Florie said of Bruno when we enjoyed a few beers afterward at the New Sheffield Café in Aliquippa. "He was like my big brother. I learned so much about organization and administration from him. The thing I respect most about him is his friendship. We ran a football camp together for 26 years. We never had an argument."

I met Florie before my visit to the hospital in Aliquippa, in front of an CVS pharmacy on Broadhead Road. I arrived twenty minutes earlier than our scheduled meeting, and stopped nearby at Wendy's for a coffee. There were four seniors sitting at a booth and table nearby, sipping coffees and sharing stories. A clerk told me they were on their third or fourth free refills and that it was a daily routine. I overheard one of them telling a story about Mike Ditka and his brother.

"Ashton missed a ball in the outfield and Mike chased him all the way home," said the storyteller. "Mike wanted to beat the hell out of him." The other men smiled and shared some of their own memories of Ditka.

(I later mentioned this story to Don Yannessa, a teammate of Ditka at Aliquippa High School and still a close friend. "I was in that game," said Yannessa. "It was an American Legion Baseball game. Mike was pitching for the Celtic Reds and I was playing for MPI. Mike's team was winning going into the last inning. We had two runners on base and someone hit what should have been a single to the outfield, but Ashton misplayed it and we scored two runs to win the game. Mike was so mad he wanted to kill Ashton. Their parents were in the stands and they had to run after them to save Ashton. Mike and Ashton broke up a lot of furniture in their home. The old man was always out buying new furniture.")

Does that sound like Mike Ditka?

Yes, Ditka is a hometown hero in Aliquippa. He was born in Carnegie, but grew up and gained fame as a four-sport star in Aliquippa. There is a baseball field named for Mike Ditka in Carnegie. There is a football field in Carnegie named for Honus Wagner. No, I didn't get that wrong. There is a room at the library in Carnegie named in Ditka's honor as well.

I wondered whether this same scene was going on in other Wendy's or McDonald's or Eat'n Park Restaurants throughout Western Pennsylvania that same morning. Beaver County can claim Namath, Ditka, Maravich and Dorsett as well as the Zernich brothers. Then, too, there were Joe Walton, John Michelosen, Frank Carver, Leo Nobile, Don Yannessa, Joe Zerilla, Claude "Tiny" Thornhill, Vito "Babe" Parilli, Mickey Davis and his brother Brad Davis, Jim Mutscheller, Ken Loeffler, Mike Lucci, John Skorupan, Po James, Bill Koman, Norm Van Lier, Simmie Hill, Dickie DeVenzio, Denny Wuycik and George "Doc" Medich.

Other local luminaries include Danny Rains, Ernie Pitts, Dr. James Frank, Jarrett Durham, Chad and Dante Calabria, Frank Kaufman, Tito and Terry Francona, Herb Lake, Jumpin' Joe Maddrey, Moe Rubenstein, Bob Taylor and Press Maravich.

No one should forget Joe Walton's father, Frank "Tiger" Walton, who played at Pitt and in the National Football League. "Tiger' Walton was Bruno's coach at Geneva College. His son Joe was an All-American end at Pitt and had a long career as a player and coach in the NFL. Now Joe is the head football coach at Robert Morris University.

Joe Namath and Larry Bruno in 1960 when Beaver Falls won WPIAL football title.

Larry Bruno was a running back at Geneve College and good enough to play in East-West College All-Star Game in San Francisco.

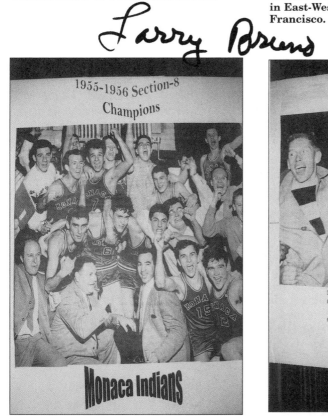

Bruno coached Monaca High School to Section 8 basketball title in 1956.

1960 BEAVER FALLS PLAYERS LIFTING COACH Larry Bruno IN LAST GAME CELEBRATING UNDEFEATED WPIAL "AA" CHAMPIONSHIP SEASON

Beaver Falls football players give Bruno a ride after AA undefeated season in 1960.

"Don't forget that Henry "Moon River" Mancini came out of Aliquippa," said Beano Cook, the ESPN analyst.

I remember traveling to Beaver County one day with Beano Cook riding shotgun to attend the funerals of John Micheloson of Ambridge and Frank Carver of Beaver. Michelosen was the football coach and Carver the athletic director during my student days (1960–64) at Pitt when Cook was the sports information director. Michelosen and Carver died on the same day, October 20, 1982.

"It was like Thomas Jefferson and John Adams," said Cook, who knows his history as well as college sports. "They died on the same day, July 4, 1826, on the 50th anniversary of the signing of the Declaration of Independence."

Beaver County can claim more great athletes than just about any similarly populated county in the country.

Darrelle Reavis of Aliquippa left Pitt a year early and was a first-round draft choice of the New York Jets in 2007. He started in the secondary as a rookie.

Some young women have made their mark in athletics as well with Candy Young (Beaver Falls) and Lauryn Williams (Rochester) starring in track & field. They were Olympic-caliber speedsters.

"I kept trying to do the best I could."

I learned a lot about Larry Bruno by reading the book *Namath*, a biography written by Mark Kriegel (Penguin Books, 2004). I'd recommend it to anyone who cares about sports.

"The son of a tailor from Naples, Bruno had grown up in East Liverpool, Ohio. The family lost its home during the Depression, and Larry and his sister were consigned to the back of their father's tailor shop. A row of clothes separated the children's quarters from the customers' domain. They had no hot water, no bathtub, just a commode.

"For Bruno, two endeavors offered respite from poverty. The first was football, which earned him a scholarship to Geneva and kept him out of the mills. The other was magic. He liked to show the tricks he taught himself.

Bruno was big on deception. "I believe in faking," he said. Bruno went to Babe Parilli, who had learned ball-handling tricks from Bear Bryant at the University of Kentucky, and he passed along his knowledge to Namath.

"Everybody said he was going to be a great quarterback — if you could handle him," recalled Bruno. "He had a bad reputation. But that was other people's version of Joe.

"My mother and dad got divorced, and I knew what that was like," continued the coach. "Of course, when something like happens, everybody goes against the father. Joe's brothers, they weren't speaking to the dad. They thought he was the worst guy in the world. They would tell Joe how bad his father was, how he was this and that. And he sort of listened. You could tell he would've wanted to speak with his dad. But his brothers said not to. Something like that.

"But I would tell him, 'Joe, you know my mother and dad were divorced. I loved my mother and I loved my dad. And nobody's gonna tell me any different.' I'd tell him, 'Joe, no matter what happens, he's still your father.'

"We were very close, me and Joe. Little stuff like that I could throw at him, and he'd listen. But you had to do it delicately."

At the hospital that day, I tried to speak as clearly and distinctly as I could so Bruno knew what I was talking about. I'd been told his memory wasn't that good, but Bruno was just fine. His recall about his days at Beaver Falls High School was wonderful. I didn't want to know what he had for breakfast, I wanted to know what he remembered about coaching Joe Namath. I wasn't out to stump the coach.

"Joe was just 5–10, 99 pounds as a freshman. But he could throw a football, a baseball, you name it. You should have seen him kick a football. He was our punter. We based our whole offense on his ability. All the plays were formulated with him in mind.

"We had a few rules, not too many. The ones we had we stuck to them. Except for maybe Joe. I tried to treat all my players well, but I admit I bent the rules when it came to Joe. I tried to treat them all the same even if they weren't a big star on the team. I tried to keep it even. I always thought of myself as a caring coach, a teacher. My first year, we had about 90 players come out for the team. Before long, we had 117 come out. You can't get that many today. My first year was 1947. I was the head coach in 1949. Joe Paterno became an assistant coach under Rip Engle in 1950. That's how far back we go."

Bruno conceded that he often looked the other way when it concerned Namath. He knew that Namath wasn't keeping the curfew he established for the night before every game. He knew that Namath was smoking cigarettes even though the players were told not to smoke. "I didn't try to catch Joe misbehaving," admitted Bruno. "I never tried to."

Bruno stayed away from the Blue Room, a recreation hall where Namath hung out and shot pool a lot. Namath knew his way around a pool table, too.

Bruno had a thin playbook, but like Lombardi, he believed in doing what they did the right way, again and again. "I tried to do some of the stuff he was doing," said Bruno in our interview at the hospital.

"I saw what other coaches were doing, and I copied what I liked best. Pete Dimperio was a great coach at Westinghouse High. He was Italian, too, so maybe that helped. He was a good one. There were three things we tried to do. We tried to win. We wanted to make football enjoyable to play. We wanted to have a football team that was exciting to watch. I tried to help my kids get recognition and get college scholarships.

"I think my guys played a little harder for me. That made me feel good. Joe was like my second son. Joe and I were very, very close. Our team was always respected by our opponents. We had enough good kids that they made the whole team look good.

"I lived in Monaca, sort of out in the country. I used to have my guys work out in the off-season. I don't think it was legal; you can figure the rest yourself. In the summer time, I took the backs and the ends down to East Liverpool and we worked out. Today, they'd call it a mini-camp. You only had to tell Joe something once. He had the right moves. He had the easy motion when he threw the ball.

"Joe was going to be a junior, and I had a good quarterback already. His name was Rich Niedbala. He went to the University of Miami. At first, I had Joe play some halfback and some defensive back. He was forty pounds lighter than Niedbala, but Rich would tell you that there was just something about Joe that you knew he was special. He had a sizzle about him. Even Rich wondered where Joe got the velocity to throw a baseball and football the way he did, not when he was so slight and skinny. After awhile, they shared the quarterback duties. Niedbala, in time, became the safety. Joe didn't start full-time until he was a senior."

Beaver Falls had two fine ends in Tom Krzemienski and Tony Goldmont, and Namath tossed touchdown passes to them on a regular basis. Namath knew what he was doing. "I never had a kid with a higher football IQ," said Bruno. "He might've been able to call the plays better than me.

"When it came to football and sports, everything he did was serious. People were jealous of him. He had his own style, and some people didn't care for it. I talked to him about that a lot. He was cocky and I wanted him to tone it down. There's a difference between being cocky and being confident. But I see that some people accuse Ben Roethlisberger of being cocky. I think he's just confident. A quarterback has to be; the team has to feed on that.

"I remember once we were playing Aliquippa. Joe was my punter, and we had a fourth down and long situation coming up. It was late in the game and some of our guys were tired. I said, "Joe, do you think you're going to be able to punt?' He put his arm around me, and looked me right in the eyes and he said, 'Coach, we're not going to have to punt.' We didn't, and we beat Aliquippa.

"Joe never forgot where he came from. When he came back home he'd stop and see me. Everything he did he wanted to do it right. Sometimes that made people mad. He'd repeat plays at practice till we got it right. Later on, he had me come and visit him in New York at his own expense. I got to meet and talk football with Weeb Ewbank, the Jets' coach. Joe did give me a lot of credit for his early development in his book.

"I didn't want to spoil anything. I wanted Joe to just be himself. I had been a pretty good athlete myself, so I knew something about what he was going through. When I was at Geneva, we had success in sports. We were the first college baseball team to play at Forbes Field.

"I coached teams where we beat Mike Ditka and his team at Aliquippa. Mike Ditka was different, too. He was so determined. He was such a tough guy, such a competitor. Hell, he scared everyone, including his coaches. Ditka played like every play was for the championship.

"In those days, you had to be undefeated to get to the playoffs. One loss and you were out of the running. They used the Gardner Points System to determine rankings.

In Joe's senior year, no one else in the same classification went undefeated, so Beaver Falls was declared the winner. In 1961, Beaver Falls went undefeated again, but didn't qualify under the Gardner Points System. Redstone High, quarterbacked by Fred Mazurek, was declared the champion without playing a playoff game this time.

"I remember Bear Bryant coming to Beaver Falls to talk to me and Joe about him going to school there," said Bruno. " Bear came to my home in Monaca and we went in the backyard and worked on some plays. He had coached Babe Parilli from Rochester when he was coaching at Kentucky. He talked about that."

"I think all his players were afraid of him."

Larry Bruno was quite the ballplayer at Geneva College in Beaver Falls. He was a 5-foot-10, 170-pound halfback and he was a standout for the Covenenters and played in the 1947 East-West Shrine Game in San Francisco.

He was the 13th round draft choice of the Pittsburgh Steelers soon after. Elbie Nickel, an end from Cincinnati, was the 15th round draft pick that same season. The Steelers also selected Frank Wydo, a lineman from Temple, and Jerry Shipkey, a back and linebacker from UCLA, in that draft class.

"I was drafted by the Steelers when Jock Sutherland was the head coach and John Michelosen from Ambridge was his assistant," said Bruno.

Bruno was impressive at camp, but left the Steelers to take a job when it was offered to him as a teacher and coach at Monaca High School. He taught social studies and coached basketball and football.

"Art Rooney called me and told me to come back to the camp," recalled Bruno as I sat at his bedside, dutifully taking notes during our time together. "He said he thought I would make the team, and that I could help the Steelers. But the money was better (about $3500 a year) at Monaca High. Imagine that. It was a different era, right?"

Some of his friends like to tell you that Bruno was not only a tough halfback, but that he could really kick the ball as well.

Pritchard also remembers Bruno punching out a guy who gave him a bad time. He also remembers Bruno giving a bad time to a football official. "He fought for his team at every turn," he said.

"When he was coaching, he ran the same plays over and over again. He was like Lombardi in that respect. He believed in power football, and getting everybody blocking for the ballcarrier. I think all his ballplayers were afraid of him."

Bruno was listening to his former players talking, and every so often he volunteered a thought of his own. "We had a few guys you had to keep an eye on," said Bruno. "Not too many. The ones we had you could talk to them. It was tough not to see some of the stuff that was going on, and you just wanted to keep it under control and make sure the kids didn't get into any serious trouble.

"Friday night and high school football were big back then," the coach continued. "The whole world came to an end on Friday night. There was no excuse for not being at the high school football game. It was like Christmas and the Fourth of July. It was big. We just wanted to make sure everyone on our team respected us and their opponents.

"We knew how to play football. People would say that Beaver Falls does this and does that. But we didn't invent that stuff. We saw what others were doing and developed our own ideas from that. People knew we were pretty good. We had teams in our conference like Butler and New Castle and the three of us were always at the top of the rankings.

"I kept trying to do the best I could."

Bruno was a proud veteran of military service. He had been in the U.S. Army during World War II and saw duty at Guadacanal as well as other places in the Pacific Theater.

"I always thought he was a better basketball coach."
— Otto Pritchard

When Karl Florie and I walked into Larry Bruno's room at the Aliquippa Community Hospital, he had two visitors at his bedside. Otto Pritchard and Kenny Woodeshick, who played on Bruno's ballclubs during their schooldays at Monaca High School, were keeping him company. I've seen a newspaper photo showing Woodeshick blocking a shot by New Brighton's Tito Francona.

Pritchard, with the kind of buzzcut he probably had back then, played on Bruno's first championship team in basketball back in 1953. Woodeshick played football and basketball for Bruno. He takes his old coach out to breakfast most Wednesday mornings, and Pritchard tags along when his schedule permits. Woodeshick coached the junior high football team at Beaver Falls when Bruno was coaching the varsity team. Bruno became the football coach at Beaver Falls when Bill Ross gave up the position and became the school's athletic director. "We had to run his system," said Woodeshick, "and Larry was always calling me with all kinds of ideas and plays."

Pritchard volunteered an opinion. "I always thought he was a better basketball coach than he was a football coach. I think he had more success as a basketball coach than as a football coach. He had three championship teams in the Top A class. We were one of the smallest schools, but we played up for years. I recall he was a strict disciplinarian.

"We had some great games with Homestead High. Chick Davies was their coach. We beat them at a gym up near Homestead Hospital and then they came back to our place and beat us. I think the score was 73–70. Jim Smith, who went on to lead the nation in rebounding at Steubenville College, was Homestead's best player."

I remembered Jim Smith. He was actually Jim Betsil from the Glen-Hazel projects, a few miles from my home. He was recruited by Davies to play at Homestead and took the last name of his grandmother who lived in Homestead. Yes, even then they did things like that. Smith was only 6–6, powerfully built with no real neck to speak of, but he led the nation's small college rankings in rebounding for Hank Kuzma at Steubenville College.

Pritchard and Woodeshick went on to play basketball at Geneva College. That was in the mid-50s. I told them that I recalled that Geneva had a real good team and often gave Pitt all it could handle. Woodeshick though Geneva had beaten Pitt seven or eight times in that era, but I checked the record book and Geneva won five of seven games from 1952–53 through 1955–56. Billy Blair was Geneva's best player. He was the leading scorer in the small college ranks for a couple of weeks in his senior season. The Covies, as they were called (short for Covenenters) to the NAIA post-season tournament in Kansas City in three of those seasons. Geneva posted a 24–3 record during the 1955–56 season.

Carnegie Tech, Duquesne, Westminster and St. Francis of Loretto all had good basketball teams in those days.

Monaca later turned out some terrific players for Duquesne in Billy Zopf and Mickey Davis, who both went on to play in the NBA, as well as Brad Davis, who matriculated at Maryland and had an outstanding and lengthy NBA career. They also spoke of Scotty Davis, another brother, who played ball at Wake Forest.

"My respect for Larry Bruno is immense."
— Art Bernardi

I called Art Bernardi in Butler to get his thoughts about Larry Bruno. Butler and Beaver Falls had fine football teams when Bernardi and Bruno were coaching those teams. Bruno had Joe Namath and, shortly thereafter, Bernardi had Terry Hanratty, who went on to be an All-American quarterback at Notre Dame and was the No. 2 draft choice of the Steelers after they selected Joe Greene of North Texas State in 1969. That was Chuck Noll's first year on the job.

"My respect for Larry Bruno is immense," said Bernardi, always eager to talk. "He had such an outstanding offensive mind. He'd drive me crazy trying to prepare my team to play Beaver Falls. You couldn't play your standard defenses against his offense. You had to do something that was difficult to execute.

"We had some great, great games over the years in the Midwestern Conference. You had Beaver Falls, New Castle, Aliquippa, Ambridge, Farrell, Sharon, Elwood City. It was quite a league. Eventually, Blackhawk and Hopewell came in," said the 77-year-old retired coach.

"I was an assistant one year (1960) at Butler when Namath was the quarterback at Beaver Falls. We looked at film of him in action. I was handling the defense. I remember saying, 'How do you stop a guy who throws like that?' We had to be disciplined. You're not going to let Joe roll out. We just had our ends run up field and not angle in at him. We were leading 12–7 at the half and we lost 26–12."

Jim Lokhaiser, the longtime sports broadcaster, promoter and late-blooming political figure from Butler, had introduced us. Lokhaiser is now a county commissioner. I wrote a story on Hanratty for *Sport* magazine before his senior season at South Bend, and visited him and Bernardi in Butler.

I remember we met at Natili's, an Italian restaurant that is a landmark in Butler. We played a little pool. We were sitting at the bar having a drink. Terry was smoking a cigarette. Ed Vargo, a National League umpire, came through the door. Hanratty moved his ashtray in front of me. "I don't want him to see me smoking," he said. "It would be bad for my reputation." I didn't smoke. "How about my reputation" I asked Hanratty. Vargo died in 2007.

I would interview Hanratty after he retired from the NFL and became a broker and investment counselor on Wall Street. He admitted he was an alcoholic, just like his dad, but that he had cleaned up his act, one day at a time. When I mentioned Art Bernardi, he said, "I was very fortunate in my football career. I had the best possible coach at every level, with Art Bernardi at Butler, Ara Parseghian at Notre Dame and Chuck Noll with the Steelers."

Bernardi's dark eyes brightened when I passed along Hanratty's observation. "I was lucky he came my way," said Bernardi. "You can win with a kid like that. It puts you one up on everyone at the start of the season. We lost only one game that year (1964). We went down to Aliquippa and lost 42–35."

"He was a most loving guy."

Nearly a thousand people showed up at Brady's Run Lodge in Beaver Falls on Saturday, May 31, 2008 to pay tribute to Bruno on the 60th anniversary of his start as a coach. It was an appreciation day and a reunion of players and associates from his days at East Liverpool, Geneva College, Monaca and Beaver Falls. Former cheerleaders and students traveled great distances to join in the tribute. Bruno's bouts with ill health had left him with some substantial health care bills and this event was aimed at helping him pay his bills.

Karl Florie escorts his dear friend Larry Bruno from a white limousine into a lodge at Brady's Run in Beaver Falls.

Vito "Babe" Parilli, a former pro football quarterback from Rochester, enjoys reunion with old friend Larry Bruno.

Babe Parilli, Tito Francona, Lindy Lauro, Joe Hamilton, Don Yannessa, Pat Tarquinio and Art Bernardi were among those in attendance.

Organizers were hoping Bruno's best known ballplayer — Joe Namath — might make the affair. Namath had a conflict with an appearance at Alabama. He had attempted to make air travel connections to get him to Beaver Falls in the early afternoon, but he was unable to do so. Namath has come to visit his coach on several occasions.

They had sold over 1,000 tickets at $30 a ticket in advance, and they never advertised that Namath would be there. It was a well organized event. The day started out ominously with lightning and rain showers, and even a threat of a tornado. But it brightened around two'clock, an hour before Bruno and his party arrived in a white stretch limousine. It was warm in the lodge, but no one was complaining.

The coach took off his mustard-colored blazer and the few who wore jackets followed his lead. Most were dressed for a picnic. And it was a good one. I'd never been to Brady's Run and it's quite a recreation complex for Beaver County's citizens. "He still looks like Mr. Bruno, my teacher," said a former cheerleader, who'd traveled from Indianapolis for the tribute.

"This is unbelievable," said Bruno, who sat in a comfortable chair and embraced everybody who approached him to say hello. He posed for countless photos. He and his wife of 62 year, Ginny Winters Bruno, both got lots of hugs and kisses, and congratulatory greetings.

I thought Bruno looked so much better than he had a year earlier when I had visited him at the hospital in Aliquippa. Otto Pritchard, who visited him regularly at the hospital and still saw him for breakfast with some buddies every Wednesday morning, was one of the organizers for the reunion celebration.

When I offered my observations about Bruno's improved appearance, Pritchard said, "I never thought he'd come home from the hospital." Ginny Bruno said she was taking good care of the coach, but admitted it was a difficult assignment.

Karl Florie was looking after Coach Bruno, making sure no one overstayed their welcome, making sure the coach got something to eat and drink from time to time. "He asked me to stay by his side all day," offered Florie, a loyal friend and admirer. Chris Vagotos, 64, came from Florida for the Bruno affair. Vegotos was a teammate of Joe Namath at Alabama in 1964 when the Crimson Tide won the national championship. He was an assistant to Howard Schnellenberger Miami when the Hurricanes won the national title in 1983.

"I recruited in this area when I was at Miami and Louisville, and that's when I really got to know Larry Bruno," said Vagotas, who stayed at Florie's home for the weekend. "He was a great football coach, a real great x's and o's guy. But he was the most loving guy. I never heard him say a bad thing about anybody."

Jim McCarl, the former owner of McCarl's, Inc., a plumbing company based in Beaver Falls for so many years, was there to pay tribute to Bruno. "People will never know how many kids — many from other schools — that he helped to get college scholarships," said McCarl, a big booster of University of Pittsburgh athletics. "We were lucky to have Larry Bruno in Beaver County. He was the best kind of coach in all respects."

There were lots of poster-size photos and memorabilia from Bruno's days at Geneva College, Monaca High School and Beaver Falls High School on display in the lodge, along with Namath's famous No. 12 jerseys and helmets from his days at Alabama and with the New York Jets that were offered in a silent auction.

"I've seen a lot of old friends and so many of my former ballplayers and fellow coaches," said Bruno. "Better yet, I recognized most of them and knew who they were."

I overhead one big fellow in line saying to his wife, "I'm going to test the coach and see if he remembers me."

I tapped him on the shoulder and said, "Just tell him who you are. This is no time to be testing him."

Larry Bruno presented his protégé Joe Namath for Pro Football Hall of Fame induction in Canton, Ohio on August 3, 1985.

Swimming with Dolphins
in early days

January 30, 2008

The undefeated New England Patriots have pulled the 1972 Miami Dolphins back into the spotlight. The Dolphins finished that season with a 17–0 record and have remained the only undefeated team in the history of the National Football League. If the Patriots can beat the New York Giants in the Super Bowl this Sunday they will finish with a 19–0 record. That's even more perfect.

Don Shula, the coach of those 1972 Dolphins, and so many of his former players, have been appearing on television and radio and in the newspapers and magazines in recent months. They don't want the Patriots to pull it off, which is understandable.

I have enjoyed the attention the 1972 Dolphins have been drawing. I know them well and it reminds me of my early days in the newspaper business. I started out at age 14 as the sports editor of my hometown weekly, *The Hazelwood Envoy*, in a Pittsburgh milltown, covering sandlot sports. I played for a midget football team called the Hazelwood Steelers.

I worked as a copy boy in the classified ad department at *The Pittsburgh Press* for my last two years at Taylor Allderdice High School, and as a summer intern in the city-side news department as a sophomore at Pitt. The next summer I worked at the *Philadelphia Evening Bulletin* as an intern in their sports department.

Beano Cook and I started a newspaper called *Pittsburgh Weekly Sports* during my senior year (1963) at Pitt and kept that going for over four years. Thanks to my efforts with that newspaper, I came to the attention of some of the best sports editors in the country. One of them, John Crittenden, offered me a job with *The Miami News* and my assignment was to cover the Miami Dolphins for the 1969 season.

George Wilson was the coach and the team finished with a 3–10–1 record in the final season of the American Football League. The players, by the way, loved George Wilson. He was a player's coach. Don Shula replaced Wilson the following season, coming to Miami from the Baltimore Colts. One of his assistants, Chuck Noll, came to the Steelers in 1969. Players didn't love Shula or Noll, but learned, as we all do, to love our sternest teachers when we get older. I left Miami after that one season and moved north to write for *The New York Post*.

I wrote for *The New York Post* for nine years and then returned home to write five more years with *The Pittsburgh Press*. I was the founding editor of *Street & Smith's Basketball* magazine and remained with that publication for 37 years until it was merged with *The Sporting News*. in the summer of 2007. I had written a column on Pro Basketball for *The Sporting News* for nine years (from 1970 till 1978). They were all great experiences.

Author Jim O'Brien enjoyed reunion with Nick Buoniconti at annoucement of Pro Football Hall of Fame Class of 2001 prior to Super Bowl in Tampa. Buoniconti captained 1969 Miami Dolphins team that O'Brien covered for *The Miami News*.

Former Miami Dolphins' Pro Bowl safety Dick Anderson is a regular participant in Andy Russell's annual celebrity golf tournament at The Club at Nevillewood and Diamond Run Golf Club

Shula turned around the Dolphins faster than Noll was able to spin the Steelers into a winner. The Dolphins were 10–4 in Shula's first season. The Steelers won their first game under Noll and lost the next 13, finishing with a 1–13 season. Noll bought a house in Upper St. Clair, less than a mile from my present home, and stayed there for 23 mostly wonderful years. It hurts to hear that he's having health challenges these days, living with his wife Marianne in Bonita Springs, Florida. In 1971, the Dolphins made it to the Super Bowl in New Orleans where they lost to the Dallas Cowboys. The next season, 1972, the Dolphins went undefeated and beat the Washington Redskins in the Super Bowl in Los Angeles. They beat the Steelers in the AFC playoffs at Three Rivers Stadium, turning the game around when the Dolphins' Larry Seiple faked a punt and made a sizable gain for a first down that led to a touchdown.

The Dolphins of 1972 had many of the same players who went 3–10–1 the year I covered them. The three main additions were wide receiver Paul Warfield of the Cleveland Browns, tight end Marv Fleming from the Green Bay Packers and a safety named Jake Scott they drafted out of Georgia. The biggest difference was Don Shula.

They had the same backfield of quarterback Bob Griese and running backs Larry Csonka, Jim Kiick and Eugene "Mercury" Morris.

Their "No-Name" defense was led by middle linebacker Nick Buoniconti, who wasn't much bigger than me, but is in the Pro Football Hall of Fame today along with Shula, Warfield, Griese, Csonka and offensive lineman Larry Little. They had a Pro Bowl safety in Dick Anderson.

I had my ups and downs with those guys. I was 26 and thought I had all the answers. I hooked up with Mercury Morris to produce a twice-weekly "Diary of a Rookie." Morris had grown up on the North Side of Pittsburgh, on the same spot where Three Rivers Stadium would later stand. He played high school ball in Avonworth.

He was brash and had a big mouth. He said whatever came to mind and I wrote down most of it in our collaborative column. I don't know which of us managed to get into more trouble with management and the players. But we had a good time.

Morris later got involved with drugs and did prison time. The nuns at St. Stephen's Grade School had told my mother I would end up in Sing Sing some day, but I managed to sidestep that prediction. So far, anyhow. I heard Morris on the "Mike and Mike" show on ESPN TV the other morning, and he was as confident and controversial and outspoken as ever. He smiled and I smiled. He's better than most of the talking heads they have on those celebrity sports panels. We had a lot of fun together when we were young and didn't know any better.

Jack Anderson

17.0 292 *#40*

Gerela's Gorillas, Dobre Shunka
enjoyed glory days of the '70s

"If I knew I was going to live this long,
I'd have taken better care of myself."
— **Ray Mathews**

January 24, 2008

O nce they were among the most visible and vocal members of the Steelers' scene. No one referred to the fans as the "Steeler Nation" during the glory days of the '70s. Not many fans were wearing a Steelers' jersey or some kind of black and gold costume in those days. Everyone wasn't twirling a "Terrible Towel," Myron Cope's creation that had special powers best reserved for playoff competition.

So they were standouts and fashion-setters in the '70s. Gerela's Gorillas were a fan club for place-kicker Roy Gerela, and Dobre Shunka (that's Polish for Good Ham) rooted, of course, for linebacker Jack Ham. Franco's Italian Army followed them.

Those three fan clubs are mentioned on the first page of the first chapter in Steelers' chairman Dan Rooney's memoir, *My 75 Years With the Pittsburgh Steelers and the NFL*, that was published in 2007. So it is obvious Rooney regards them as an important part of the team's history.

Then came Lambert's Lunatics, the Banaszak Bunch, Kolb's Cowboys and the short-lived Rocky's Squirrels. They were all part of the setting at Three Rivers Stadium during the decade in which the Steelers won four Super Bowls. They resided in STEELER COUNTRY, according to a huge banner that hung from the second level in the western end zone.

Bob Bubanic, who founded Gerela's Gorilla's in 1971, and wore a gorilla costume to all home games and some road games as well for the next eight years, was sitting beside Thaddeus "Teddy" Majzer at the Eat'n Park Restaurant on Lyle Boulevard in McKeesport earlier this month. They were reminiscing about those glory days. Both have those Mon Valley monikers. Talking about the Steelers of the '70s put a gleam in their pale blue eyes. Majzer told me he was half Polish and half Slovak. "My dad was Polish and my mother was Slovak," he said. Bubanic is a Slovak. He has more vowels in his surname than most Slovaks.

They were sipping coffee and catching up on old times. They both brought some prized photographs and time-yellowed newspapers and displayed them on a corner table. They certify their crazy days when they were something else. One of the newspapers was from August 22, 1979. It was the sports section of *The Pittsburgh Press*. The banner story was one I had written about Roy Gerela getting waived by the

Steelers, and I also had a column about Tony Dungy, a popular defensive back, getting traded to the San Francisco 49ers the same day. It's always an adventure to come across those old newspapers and see stuff you'd forgotten you'd written; yet the layout looks so familiar when you scan the stories.

My picture accompanied the column. My hair was jet black and so was my mustache. Not gray and white as it has been for many years now. I was 37 then. The thought struck me that perhaps this was my heyday, too. There were two other stories on that front page, a column by sports editor Pat Livingston and a feature by Russ Franke. Both are deceased. Of all the bylines on that page, I'm the lone survivor. The Steelers would go on that season to win their fourth Super Bowl in six years. The Pirates had won the World Series in 1979 and Pittsburgh was celebrated as "The City of Champions." Those were the best of times in Pittsburgh, for sure.

I had returned to town that April of 1979 — talk about good timing — after nine years in New York and a year before that in Miami. I'd missed out on most of the '70s in Pittsburgh when the Steelers were named "the NFL's Team of the Decade." I'd gotten to New York right behind Joe Namath's "I guarantee it!" boast while leading the AFL's Jets to a Super Bowl victory over the NFL's Baltimore Colts, and the Amazin' Mets 1969 World Series triumph.

I was able to interview the likes of Namath and Tom Seaver and Weeb Ewbank and Gil Hodges and Yogi Berra, and then be a close-up observer when the Knicks won NBA titles in 1970 and 1972, and when Dr. J and the Nets ruled the ABA, and the New York Islanders under Billy "Bowtie" Torrey was drafting the kind of talent that would lead to four Stanley Cup winners at Nassau Coliseum, not far from my home in Baldwin, N.Y. I knew Torrey from his earlier years with the Pittsburgh Hornets. Ralph Kiner was in the broadcast booth for the Mets. When I told him of my friendship with Frankie Gustine, someone he admired when he was the NL's home run king with the Pirates, Kiner couldn't do enough for me to make me feel welcome to the club.

That was a great decade in The Big Apple. By leaving Miami when I did, however, I missed out on the turnaround of the Miami Dolphins that peaked with their undefeated (17–0) run in 1972.

Judy Black, a waitress from White Oak, was curious about what was transpiring at her corner table at the Eat'n Park Restaurant, and poked her head in to get a better look at the photos and sports pages from the local daily newspapers. "He was Gerela's Gorilla," I told her, pointing to Bubanic.

"I'm sorry," she said with no hint of recognition, "but I'm not into sports. Gerela's Gorillas, huh?"

A regular at the next table, Pat Toth of Dravosburg, kidded her friend Judy Black. "You said Gerella's Gorillas like it was some kind of foreign language!" Looking at Bubanic, she added, "So you were Gerela's Gorilla? That's cool."

I talked to Toth later. She was a friendly sort and she was wearing a white T-shirt with an image of Ben Roethlisberger above the

**Teddy Majzer and Bob Bubanic of Port Vue still dress the part of rabid Steelers'
fans as they stand in front of McKeesport industrial park.**

Photos by Jim O'Brien

Majzer's home is full of Steeler stuff. Here's the couch in the family room.

wording ROETHLISBURGER. Yes, that's the way it was spelled. She had picked it up at one of those Pittsburgh restaurants — Peppi's on the North Side and in The Strip and Brentwood Express, a take-out oasis on Rt. 51 — that feature a special hamburger concoction named in honor of the Steelers' popular quarterback.

"I have season tickets for the Steelers, season tickets for the Pirates and partial season tickets for the Penguins," she said proudly. " I'm a real sports fan. It's 35 days till the pitchers and catchers report to spring training for the Pirates. I can't wait. I just wish they'd write about each sport in its season. The Steelers shouldn't be in the news every day."

Both Bubanic and Majzer are long retired from their jobs, Bubanic after 41 years working in a greenhouse for Allegheny County Parks & Recreation Department at South Park, and Majzer, after 31 years with U.S. Steel. Majzer started out as a bricklayer at the National Tube mill he could point to, just across the railroad tracks, from the parking lot at Eat'n Park. He was there for 18 years and then he worked as an engineering technician at the U.S. Steel Tower in Downtown Pittsburgh for another 13 years.

Bob was 70 and Teddy was 77 when we met for a breakfast interview. They are both soft-spoken in conversation, a far cry from their days as among the most animated Steelers' fans. When Bob took his ballcap off, I saw that he was bald. But he was bald when he wore that gorilla costume as well, I noted from a photo of him that had appeared back then in *The McKeesport Daily News*. Teddy has a wave in his brown and gray hair. They were friendly enough, but they didn't smile much at our meeting. Like they'd lost their steam.

Bubanic told me he had worked for Joe Natoli at the county park. I knew Natoli well. Natoli had also gained fame as the coach of the Morningside Bulldogs, a powerhouse midget football team, and he was one of the founders, along with Dan Marino Sr., of the Pittsburgh chapter of the Italian-American Sports Hall of Fame.

Teddy Majzer and Bob Bubanic both live alone in modest homes in Port Vue, a community of 4,700 people, located on the southeastern border of McKeesport, overlooking the abandoned mills and the Monongahela River and Youghiogheny River. Bob said he never married and lived with and looked after his mother before her death a few years earlier. Teddy's wife, Terry, died in 2004. It was evident, by little things he said, that he missed her a great deal. Teddy and Bob live within two blocks of each other, and say they bump into each other at the local supermarket or gas station from time to time.

They remind you that Port Vue is the hometown of Ray Mathews, a great Steelers' receiver from 1951 to 1959. Mathews was the Hines Ward of his day. He even played one season with the first-year Dallas Cowboys in 1960 to finish out his NFL career. Mathews likes to say, "If I knew I was going to live this long I'd have taken better care of myself."

Majzer remembered that Mathews "was a year ahead of me at McKeesport High School and, before that, at Port Vue Junior High

Terry and Teddy Majzer were major fans of Steelers' Jack Ham.

Teddy Majzer and his brother, Dan, flank Jack Ham and his wife, Joanne, at Dobre Shunka party at The Blue Rock Club Bowling Lanes in Port Vue.

School." Majzer said he played one year on the junior high basketball team with Mathews. "Then we went to McKeesport High for 11th and 12th grade. My brother George hung around with Ray Mathews. I have a bubble gum card of Ray Mathews that's supposed to be worth $25. When he played football and basketball at Port Vue Junior High, his coach in both sports was a woman named Thelma Smith. When Ray was in the NFL he was the only player who could say a woman coached him in both sports. She was something.

"We also had a guy named George Mrkonic on our football team who went on to be an All-American at Kansas and later played for the Philadelphia Eagles," added Majzer.

Teddy showed me a photo of his wife Terry and him with a large DOBRE SHUNKA sign they displayed in their back yard. He showed me a photo of his brother, George, and him standing behind a bar in his home, flanking Jack Ham and Jack's wife, Joanne. Those were wonderful days. He had another brother, Fran, who was one of Gerela's Gorillas.

Now Teddy's and Bob's homes seem so empty, even though there is what I'd call organized clutter wherever one looks. There are afghans spread across most of the furniture in their respective living rooms. Both settings are stale. A woman's touch and care are missing in their modest abodes.

Maybe it's my hang-up, but I can't stand the solitude. It reminded me of how I felt when I visited Steelers' great Elbie Nickel, a member of their All-Time Team, at his home in Chillicothe, Ohio. Nickel died during the 2007 season, but I can still see him standing inside the door of his home waving to me as I departed his place. When I had arrived, Nickel had apologized that the place wasn't as neat as it was when his wife was alive. I thought it looked just fine. Such scenes made me appreciate my wife Kathie even more.

"We're not as crazy as we used to be."
— Bob Bubanic

Teddy Majzer came to breakfast that Tuesday morning at Eat'n Park wearing a vintage Jack Ham No. 59 jersey. It was bright white with black numerals and fit him snugly. It looked like it had just come from the dry cleaners. He brought along a nicked-up black steelworker's hardhat he once wore to games. Bubanic was wearing a Notre Dame ballcap. He has a wall dedicated to the Steelers and another one dedicated to Notre Dame on the first floor of his two-story home.

"I've been a Notre Dame fan since I was eight or nine years old," said Bubanic. "I go back to when they had Johnny Lujack from Connellsville and Leon Hart from Turtle Creek. They both won the Heisman Trophy (in 1947 and 1949 respectively). I remember when Leon Hart was a rookie with the Lions and they played at Forbes Field.

Chuck Mehelich of the Steelers tackled him on a kickoff return and broke his leg."

I mentioned that Mehelich, a graduate of Duquesne University, was the uncle of Bill Fralic, an All-American tackle at Pitt and a Pro Bowl performer for the Atlanta Falcons.

I checked out some pamphlets Bubanic brought to my attention that had profiles of Notre Dame legends Knute Rockne and George Gipp. He seemed impressed when I told him I had visited Laurium, Michigan, the hometown of Gipp, and seen a memorial park named in his honor. I told him Gipp was Notre Dame's first All-American football player. He wasn't aware of that. Neither was I until I visited Laurium.

I was visiting different sites several years earlier in Michigan's Upper Peninsula with my buddy, Alex Pociask, who had played football and graduated from Michigan Tech. The Tech campus is in Houghton. Pociask had never been to Laurium during his school days, but I insisted we had to go there since it was so close. We'd already visited the Green Bay Packers Hall of Fame and been to a bar in Appleton that had belonged to Rocky Bleier's parents. Bleier and his family had lived above the bar. We also went to Wrigley Field to see the Cubs play the White Sox, and had lunch at Mike Ditka's Restaurant in Chicago. Ditka came to our table and greeted everyone. We saw the not-yet-finished Ford Stadium in downtown Detroit. We went to the Lindell A.C., a dimly-lit bar where Bobby Layne and the Lions hung out in their heyday. Bubanic and Majzer and any self-respecting Steelers' fan would have enjoyed that Midwest excursion.

Bubanic's gorilla costume is draped over a gold-covered chair in the living room of his gray siding home, like someone had been sitting in the chair and shed it when they rose to leave the room. There is dust on the fur because it's been quite a while since Bubanic wore it anywhere. It looked a little eerie. The head is missing. A mustard-colored tam he used to wear was displayed where the head should have been. He said the head got battered and ugly, so he tossed it into the garbage can one day. "Imagine what the guy must have thought when he picked up my garbage that day," said Bubanic. "I'll bet he got a thrill." Bubanic once wore that costume to Canton to witness several of the Steelers being inducted into the Pro Football Hall of Fame. For some reason, I recalled the classic horror movie "Psycho," and pictured Norman Bates' mother sitting in a rocking chair on the second level of that house on the hill above the family motel.

"I used to put that gorilla costume on around 11 o'clock in the morning and not take it off until 8 at night," said Bubanic. "Even in cold weather I would be sweating. The sweat would be pouring off my head. We paid $260 for that costume and we raised the money by holding a raffle."

Majzer has an entire room, more of a half room in size, full of Steelers and Ham mementos. The entire display looked like it had been flash frozen back in the '70s. He attended three of the Steelers' first four Super Bowls. So did Bubanic.

In fact, Bubanic appeared in his gorilla costume in a photograph on the front page of the *Times-Picayune* of New Orleans the day after the Steelers' first Super Bowl triumph, by 16–6 over the Minnesota Vikings at Tulane Stadium. He was seen being confronted by a sword-yielding Viking mascot in the Monday, January 13, 1975 issue. The price on the newspaper was 10 cents. Of course, the game tickets cost only $25. Some members of Gerela's Gorillas and Dobre Shunka had driven 1200 miles to get to the game. Some went by airplane. The last time they went to see the Steelers in the Super Bowl, against the Dallas Cowboys in Tempe, Arizona, they paid $700 for a game ticket.

"I paid $700 for a seat to see Neil O'Donnell give away the game with those interceptions," blurted Bubanic. Poor Neil. They'll never forgive him that unfortunate football outing.

There were 80,897 fans for the final football game to be played at Tulane Stadium when the Steelers won their first Super Bowl. Pittsburgh mayor Pete Flaherty was among them, as a guest of Steelers' founder Art Rooney Sr. The great Grambling University marching band performed a salute to Duke Ellington at halftime. It was the first championship in the 42-year history of the Steelers, and the fan clubs from Port Vue were both well-represented in the stands.

There was a friendly competition among the members of Dobre Shunka and Gerella's Gorillas, I learned from talking to Teddy and Bob. The Gorillas had front row seats in the western end of Three Rivers Stadium. Dobre Shunka sat in the opposite end of the stadium.

They especially got after the place-kickers for the opposition when they were attempting kicks at their respective ends of the stadium. They kept track of how many points the Steelers and the opposition scored at their end of the stadium. They used that to determine which fan club had the greatest impact on the outcome of a contest.

"We went easy on George Blanda of the Raiders because he was from Youngwood," said Bubanic. "Two of his brothers came down out of the stands to tell us not to get on George. When George came out on the field, he looked up our way and acknowledged us."

Gerela's Gorillas didn't go easy on Ted Colton, the sports editor of *The McKeesport Daily News*. Colton was the sports editor of *The Pitt News* when I was a freshman reporter at the University of Pittsburgh. At the urging of Murray Chass of *The New York Times*, one of his mentors during his days at Pitt, Colton named me the sports editor in my sophomore year. It had previously always been a senior position. So I have always been grateful to Colton.

He called me on the telephone from Florida in late April, 2008, and I told him about some of the stories in the book I was writing. "I knew Bob Bubanic well," he said. "I knew all those guys. One year I wrote a prediction in the game program that had the Houston Oilers winning the AFC Central Division. When I came out of the stadium after the game, Gerela's Gorillas chased me to my car. They were hollering at me all the way. They were really upset with me. That incident was mentioned in Roy Blount Jr.'s book, *About Three Bricks Shy of a Load*. I'll never forget that."

Bob Bubanic displays front page of New Orleans Times-Picayune that shows him in his Gerela's Gorilla costume at Super Bowl in New Orleans.

Bubanic sits on arm of chair that has his old gorilla costume draped over it.

Steelers' place-kicker Roy Gerela in black leather jacket greets Gerela's Gorilla outside Three Rivers Stadium.

Majzer once had 13 Steelers' tickets in his name. Now he has two in the eastern end zone. He says they cost him $70 a seat. He still goes to most of the games at Heinz Field. He watched the Steelers' defeat in the playoffs in 2008 by the Jacksonville Jaguars at the home of his son, Thomas, during a two-week visit to his home in Las Vegas. "Tommy had a signed jersey of Jack Ham's and some other Steelers' stuff in his game room in Las Vegas," said his proud father. "That jersey cost him $200. It's signed to Tom M., Jack Ham. He has an NFL football signed by Art Rooney. He has a big Sony TV in his game room. He gets Direct TV and he gets all the games he wants to watch. He's still a big Steeler fan."

Bubanic doesn't go to the Steelers' games anymore. He said he stopped going in the early '90s. He watches them on television at his home. "But I turn down the sound and listen to Hillgrove, Tunch and Wolfley on the radio," said Bubanic. "You learn more from them."

He says he doesn't miss going to the games, and that Heinz Field isn't the same as Three Rivers Stadium. There's another difference.

"We're not as crazy as we used to be," said Bubanic.

"Roy was like part of my family." — Bob Bubanic

Bubanic can still remember that dark day in late summer of 1979 when he heard on his car radio that Roy Gerela had been let go by the Steelers in favor of a rookie place-kicker from Penn State named Matt Bahr.

Gerela had kicked two 48-yard field goals the weekend before in a 27–14 exhibition game victory over the New York Jets. "I was shocked," Bubanic recalled. "I thought he had made the team. They cut him before their final exhibition game at Dallas. I didn't understand why they didn't wait until after that game to make up their minds.

"I didn't understand it. Roy was like part of my family. I was bitter. I wasn't convinced Bahr could do the job."

Gerela used to come and drink with Gerela's Gorillas. There were 33 of them. There were about a dozen members of Dobre Shunka. They all got together at the Blue Rock Club in Port Vue. It had been a club for Bohemians way back when. Now it's the Brown Derby Pizza. Ted Majzer moonlighted as the manager of the bowling lanes there for 25 years. He coordinated leagues for adults and kids on the four lanes. It was rubber-band duckpin action, popular in Pittsburgh and western Pennsylvania bowling alleys back then. The club has been closed for some time now. "There weren't enough members," said Majzer. "We closed it and sold it."

Then Teddy had another thought; that's the way the conversation went, back and forth, like bowling balls at the Blue Rock Club.

"They had a big banquet for Jack Ham in his hometown of Johnstown," said Majzer, "and we all went to that. We got to meet Jack's parents." Bubanic went to that banquet as well. "They had me roll out a cake for Jack in my gorilla outfit," he recalled. "Those were great times. I root for the Steelers now, but not like in the '70s. We were so good then. We could have won six Super Bowls in a row. I remember that one season (1976) when Franco and Rocky Bleier both got hurt in a playoff game in Baltimore and we went to Oakland without our top two running backs and lost in the AFC championship game. We had the best team in the league that year. Art Rooney thought that might have been our best team ever.

"It was a special time, winning all those Super Bowls. The way they played then. They had the same team for a long while. I hate this free agent stuff, where they sell out to the top buyer and break up a winning combination. Back then they all stood up for each other. They seemed like they were more approachable in those days. It's different today. I do think Charlie Batch has become a real goodwill ambassador for the team, the way those guys in the '70s did. He's done a lot for the kids in his hometown of Homestead."

A bus pulled up to the curb on the other side of Lyle Boulevard as we were talking at Eat'n Park. The entire side of the bus had a billboard-like promotion relating to Steelers' Coach Mike Tomlin and his weekly TV show. I could see an image of Tomlin over the shoulders of Majzer and Bubanic. I could also see what appeared to be a brand new American flag flying from a pole across the street. McKeesport is the kind of community where one sees a lot of American flags flying from porches and in front of buildings. "I like Tomlin so far," said Bubanic, and Majzer nodded in agreement. "I liked Noll and I always liked Cowher, too. They were different, but they were both good coaches. This guy is different, too." Bubanic, as Gerela's Gorilla, got a lot of TV time in the glory days of the Steelers. "I did some TV commercials with Sam Nover for Iron City Beer and for Oldsmobile," Bubanic continued. " So people knew us."

Bubanic mentioned that the students at South Allegheny High School did a mural about Gerela's Gorilla's for a special display of murals by area school kids that they have on display at Heinz Field. There are 60 such murals from schools that have won some kind of sports championship.

"We were before Dobre Shunka and Franco's Italian Army," Bubanic reminded us. "We sat in the front row of section 247 in the end zone at Three Rivers. We had great seats. We could see everything and everyone could see us.

"I remember once that Mr. Rooney talked to us for 45 minutes. Where else but Pittsburgh would you get an owner who would stop like that and talk to us? This was during a practice one day when the equipment man let us come out on the field. People probably said, 'Who are they?' Without my gorilla costume, I was just another Pittsburgh guy. But that was good enough for Mr. Rooney."

Steeler Nation
Passionate fans put on game faces

December 6, 2007

A couple from Lancaster, Ohio was keen on showing me their infant son. This was back on Saturday, September 15, 2007. They told me he would be a month old in two days. They were taking him to his first Steelers' game the next day, as sort of a baptism in becoming a Steelers' fan.

The little boy was wearing a white tassel cap with Steelers in gold script across the front, a black and gold jacket, and a gold blanket. They said they had named him Tré Rivers. This is a good indicator of how passionate and often how zany Steelers' fans have become.

Shawnta Kemmerer, the mother, smiled when she told me the baby's name. Jeff, the father, opened the blanket so I could see Tre' Rivers better. The name, of course, was a play on Three Rivers Stadium.

We were talking in front of Hometowne Sports in Station Square the day before the Steelers' game with the Buffalo Bills. I wouldn't take a one-month-old baby to Station Square or any other mall, but I've backed off lecturing young couples about such ill-conceived conduct.

I hear and see a lot of strange things when I am signing my books in front of the main store in the Hometowne Sports complex of shops at Station Square. This is where many of the team's fans come before the Steelers' home games. When the Steelers play night games, such as they did on a Monday and Saturday the past two weeks with the Miami Dolphins and Cincinnati Bengals coming to Pittsburgh, it's a day-long parade of people wearing all manner of black and gold costumes. Ponchos and rain gear were big sellers the night of the Dolphins' game. It's worth visiting Station Square on the weekend of a home game even if you don't have tickets to the game.

You wouldn't believe the scene. Fans from opposing teams show up, too, and receive mostly good-natured ribbing for daring to wear their colors in public in Pittsburgh venues. Station Square is a popular place, especially with out-of-town visitors. I've met Steelers' fans from the United Kingdom, Germany, France, Mexico, Canada, as well as Wyoming, California, Arizona, Maryland, South Carolina, North Carolina, Delaware, West Virginia, Ohio, Illinois, Minnesota and you name it. Linda and Frank Meyer, the owners of Hometowne Sports, introduce me to everyone. Willie Parker's mother and her family are frequent visitors. They buy everything with No. 39 on it.

Station Square is where I met Rose and John Allen of Washington, D.C. Rose was very pregnant. She told me she was scheduled for Caesarian section delivery in two weeks. "We drove up from D.C., and I really shouldn't be traveling like that right now," she said. "It would

Steelers' fans make sure everyone knows where their loyalty lies .

Photos by George Gojkovich

be my husband's dream for me to deliver our baby at Heinz Field. But it's his dream, not mine."

She said they had taken their son Zach to his first Steelers' game when he was six months old, and that they had to buy a ticket for him when they entered the stadium.

Kim and Steve Sutley of Rochester, N.Y. told me the details of their Steeler wedding, in which the wedding party was dressed in black and gold.

Dan Frank of Morton, Ill. has attended several Steelers' games in Pittsburgh this season. He and his fiancée Ann Knapp stayed at the Renaissance Hotel for a week between home games with the Baltimore Ravens and Cleveland Browns.

They were also here for the season opener. Dan took Ann up to Mt. Washington "where the view is just awesome," he recalled. As they stood looking at Heinz Field from a viewing platform along Grandview Avenue, Dan asked Ann to marry him and gave her an engagement ring. When Dan retires, they plan to relocate to Pittsburgh.

Guido Emde, 36, who grew up in Mexico and now lives in Cologne, Germany, told me he became a Steelers' fan when he was six or seven years old because he loved the Steelers of the '70s so much. He was in Pittsburgh for the first time to see them play. Gene Musial of Upper St. Clair, who tends the door at Hometowne Sports, introduced us.

Jane and Bill Lebeda of West Homestead show up at Station Square before most home games. Jane is there more often than Bill. But she only comes there to talk to other fans. She buys all her Steeler stuff at Hometowne Sports at Century III Mall. "It's too busy here," she explained. The Lebedas have devoted two rooms in their home to displaying their Steelers' memorabilia. They have several black and gold trains and trolley cars set up with a Christmas tree completely decorated with Steelers' stuff.

Susie Campbell of Coraopolis comes to every home game in costume, with lots of black and gold bling. There's a twinkle in her eyes because her contact lens have Steelers' insignias on them. her nickname is "Crazy Woman."

Many of the fans that come to Station Square eat at restaurants nearby and they take the Gateway Clipper to the games. They rave about the landscape and the passion of Pittsburgh sports fans. "There's nothing like it where we live," said a woman from Minneapolis.

Pam and Larry Butcher and their son Eric were excited to be here for the Monday Night game with the Dolphins. They live in Portland, Oregon and have a business in Vancouver, Washington.

They became Steelers' fans three years ago, according to Larry, and they love Pittsburgh. They have put money down on an apartment in the Carlyle in the center of downtown. "We come in for about three games a year," said Pam, "and we want our own place in Pittsburgh. We just love your city, and the real estate costs about one-third what it would cost on the West Coast." It gives you some idea how important the Steelers are to this city, and that they have some well heeled fans.

Hometowne Sports proprietor Frank Meyer hosts Ann Knapp and Dan Frank who visit his store regularly when they come to Pittsburgh to see Steelers' games. They have since been married and eventually plan to move here from Illinois.

Jerome Bettis fans brought their own "Bus" to stadium to show their affection for the Steelers' Future Hall of Fame back.

Jack Lambert's fans show their signs at Three Rivers Stadium.

Kevin Greene look-alike roars in stands.

Fan expresses feelings for last Steelers' game at Three Rivers Stadium.

Steelers' front four was one of NFL's finest defensive lines. Dwight White (78) and Ernie Holmes (63) both died in first half of 2008.

Fans wear their favorite player's jersey when they get warmed up for games at Station Square.

Steeler Nation

Steelers' fans and Saints' fans
come marching in

November 15, 2006

A married couple came all the way from Austin, Texas to see their beloved Steelers play the Saints at Heinz Field this past Sunday. "It's our anniversary present to each other," said Devin Shelgren, 38. "It was my wife's idea."

Candi Shelgren just grinned in acknowledgment.

Devin said he was originally from Iowa and had always been a Steelers' fan. He had no relatives or roots in this area. He was simply a Steelers' fan. He and his wife were wearing Steelers jerseys, the uniform for the day in Pittsburgh.

A few brave souls came marching by in New Orleans Saints garb, just a jersey in most cases, but nothing to compare to the costumed folks who follow the Steelers.

I sat in front of Hometowne Sports, a store at the Station Square Shops on the South Side that sells everything that relates to the Steelers, and was signing my Steelers' books on Saturday evening and Sunday morning and afternoon. What I witnessed at the Shops at Station Square complex was both fascinating and frightening.

I'd recommend to Pittsburghers that they go there before a Steelers' game just to check out the scene. You'd get a different appreciation for the Steeler Nation. I'm wondering if anyone who lives in Pittsburgh goes to Steelers' games. Everyone seemed to be from somewhere else.

Two older women were spotted who weren't wearing Steelers' stuff. "We're from Philadelphia," one of them said. "We're foreigners."

Otherwise, it was like one continuous Halloween Parade. In New Orleans, they'd call it Mardi Gras. Steelers' fans wore every manner of black and gold garb, with some crazy hats, strings of beads about their necks, Terrible Towels in their belts. Some were covered from head to toe in black; some wearing Steelers' pajama bottoms. Some wore black and gold face paint, and one had a black and gold Mohawk-style hairdo.

I met fans from California, Canada, Mexico, Mississippi, Louisiana, Texas, Ohio, Michigan, Missouri, Idaho, New York, New Jersey, Vermont and even England. Simon Chester made my day when he told me he lived in London, and that he had all my books about the Steelers. He belongs to the Black & Gold Brigade of the United Kingdom. He bought the latest offering called *Steeler Stuff.*

The title is appropriate, and the inspiration came from hearing so many passersby through the years pointing to Steelers' paraphernalia and shouting, "Look, Steeler stuff!"

I don't pretend to understand this phenomena of the fans. My main thought about getting ready for a football game at night in November would be to dress warmly. I'd prefer a parka and a heat pack to anything black and gold. There's something else going on here. "This is the closest I'll ever get to playing for the Steelers," said one huge man. The ones from Texas said their parents were Cowboys fans, so this was their way of rebelling when they were young. They have stayed Steelers' fans. Many were turned on to the Steelers during the glory days of the '70s.

One told me he was a Vikings fan because when he was eight years old he saw the Vikings play the Rams on television and he fell in love with the Vikings' helmet logo and Fran Tarkenton, their quarterback. "Then I became a fan of the Minnesota Twins as well," he said. "I even root for their basketball and hockey teams now."

I told him that when I was a kid I had a gold helmet and I painted blue horns on it because I liked the Rams helmets so much. I told him I thought the Rams were the first NFL team to wear logos on their helmets. The Steelers, of course, are the only team to have a logo on just one side of their helmet.

The wind was blowing stiffly off the three rivers—or what a Louisiana boy named Bubby Brister who played quarterback for the Steelers once referred to as "the lake"—and it had to be cold sitting in the stands at Heinz Field for the nationally-televised NFL contest.

There were eight people who looked like they'd bought out the store who said they were from Winnipeg and Thunder Bay. I asked them if they could clear customs to get back into Canada if they remained in costume. They took in the Penguins game with the Ottawa Senators on Friday evening at Mellon Arena, and then traveled to Canton to visit the Pro Football Hall of Fame. They said that was a real treat.

I met some other fans from Montreal who said they were staying in Pittsburgh to see the Penguins play the Philadelphia Flyers on Monday night. They were all staying at local hotels and spending a lot of time at local bars and gift shops so they really do stir the Pittsburgh economy. Pat Ulens, who grew up in Charleroi and now lives in Maryland, told me he caught me on the Guy Junker & Eddy Crow Sports Talk Show on ESPN radio talking about my book the previous week. I asked him how he did that. "I listen to them every day on the Internet," he said. Unreal.

Ulens was among about 200 members of the Steelers Fan Club of Maryland who were staying and partying at the nearby Sheraton at Station Square. They come to one game a year and otherwise watch the Steelers' games on TVs at five designated bars in the Baltimore area.

There are Steelers' bars everywhere in the world, or so it seems. No other team has this kind of following. As the Steelers were struggling against the Saints, blowing an early 14–0 lead, and looking like a team that might lose another heartbreaker, I thought about all those fans who'd come so far to see the Steelers play. They were desperate for a win.

According to a Los Angeles Times survey in 2006, one fifth of former NFL players from the 1970s and 1980s who died through that year were former Steelers. That should merit a study of Steelers alumni by an independent research team.

My wife Kathie and I were sitting in the warmth of our family room, perched at opposite ends of a couch, and sharing a blanket as we watched the game. I wanted the Steelers to reward us all with a victory. This city gets in a weeklong funk when they fail. Thank God it was the Saints who slipped up this time. The Steelers Nation needed this one.

A new generation of Steelers' Nation show their stuff at summer training camp at St. Vincent College.

Troy Polamalu
Goes on holy pilgrimage
To Greece and Turkey

April 18, 2007

The Steelers' Troy Polamalu moves to the beat of a different drummer. When the Steelers are doing conditioning drills, Polamalu is seldom in step with the rest of his teammates. He gets ready in his own way. Bill Cowher left him alone to do his own thing. I remember watching Polamalu during a calisthenics session at St. Vincent College and being intrigued when he was doing something completely different from the exercises everyone else was doing.

I thought about old-school coaches such as Jock Sutherland and Buddy Parker and Chuck Noll and how they'd have gone nuts if they observed such behavior. In their day, everyone was expected to do the same drills. It was a team thing, a discipline thing.

While most of the Steelers have been participating the past few weeks in "voluntary" conditioning sessions at their South Side complex, Polamalu took a break to go on a religious pilgrimage, visiting shrines in Turkey and Greece.

Most serious Steelers' fans know that Polamalu is of Samoan descent, but few know that he was baptized an Orthodox Christian and joined the Greek Orthodox Church. He was married to Theodora in services at Holy Trinity Greek Orthodox Church on the North Side, and he was baptized by total immersion in a baptistery pool at a Greek Orthodox church in Oakmont. His wife's mother is of Greek heritage.

Polamalu is now nearing the end of a 12-day religious tour with a group of men from the Greek Orthodox community in Pittsburgh. Among those accompanying the group are Father George Livanos of All Saints Greek Orthodox Church in Canonsburg and Father John Touloumes of Holy Trinity Greek Orthodox Church.

It is a period for meditation and prayer and a renewal of faith.

I remember Polamalu telling me when we spoke at St. Vincent College that he liked the campus because priests and brothers were visible there, and it had a religious spirit about the grounds. The Rooneys regarded it in the same way, one of the reasons they have stayed there so long when it would be easier just to conduct all their practice sessions at their more convenient complex on the South Side.

I learned about Polamalu's pilgrimage involvement from an old friend. Manuel "Buns" Pihakis was serving patrons at the annual two-day Greek Food Festival at All Saints Greek Orthodox Church last Thursday when I paid a visit to see him and his friend Frank Sarris. Both are pillars of this beautiful church.

Pihakis provided me with a printout of the scheduled tour and it summarized all the holy places they were visiting. One of the most

Jim O'Brien

Troy Polamalu poses beside statue of St. Vincent in reception hall at college named in his honor, and flashes familiar smile on sideline at Steelers' game at Heinz Field.

George Gojkovich

prominent was Mount Athos on a peninsula in Greece. It is heralded as the "oldest surviving monastic community in the world." There are 20 monasteries located there. Monks live there in hermit-like environments and are constantly praying. The summit of Mount Athos is usually snow-covered and crowned by white clouds and is said to be an awesome sight. They say "miracles mix with reality" on Mount Athos.

Pihakis also introduced me to Dorothea Livanos, the wife of Father George. She was reluctant to discuss what Polamalu was doing, for fear she was intruding on his private life, but she talked enthusiastically about what her husband and the other men were doing in Turkey and Greece.

I told her I had been talking to Polamalu two weeks earlier when he played for the Steelers' basketball team in Bethel Park, and how I had been struck by his demeanor when I met and talked with him three years ago at St. Vincent College in Latrobe. He seemed so different from most of the Steelers and pro athletes in general.

He is quiet, soft-spoken, quick with a smile, pleasant with people of all ages, engaging once you break through the barrier, and deeply spiritual. Yet he's a Pro Bowl demon on the football field. There's more to Troy Polamalu than that long black hair of his.

I compared him to a Greek pastry they were offering at a nearby table. "He seemed so sweet, like baklava," I said.

"And they both pack a lot of power," declared Dorothea, and she smiled at her own observation.

I checked with other friends of mine to learn more about Polamalu's conversion to the Greek Orthodox faith. Stella and Gus Kalaris operate a popular ice ball stand at West Park on the North Side, not far from the Holy Trinity Church they attend and support faithfully.

They confirmed that Polamalu was, indeed, a member of their church. "He participates in a lot of the services," said Gus Kalaris. "He's even taken an active part in processions during Easter. Everyone respects his space, but they are happy to have him there."

To which Stella added, "He's such a nice young man. He seems almost shy." (Holy Trinity Church, by the way, is relocating to a new site in the North Hills on the LaRoche College campus.

I told them about an experience I had with Polamalu, a few months after I met him for the first time. He approached me as I was signing books during the holiday season of 2004 at Monroeville Mall. He said hello and introduced me to Theodora, then his girl friend. That's so unusual for a ballplayer to do that.

Later, he waved to me and smiled as he passed on the other side of the walkway. Fifteen minutes later, he showed up in front of me and set a steaming hot cinnamon bun on the table. He smiled and walked away without a word.

Bob Milie of Mt. Lebanon, a trainer with the Steelers in the glory days of the '70s, shared a story about Polamalu: "My cousin was out to dinner at an Italian restaurant in Sarver, up beyond New Kensington. Troy Polamalu and his wife were eating there that same evening. Everyone was discreet enough not to disturb them during dinner.

"After finishing his meal, Polamalu rose and asked for everyone's attention. He thanked everyone for not disturbing him and his wife while they were dining. He then announced, in appreciation, that he was picking up the tab for everyone, and that he'd sign autographs for a few minutes before he left. How about that?"

Yes, indeed, Troy Polamalu moves to the beat of a different drummer. And the music has a festive Greek sound to it.

News item from June 6, 2008:

Former Steelers' defensive end Dwight White died at age 58 of a blood clot following back surgery at a UPMC hospital in Oakland. At least 39 former Steelers have died since 2000, 17 of them were 59 or younger.

Troy gets late invite to gala event

It was January, 2007, right after the Steelers had completed a disappointing 8–8 season. Troy Polamalu had missed some games late in the season because of wear and tear on his body.

He and his wife Theodora were enjoying a relaxing getaway at the Nemacolin Woodlands Resort and Spa. She was getting a massage and Troy was relaxing in a steam room.

"Then this man comes walking up," recalled Polamalu.

So Polamalu, polite as always, chatted with the engaging guy.

"I asked him where he's from?" Polamalu recalled. "He said he lives all over the world. I say, 'So seriously, what do you do?' He says, 'I own this place.'"

The garrulous guy was none other than Joe Hardy, who also founded and owned 84 Lumber Company.

"Listen, they're having a surprise 84th birthday for me today. How would you like to come?" Hardy asked. And that's how the Polamalus came to be in attendance at Joe Hardy's 84th birthday and shared a table with the birthday boy and Robin Williams, Governor Ed Rendell and former Governor Tom Ridge, listening to Bette Midler and Christine Aguilera sing, and star-gazing at all the important people Hardy attracts for such events. Some people just live right.

Al Vento Sr.
Still a Four-Star General
in Franco's Italian Army

*"He's a good man.
I love that kid."*

Al Vento says Franco Harris has never forgotten where he came from, and that Franco Harris has never forgotten old friends from his earliest days with the Steelers.

"He's a first-class individual," Vento says of Harris. "He never forgets me. He respects me. He was always good to me. If he's celebrating something — like the anniversary of his Immaculate Reception or some kind of Steelers' reunion — he invites me and my wife Rita and he always seats us with the best people. He always has time for us. He's a good man, so sincere. I love that kid."

Vento, who would turn 80 on July 26, 2008, has owned and operated a pizzeria in East Liberty for 57 years. He and the late Tony Stagno, who owned a popular bakery on Auburn Street in the same neighborhood, founded Franco's Italian Army, a fan club like no other, to root for the rookie running back from Penn State during the 1972 season.

Vento grew up in that neighborhood. He and Rita rented a second-floor apartment there on St. Clair Street for $7 a week in the early years of their marriage. The building is still there and one of his workers lives there now. "It didn't have running water in the apartment when we were there," recalled Vento. "You had to go down the hall to a bathroom." They soon moved to a beautiful home in Whitehall, where they have lived the past 54 years.

Franco's Italian Army comes in for a mention on the first page of Dan Rooney's book, *My 75 Years With The Pittsburgh Steelers and the NFL*, and a full chapter in Myron Cope's memoir, *Double Yoi!* So they are part of the Steelers' story, the team's history.

Franco's Italian Army came to the Steelers' games in full gear, wearing Army battle helmets, waving a full-size Italian flag, and bearing baskets of Italian cheeses and, buried beneath that, some homemade Italian wines. On one occasion at Three Rivers, they came onto the sidelines in Army tanks and jeeps they borrowed — hey, Vento has connections — from the Army Reserve unit at Hunt Armory in East Liberty.

When the Steelers spent a week in Palm Springs prior to a late-season contest with the San Diego Chargers late in the 1972 season, Cope arranged for Frank Sinatra to come to a Steelers' practice. Ol' Blue Eyes was properly inducted into Franco's Italian Army by Vento and Stagno who flew there on a half-day's notice to conduct the ceremonies.

Franco Harris, Bruno Sammartino and Al Vento were among 300 men who attended Armand Dellovade's annual "Italian Stag" party at his home in Lawrence, Washington County.

Armand Dellovade, third from left, welcomes five one-time Pitt head football coaches to his home. From left to right, they are Dave Wannstedt, Walt Harris, Foge Fazio, Jackie Sherrill and Carl DePasqua. Someone said that Dellovade "cursed every one of them at one time or another." To which, Sherrill said, "He probably did. But he was always there when you needed help."

"Those years were the greatest time of my life," allows Vento. "I met a lot of nice people. It's something that will be in my memory bank forever. And I became a friend for life with Franco."

Vento is still waving an Italian flag for his friend Franco.

I visited Vento at his current restaurant at 420 North Highland Avenue, his fifth location in that time span. City officials are always attempting to change the landscape in East Liberty and Vento's Pizza is one of the places that keep getting moved.

"It's 'For the Betterment of East Liberty' deal," he says with more than a hint of sarcasm in his voice, "and it just keeps getting worse. Right now, though, the neighborhood around our place never looked better. So I guess we're making progress."

Vento voices a lot of opinions about Pittsburgh. He loves to vent. But he's fun to be with, and one can learn a lot about running a business successfully in the unforgiving streets of the inner-city, the Pittsburgh sports scene, the Pittsburgh political scene and the powers-that-be that call the shots. Vento and his pals are power brokers as well as hard-working citizens.

Vento has huge hands, working man's hands, and huge brown eyes. His hands and eyes are always moving to the beat of his stories, and he commands and holds one's attention. Anyone would be comfortable in his company. He likes to say he's for real. He's a Pittsburgh guy, genuine to the core. He once was nearly 6-feet tall, but his shoulders are rounded now and he's a little stooped, probably from bending over to embrace his customers so often.

He once worked 18-hour days six and seven days a week. He's cut back to four-hour days. "I can't quit cold turkey," he tells everyone. His son, Al Jr., 51, and his wife, Sherry, manage Vento's Pizza these days, but the old man remains the heart and soul of this East End institution. Al Jr. jives with the patrons non-stop at the front counter. He can speak Ease-sliberty with the best of them.

I love the sounds and smells of Vento's Pizza. Everybody's talking at once. The pots and pans are banging in the back of the kitchen. The aromas are wonderful, the red sauces, the hot sausages, the calzones, the garlic. One of my favorite writers, Ernest Hemingway, told a friend in 1950, "If you are lucky enough to have lived in Paris as a young man, then wherever you go for the rest of your life, it stays with you, for Paris is a moveable feast."

Vento's Pizza is like Paris, or maybe Rome, in that respect. The garlic goes with you, that much is certain. So does Al Vento's version of the world.

Al Sr. sold newspapers as a kid, and always hustled, doing whatever jobs he could find to make a few extra bucks. He saved some of it, and bought his own first car, a black 1950 Plymouth for $800. "I went to a Chrysler dealer on the North Side with Chippy DeStout, the old police chief," he recalled. "He knew the owner and he thought he could get me a good deal. I wanted a red car, but they couldn't get it for me. I went back with Chippy a couple of times, but no luck with getting a red one. So I took the black one. It was right there on the floor in front of me. Hey, when you're 16 years old your eyes light up at the sight of having your own car."

I visited Vento the first time on Tuesday, January 29, 2008 to do an interview and returned a second time on Tuesday, March 18 to pick up some classic photos. We celebrated St. Patrick's Day one day late.

There are photos of Franco and Rocky Bleier and Terry Bradshaw on every wall at Vento's Pizza. There are even photos showing Vento as a teenager with some of the sandlot football teams he played for, such as Help of Christian, St Peter and St. Paul, the Butler Cubs and Sto-Rox Cadets. He's one of the biggest fellows in most of the photos, the one with the dark-hooded basset hound eyes.

There are more framed photos in his back office, some showing him with the late Mayor Bob O'Connor, one of his favorites, and a photo with another late mayor, Richard Caliguiri. Vento can be viewed with other Pittsburgh dignitaries such as County Executive Dan Onorato and sports celebrities such as Steelers' quarterback Ben Roethlisberger and Rams' quarterback Marc Bulger, a local boy who followed in the Dan Marino tradition at Central Catholic High School.

Most of them have been to Vento's Pizza on more than one occasion. Vento and his friends have backed them all at one time or another.

I remember running into Al Vento in the fall of 2006 at Mayor O'Connor's funeral at Freyvogel's on Centre Avenue in Oakland, and he called out from the other side of the room, "You missed Myron Cope. He was just here. He doesn't look so good."

"He's the last of the Mohicans."

It's a pleasure to visit Vento's and to enjoy the pizza and hoagies and the owner's warm company. I brought along two good friends of Italian heritage that I thought would particularly enjoy him and his pizzeria. I told Al they were my bodyguards. Bob Milie, 81, was a part-time trainer with the Steelers when they won four Super Bowls in the '70s and a former trainer and sports information director at Duquesne University, and he had good stories to share with Al Vento. Baldo Iorio, 92, is the grandfather of my son-in-law, Dr. Matthew Zirwas. He was a car salesman in Bridgeville most of his working days and he can appreciate how Vento treats his loyal customers. Iorio and Vento spoke a little Italian to one another just because they can.

"He's the last of the Mohicans," said Iorio, after seeing Al Vento in action, shaking hands and patting customers on the back, and even reminding one of them that it was time to take his medicine. His place can seat about 50, counting the patio. On both of my visits, his customers looked about two-thirds African-American and one-third Caucasian. "Make that 60/40," advised Vento when I told him my observation. It was packed for lunch on both occasions.

He pressed the flesh with everyone, coming and going. "Thank you for coming," he'd say. "I appreciate you coming. Don't be a stranger."

His work ethic and the way he treats his customers — like family — is similar to that of Gus Kilaris, a proud Greek who operates an outdoor ice ball stand in West Park on the city's North Side and counts Dan Rooney and several Steelers, past and present, as customers and good friends. Tony Accamando, Sr., 88, was cut from the same cloth. He owned the Pizza Time Shoppe in Mt. Oliver from 1940 to 1980 before retiring.

"We're for real," says Vento. "I treat people the way I want to be treated. We treat everyone with love and respect. It's that simple and that demanding. The restaurant business is a tough business. You've got to be there all the time to make it work. And you've got to have good product. If your food isn't good the customers won't come back."

At my request, Vento inducted Milie and Iorio into Franco's Italian Army during our visit. They are both lieutenants now. He brought out some glasses of homemade Italian red wine and calzones to mark the occasion. So it's official. He said, "Salute" as they sipped the dark red wine from plastic cups. "Good luck for a hundred years," he said. He repeated the toast in Italian. Iorio and Milie just smiled appreciatively.

They had some good stories of their own. Milie was telling us how Franco always wanted him, and him alone, to tape his ankles before a game. "He had the flattest feet I ever saw," said Milie. "I had to tape his arches up first, to give him a little boost."

Both Milie and Iorio served in the U. S. Army in World War II. Milie was in the Pacific Theater along with two of his brothers, Jack and Louis, and Iorio was in Europe. (Al said his brother John served in the Pacific as well.) Milie was with the 24th Infantry Division that came into Southern Japan right after the peace treaty had been signed in 1946. He visited Hiroshima and Nagasaki, the cities that had been hit by the Atomic Bomb. "There were steel structures that melted to the ground, the heat was so intense from the blast," said Milie. "Everyone you saw in those two cities had some kind of bandage on them. It was unreal." Iorio served in England, North Africa and Sicily. He's shown me photos from those days, and he's proud to have served his country. He was with the 431st automatic weapons (anti-aircraft) battalion. He was an NCO. He smiled and said he was also proud to be a lieutenant in Franco's Italian Army. "Now I'm an officer," he declared. "I'm moving up in the ranks."

Milie grew up in East Liberty and graduated from Peabody High School, a block away from Vento's Pizza. Milie was a good guide in that neighborhood, pointing out homes where Franco and Rocky Bleier once lived, where Sam Davis and Frenchy Fuqua once resided, as well as the boyhood homes of light-heavyweight boxing champion Billy Conn (Aurelia Street), singer-dancer Gene Kelly (Mellon Street) and singer Billy Eckstine (Bryant Street). We saw Motor Square Garden where Conn and Fritzi Zivic of Lawrenceville once fought.

There are a lot of stately, still-magnificent mansions lining Negley Avenue. "I'll bet Italian brick-layers built those homes," said Iorio.

Photos by Jim O'Brien

Al Vento gets close-up of picture of one of the sandlot football teams he played for as a young man. He's the big guy (No. 40) on the far right.

Al Vento inducts two new members of Franco's Army. Baldo Iorio of Heidelberg and Bob Milie of Mt. Lebanon were visitors at Vento's Pizza in Milie's boyhood neighborhood in East Liberty.

We passed the corner of Penn and Negley where the Pennley Park Apartments once stood. They have given way to strips of townhouses in yet another renaissance in East Liberty. My wife Kathie and I lived at Pennley Park for a year-and-a-half when we first were married in 1967 and 1968. Our fellow tenants included Roberto Clemente, Maury Wills, Juan Pizzaro and Alvin O'Neal McBean of the Pirates, and legendary basketball coach Moe Becker of Braddock High School. Those were great days, too.

I remember watching Sonny Liston train at a local gym there for a fight with Roger Rischer at the Civic Arena (November 12, 1968). He skipped rope to the sounds of "Night Train." Liston took pride in his rope-skipping skills.

Rischer had declared before the fight that he was not afraid of Liston, despite his menacing reputation and baleful mask. "I fear no man who walks this earth," Rischer said in a pre-fight interview.

Liston KO'd Rischer in the third round with a lethal blow to the kidneys. I mentioned Rischer's remark to Liston after the fight, and Liston allowed, "Once he got up into that ring he wasn't on this earth no more." You don't forget lines like that. That fight was for the benefit of Ben Anolik, a veteran fight promoter in Pittsburgh, who was one of the first heart transplant patients in America. Within two years, Liston, Rischer and Anolik all were dead.

We saw the East Liberty Presbyterian Church. It's still such a statuesque landmark. It was often referred to as "Mellons' fire escape" because it was built with Mellon money. Some thought it was built to keep the Mellons out of hell for their lending practices.

There's a lot of history in East Liberty. "There's no place quite like it," said Al Vento.

Al Vento Sr.:

The Steelers went to Palm Springs, California late in the 1972 season for a big game with the San Diego Chargers. Chuck Noll wanted his team to get used to the warm weather in December, so they went there for a week to get ready.

My buddy Tony Stagno told Myron Cope that Frank Sinatra lived in Palm Springs. Stagno suggested that Cope use his connections to get hold of Sinatra, have him attend a practice, and induct him into Franco's Italian Army.

When the Steelers' party arrived in Palm Springs, Cope, quite by accident, spotted Sinatra at a dinner club. He wrote him a note explaining his mission and had a waiter deliver it. Sinatra came over to Cope's table and said he'd do it.

I remember Myron Cope calling me and telling me he had arranged for Frank Sinatra to come to a Steelers' practice in Palm Springs to meet Franco Harris. We jumped on a plane to get there. When we arrived, Sinatra hadn't shown up yet.

Singer Frank Sinatra, at left, is officially inducted as a general in Franco's Italian Army by Al Vento Sr. and Tony Spagno at Steelers' practice site at Palm Springs, California.

Members of Franco's Italian Army celebrate a Steelers' victory in December of 1972. They are, left to right, Al Vento Jr., Al Vento Sr., Tony Spagno, Armand Zottola and Dom Stagno

Jim Boston, the business manager for the Steelers, made a flip remark to Myron.

"Where's your Frankie-boy now?" Boston said. "Sinatra's a no-show. Cope's a loser again."

No sooner had Boston berated Cope than Sinatra was there, tapping Boston on his shoulder. "When Sinatra says he'll show," said Sinatra, "he shows."

That was great and there were newspaper photographers there to capture the moment.

That was one of the highlights for Franco's Italian Army.

"It was a great day."

I had a special time this season, too. When Miami came here for a Monday night game (November 26, 2007), a lot of the former great Steelers were in town to mark the 75th anniversary season of the Steelers. They had a program that afternoon at the Heinz History Center to call attention to Dan Rooney's new book about his life with the Steelers during that time. He was born the year before (1932) the Steelers came into being.

My daughter, Mary Ann, bought a pair of tickets for my wife and I to go, and surprised us with this gift. She went with us. They have a display of all my stuff from Franco's Italian Army at the Sports Museum at the Heinz History Center. I gave them everything.

When we arrived just before the noon start, the Steeler Nation got there earlier and we had to sit in the back row of seats. We were split up, at first, but then someone moved so we could sit together.

Stan Savran interviewed Dan Rooney, and many of the Steeler greats were up there on the stage. Terry Bradshaw and Joe Greene were up there. When I saw Franco come out, I went up to say hello to him during a break in the program. I wanted to let him know I was there. Franco was sitting on the end.

His wife Dana stops me and gives me a hug and a kiss. She tells me to get my wife and daughter and bring them down to the second row. There were more players sitting in the front row. Bradshaw told a good story about how he had once been asked to pose for a picture with someone and their baby in Ligonier. He said that 30 years later, he was in town and a guy came up to him, and said he had a picture to show him. The guy said, "I was the baby you were holding years ago." Bradshaw said stuff like that catches you up short. "That reminds me how long ago I was playing for the Steelers," Bradshaw said.

Then Dan Rooney says that Franco never should have been allowed to leave the Steelers to go to the Seattle Seahawks in his last season (1984) in the NFL. He said if he'd known what was going on he'd have paid Franco out of his own pocket to keep him here. What a bullshit story that was! I nearly fell out of my chair. Who was the owner of the Steelers then? Who was signing all the checks? That hit me the wrong way. Who'd he think he was talking to?

Franco shouldn't have been playing anywhere but Pittsburgh. He did so many good things for the Steelers and this community. The same is true now with Alan Faneca. These guys should be Steelers forever. Franco went to Seattle and they didn't want to block for a new guy. He'd taken the place of a teammate of theirs.

When Franco got up to speak at the History Center, he said, "We're fortunate today to have one of the generals of Franco's Italian Army with us." I stood up and the place went into an uproar. I hollered out, "Go, Steelers!" After the program was over, people asked me to sign Dan Rooney's book. They had me posing for pictures. My daughter had me posing and she was taking pictures for them.

This one family was from Mexico and they asked, "Mr. Vento, will you take a picture with my family?" It made me feel pretty important. I shook hands with all the Steelers. It was a great day.

"They were so bad we rooted for the other team."

I remember when Franco had a one-room apartment near my pizza restaurant. It was a dingy-ass room, too. He liked my place and he was a regular. Sam Davis ate here all the time and I got to know him and his wife and kids. Her name was Gladys. It seemed like Sam was in here every day. They lived right behind that Home Depot building over there. That building wasn't there then. He was on Sheraden, I think. Rocky lived on Baum Boulevard, not far from here. Frenchy was on Negley. Willie Stargell and L.C. Greenwood came in a lot. I still see L.C. once in a while.

I asked Franco one day soon after I met him if he would mind if we would form an Italian Army to be his fan club, and he said it was okay with him. They already had fan clubs for Jack Ham and Roy Gerela. I'm not sure he knew what he was getting into. Our guys loved him. His mother was from Italy and his father was a black Army sergeant when he met her in Italy. When Franco had a big running day, we said he's all-Italian.

Tony Spagno and I started to go to Steelers' games in 1969 at Pitt Stadium. That was Chuck Noll's first season. They won their first game and lost the next 13. They were so bad we rooted for the other team so we'd be on the winning side.

Things got better when Franco came to town.

Franco had a one-room place on Stratford Avenue. I would bring him two hoagies and a half-gallon bottle of Pepsi every other night. He went to the stadium by bus. He had no money. Dana was his girlfriend at Penn State and I got to meet her when she came to town.

"Joe got shafted real good."

One night I went with Joe Chiodo to a dinner for Bishop Wuerl at the Pittsburgh Hilton. We were sitting down front and all the Rooneys came by and they stopped at our table and they hugged and kissed Joe. You would have thought he was The Pope.

Some of the younger Rooneys were calling him "Uncle Joe" and stuff like that. I couldn't believe it. This is nice, I thought.

Joe Chiodo was one of their most loyal fans. He had season tickets — 36, I think — when not too many people in Pittsburgh had season tickets. He sponsored bus trips to away games in Philadelphia, Cincinnati and Cleveland. He'd take two or three busloads of fans to those games.

Comes the seating for the new stadium (Heinz Field), he ends up with seats alongside the scoreboard, in the far corner. He couldn't get any of the Rooneys to change his seats. He called and no one called him back. He went to their offices on the South Side and no one would come out and see him. Joe got shafted real good. He was so upset about that. Finally, he gave up his seats. They put his picture on tickets for one of their games, but they didn't give him the time of day when he asked them to change his seats.

He was out in the sun and he wanted to be on the shady side of the stadium, and closer to the action. He deserved that much consideration. I told you about all the Rooneys hugging and kissing him, but where were they when he needed them? That wouldn't have happened, he said, if Mr. Rooney, the old man, had still been alive.

When Art was there Joe Chiodo could walk right into his office and talk to him about anything. Joe was proud of that.

Joe used to take me once in a while to the annual sports dinner at the Thompson Club in West Mifflin. There was nothing quite like it. Bob Prince and Pete Dimperio used to hold court there and they had everyone in stitches. Then Myron Cope and Bill Hillgrove became the big stars on the program. Lots of sports celebrities came to that dinner. I haven't been there since Joe died.

I arranged through Darrell Hess for Al Vento Sr., and his son, Al Jr., to get two tickets at Chiodo's old front row table for the 2008 Thompson Club Sports Night Dinner.

"I was making real money then."

Pizza goes back to 1937 or 1938. The first place around here I can remember where you could get pizza was at Delpizzo's Restaurant in East Liberty. That's the family that now owns Del's in Bloomfield. You could get a whole pie for a quarter. When I started in business in the '50s (1951), they were throwing surplus cheese in the ocean. They were giving every American family a five-pound block of American cheese. People would give it to me. I was selling it for 80 cents a pie, or 10 cents a slice. I was making real money then. Today, it's tough to make a buck. Everybody is greedy today. Everything costs so much. There's no way to make real money.

I got to meet a lot of good people. When I first met Bob O'Connor he was working for Lou Pappan. He had those Pappan's Restaurants and the Roy Rogers' Restaurants, and O'Connor oversaw their operations.

We have an Italian Club on Chislett Street in Morningside. My friend Joe Natoli lives on that same street. You can't belong to our club unless your family comes from Spingo, a town near Mt. Casino and Rome in Italy. We have about a hundred members and 47 of them are millionaires. There are some tremendous people that belong to the club.

Bob O'Connor came to me and said, "Do you know any people who can help me get on city council?"

My brother, John Vento, was the secretary-treasurer for the AFL-CIO union in Pittsburgh. We had a meeting among ourselves and Bob got the endorsement from the union. That helped. I got some of my friends to pool some money for his campaign. We liked Bob and what we liked best about him was that Bob's closet was clean.

He could have been the president of City Council right off the bat, but he'd given his word he wouldn't run for that office. His word was his bond. I told him he was foolish. This is politics, I told him. He might've been mayor one term earlier if he'd been the president of City Council right from the start.

Bob O'Connor used to come to our club when he was the mayor for special events. When he saw a photo of Mayor Caliguiri on the wall he asked if we'd put his picture up there, too. So we're going to do that this year. I've had Dan Onorato at our club, too. The drink tax didn't win him many friends, but he's a good man and he can go far in politics. We liked Mayor Caliguiri. We went to him once to see if he could promote one of our guys, who had all the qualifications, for a higher position in the police department. He said he couldn't do it. When we asked him why, he said, "Because he's an Italian. Because I'm an Italian." Most of the time — you can check it — the Irish have held the top political positions in Pittsburgh. Yeah, your guys. The Irish were calling the shots. Who had all the jobs?

When I was growing up, Italians had three options in this town. You could be a numbers writer, you could be a pickup man, or you could join with the boys. Don't say "mob" because people don't like that connotation. I have friends in high places; you never know. Some of my best friends have done me big favors, and I try to pay them back.

We had a friend named Col. John Danzilli. He went to school with me and graduated from Peabody High School. He was in charge of the Reserve Unit at Hunt Armory. That's how we managed to get those tanks and jeeps that we took to Three Rivers. We made him a Colonel in Franco's Italian Army. Maybe he was a general, I'm not sure.

Things are improving in this neighborhood. We have a lot of new stores that are thriving and drawing people from other places in Pittsburgh. They built some new homes nearby. I'm told a Target store is in the works. They're going to build a few hotels. There's money here now. It's headed in the right direction. It's coming back. I'm optimistic. I always think the Steelers are going to win the Super Bowl.

Photos by Jim O'Brien

Al Vento Jr. and Al Vento Sr. take a break beneath *Sports Illustrated* cover that featured Franco Harris at their pizza restaurant in East Liberty.

There's a sign outside singer Billy Eckstine's boyhood home in East Liberty calling attention to his achievements. Pittsburgh produced many of the world's greatest jazz musicians and singers. Eckstine sang the National Anthem at Forbes Field to open the 1960 World Series.

Basketball world
suffers several losses

August 1, 2007

I lost some friends in the world of basketball in recent weeks. Jimmy Smith of Duquesne and Jimmy Walker of Providence both died at age 63. Then Skip Prosser, the popular basketball coach at Wake Forest, died last Thursday at age 56.

Those losses hurt a lot more than the news that a greedy NBA referee had been betting on league games, some that he was officiating.

I also learned via an e-mail message that *Street & Smith's Basketball* magazine would cease publication. Its parent company had purchased *The Sporting News*, and henceforth all the sports annuals will be published under the banner of *The Sporting News*.

Street & Smith's Basketball was known as "The Bible of Basketball," and *The Sporting News* was once known as "The Bible of Baseball." I thought this was going to be my last year to do the Big East report, but the end came sooner than expected.

I was the founding editor of *Street & Smith's Basketball* back in 1970. I wrote a column on pro basketball, first about the ABA and then the NBA, for nine years in the decade of the '70s for *The Sporting News*. I served as the editor of *Street & Smith's Basketball* for 23 years, and have continued as a contributing writer for another 14 years. A few years back the editor gave me the title of Editor Emeritus.

"That just means you're getting old," said my wife Kathie when I told her of the honorary title.

When I was the editor of the magazine, Kathie and my mother, Mary O'Brien, used to proofread the entire issues. Kathie also typed all the college basketball schedules for me for twenty-some years. In doing so, she learned and memorized the location of all the colleges, their nicknames and colors. It made her a big hit at parties in our New York days.

I did the magazine and other basketball-related publications and books in those early years in New York, while covering sports for *The New York Post*. It made for busy summers, and we were never able to take extended vacations.

I saved much of the money I made from such free-lance activity, and it paid for tuition, room and board when it came time for our daughters Sarah and Rebecca to go away to college. It also provided funds for their weddings. Rebecca's money is still earning interest in that respect.

I met a lot of great people in the basketball world by being the editor of *Street & Smith's* magazine. I was allowed to publish the kind of magazine I thought was best for the marketplace. We were the first basketball annual to provide extensive coverage to women's basketball, back when Immaculata College, Delta State and Wayland Baptist were the big powers. My magazines were the first in the *Street & Smith's* annuals field—there were baseball and football magazines as well going back to 1940—to feature black players on the regional covers in the Deep South.

There were interviews with the likes of Wilt Chamberlain, Bill Bradley, Adolph Rupp, Bobby Knight, Dean Smith, Hank Iba, Jerry West, Red Holzman, Bob Cousy, Bob Pettit, John Thompson, Dave Gavitt, Elgin Baylor, Bill Russell, Press and Pete Maravich, Bill Sharman and so many others.

Jimmy Walker was a two-time All-America at Providence. A slick 6–3 guard, he led the nation in scoring with 30 points as a senior in 1967, and was a No. 1 pick of the Detroit Pistons. Jimmy Smith, who was living in Bethel Park, led Duquesne in scoring as a senior that same season with 16.5 points. He was a chunky 6–5 guard. He was a fun guy, always with the bright eyes and big smile, a funny story.

He was a friend and teammate of my boyhood friend and CYO teammate Jack Fitzhenry. Fitz died several years ago. He was also living and working in the South Hills when he died. Smith had starred at South Hills Catholic, helping Coach Jerry Conboy win the 1971 PIAA Catholic Class A championship.

About five years ago, Skip Prosser was a strong candidate for the Pitt basketball-coaching job after Ben Howland left in favor of his all-time dream job at UCLA. Prosser was ready to take the Pitt position, but changed his mind because Wake Forest didn't want to let him go. They didn't want to let him go last week either.

Prosser was jogging in an athletic center on the Winston-Salem campus and returned to his office in the early afternoon. He suffered a heart attack and slumped onto a couch where he was later found. He was just 56. It was only a few years ago that Prosser had Wake Forest ranked No. 1 in the country for the first time in that school's history.

He grew up in Carnegie, and remained a fan of the Pirates and Penguins and Steelers, especially the Steelers. He was a good guy. Everybody liked him. He used to come back and speak at the YMCA Scholar-Athlete Awards Dinner at the Hilton. And he was only 56.

That sort of news makes you think twice when you are going to turn 65 this August 20. Like Jimmy Smith and Jimmy Walker, my dad, Dan O'Brien, was only 63 when he died. That's why I was eager to turn 64.

I have loved the sport of basketball since I was nine or ten years old. I used to have the *Street & Smith's* baseball and football annuals on my nightstand back then, along with *Sport* magazine and *The Sporting News*. I had a league of my own in front of my house where I had put up a basketball hoop on a telephone pole across the street.

I was the smallest kid my age and Wilt Chamberlain was my hero. This background might help explain why it hurts to think that I will never see another *Street & Smith's* sports magazine. It was a good run, though—36 years—and I have no complaints.

Getting mistaken at malls for Art Rooney,
Bill Mazeroski and Jack Lambert

January 2, 2008

A woman walked up to me in front of Waldenbooks at South Hills Village and asked me if I had a book about Andy Rooney. I smiled. I told her I had written a book about Art Rooney, the founder of the Pittsburgh Steelers, called *The Chief*. I told her I enjoyed Andy Rooney's acerbic and cynical commentaries on CBS's "60 Minutes," but that I believed she was looking for a book by Art Rooney's oldest son, Dan Rooney, the Steelers' chairman of the board.

It was about the 75 seasons of the Steelers and was, by far, the hottest-selling local sports book on the market this holiday season. She positively blushed and thanked me for not being too acerbic or cynical about her gaffe. In the spirit of the season, I even escorted her to where she could find Dan Rooney's book

Another woman, this time at Borders Express at Century III Mall in West Mifflin, approached me and asked me if I were Art Rooney. I knew my hair was grayer than ever, but I didn't think I resembled the cover drawing on *The Chief* that much. It wasn't the first time I was asked that same question. I have also been mistaken for Bill Mazeroski, the cover subject for *Fantasy Camp: Living the Dream with Maz and the '60 Bucs*.

I patiently explained to the woman that Art Rooney died in 1988 after a stroke at the age of 87. If he were alive today, he'd be turning 107 at the end of this month. "If you do see him," I said, "please call me because it would be a good scoop."

A blonde at Borders Books & Music Store at Pittsburgh Mills apologized for not being sure about my identity, but asked, somewhat sheepishly, if I were Jack Lambert. I only wished that Lambert had been there to overhear it, but he was, more than likely, safely in seclusion at his 128-acre hideaway in Worthington, Pa., close to Kittanning. Overhearing that remark would have made his day, and given him something else to be annoyed about.

I've authored a book called *Lambert: The Man in the Middle*, much to Lambert's annoyance. Lambert, like the late Greta Garbo, wants to be left alone, and to lead a life unexamined, especially by a sportswriter, and someone who isn't a qualified psychiatrist.

The question I was asked the most at malls this holiday season was "Why didn't Lambert show up for the Steelers' 75th anniversary celebration at Heinz Field?" As succinctly as possible, I told the inquiring folk that "Jack" wasn't the only four-letter word that began and ended with "J" and "K." Along the way, I also learned that Lambert was unhappy with the Steelers about the lack of compensation for commercials that called attention to the anniversary and had a brief highlight of him in the accompanying footage. He also feels improperly compensated by the team's marketing department. And he's upset with the NFL Players Association because the NFL pension isn't nearly as golden as the ones doled out to retired pro baseball and basketball players.

This is a man who was the best-paid defensive player in the league at his heyday, has never worked at a real job since he retired from the Steelers, and makes more money than most of us just for signing autographs at $50 a clip and more when he comes out for his rare public appearances. He is a selective recluse, at best. His failure to attend the Steelers' celebration left a lot of fans keenly disappointed, to say the least. He may live to regret his decision, or just get more paranoid.

Lambert had put in a stint as a volunteer game warden, but wore out his welcome. He was too intense. He wanted to hang anyone who didn't have a proper hunting or fishing license from the nearest tree.

He was involved with his kids' athletic activities. He umpired some baseball games, but hollered at a noisy fan in the stands and told her to leave the ballpark. He was in charge of cutting the grass on the same ball field, and handed out directions with illustrations on just how the grass should be cut.

When Lambert failed to show at a Dapper Dan Sports Dinner that honored the Steelers' 1980 Super Bowl team on its 25th anniversary, defensive coordinator Woody Widenhofer was disappointed. "It's time he quit playing the role," said Widenhofer. "He should be here with his teammates. They'd like to see him now and then."

I told the lady who mistook me for Lambert that I was not Lambert. "If I were Lambert," I informed her, "I'd be wearing a black state trooper's ballcap pulled down over my forehead to hide my dark sunglasses, and I wouldn't be looking you in the eyes and being as pleasant as possible. And I wouldn't be personalizing the remarks over my signature, and it would cost you a lot more money."

TV host and book author Art Linkletter liked to say that kids say the darnedest things. He even authored a best-selling book by the same name with some amusing anecdotes. So do adults say the darnedest things, and I can attest to that. I see and hear the strangest things every year during my holiday season signing siege. I'm in the bookstores at the malls every day from Thanksgiving to Christmas Eve.

A red headed man who looked like Leif Eriksson, the Norse explorer, told me he might have been the only person in the bookstore who had read only one book in his life. "When I was in eighth grade," he said, "I read *Old Yeller*, and when that beagle died at the end, I just cried and cried and cried. I never picked up another book after that." I didn't want to ruin his once-in-a-lifetime reading experience by pointing out that the title subject wasn't a beagle, but why spoil his good story?

Another man, who looked a bit crazed, offered an interesting observation when he saw my book *Steeler Stuff*, hoping perhaps to get a mention in a sequel. "It's a shame the Steelers weren't called the

Gladiators," he said through blood-shot eyes. "All my early ancestors were gladiators."

He asked me if I had ever seen the movie "Spartacus," which was about gladiators. When I nodded positively, he noted, "Remember the gladiator played by Tony Curtis?" How could I forget that bit of mis-guided and creative casting? "Well, that was one of my ancestors," the man said with a straight face.

I just smiled. I wanted to shake him, and ask him if his mother told him that when he was on her lap. It helped to explain why there are still UFO sightings reported to police stations regularly, especially when there's a full moon.

I overhead a lot of people saying "I seen this..." and "I seen that..." enough to get my boxer shorts in a knot. I watched a constant parade of people pressing cell-phones to their ears, or staring at them trying to figure out whom they should call next. So many of them asked the per-son they were talking to, "Where you at?" Or worse, "Where yunz at?"

"In Pittsburgh, naturally," I muttered more than a few times under my breath.

I shouldn't feel bad about being mistaken for so many different sports stars. A few years earlier, Oprah Winfrey recommended to her viewers that they check out John Steinbeck's classic, *East of Eden*. She had put her official Oprah stamp of approval on the cover of recently released copies of the book.

A woman came into the bookstore at Monroeville Mall and told the clerk she had enjoyed the book immensely. "Has he done anything else?" she asked. The clerk wasn't sure.

Three local coaches who attended Pete Dimperio's 2008 football clinic at the Raddison in Green Tree were, left to right, Bob Colbert of St. Vincent College, Ray Reitz of WPIAL Class A champion Jeannette High School, and Ray Radakovich, former assistant to Joe Walton at Robert Morris University. Bad Rad retired prior to 2008 season and was replaced by former Steelers' defensive lineman John Banaszak.

Mayor O'Connor
Pictures of mayor spark memories

September 6, 2006

I placed a photo of me with Mayor Bob O'Connor on my writing desk a few weeks ago. I wanted to see him and be with him, but visitors outside of the family and closest friends weren't permitted at the Hillman Cancer Center at UPMC Shadyside Hospital. I called and left him a message at his home in Squirrel Hill.

We are both smiling in that photo. Our hair is white-gray, combed straight back and then pushed forward for a little pompadour above the high brow. We're both Irish and have been told we look alike. We had some bonds.

Bob O'Connor grew up in Greenfield, a neighboring community to my hometown of Hazelwood. The guys and gals in Greenfield always felt they were better than we were, indeed, a superior breed. I bought into that boast and thought I was moving up when I dated girls from Greenfield in the late '50s and early '60s. As we grew older, we matured and began to realize we were all in the same boat.

The picture had been taken at The Club at Nevillewood where Mayor O'Connor and I were attending the Mellon Mario Lemieux Celebrity Golf Invitational. As kids, Mayor O'Connor and I never thought we'd be invited to a country club someday or be able to mix with sports stars.

He always had time to talk to me. If he'd spot me in a crowd he'd come over and say hello, and start a conversation. He made you feel like a big deal. I was lucky to know a lot of men and women in this town who had that quality, such as Art Rooney and Frankie Gustine and Baldy Regan, all Pittsburgh guys, and Elsie Hillman and Jeannie and Dick Caliguiri. Art Rooney would have regarded Bob O'Connor as being "a real Pittsburgh guy." To the Steelers' owner, there was no higher compliment.

Mayor O'Connor graduated from Taylor Allderdice High School three years after I did. I was in the graduation class of 1960. We'd gone to the same movie theatres in Hazelwood and Squirrel Hill, the same dances at St. Rosalia's in Greenfield and St. John's in the nearby Four-Mile Run, as well as St. Stephen's in Hazelwood. We danced to Jimmy Clanton's "Just A Dream," and we both had dreams of what we wanted to be. The same was true with Dick Caliguiri, another favorite mayor of mine.

We played ball on the same fields at Magee Recreation Center and Burgwin Recreation Center and the same CYO gyms throughout the area. We hung out in the same bowling alleys and poolrooms.

I was talking to Tony Ferraro, one of the top sales executives at the beleaguered Pittsburgh Brewing Company, during a Pirates-Cubs game at PNC Park last Wednesday afternoon. "Mayor O'Connor is a

Mayor O'Connor and his wife, Joan, are flanked by Mel Blount and his wife TiAndra at downtown dinner. At right, Mayor O'Connor and author meet at Mario Lemieux's golf outing at The Club at Nevillewood.

Mayor O'Connor and former Steelers' star Merril Hoge have reunion at Caring Foundation golf outing at the Southpointe Golf Club in Canonsburg.

common man, just like us," said Ferraro, who grew up in modest circumstances in Etna and worked his way up the corporate ladder. "He's a good man and he's gotten out and tried to turn this city around. He's been with us at the brewery, trying to help us get straightened out. It's a shame what's happened to him."

Mayor O'Connor, of course, was in the hospital as we spoke, battling for his life. Some said he might not survive the day; that's how sick he was. Mayor O'Connor had been hospitalized for two months for treatment of primary central nervous system lymphoma. In layman's terms, the way he has always spoken, he had brain cancer.

I attended a Pitt pep rally hosted by Armond Dellovade of Lawrence at Piccalina's Restaurant in Upper St. Clair last Thursday night. It was the kind of party Mayor O'Connor would have enjoyed. There were lots of familiar faces there, people who felt close to Mayor O'Connor. Many were talking about him. One of them was Mike Fisher, the former state attorney general who was now a judge. Mayor O'Connor has been the subject of many similar conversations ever since he became ill. He's been on the minds and prayer lists of so many people here.

Former Pitt football coach Foge Fazio was at the pep rally. He's been receiving chemotherapy treatments for cancer at the Hillman Center in recent months. Dr. Stanley Marks, a big Pitt booster, is the oncology specialist for both Mayor O'Connor and Coach Fazio. "I've been asking about Bob," offered Fazio. "He's always been a big fan of Pitt football and I'd see him everywhere. You just never know. There was no warning that he was sick. That's why you better enjoy life as best you can."

Foge Fazio is just one of many friends who are battling some kind of illness. I received back-to-back e-mails from good friends in Mt. Lebanon and Atlanta last week that are both in constant pain. "The golden years haven't been treating me too well this year," wrote one of them, former Pirates' pitcher and broadcaster Nellie King.

Mayor O'Connor got sick just before the Major League Baseball All-Star Game was held at PNC Park in mid-June. He had been looking forward to that, eager to participate in all the All-Star activities, eager to show the best face of Pittsburgh to the world.

Back in February, Mayor O'Connor had ridden in an open car in the parade that celebrated the Steelers' Super Bowl XL championship. "It doesn't get any better than riding as the mayor in a victory parade in Pittsburgh," he said.

A year ago I saw O'Connor walking in the Labor Day Parade. He wasn't the mayor yet. But he was walking with Bishop Donald Wuerl and Governor Ed Rendell, and he was walking with his head held high. Pittsburgh was always his city, but soon he would be the mayor of his hometown. He was so proud to be the mayor of Pittsburgh. He paid his dues and waited his turn.

When I saw him that day downtown, walking on the Boulevard of the Allies near the end of the parade, he looked like he was walking on air. I had gone to the parade with my wife Kathie—who's not big on parades or Kennywood Park, mind you—and our granddaughter

City Council member Bob O'Connor with Franco Harris.

Mario Lemieux welcomes Bob O'Connor to golf outing.

Arnold Palmer signs scorecard for Bob O'Connor. That's Doc Giffin, Palmer's aide-de-camp, in the background. Mayor O'Connor loved to play golf. The Schenley park course has been named in his honor.

Margaret Zirwas, who was 16 months old at the time. It was her first downtown parade.

Bob O'Connor broke from the ranks to come over and say hello. He's just always been that kind of guy. I told him he was in good company. I'd seen him marching in St. Patrick's Day parades as well.

I have photos in my home of Mayor O'Connor on many occasions. He often came to the wall that remained of Forbes Field on Oct. 13 to celebrate the 1960 World Series triumph of the Pirates over the New York Yankees and to mark Maz's game-winning home run. He mixed with everybody, talked to everybody and, like Maz, couldn't understand why anyone would make a fuss over him. He had his son Corey with him and introduced him to everyone.

When I was standing near the end of a long line of visitors at the Freyvogel Funeral Home in Shadyside when Mayor O'Connor was laid out there, I recall Corey coming by me and smiling at me, "You're the guy who writes the books. My Dad has all your books." It was good to hear that.

I will never forget that it was Bob O'Connor who introduced me to Roy Rogers, one of our favorite cowboys. That was back in 1987 when I was the assistant athletic director for sports information at my alma mater, the University of Pittsburgh. Pitt was celebrating its bicentennial and during the year they paid tribute to special people. Roy Rogers was one of them. Bob O'Connor was a regional manager at the time for a local chain of Roy Rogers Restaurants and Lou Pappan's Restaurants.

O'Connor brought Roy Rogers to the press box at Pitt Stadium. A photographer from Bloomfield named Bill Kovach took a picture of the three of us together.

I have thought about Bob O'Connor these past two months and said a prayer from time to time for his recovery or for his deliverance to peace. He's always had a strong faith. Bob is Catholic and married to Judy, who is Jewish. They have a son who is a priest and a son-in-law who is African-American. Bob boasted that he had his own Rainbow Coalition.

None of that was a big deal with Bob O'Connor. He always got along with everybody. He was just 61 when he was hospitalized. I was about to turn 64 so it hit close to home for many reasons. His illness and how suddenly it hit him has left many of us feeling a lot more vulnerable, a lot more fragile.

I have all my photos of Bob O'Connor. He's got his beautiful hair, his beautiful smile and his glad hands. He's with Elsie Hillman in one of them. They were present the day they honored "The Pittsburgh Kid" —East Liberty's Billy Conn—by naming a street after him next to St. Paul's Cathedral in Oakland. Conn was light heavyweight champion of the world as a boxer back in the '40s. He was one of Pittsburgh's all-time most popular athletes. Tom Murphy was the mayor at the time.

O'Connor has always been a Democrat and I have always been a Republican. But I always sent him a check for $100 whenever his staff sent a letter soliciting funds for his latest campaign. I attended many of his annual "Cookie Cruises" on the Gateway Clipper.

There were always boyhood friends from Hazelwood, Greenfield, Squirrel Hill and Oakland on board the boat. It was always a good time. I have mental photos of Bob O'Connor kissing the cheeks of every woman who went on board that boat, and a hearty handshake and sometimes a hug for his male supporters. He was an old-time politician, a real schmoozer. Yes, to Bob O'Connor, we were all in the same boat.

Bob O'Connor escorted Roy Rogers to Pitt press box and introduced him to the author during Pitt's Bicentennial Celebration.

Mayor Bob O'Connor matches smiles with Pirates' Jack Wilson and Jason Bay.

Red Auerbach & Company
Lit cigars and music are good memories

"I never thought he'd die."
—John Feinstein

November 8, 2006

I played in a doubles tennis match once with Red Auerbach one of the opponents on the other side of the net. The Hall of Fame coach and general manager of the Boston Celtics was a crafty competitor, as I remember, full of guile and cut shots and he kept the ball in play.

I don't remember our partners—I think they were also NBA coaches; they might have been Kevin Loughery and Rod Thorn of the Nets—but I remember that Red Auerbach's team won. Of course. Red's teams always won, or so it seemed during the days of the Celtics' championship reign in the National Basketball Association. Red lit up a cigar after his team beat mine in that tennis match, just like he did late in games the Celtics were going to win. His smile was always that of a smart-ass bully from Brooklyn's Bedford-Stuyvesant streets.

As good as the Steelers were in the '70s, winning four Super Bowls, they never dominated their sport the way the Boston Celtics did. No one has. They won the NBA title nine of ten years (1956 through 1966) when I was a schoolboy. I read magazine stories about the Celtics back then.

"Red Auerbach knew how to coach, and he knew how to handle talent and egos," said Bill Sharman, a member of the Basketball Hall of Fame as both a player and coach, when we had lunch at a Marriott Hotel in Los Angeles in the summer of 2007. "There was no one quite like him."

I remember that Arnold "Red" Auerbach was a brash, often-boisterous guy, and an argumentative sort. You'd have thought that he and not Dr. James Naismith had invented the game of basketball. He was an NBA man at the time, and I was writing a column about the rival American Basketball Association in *The New York Post* and *The Sporting News* at the time.

Red didn't think much of the ABA and told me so. This was at a gathering of pro basketball people for the annual Maurice Stokes Basketball Game in the summer at Kutsher's Country Club in New York's Catskill Mountains. The game was held to raise money for Stokes who had been left paralyzed by a bad fall during an NBA game. Stokes had played at Westinghouse High School in Pittsburgh and St. Francis of Loretto (Pa.) College before becoming an NBA All-Star.

As a kid I had my own three-man basketball league in front of my home on Sunnyside Street and my team was the Royals. You had to play a zone defense because I hated going up against man-to-man defense. The Rochester Royals were my favorite team in the mid-50s, when I was 13 and 14 years old, because their lineup had so many Pittsburgh connections. The Royals included Stokes and Ed Fleming, who played at Westinghouse High School in Pittsburgh, and Jack Twyman, who played high school ball at Central Catholic, and Dick Ricketts and Sihugo Green, both All-Americans at Duquesne, and Dave Piontek of Bethel Park and Xavier.

Years later, at an NBA All-Star Game in Miami, I ran into the Royals' owner Lester Harrison in the lobby of the hotel and introduced myself, and told him what a fan I'd been of his team back in the '50s. I introduced him to my daughter, Sarah, who accompanied me on the trip. Harrison, one of the NBA pioneers, was inducted into the Basketball Hall of Fame in 1979.

Wilt Chamberlain always played in this Stokes benefit game at Kutsher's and it was always a thrill to see him and spend time with him at the hotel bar late at night. He commanded everyone's attention and told great stories in a deep-throated but warm voice. A friend of mine, Jim Bukata, who grew up in Munhall and became a basketball p.r. man in New York, knew that Chamberlain had been my boyhood hero. He sent Chamberlain to my room at Kutsher's one day. I was stunned when I opened the door and Wilt walked in, bowing so as not to hit his head on the doorway. He stayed awhile and I took some pictures of him that I still have in a scrapbook. It's a great memory.

Red Auerbach was one of Wilt's foes. Auerbach always argued that his center, Bill Russell, was the best in the league, and that his teams nearly always beat Wilt's teams. Red liked to razz Chamberlain.

Red Auerbach died of a heart attack at age 89 in late October of 2006. Sports author John Feinstein said, "I never thought he'd die." If you want to truly appreciate Auerbach you should read Feinstein's wonderful book about him. It's called *Let Me Tell You A Story*.

Too many people whom I've known somewhere along the way have died during the past three months, and it gets you thinking.

A week ago I went to a viewing at the Freyvogel Funeral Home on Centre Avenue in Shadyside for the third time in as many months. This time it was for Jack McGinley, who died of cancer at 86. He had been a silent partner of the Rooney family in the ownership structure of the Pittsburgh Steelers. Few fans knew about McGinley, but he was a great guy, as good a man in so many ways as Art Rooney Sr., the founder of the franchise and one of the most beloved figures in the history of the National Football League or The City of Pittsburgh.

McGinley was always close-mouthed when I asked too much about Art Rooney's early days. He'd smile and switch the subject. He was a gem. Whenever he'd see me at Three Rivers Stadium, he'd invariably say, "Come up and see us after the game. Have a glass of wine with us."

When I'd show up, there was usually a priest at his side. Monsignor Rice, the fiesty "labor priest," was a regular at the table. Jack McGinley would take me to lunch at the PAA or to Del's in Bloomfield. He was a kind and generous man. I had a chance to talk to him when he was ill, just about two weeks before he died.

There was a photo of Jack McGinley and his family on display near the casket. It was a photo I had taken of the McGinley clan in their private box at Three Rivers Stadium. I was proud to see that photo there that day.

Walt Harper, the legendary Pittsburgh jazz musician, had been in the same viewing room before McGinley. Harper was known as the "Prom King of Pittsburgh" and, indeed, he had played at my Allderdice High School prom at the Pittsburgh Hilton in 1960. I'd played in a celebrity tennis tournament with him in Monroeville along with Franco Harris and—get this—Ethel Kennedy—once upon a time. Yes, the wife of the late Bobby Kennedy.

I'd been in that same main viewing room at the Freyvogel Funeral Home each of the previous months, first for Tom "Maniac" McDonough and then Mayor Bob O'Connor. McDonough was a funny guy, a highly successful insurance salesman and sports fan who got a kick out of getting into games for free. He was known as "the greatest gate-crasher since Genghis Khan."

Usually the deceased is the dominant figure at such a funeral, but that was not the case for McDonough's viewing. One of his long-time friends, former Pirates' slugger Frank Thomas, commanded my attention that afternoon.

Thomas had grown up near Magee Womens Hospital in Oakland, where his dad worked in the laundry. McDonough had befriended him when Thomas was playing for the Pirates. Thomas is probably the greatest major league baseball player ever to come out of Pittsburgh proper. He is the second greatest Lithuanian athlete from Pittsburgh, right behind Johnny Unitas. His family name was originally Tumis.

"He doesn't look like himself," Thomas thundered as I approached him to offer a greeting. "He doesn't look like himself."

I remembered that Art Rooney had often remarked, "No one looks good in the box."

There were a lot of Irish people present at the McDonough funeral. One woman wore about six different shades of green, including a green boa, and looked like she'd just come from the St. Patrick's Day Parade. She looked like she had put on her bright red lipstick in a dark room.

I saw Thomas going around the room, putting his right hand on their shoulders. No one can put the arm on someone, as the phrase goes, quite like Frank Thomas. He was taller than anyone around him. He had a notepad in his hand, and he was writing information as he spoke to the mourners. It took me awhile to realize he was taking orders for his biography, a book he'd written and published that year.

I think Maniac McDonough would have approved of what Thomas was doing. After all, McDonough, no doubt, sold some insurance policies at such gatherings in his heyday. He could be aggressive. He amused most with his non-stop routine and turned off others with his maniacal spiel. He was a funnyman who ended up suffering from depression.

He used to say, "I don't push insurance on my friends. To hell with them, if they don't want to buy a policy from me I'll let them die

Jack McGinley was silent partner in Pittsburgh Steelers' organization.

Tom "Maniac" McDonough enjoys Pirates' game with good friends, right to left, Joe Gordon and Bert "Porky" Caplan.

Wilt Chamberlain visited author's room at Kutsher's Country Club in New York's Catskill Mountains during the Maurice Stokes Memorial Basketball game.

Photos by Jim O'Brien

without insurance." I had to smile. I think I hustle pretty good to sell my books, but I've never tried to peddle them in a funeral home.

"He got me at another funeral," offered former state legislator Bill Coyne, who also lives near Magee Womens Hospital.

I spoke to Thomas several weeks later when he was selling and signing his books at a more appropriate place, a book fair at the Heinz History Center in The Strip. I've always been intrigued by Thomas. He could get under your finger nails real good, yet former teammates such as Bob Friend felt he was, deep down inside, a good man and a terrific competitor.

"He was a Maniac all right," Thomas said of his dear friend, Thomas McDonough. "I never saw anyone who could get into more sports events and not pay as Tommy. He could probably get into the Vatican without a ticket.

"He had a heart as big as gold, and a gift for gab. He told good stories. He was a salesman who'd follow up with three calls until he got your business. He remembered everyone's birthday, stuff like that."

I digress, now back to some other funerals of recent vintage...

Mayor O'Connor was a contemporary of mine. He grew up in Greenfield near my hometown of Hazelwood. When I was working at Pitt and he was working for Roy Rogers Restaurants he introduced me to Roy Rogers—"The King of the Cowboys"—in the press box at Pitt Stadium. You would never forget something like that.

Leo Koeberlein of Pleasant Hills, the former managing editor of *The Pittsburgh Press*, also died last month. He hired me twice, for a summer internship during my student days at Pitt, and later when I returned to Pittsburgh in 1979 after one year in Miami and nine years in New York. Like Auerbach, he was a demanding boss, but a fair one.

Beckley Smith Jr., who grew up in Mt. Lebanon, also died last month. He had been the P.A. announcer at Penguins' games in the '80s, but I knew him better from the final season of the Pittsburgh Hornets —in 1966—when we teamed up to broadcast about ten of their games on WEEP Radio. He called the action and I provided the color.

I mentioned to my friend George Schoeppner, a retired insurance salesman from Mt. Lebanon, that when you got into your 60s you started recognizing more of the names in the obituary notices. "I went to 42 funerals last year," said Schoeppner, "and 30 funerals so far this year."

My pal Bill Priatko told me he'd gone to as many as ten funerals in a month. "You've got to go and pay your respects," he said, sounding like a disciple of Art Rooney.

My friend Baldo Iorio of Heidelberg, who turned 90 last month, told me, "When you get to be my age you don't go to many funerals. All your friends are gone."

I remember once accompanying the West Virginia University basketball team to Logan, Utah for an NCAA first round championship tournament (March 11–12, 1982). It was held on the campus at Utah State University. I knew that had been the school of Merlin Olsen, the former great of the Los Angeles Rams who became a TV actor.

One day I went to the campus library and picked out a black leather-bound book called *Obituaries*. It was written by William Saroyan. I had met Saroyan once in New York at Gallagher's Restaurant for a media luncheon that preceded "The Greatest Fight of the Century" between Joe Frazier and Muhammad Ali at Madison Square Garden.

Saroyan had written this book when he was dying in a hospital. Someone had brought him a copy of the year-end edition of *Variety*. It contained a necrology—a list of all the people associated with show business who had died during the year. Saroyan bet a nurse he had personally known about 30 of the deceased and had enjoyed a personal experience in their company. *Obituaries* is Saroyan's off-the-cuff recollections of these famous and not-so-famous folks and it made for good reading on the road. I have often thought about his book when I've seen a list of sports people who died during a particular year. Such lists bring back mostly great memories.

Before the year was up, I would read in the newspaper about the death of Gordon Parks. He was a famous photographer, one of the first blacks to gain national acceptance and celebrity in that role in this country. I had first met Parks at the West Side Tennis Club in Forest Hills, New York. We were among the 80 some participants in a media-celebrity tennis tournament that preceded the U.S. Open Tennis Tournament.

Parks had luminous white hair. It was curly and reached his shoulders. It provided quite a contrast to his coal-black face. He had a theatrical look about him, like Franco Harris does. You figured Gordon Parks worked at that look. It was not merely a mask. He had deep penetrating eyes, better to see you with, but an easy smile. I was pleased and impressed to make his acquaintance.

The media tournament was all doubles competition. I didn't get to play with or against Gordon Parks, but I did get to play in a mixed doubles match against Sarah Palfrey Danzig. She had won a title or two at Wimbledon. Our team beat hers and I was eager to tell my wife about my latest tennis triumph.

"How old is she?" Kathie came back on the telephone. Kathie likes to keep me humble. I was in my early 30s at the time. Mrs. Danzig was in her early 60s. Who needed to know such information?

A few years later, I was on the winning doubles team in that same tournament when they were opening the new U.S. Open Tennis Center —now the Arthur Ashe Tennis Center—at Flushing Meadow, near Shea Stadium. So I was on the winning team in the first tennis tournament ever conducted there.

I wait each year for John McEnroe or Mary Carillo, two former tennis stars from the same hometown of Douglaston, New York, to recall that bit of trivia during the telecast of the U.S. Open. I'm still waiting. "Don't hold your breath," counsels Kathie.

I saw McEnroe make his professional tennis debut, by the way. It was at the West Side Tennis Club in an exhibition match against the great Pancho Gonzales.

That's a great memory, too.

When I was working at *The New York Post*, I covered the U.S. Open that same year at the West Side Tennis Club. We didn't have a Sunday newspaper, but I showed up anyhow on the final Saturday to see the men's final match between Jimmy Connors and Ken Rosewall.

The U.S. Open setting was much more sublime in those days. The press box took up one side of the court. It was a wooden affair, painted dark green, with a roof over it. There were about five or six rows with tables and chairs. The press box was even air-conditioned, a retreat from the harsh summer sun. I was sitting in the back near a cooler that had all kinds of beer chilling in water that was filled with ice cubes. I chose to drink the Rolling Rock brand in the green bottles that afternoon. A young writer from *The New York Daily News* came upon me—it was Gene Ward's son and I believe his name was Greg—and asked, "Why would you come here on your day off?"

"If you can tell me something I'd rather do on a Saturday afternoon," I replied, "please tell me what it might be. I'm all ears."

I remember one of my mentors in my New York days, Dick Young of the *Daily News,* the best baseball writer of his time, telling me, "I don't want to be a millionaire. I just want to live like one."

Young and I were both sitting in lounge chairs at poolside of a San Diego Hotel when he said that. We were staying in the same hotel as the New York Mets. We were typing away as we sunned ourselves. A story had broken that day, about a trade, and we were on the scene to get the news first-hand. The rest of the reporters were staying at a newer, swankier hotel on the outskirts of San Diego. They had made their own travel arrangements. They had to hustle into town for the impromptu press conference.

"We're supposed to be with the team," declared Dick Young. "My paper didn't send me out here to be on vacation."

Arnold "Red" Auerbach, John Havlicek and Tommy Heinsohn are all smiles in Boston Celtics' team photo in 1971.

Bruce Van Dyke and Jack Butler
On Steelers' Legends Team

I see Bruce Van Dyke from time to time when he is walking along the Peters Trail not far from his McMurray manse. He walks there occasionally on weekends with his wife Maureen. My wife Kathie and I always say hello. He smiles, happy to be recognized. Most trail travelers have no idea that he played for the Steelers once upon a time.

His hair may be thinner at 63, but he still looks a lot like the guy who played guard for the Steelers from 1967 to 1973. He was in the Steelers' starting lineup when they reached the playoffs in 1972 and 1973 for the first time in the team's history.

His best season might have been 1972 when he was named first team All-AFC by *The Sporting News* and second team by the UPI and Football Writers. He had come to the Steelers in 1967 along with full-back Earl Groh from the Philadelphia Eagles in exchange for running back/receiver Gary Ballman.

At 6–2, 265 pounds, Van Dyke was definitely a first-rate football player. That's why Steelers' chairman and owner Dan Rooney selected Van Dyke for the team's "Legends Team," those who played in Pittsburgh prior to the Steelers' Super Bowl seasons of the mid-to-late 70s.

"Bruce Van Dyke was definitely our most valuable player that season," said former teammate Andy Russell. "He was a key factor on the field and certainly in the clubhouse. He set a competitive tone and was part of our turnaround from a bad football team to a good football team."

That's why Van Dyke was among those outstanding Steelers of the past who were honored at halftime of last Sunday's Steelers' game with the Buffalo Bills. It's part of a yearlong celebration of the Steelers' 75th season in the National Football League.

The late Art Rooney founded the team in 1933 and they were called the Pirates until 1940.

Van Dyke is the lone "Legend" who lives in the South Hills. His son Brad, 18, is a senior and plays on the lacrosse team at Peters Township High School. One of the benefits of this year's anniversary is that fans that are paying attention will learn more about Steelers such as Van Dyke.

Most of the individuals who masquerade as modern day Steelers' fans by wearing black and gold garb from head to toe and waving Terrible Towels couldn't pick Van Dyke or most of the living "Legends" out of a police lineup. If one is to truly appreciate the Steelers' story he or she must learn the team's tradition and history.

"It's an honor to be recognized on a team with Pro Football Hall of Famers like 'Bullet Bill' Dudley, Bobby Layne, John Henry Johnson and Ernie Stautner," said Van Dyke last week when I interviewed him at his home in McMurray. "It's great to be in the same lineup as 'Big Daddy' Lipscomb, Jack Butler, Dick Hoak and Roy Jefferson."

Butler, who has lived with his wife Bernie in Munhall for many years, should be recognized in the Pro Football Hall of Fame. He's always been a humble, low-key sort and he'd never complain about the oversight. "I'm happy to have played for my hometown team all those years, and to have lived in Pittsburgh so many years," said Butler at a press conference at the Steelers' South Side training complex last week.

On a personal level, the Butlers bought their home in Munhall from the Thomas family. My sister-in-law, Diane Thomas Churchman, grew up in that home. It's a big place, but the Butlers needed the space since they had eight children—four boys and four girls. It's one of those mansions that sit on a knob behind the Carnegie Library of Homestead. I had a chance to check it out when I was visiting the library for a tour in late 2007.

Jack Butler retired this year, at age 79, from his position of the director of the Blesto Scouting Service. It was the second scouting combine in pro football. His work as a talent scout should count toward his qualification for Hall of Fame honors as well as the interception numbers he recorded as a defensive back in nine seasons with the Steelers (1951–1959). Butler pointed the Steelers in the direction of many outstanding players for the college draft.

He and Dick LeBeau, the defensive coordinator of the Steelers, should have been inducted into the Pro Football Hall of Fame in Canton many years ago. When LeBeau retired from the Detroit Lions he was third in career interceptions in the NFL and still ranks among the leaders. His innovative work as a defensive coach and his 50-year career as a stellar citizen in the NFL should be on his resume as well.

A Veterans Committee recently nominated two defensive backs, Emmitt Thomas of the Kansas City Chiefs and former Pitt legend Marshall Goldberg of the Chicago Cardinals, for consideration by the voters for the Hall of Fame. Neither one of them has credentials that can compare with the achievements of Butler and LeBeau. (Thomas was inducted into the Hall of Fame in the summer of 2008.)

Some others with local ties might have been in the "Legends" line-up that was recognized on Sunday. Andy Russell, who like Van Dyke played at the University of Missouri, would qualify as one of the linebackers. Russell resides near the clubhouse at Nevillewood. Hopefully, Russell, who played in seven Pro Bowls, will be on the All-Time Team.

Russell's good friend, the late Ray Mansfield, who lived in Upper St. Clair, could have been the center for the "Legends."

Chuck Cherundolo, a Penn State grad, was Rooney's selection there. Nobody asked me but I believe the team's best center before Mike Webster was Notre Dame grad Bill Walsh (1949–1955). Dudley, who's in the Hall of Fame, should be a running back on the "Legends" team as well as the All-Time Team. Dick Hoak was a plugger; Dudley was twice the league's MVP and led the league in rushing, intercep-

Bruce Van Dyke spends time with Lloyd Voss at Steelers' Alumni Golf Outing at Diamond Run in North Hills.

Rocky Bleier, Bruce Van Dyke, Jack Ham and Mel Blount attend wine tasting fund-raiser at Grand Concourse Restaurant at Station Square.

tions and punt returns, as well as being the team's punter back in the '40s. Dudley and Franco Harris both lifted the Steelers to the elite ranks in the NFL. There's a difference between being great and being good.

Van Dyke was traded to the Green Bay Packers after the 1973 season. Dan Devine, his coach at Missouri, wanted him and Russell on his team when he became the coach at Green Bay. "I got on the bad side of our line coach Dan Radakovich," said Van Dyke, explaining the reason behind his departure. He and Mansfield were famous for sneaking out of training camp after curfew and frequenting bars on Route 30 late at night. Asked to characterize himself in those days, Van Dyke confessed with a smile, "I guess I was kinda carefree. I had a good time."

He and Bill Saul used to hang out at Dante's, a watering hole in Brentwood-Whitehall that had been the favorite haunt years earlier of Bobby Layne, Ernie Stautner and others. "We had some good players. I got to play with Andy Russell, Dick Hoak, Clendon Thomas, Ben McGee and Roy Jefferson, among others, with the Steelers. I played against them when they had John Henry Johnson and I was with the Eagles."

Asked if he was disappointed that he missed out on the Super Bowl years here, Van Dyke cracked a funny line that I missed. "That was a joke," he came back. Oh well, Chuck Noll didn't get his humor either. Noll wanted his veterans to set a better tone, which is why he also traded away Roy Jefferson, the team's best player in that period. "Of course, I was crushed," said Van Dyke. "I would have liked to have been part of those Super Bowl championship teams. Actually, I was crushed that I missed out on that."

He also missed out on the big money. "I see how Chucky Okobi was making $2.5 million a year as a backup center with the Steelers, and he never even played," said Van Dyke. "I didn't make $500,000 in eleven years. It's nice when you can make millions and you don't even have to do anything."

Van Dyke has been working as a sales manager the past 20-some years for Golden Eagle Construction, a Uniontown firm that sells stone and asphalt and paves roadways. "We just got everybody upset by repaving a long stretch of Route 19 in McMurray," said Van Dyke.

I suggested that there should be a stretch of Route 19 in Upper St. Clair named after Chuck Noll. He lived in the same house in that community all of his 23 years as coach of the Steelers.

I told Van Dyke I'd been to Green Bay and that I'd seen streets and avenues named after Packers' luminaries such as Vince Lombardi, Mike Holmgren and Brett Favre. "They have an alley somewhere here (Crafton) named after Bill Cowher, don't they?" said Van Dyke. "Maybe we could do better by Coach Noll." I later learned from Van Dyke's father-in-law that when Bruce was a boy he lived on Van Dyke Road, named for his family who once had a farm there.

Bruce Van Dyke

352

A footnote: my pal Bill Priatko remains so proud of his playing days at North Braddock Scott, Pitt and with the Steelers in 1957. This is his 50th anniversary of his rookie season with the Steelers. Better yet, he and his wife Helen recently celebrated their 50th wedding anniversary.

Priatko and Dick LeBeau were teammates at training camp of Cleveland Browns in 1959, and they have remained close ever since. Priatko also played with the Green Bay Packers. They compare notes before and after every Steelers' game.

An ardent member of the Steelers' Alumni organization, Priatko knows and appreciates the Steelers' history more than most. He was hoping his boyhood hero, Fran Rogel, would be recognized during the Steelers' 75th season celebration. Bobby Layne once said Rogel was the toughest player he ever had for a teammate. In our view, however, Rogel was a plugger, a gritty gridiron competitor of the highest order, but not a great player.

Rogel, who played and coached at North Braddock Scott, starred at California (Pa.) State College, Penn State and was the leading rusher for the Steelers for five of six seasons in the early '50s, losing out one year to Ray Mathews of Port Vue in one of those seasons. Mathews is a member of the Steelers' "Legends" team as a receiver. He still plays in a lot of charity golf outings in this area.

"If I knew I was going to live this long," admits Mathews, "I'd have taken better care of myself."

Jim O'Brien

Bill Priatko joins his pal Dick LeBeau at Steelers' training camp at St. Vincent College in Latrobe.

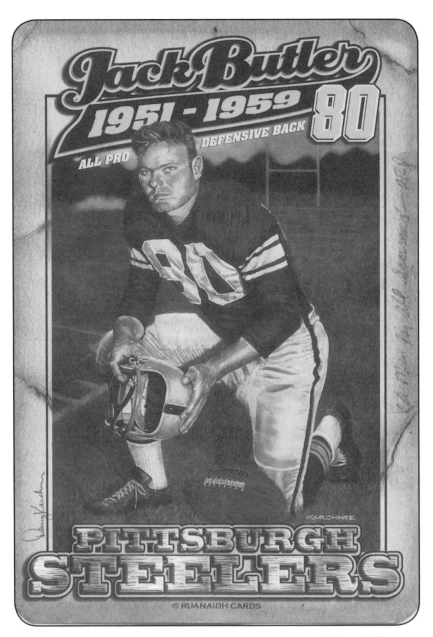

Jack Butler's Steelers career is celebrated in this special card that was commissioned by his friend and fellow scout, Art Rooney Jr. of Upper St. Clair. The artwork is by Denny Karchner.

354

Peyton Manning
There were reasons
to root for the Colts

February 7, 2007

I was pleased that Peyton Manning and Tony Dungy directed the Indianapolis Colts to a 29–17 victory over the Chicago Bears in Super Bowl XL. I was rooting for them because of Manning and Dungy as well as Tom Moore and Tyler Frenzel, and because our Steelers weren't there this time around.

Moore is the offensive coordinator of the Colts. Moore was an assistant coach on Chuck Noll's staff with the Steelers from 1977 to 1989. I first met Moore when he was an assistant coach on Babe Parilli's staff with the New York Stars of the old World Football League. That's also where I first met Lloyd Voss, who had played for the Steelers under Bill Austin and Noll. Voss and I would later return to Pittsburgh and reside in the South Hills and become friends.

Moore lived in Upper St. Clair as Noll and most of his coaches did. Moore still owns a home there, where his daughter Terry Dasdorf lives.

"When I retire," Moore told me when we met a while back at South Hills Village, "I'm coming back here. I love Pittsburgh. Chuck Noll was the greatest influence in my career and my life. There's a lot of Chuck Noll on the sidelines with Tony Dungy as the head coach. He was a Noll disciple too. And there's a lot of Terry Bradshaw in Peyton Manning. They both call their own game."

I first met Dungy when I covered the Steelers for *The Pittsburgh Press* in 1979. He was different, quieter and more humble and spiritual than most pro players. To hear the reports, he remains that way. That's what really sets him and Bears' coach Lovie Smith apart from the pack, not that they are both black. I was never a fan of in-your-face coaches or loudmouth ballplayers. That's one of the reasons I was never completely enamored with either Bill Cowher or his pet player Joey Porter though both served the Steelers well.

I wasn't a fan of Peyton Manning or any of the Mannings—father Archie and brother Eli—for several reasons until my friend George Schoeppner told me stories about Peyton Manning and how he was such a blessing in the young life of his grandson, Tyler Frenzel of Carmel, Indiana.

Schoeppner is a former Pitt All-American baseball player (in the late '50s) and a retired insurance man from Mt. Lebanon. Tyler was the son of Schoeppner's daughter, Pam Frenzel and her husband Eric. Tyler was diagnosed at age seven with leukemia. He was a big fan of Peyton Manning and wore a Colts' jersey with No. 18 on it.

When Peyton Manning learned of Tyler Frenzel and his fight with cancer he began exchanging cards and letters and autographed Colts' stuff. They became pen pals. Peyton sent Tyler a cake for his 9th birthday and a $200 gift certificate for the Colts' Store. Peyton has contributed a great deal of money and personal time to a children's hospital in Indianapolis.

My wife Kathie and I had lunch the Friday of Super Bowl Weekend with George Schoeppner and his wife Barbara at Atria's Restaurant & Tavern in Peters Township, about 15 miles south of Pittsburgh. Barbara said that Tyler attended a holiday party hosted by Peyton Manning five days before Tyler died at age 9 on Dec. 11, 2004.

I can't imagine how much the death of a grandchild can hurt. Yet George bites his lip, winces a bit, and allows a smile to form any time I talk to him about Tyler.

"We'll be rooting for Peyton and the Colts," said George, "and I think Tyler will be looking down on him, too."

I've long been a Colts fan. Back in the '50s, the Steelers and Colts shared a TV contract with DuPont, and Pittsburgh football fans got a steady diet of either Steelers or Colts contests on TV each Sunday. John Unitas, a Pittsburgh-born and bred ballplayer, was the Colts' quarterback. He was the best quarterback in football. He'd been cut by the Steelers after seeing no action in exhibition games his rookie year in the NFL.

He played for the Bloomfield Rams in a Pittsburgh heavyweight sandlot league. He gave all of us sandlot ballplayers hope. When I was playing for the Hazelwood Steelers in a Greater Pittsburgh Midget Football League I wore his No. 19, wore my hair in a crew cut, wore black hightop football shoes, practiced throwing the ball just past my ear as if I were throwing a curve in baseball. If I had been taller, more talented athletically, quicker, stronger armed and wasn't near-sighted I, too, might have been another kid from Pittsburgh to make it big in the NFL. In short, and I was quite short, Johnny Unitas was my boyhood hero as far as football went.

I had thought about traveling to Miami for Super Bowl XLI. There were some people I wanted to see, like Mike Ditka and Dan Marino, and Marino's dad, Dante, and their good friend and neighbor Angelo Dundee, the legendary trainer for Muhammad Ali. Dan Marino does the same kind of things for ailing children in South Florida as Manning does in Indianapolis. There is a wing in a children's hospital dedicated in Marino's name.

I had worked for *The Miami News* in 1969, covering the Dolphins. I thought I'd visit some old haunts, and talk to some old sportswriters and friends in the sports world. I did that when the big game was in Tampa six years earlier.

When Kathie told me that our older daughter, Sarah, and our granddaughter, Margaret, were coming to our home that same weekend, I scrapped the Miami trip.

I didn't watch the Super Bowl game with the attention I have always preferred. I ended up reading a half dozen children's books to

Margaret, helping her—not much mind you—assemble jigsaw puzzles, and watching her decorate cookies that Kathie baked with her.

It was great just to have Margaret sitting next to me on one of the couches in our family room to watch the Super Bowl. I felt especially smart when I saw there was a steady downpour at the stadium in Miami. I wouldn't have been happy sitting in the auxiliary press section, out in the stands, out in the rain.

I don't know who looked more perplexed in the rain, Bears' quarterback Rex Grossman or Prince, who sang his hit "Purple Rain" during the halftime extravaganza. Prince was playing an electric guitar and I prayed he didn't get electrocuted.

There were constant bulletins at the bottom of the TV screen about the little girl who was missing in Braddock. She was about the same age as Margaret. I feared the worst and was not surprised, just terribly saddened, to learn she was later found dead in woods near her home. She died from the cold. Her father was upset with her and left her there to die. It's the kind of senseless tragedy that brings everybody back to the real world. It's the dark side of life as opposed to the bright side where celebrated ballplayers such as Peyton Manning and Danny Marino do what they can to help ailing children and their families during difficult times. It should make us all count our blessings. The Super Bowl, after all, is just a game.

In honor of Tyler Frenzel
1995-2004

Tyler Frenzel lost his fight with cancer, but he always said, "No limits. Fight hard. Never give up." Peyton Manning of the Colts befriended young Frenzel and has contributed his money and time to help ailing children in Indianapolis.

Ernie Buccini
Praying for the Steelers
with black and gold rosary beads

Ernest Buccini was packing his bags for a vacation trip to Florida with his wife Helen. They were in their home in McKeesport on a morning when the sun was slow to get out of bed and the temperature outside was creeping toward 40 degrees. It was a gray day in Pittsburgh on April 1, 2008 and the Buccinis were both looking forward to spending some time in the sun.

I had first met them several years earlier when they were buying one of my books at Waldenbooks at Century III Mall in West Mifflin. They became regular customers and, on one of their visits with me, Ernie gave me a set of rosary beads he had made. They were black and gold rosary beads.

They were mostly black beads with an occasional gold bead breaking up each set of ten beads. "There are 59 beads in a rosary," Ernie informed me.

"I've been making rosary beads for people for a long time," he said, "and I'm such a big Steelers' fan I felt it would be a good thing to make some black and gold rosary beads. I make them and give them away, and some people buy them from me."

The Buccinis are members of St. Mark's Church in neighboring Port Vue. He mentioned that Port Vue was the hometown of Ray Mathews, a star receiver for the Steelers in the '50s. He remembered that George Hays, an end from St. Bonaventure who played for the Steelers (1950–52), was a neighbor of his brother-in-law in Elizabeth Township, and was the first Steeler he ever met. I had met George Hays a few years earlier during an autographing session for Steelers of the '50s at Robert Morris University.

George Hays later served as an assistant coach to Chuck Klausing during his successful run at Braddock High School. "I was fortunate to have a great assistant coach," said Klausing. "I knew the linemen were impressed with what they were learning from George. Even in 1954, the players had the dream of playing in the NFL."

I asked Ernie if he ever prayed for the Steelers on those black and gold rosary beads. He ran his fingers through his thinning hair before he answered my question.

"I cuss at them once in a while," he said with a smile. "Sure, I pray for them. Everybody prays for the Steelers, don't they?"

Ernie Buccini has been a devoted Steelers' fan for most of his 75 years yet, oddly enough, he has never seen a single game in person. "I watch them on television," he said. "When I was a kid, I listened to them on the radio."

He was born in late 1932, the year before Art Rooney founded the Steelers, who were originally named the Pirates. So the Steelers' 75th anniversary season was special to Ernie as well. He would turn 76 in November, 2008. He was long retired from Equitable Gas Company. "I started out digging ditches for them, and ended up in gas control in their downtown offices," he said. "One year I made several black and gold rosary beads and sent one to Art Rooney, one to Dan Rooney, and one to Chuck Noll," recalled Ernie. "A relative of ours was working for Dan Rooney at the time, and I gave them to her to take to the office. I got a nice letter back from Art Rooney thanking me for the gift and saying he would put them to good use. I still have it. I treasure it."

Buccini brought the letter from Art Rooney to show me. I recognized the signature. It was the real deal. Rooney told him he'd get the rosary beads blessed and say some prayers on his behalf.

I wonder what happened to those rosary beads. I recall that Art Rooney Jr. told me that his family held a draft to dispense with his dad's personal belongings when he died. "I got his Bible with my first pick," said Art Jr. "It was full of prayer cards. My dad used the cards he picked up at funerals for bookmarks."

I told Ernie Buccini that Art Rooney used to take out what they call a short set of rosary beads late in ballgames at Three Rivers Stadium, and say some prayers. He was usually flanked by Catholic priests in his private box, just for good measure.

Ernie smiled and shared a story about those rosary beads. "Some one asked me if they were called 'Terrible Rosary Beads,' and I told him I didn't think that would sound right," Ernie explained. After all, he suggested, there's a big difference between rosary beads and a towel.

"I still root for them," said Ernie. "My favorite players now are Troy Polamalu, Hines Ward and Ben Roethlisberger. I'm still watching them on TV at my home in McKeesport."

Ernie Buccini displays a pair of black and gold rosary beads that he fashioned for Steelers' fans.

Art Rooney Jr. commissioned California artist Merv Corning to create a series of cards honoring Steelers in the Hall of Fame.

Wellington Mara
A real Giant in Pleasantville

*"The Irish were not meant
to be out in the sun."*

November 2, 2005

Ishared some magic moments with Wellington Mara. He was the co-owner of the New York Giants football team and one of the most respected leaders in the National Football League.

He brought dignity and integrity to a league that needs it more than ever because of the owners, coaches and ballplayers who bring it down with their bad behavior and bad judgment.

He was a close friend and admirer of Art Rooney, the owner of the Pittsburgh Steelers. Wellington's father, Tim, was more of a contemporary of Art Rooney. Tim Mara was a licensed bookmaker. He handled some of the bets Mr. Rooney placed the day he made the big killing betting the horses at Saratoga in the late '30s.

Wellington Mara always said he was the son of an Irish bookmaker. He was nicknamed "Duke" because it went with Wellington, and the way he carried himself. I was fortunate as a young man to walk with Wellington Mara and Art Rooney.

Wellington Mara looked at the world through squinted eyes and with a thin smile. He was Irish through and through, like the Rooneys, and wore his Irishness on his sleeves.

I went to Mass with Wellington Mara and Art Rooney and their wives, Ann and Kathleen, on St. Patrick's Day in Maui in March, 1981. We were there for the NFL Owners' Meeting. The Maria Lanakila Church in Lahaina was a modest white-walled edifice, beautiful in its simplicity. Mr. Mara and Mr. Rooney attended Mass every morning, no matter where they were. They recruited others to join them. It is a treasured memory.

Mr. Mara said he was "always comfortable in the company" of Art Rooney. He said his father Tim had told him that track people were honest and you could take them at their word. One of Mr. Rooney's granddaughters married one of Wellington Mara's sons.

I always cherished the times I spent on the sideline at football fields with Mr. Rooney at the South Park Fairgrounds, when I was 19, and at Three Rivers Stadium, when I was 38 and 39 and 40. I also stood on the sideline with Mr. Mara during Giants' practices at Yankee Stadium in The Bronx, not far from Fordham, where he'd gone to school, or at Pleasantville, not far from his home in Rye. Pleasantville was the home of Pace University, where the Giants held their summer training camp, and where *Readers Digest* was produced. Just for the record, though, *Readers Digest* was founded in Pittsburgh by a former Westinghouse employee, DeWitt Wallace and his wife Lila Bell.

Two famous writers, Dashiell Hammett (*The Maltese Falcon*) and Lilliam Hellman (*The Children's Hour*), also resided in Pleasantville and were romantically linked. It was fitting that Mr. Mara was in a place called Pleasantville. It suited his personality perfectly. I last spoke to him when I went to Tampa to attend the Super Bowl three years ago (his Giants were playing for the championship). I talked to him for a book I was writing about Mr. Rooney called *The Chief*.

His large family surrounded Wellington Mara when he succumbed to cancer at age 89 last week at his home in Rye. It caught my eye when I read that he had been battling skin cancer for over 25 years.

Mr. Mara and I both were Irish with blue eyes. We were both squinting into the sunlight one afternoon on a particularly bright day in Pleasantville. Mr. Mara always had three smiles on his face, one with his mouth and two more with his eyes. They were in a perpetual squint it seemed. "The Irish were not meant to be out in the sun," he told me one day as we stood on the sideline. "We're fair-skinned, and we're better built to be in peat bogs, caves and other dark places. That may account for why the Irish spend so much time in pubs, taverns and bars." He smiled at his own story.

Mr. Mara had a sense of fairness about him. He knew the difference between right and wrong. He knew the NFL would only be as strong as its weakest member. He had the richest franchise, but he shared the wealth with the Green Bays and Baltimores and Pittsburghs.

WELLINGTON MARA
A giant among Giants

New York Giants archives

It's unlikely the Steelers would have been playing the Baltimore Ravens in a nationally televised game on Monday night if there were no Wellington Maras showing the way. He helped convince Art Modell and Art Rooney and Carroll Rosenbloom to take their NFL teams into the AFC part of the merged pro football leagues back in 1970.

Modell is often cast as a villain because he later moved his Cleveland team to Baltimore, but it was the only way he could save his franchise. He, too, is a good man. And he spoke last week of his high regard for Wellington Mara. So did Dan Rooney.

Wellington Mara was a man's man. He walked tall and when he spoke everyone listened. Walking with his likes was a gift from the God he loved and honored every day of his life.

Paul Waner
Wore No. 11 with dignity

Any self-respecting Pirates' fan should know about Paul Waner. He was certainly one of the greatest ballplayers in Pirates' history. He was their all-star rightfielder before Roberto Clemente came to Pittsburgh from Puerto Rico. They both knew every nook and cranny in the angular right field wall at Forbes Field, a wall that lent character to the revered ballpark in Oakland. Those two gifted glovemen instinctively knew where to position themselves to catch any ball that caromed off the wall or the screen above it, and they knew where to throw it.

Waner played for the Pirates for 15 seasons, from 1926 to 1940, and played five more seasons with the Brooklyn Dodgers, Boston Braves and New York Yankees. He joined the Pirates at the age of 23. His career batting average was .333. His batting average with the Pirates was .340—still the best in club history. He won three National League batting titles in the '20s and '30s.

He batted .336 as a rookie and led the league with 22 triples. Some baseball historians say Waner's rookie season was the best by a right fielder in National League history. The following season, he won the first of his batting titles with a .380 average, led the league in hits with 237 and in triples with 17.

He holds another record that is even more stunning. In that second season with the Pirates, the pennant-winning year of 1927, Waner led the way with 131 runs batted in. That record remains in the Pirates' guidebook, even though the team claims such run producers as Ralph Kiner, Willie Stargell, Roberto Clemente, Honus Wagner and Barry Bonds.

Only Wagner scored more runs—1,520—than Waner's 1,492. He and Wagner both top the Pirates' all-time list with 556 doubles. Waner's 186 triples are second only to Wagner's 231. In the extra-base hits category, Stargell leads with 953, with Wagner second with 869 and Waner third with 850.

A left-handed hitter, Waner usually batted third in the Pirates' lineup.

He represented the Pirates, along with Pie Traynor, in the first All-Star Game in Chicago in 1933 and with Traynor and Arky Vaughan the following year. Some of his teammates on the Pirates included Gus Suhr, Babe Herman, Elbie Fletcher, Woody Jensen, Bob Elliott and Mace Brown. He played in a golden era when the likes of Babe Ruth, Jimmie Foxx, Mickey Cochrane, Frankie Frisch, Rogers Hornsby, Hack Wilson, Al Simmons, Tony Lazzeri, Bill Terry, Lefty Grove, Dazzy Vance, Chuck Klein, Lefty O'Doul and Dizzy Dean were in the majors.

All Pirates' fans know that Clemente closed his career with an even 3,000 hits in regular season play. Waner had 3,152 hits. He got his 3,000th hit, interestingly enough, against the Pirates in 1942. He played for the Braves that year.

LLOYD WANER, showing his left-handed batting form in 1940, was a Hall of Fame rightfielder for Pirates.

Waner was inducted into the Baseball Hall of Fame in 1952. In 2007, the Pirates retired his number—11—and that honor should help make present-day fans become better acquainted with this legendary ballplayer. Waner wore No. 11, for sure, from 1932 to 1939 and No. 9 in 1940. Records for player numbers are not available before 1932.

Bob Smizik, the veteran sports writer of the *Pittsburgh Post-Gazette* and a long-time voter for the Baseball Hall of Fame, has urged the Pirates to retire Paul Waner's number for a long time, believing him well deserving of the honor.

Waner was known for having exceptional bat control. In his book, *The Pittsburgh Pirates: An Illustrated History*, Smizik shares an observation from Frankie Gustine, who joined the Pirates in 1939 and became a roommate of Waner.

"It was unbelievable," said Gustine, who owned and operated a popular restaurant near Forbes Field for over 30 years. "He would stand up there and announce he was going to hit everything down the left-field line. And that's what he would do. Pitch after pitch almost to the exact same spot, right down the line."

Paul Waner was called "Big Poison." Yet he was small in stature, standing just 5–8^1/$_2$. He was listed at 155 pounds, but he said he never weighed that much. "I never weighed more than 145 pounds in my life," Waner said years after he concluded his major league career. "When I started out in the minors in San Francisco I weighed more like 139 or 140 pounds."

Hyperbole or exaggeration was the name of the game in sports back then. Everyone had a nickname. The Steelers had "Bullet Bill" Dudley. He was also slight in stature and, by his own admission today, not very fast. Alliteration meant more than accuracy in those days.

Ballplayers were smaller back then. Paul's brother Lloyd also starred for the Pirates. He was the same size and he was called "Little Poison." The Pirates would later have some other brother acts—Johnny and Eddie O'Brien and George and Gene Freese —but none could compare to the Waners. Lloyd Waner's career batting average was .319. He was inducted into the Baseball Hall of Fame in 1967.

The Waner brothers came out of the dust fields of Oklahoma to make their mark in the major leagues. As kids, they used to play baseball by hitting corncobs with sawed-off broomsticks. They'd break off a piece of a corncob about the size of a baseball. "You could really make them curve," recalled Paul Waner.

With the Waners, they never worried about the equipment. They could hit anything thrown their way.

"The constant practice of hitting the strange curves of the corncob did more than anything else to build up my batting," Paul Waner once said. "You had to keep your eye on the cob because it could blind you. If it hit you in the eye or if it hit your head it hurt like hell. There were more curves in those corncob games than I have ever seen in a real baseball game."

Waner, it was reported, used to let the baseball bat rest on his shoulder until the pitcher released the ball. He had powerful lightning-quick wrists and he hit line drives. Like many players of that era, he looks older in his photos than he was.

The Pirates take pride in their archives. They keep voluminous records and newspaper clippings on players past and present, but material from the early days is hard to come by. The teams simply didn't pay attention to such details in the early days.

So the file on Paul Waner is a slim one. Through the years, whatever materials might have been in that file have been lost or misplaced, or borrowed and not returned by baseball researchers.

Here's one historical note that places Waner's feats in their historical perspective: On May 20, 1932, on the day Amelia Earhart began her trans-Atlantic solo flight from Newfoundland to Ireland, Paul Waner stepped up his assault on Chuck Klein's record for doubles in a season—59 for the Phillies in 1930. Waner hit four doubles that afternoon and finished the season with a record 62 doubles.

In August of 1937, Waner was experiencing early difficulty in picking up the ball as it was pitched. He was given some advice by pitcher Carl Hubbell of the Giants: "Just hit what you see," said Hubbell. Waner went three-for-four that day.

Waner was known for partying and staying out late at night. "They say money talks," he said, "but all it's ever said to me is 'Goodbye.'" He had a serious drinking problem, but he showed up at the ballpark ready to perform. He didn't always look so good, but it didn't seem to hinder him from hitting a baseball or catching a ball that ricocheted off the wall at Forbes Field.

They told stories about Waner's weakness for hard liquor. He drank too much and smoked too much. He died in 1965 at age 62. Branch Rickey at age 83 died that same year of a heart attack. Rickey was reputed for his tee-totaling ways. Waner died from emphysema. My father died at age 63 from emphysema. Yes, he also drank and smoked too much, and he was small and slim like the Waner boys.

Late in Waner's career, when Frankie Frisch was the manager of the Pirates, Frisch found a whiskey bottle in the clubhouse. "Waner," he shouted in Paul's direction. "Is this your bottle?"

"What's in it?" Waner wanted to know.

"It's half full," offered Frisch.

"Then it's not mine," Waner replied. "If it was mine it'd be empty."

They say that the ballclub convinced Waner to go on the wagon once, and refrain from drinking, and that he went into the worst batting slump of his career. He often came to the ballpark with a bad hangover and he did somersaults on the field to clear his head. It was a different era.

I remember talking to Mace Brown, who was an all-star caliber pitcher for the Pirates in 1938, while visiting him at his home in Greensboro, North Carolina. He remembered the Waners well.

"Paul and Lloyd Waner were two of the great ones I played with," said Brown back on October 25, 1998. "Lloyd could fly to first base. He had some hands and he had a good strong arm. He wasn't the hitter

Paul was, but he could run, and he got a lot of singles that way. I think he had 199 singles one year. Paul was the best hitter I ever saw until I played with Ted Williams. He was one of the few hitters who could tell you where he was going to hit it. He'd foul off balls until he got his pitch. There were several years (three, in fact) when they both had 200 or more hits. Pound for pound, the Waners were as good as anybody."

Fortunately, there are some former Pirates players and managers who had first-hand experiences with Waner.

Frank Thomas and Dick Groat grew up in Pittsburgh. Thomas lived in Oakland, only a few miles from Forbes Field, and could walk to the ballpark. Groat lived in Swissvale, just east of Pittsburgh.

"I was struggling at the bat my rookie year," recalled Groat of that 1952 season when he reported directly to the Pirates from the Duke campus. "Paul Waner owned and operated a batting cage out in Harmarville. I went out there to see him, and he really helped straighten me away. I was hitting .180 or something at the time, and I got up to .284 by the end of the season."

Groat won the National League batting title with a .325 average in the 1960 season and was named the league's MVP as the Pirates beat the Yankees in seven games to win the World Series. He once batted .319 for the St. Louis Cardinals after Joe Brown traded him.

"When I was a schoolboy, I used to go to games at Forbes Field," said Groat, "and we'd sit out in the cheap seats in right field. Paul Waner played that wall like a magician. No one ever played it as well until Bobby Clemente came along. He was pretty good out there, too."

Bob Friend, a star pitcher on that same Pirates' team, also remembered Waner having a batting cage in Harmarville, just east of Pittsburgh on old Freeport Road. "A lot of guys got help from him," recalled Friend. "We had a pretty good hitting instructor with the Pirates in those days in George Sisler. He was in the charter class of the Baseball Hall of Fame, and he helped a lot of guys, too."

Friend mentioned that Honus Wagner and Pie Traynor often were in the Pirates' dugout in those days, in the '50s, and offered tips and words of encouragement to anyone who approached them. Sometimes they put on a Pirates' uniform and sat on the bench with the ballplayers. That was a big thrill to many of the young men who played for the Pirates.

Frank Thomas, who calls himself "the original Frank Thomas" to differentiate him from the American League slugger of the same name of more recent vintage, also remembered Waner.

Thomas played for the Milwaukee Braves in 1961 when Waner was the team's hitting coach. "He still had great bat control, and he tried to get us all to spray the ball to different fields," said Thomas. "I was a power-hitter and a pull hitter and that wasn't for me. But I do remember that Waner thought you should try to hit the ball down the baselines. He said there were more players up the middle—the pitcher, the shortstop and the second baseman—and that you had a better chance of getting it past one player—the third baseman or the

Harold "Pie" Traynor

Pirates alumni lineup includes, left to right, Frankie Frisch, Waite Hoyt, Lloyd Waner, Pie Traynor and Max Carey.

Lloyd Waner, at left, with mother, sister Ruth, father, and brother Paul pose formally at Forbes Field

first baseman. He could hit the ball wherever he wanted to, even as an old man."

Chuck Tanner, who managed the Pirates when they won the World Series in 1971, comes to PNC Park regularly and sits behind home plate taking notes on the players. He has scouted for several major league teams since his managing days.

Tanner is a delightful fellow, always upbeat, and always with a story. He never disappoints. "No one's ever asked me for a Paul Waner story," he began. "You're the first writer I've ever told this story."

Tanner knows how to make a sportswriter feel special, you see. "I broke in with the Braves in the mid-50s when they held their spring training in Bradenton, where the Pirates are now," continued Tanner.

"In fact, Paul Waner is buried in Bradenton. I've been to his gravesite. One day, when I was at spring training there with the Braves, we're all around the batting cage taking our turns.

"The Braves in those days included Henry Aaron, Eddie Mathews, Del Crandall, Joe Adcock, Johnny Logan, Andy Pafko, Bobby Tompson, Red Schoendienst, Bill Bruton and Wes Covington. And don't forget Warren Spahn. He liked to get in his licks, too. He was a good hitter for a pitcher. So was Lew Burdette, the other ace pitcher.

"Paul Waner was our hitting instructor. He was standing there holding a 3/4˝ steel pipe in his hand. He leaned on it now and then like it was a cane. He was telling us to try to hit the ball to different spots in the outfield. He wanted us to be able to hit to all fields, whatever the situation dictated we do. He wanted us to be more versatile.

"He's hollering out advice and, finally, Del Crandall…I think it was Crandall…came over and went to hand Waner his bat. He said, 'Here, you show us how to do it!' Waner said, 'I don't need your bat.' Waner went into the batting cage with that 3/4˝ pipe, about half the diameter of a baseball bat. He'd tell us where he was going to hit it and that's where he'd hit it, over and over. Then, he stopped and said, 'That's enough.' And he went back to leaning on that steel pipe.

"I remember he told me to hit the ball down the line. 'Hit it like you're trying to hit it foul. It's either going to go foul and be a strike or it'll go right down the line and you might end up with a double.' He had all kinds of theories about hitting.

"I grew up in New Castle, and I read about those Pirates in the papers each morning. We didn't have enough money to afford the Sunday paper so an aunt would give it to me. I loved to read about the Pirates. So it was always a big deal when I'd meet one of those old-timers.

"So I always paid attention when someone like Paul Waner was talking."

Tanner, of course, was born on the 4th of July, hit a home run in his first major league at bat, and once pinch-hit for Henry Aaron in a runaway victory for the Braves. So being upbeat and positive comes naturally to him. So do stories about the likes of Paul Waner. They are both Pittsburgh baseball treasures.

Will Smith and Joe Montana
Big stars pay a visit
to Atria's in Mt. Lebanon

May 16, 2007

A burly fellow stuck his head inside the front door at Atria's Restaurant & Tavern in Mt. Lebanon and asked the hostess, "Can you handle a party of 12 for dinner?"

When the burly fellow got a positive response, he leaned closer to the hostess and whispered, "I've got Will Smith out there."

The hostess nodded again. She didn't pick up on the name right away. After all, Will Smith is a rather common name. It's not like Tom Cruise. Then, Will Smith stood in the doorway with his family and friends close behind.

Will Smith's nine-year-old son, Jaden, was close by his side. Yes, it was that Will Smith, tall and lean and all smiles. The 38-year-old movie star didn't look much different from when he first came to our attention on the TV sitcom "The Prince of Bel-Air." He and Jaden were the stars of a movie my wife Kathie and I had just seen at The Star City movie complex in Bridgeville. "Pursuit of Happyness"—that's how it's spelled on the marquee—was up for some Academy Awards.

If you haven't seen this movie, it's worth checking out. It's a different role than we're accustomed to seeing from Smith, now thought to be the No. 1 male movie star in Hollywood.

Will Smith and his son had been attending an all-star camp for young quarterbacks at Keystone Oaks High School in nearby Dormont.

Greg Dearolf, the proprietor of Atria's in Mt. Lebanon, and his wife Marlene rolled out the red carpet for Smith & Co. Dearolf said Smith told him his mother was from the North Side of Pittsburgh and now lived in the North Hills.

"He was nice with everyone," declared Dearolf. "He posed for some pictures, and exchanged greetings with anyone who said hello or smiled his way."

That was on the first Saturday in May. The following day Smith sent another famous fellow to Atria's with his wife and two sons. That was Joe Montana, the Hall of Fame quarterback from Monongahela. He was also in Pittsburgh for the quarterback camp. Ben Roethlisberger of the Steelers made a cameo appearance as well at the camp.

Joe Butler, one of the regulars at Atria's, had checked out the camp, and saw Roethlisberger there. Butler, who operates Metro Index, a scouting service, runs his own football camps in this area, most recently at the Steelers' training complex on the South Side.

Butler drinks iced tea with about a dozen guys who can be found at Atria's most Friday afternoons. I tell Kathie I am going to "the club," when I go there to check out the scene and get into some lively sports debates.

On the first Friday of this month all the regulars at the bar were eager to tell me what I missed while I was away that week. In addition to Smith and Montana, there were some other famous and semi-famous sports people who frequented Atria's in my absence.

Reggie Warford, a friend from my days working at Pitt when he was the assistant basketball coach on Roy Chipman's staff and more recently the head coach at Seton LaSalle High School, brought Kevin Young and Bob Lanier to Atria's on a Wednesday afternoon at the end of April.

The regulars recognized Young, a former first baseman with the Pittsburgh Pirates, but few knew Lanier. He should have been the easiest to recognize. Lanier is a husky 6–11, and wears size 22 shoes. His sneakers were on display in the Basketball Hall of Fame before Big Bob was inducted himself in 1992.

He was a dominant center for the Detroit Pistons and Milwaukee Bucks and had served in recent years in community service and as an ambassador for the National Basketball Association.

One female customer, I'm told, did look up at Lanier, now age 58, and ask him if he'd been a basketball player. How many times do you think he's been asked that question?

Debbie Tomich, one of the hostesses at Atria's, was especially pleased to see Joe Montana. They were classmates at Ringgold High School. "He signed my yearbook, but it was just Joe and not his full name."

This time Debbie got Joe Montana to sign a note to her sons. They didn't believe her when she came home the previous night and told them that Will Smith had been to Atria's. So Montana signed a note saying Smith was, indeed, there, as their mother told them. This time he signed his full name.

I missed this celebrity parade at Atria's because I was in Southern California visiting our younger daughter, Rebecca. We drove through Hollywood and Beverly Hills. I'd seen Brad Garrett, the big brother on "Everybody Loves Raymond," on a previous visit. Garrett grew up in Woodland Hills, where Rebecca now resides.

I had lunch in L.A. with Bill Sharman, a member of the Basketball Hall of Fame, as both a player and coach. He was an old friend from our ABA days and one of the classiest people I'd met in sports. The waiter asked to see Sharman's ring that he'd won as a front-office official of the NBA champion Lakers.

I spotted Danny Bonaducci at the Los Angeles Airport on our return home. He was a member of "The Partridge Family." About five or six years ago, I spotted Shirley Jones, the star of that TV show, at the Pittsburgh Airport and sat down and talked to her for 15 minutes.

Now that was really special. A friend of mine had Shirley Jones sign a CD cover of her hit songs for me on a recent appearance in Greensburg. He said she asked how I was doing. Hey, he's my friend, right?

Imagine the reaction when Will Smith and his son Jaden showed up at Atria's Restaurant & Tavern in Mt. Lebanon hoping to get a table for dinner. Owners Marlene and Greg Dearolf flank their celebrity customers.

One day later, Joe Montana, the Hall of Fame quarterback from Monongahela, came to Atria's after Will Smith recommended it and told him to see owner Greg Dearolf, a serious Steelers' fan.

Pittsburgh is still
City of Champions

"I got a second chance. I never gave up."
— Amy Palmiero-Winters

April 10, 2008

Bennie Cunningham and Randy Grossman were a great one-two combination as the tight ends on the Steelers in the '70s and teammates on the last two Super Bowl teams in that decade. Both had lots of hair then. Now they are both bald, Bennie as clean-shaven as his host, Mel Blount, as they appeared at a dinner last Friday night at the Pittsburgh Hilton.

"It's the style," claimed Cunningham, who along with Blount, offered big hugs to a sportswriter who had covered the club in those days. It was so good to see them, as well as 13 other members of that glorious cast at the Mel Blount Youth Home 10th Annual All-Star Celebrity Roast. There were 33 former Steelers on the scene.

They all looked a little different, and so did that sportswriter, from when they first met. Time flies and so does the hair in some cases when you're having so much fun. I had blow-dried my hair before going to the dinner, and had if puffed up just so, and was scolded by one old friend for having "that Jimmy Johnson look."

Jimmy O'Brien was happy being himself and being in such distinguished company at this black-tie affair that has raised millions of dollars to help Mel Blount and his wife TiAnda look after and help straighten out wayward kids at their horse farm out in Claysville and Taylortown in Washington County.

Agnus Berenato and Amy Palmiero-Winters are two women who stood tall at two different sports-related dinners last week. Berenato, the women's basketball coach at Pitt, was honored as the Sportswoman of the Year at the 2008 Dapper Dan Dinner & Sports Auction at the David L. Lawrence Convention Center on Tuesday, and Palmiero-Winters was honored as the Sportswoman of the Year at the 22nd Annual Awards & Scholarhip Banquet held by the Pittsburgh chapter of the National Italian-American Sports Hall of Fame.

Berenato had just returned from Spokane, Washington where she had led her Pitt women's basketball team to the NCAA Sweet 16 for the first time in the school's history. She's become a big hit here already and the best is yet to come. Her great gusto and genuine warmth attract admirers. She's made women's basketball relevant in this town. Suzie McConnell-Serio, the women's basketball coach at Duquesne, was also on the dais. She's enjoyed great success every step of the way in her wonderful career, including a gold medal (1988) and a bronze medal (1992) from the Olympic Games, and she's going to do great things as

Coach B. with Sidney Crosby

With Dr. Freddie Fu

Sportswoman of the Year

With Pitt Chancellor Nordenberg and star player Mercedes Walker

Agnus Berenato

Like a little kid at the circus, Agnus steals a peek at Dapper Dan Dinner scene.

With Suzie McConnell Serio, the women's basketball coach at Duquesne University.

well at Duquesne. Berenato embraced her, as she does everybody, at the pre-dinner gathering of sports celebrities at the Convention Center.

People need to know more about Palmiero-Winters. She was standing tall on a right leg of her own and a prosthesis that replaced the left leg she lost following a series of surgeries over a three-year period after she was badly injured in a motorcycle accident 14 years ago. She may be the best comeback story in sports this side of Rocky Bleier, and she is a reminder of what might have happened to Steelers' quarterback Ben Roethlisberger when he got banged up in his motorcycle accident.

Palmiero-Winters is a 35-year-old welder from Meadville who has set world records in the marathon for female amputees on two occasions. She was 21 when she was involved in the accident and 24 when her left leg had to be amputated below the knee. "I never gave up," she said. "I had a second chance to compete at what I loved to do." Her courage is such an inspirational story.

Her current record in the marathon is 3 hours and 4 minutes. That's about how long most sports banquets last.

I went to three sports-related banquets last week. It not only expanded my waistline, unfortunately, but it also expanded my regard for the great sports successes we have enjoyed in this city that is now celebrating its 250th anniversary.

For someone who liked to read inspirational stories about sports heroes as a student who often retreated to the library at Taylor Allderdice High School and has written 23 books about sports achievement it was quite a revealing and satisfying week. My buddy Bill Priatko went to four funerals in the same time span. Banquets are better than burials, I know, but both point up the passing of time and that we had better enjoy these special evenings when we can.

Those sports banquets are reminders of the great sports legacy this city has enjoyed since it was founded. We've come a long way in so many respects.

Terry Bradshaw was unable to get to Pittsburgh because of airplane cancellations and delays, so Lynn Swann took his place as the emcee of the Mel Blount Dinner. Former strong safety Donnie Shell was the honored (or dishonored) guest for the program.

Swann mentioned that when Shell signed with the Steelers as a free agent out of South Carolina State that he was paid the munificent salary of $12,500 that first season (1974). Shell now serves as the Carolina Panthers Director of Player Development.

Swann told Max Starks, tagged as the Steelers' "transitional player," that minimum wages have improved in the National Football League. The lowest-paid Steeler now makes more money than Bradshaw did during most of his stay with the Steelers. Starks, by the way, was impressive looking in a black tuxedo. He has had his hair cut close, getting ahead of the NFL dictum that long hair will no longer be permitted to cover the shoulders of the league's players.

Starks is a slimmed down 6–8, 300-pound-plus lineman these days, but still the biggest Steeler of them all. A woman posed for a

Sidney Crosby was honored as the Sportsman of the Year at the 2008 Dapper Dan Dinner & Sports Auction at the David L. Lawrence Convention Center.

Max Starks and Jeff Hartings look classier than ever at 2008 Mel Blount Youth Home Celebrity Dinner at Hilton Hotel.

picture with Starks at the VIP reception in the Kings' Garden at the Hilton. Her husband took the picture. Then he turned to me and asked, "Who is that?"

Did it really matter? He was one of the Steelers and that's good enough to get you royal treatment in most establishments in Pittsburgh. Speaking of changing faces. I spoke to Don Lee, the banquet director at the Hilton, who knew Connie Hawkins when they were growing up in Brooklyn's Bedford-Stuyvesant neighborhood. Lee looked after my daughter Sarah's wedding reception in that same King's Garden ten years ago this summer. Now Sarah is expecting our second granddaughter in the middle of May. Yes, time flies.

It was good to have a reunion with so many of the Steelers I came to know when I was reporting on the team for *The Pittsburgh Press* from 1979 to 1983. We shared a lot of good times together.

One of the most gracious remains Tony Dungy, now the celebrated head coach of the Indianapolis Colts. He couldn't have been friendlier. He had a hug for me as well. I told him I had recently come across a newspaper clipping of a column I had written about him the day he was sent packing at St. Vincent College and was traded to the San Francisco 49ers in the summer of 1979.

"Everything I wrote about you then," I told Dungy, "has stood the test of time. My perception of the kind of man you were then is still the special person you are today."

Dungy smiled. "I remember that article," he said.

As a boy of eight-to-twelve-years old, I delivered the *Post-Gazette* newspaper in my hometown of Hazelwood and Glenwood. I'd read the stories about the Dapper Dan Sports Dinner with all the distinguished sports greats who appeared there. So it means a great deal to me.

I was the smallest kid in our neighborhood, not that good at sports, but always an eager competitor. That sums me up nowadays as well.

So it was a real honor to be seated in the first row, even at the extreme end, of the three-tiered dais of sports dignitaries at this year's dinner.

I was up there with Mario Lemieux and Sidney Crosby. The words "gifted" and "debonair" describe them both so well. They represent the Penguins' past and present. Lemieux was honored as the city's greatest-ever athlete. He wasn't, but the choice made sense on this occasion. Swissvale's Dick Groat and Donora's Arnold Galiffa were greater athletes, and so was the oft-overlooked track & field star Roger Kingdom, now a coach at California (Pa.) University, but they weren't even among the nominees for the award.

Tony Dorsett was sitting in the front row at the Dapper Dan Dinner. He was one of the nominees for the city's greatest athlete. He single-handedly, with a little help from Johnny Majors, led Pitt back from the dead to win a national championship in 1976. Dorsett won the Heisman Trophy that year and helped the Dallas Cowboys win the Super Bowl in the same building — the Superdome — to complete a parfecta.

Lemieux led the Penguins to two Stanley Cup championships in the '80s, and Crosby could repeat that accomplishment in this decade. There's excitement and hope for another title as the Penguins are one of the top seeds in the Stanley Cup competition that just got underway.

Several Pirates from the 1960 World Series winning champions were on the dais. They included Bob Friend, Bill Mazeroski and ElRoy Face, who all still live here, and later Pirates were present such as Dave Giusti, Steve Blass, Kent Tekulve, John Candelaria and Grant Jackson. Maz was honored for delivering the "greatest moment in Pittsburgh sports history," hitting the home run leading off the bottom of the ninth in the seventh game of that 1960 World Series to beat the mighty New York Yankees. The 1978 Steelers were named the greatest team in history, though those 1960 Pirates remain the most popular team this town ever produced.

J.T. Thomas, a member of those four Steelers' Super Bowl teams, took exception to the choice of Maz's home run as the greatest moment in Pittsburgh sports history. He held out for teammate Franco Harris and his "Immaculate Reception." I told Thomas a few nights later why Maz's moment is the greater of the two. I've researched and studied Pittsburgh's sports history pretty thoroughly. Thomas wasn't in town when Maz turned it upside down with his heroics. There's never been a public reaction to anything quite like it here. no one over 55 will ever forget it.

The home run came in the final and deciding game of a World Series. Franco's came in a playoff game, not even the AFC championship game and not the Super Bowl. The World Series was shown on television here, and that 1972 playoff game with the Oakland Raiders was blacked out in Pittsburgh. Everyone knew what Maz had done when it happened. They are still debating exactly what happened when Franco scooped up the deflected pass from Bradshaw to Frenchy Fuqua. Most Steelers' fans felt the game was over and that the Steelers were going to lose when it happened. Many weren't even looking out on the field, but rather at their shoetops as they left their seats at Three Rivers Stadium. Fans still gather every October 13 at the wall that remains from Forbes Field to mark the anniversary. No one comes to the parking lot between the ballparks on the North Side each December 23. Who even remembers that date? Except Franco, of course.

Both were great moments. There were so many wonderful images of Pittsburgh's sports accomplishments on banners and on big screens at the Convention Center. Seeing all those sports figures in one big room was like seeing the characters in my books come to life.

I flip through those books now and then, looking up an incident, a date, and I still marvel at how much has happened here, and how good we've had it. Pittsburgh sports fans are, indeed, a fortunate bunch.

"To me, Maz's home run comes first as far as special moments in Pittsburgh sports history. Luckily, there were other special moments that came later."
— **Franco Harris**

Three good men who
left their mark in Pittsburgh

"It was a good town for me."
— Lloyd Voss

March 7, 2007

I write books about the best and brightest ballplayers from these parts, or those who come here to play for our Pittsburgh teams. I do my best to pick people we can all learn from, the good guys who have set a high standard for the way they conduct themselves on and off the field. After you have visited them in their homes, seen them in their own surroundings, and listened to their stories, you get more comfortable in their company. In the best situations, you even become friends.

That's why it hurts when you hear that they are not faring well, or they are hospitalized, and, of course, when you learn that they have died. I remember something in that regard from the late Red Holzman, the Hall of Fame coach of the champion New York Knicks of the early '70s. About a week before I departed New York to return home to Pittsburgh to write for *The Pittsburgh Press*, I received a phone call at home from Holzman.

I hadn't covered the Knicks on a full-time basis, only from time to time, yet Holzman called me with a stern admonition. "You trying to run out of town without saying goodbye?" he asked.

Holzman invited me to join him at his tennis club on Long Island. We'd play a few sets of singles tennis, have a few drinks and say goodbye properly. I appreciated his gesture so much. There were other sports figures I thought I was closer to who never bothered to say goodbye. I took along a copy of a book my *New York Post* colleague, Leonard Lewin, the regular beat-writer, had written called *Holzman's Basketball*. I asked Red if he would sign it for me.

Holzman's message reads: "Best to Jim in Pittsburgh. Once a sportswriter, now a friend. Red Holzman." I treasure it and keep it on a shelf with my most prized books. It's next to one autographed for me by Muhammad Ali. It's not always easy to say goodbye. I've learned from folks like Holzman and Art Rooney, another Hall of Famer, how to do that.

I felt sad this past Sunday because three men I'd written about in my books had died that week. Pittsburgh provided a perfect backdrop for anybody who felt sad. It was cold and windy and occasionally some snowflakes flew this way and that way against a steel gray sky.

I drove my car across the Fort Pitt and Fort Duquesne bridges and saw our new ballparks, Heinz Field and PNC Park, but I was thinking about these three men who had played at Forbes Field, Pitt Stadium and Three Rivers Stadium. None of them is a part of the Pittsburgh scene these days. They are all gone.

Emil Narick was the starting quarterback in a single-wing offensive scheme for the 1939 Pitt football team that is believed to be the first college team that flew in an airplane to an away game, traveling all the way to Washington on the West Coast. He was the son of a coal miner from West Virginia and believed he was the only Pitt football player ever to become a judge. He was a long-time resident of Upper St. Clair. He died on Saturday at the age of 90 from Alzheimer's Disease.

I had seen him and his son Kirk when Narick was living the past two years at the Sunrise Assisted Care of Upper St. Clair complex near South Hills Village. A few years earlier, I'd caught Narick at the James Street Tavern, tapping his fingers on a table to the music of the Pittsburgh Banjo Club. He was a regular at their Wednesday night jam sessions. He loved to dance as well. He moved with them when the James Street Tavern closed and they moved their practice session to the Elks Club a few blocks away on the North Side.

Narick had played for the legendary Jock Sutherland, and was a teammate of "The Dream Backfield" foursome that included Marshall Goldberg, Dick Cassiano, Curly Stebbins and John Chickerneo. They had won national championships and the Panthers were among the nation's elite teams in the mid-to-late '30s. His name was Naric when he first enrolled at Pitt. He was proud of his Croatian heritage. I'm not sure why the "k" was added to his surname. One of the backs who preceded him at Pitt was Mike Niksik, who became Mike Nixon, and there was a lineman named Al Lezouski who became Al Leeson. Mike Nixon was later a coach at Pitt and with the Steelers. Al Leeson was the father of Rick Leeson, a star running back when I was a student at Pitt in the early '60s.

Lloyd Voss played for Vince Lombardi in Green Bay and Bill Austin and Chuck Noll in Pittsburgh. He left Green Bay before the Packers became the most dominant team in pro football and played for the Steelers before they succeeded the Packers as the best team in the NFL.

He grew up on a farm in Minnesota, played six-man football in high school and then at the University of Nebraska. He lined up alongside Joe Greene, L.C. Greenwood and Dwight White on the Steelers' defensive line. They all say they learned a lot from Lloyd Voss.

"I may have missed out on the Super Bowl years," said Voss, "but maybe I helped get those guys ready for all those championships. I don't regret coming to Pittsburgh. It was a good town for me. I enjoyed every moment of my pro football career."

He died at age 65 on Friday from liver and kidney failure at UPMC's Montefiore Hospital. He had a kidney transplant there three years earlier, and had some health challenges in the ensuing years. I had visited Voss on two occasions in the company of Tom Averell, an ardent member of the Steelers Alumni Club.

I could see that Voss was in bad shape. What was that like? Once he was one of the strongest boys on the block. He had played at

Nebraska, one of the storied programs of college football, and with the Green Bay Packers and Pittsburgh Steelers. Now he was having trouble getting out of bed. He was wearing one of those godawful paper-thin hospital gowns, with the open backs that show your ass every time you amble down the hallway. That's the way we all end up. I wanted to ask him about his feelings, but didn't feel I could do it when Averell and the nurses were also in the room. I preferred one-on-one sessions to get my stories. The problem with being a writer is that you are always working. Everything becomes a story. And I realize sometimes that this isn't right.

For a writer, I must confess, you always want that one last interview, in case you missed some stories. Before it's too late and they are lost. I thought Lloyd Voss was vulnerable when I learned that his wife, the former Diane Kruger, had died. She was his second wife. His first wife, Jan, had died in 1995 after they had been married for 27 years.

He met Diane Kruger when she was caring for his ailing father back in Minnesota. She was a registered nurse. She took good care of his father and I knew she took good care of Lloyd. I had visited them twice in March and April of 2002 at their home in Carnegie, on the border of Mt. Lebanon and Scott.

Diane Kruger is in my Hall of Fame as far as hostesses go in my history of visiting the homes of sports stars to interview them. She offered me fresh-cut fruit and cheese and crackers and wine, and had a candle display lit in the dining room table. She did this on both occasions. She told Ann Nobile, the wife of former Steelers' lineman Leo Nobile, to do the same when I visited them in their home in Moon Township. I usually have to ask for a glass of water or Diet Coke when I am at most sports stars' homes. I also saw how Diane looked after Lloyd and reminded him about what he had to do to follow his doctor's instructions. Lloyd's legs were swollen at the time, and he had to keep them elevated on one of those extended Lazy-Boy chairs. I sensed that Lloyd would be lost without her.

Elbie Nickel was the best tight end in Steelers' history, starring for the team from 1947 till 1957. He was the son of a carpenter in Chillicothe, Ohio. His father built the home where Nickel was living when I visited him at his home in late February of 1999 to interview him. He was a favorite of club owner Art Rooney who named one of his racehorses after Elbie Nickel. He had framed photos and Steelers' mementos on display in his game room. He died at age 84 last Tuesday of Alzheimer's Disease.

When I was in Nickel's home, he was quick to take me to his game room and show me all the framed photos on the wall from his days with the Steelers. I was stunned to find my own image in one of the photos. It showed me standing in a lineup with Mr. Rooney, Nickel, Pat Brady, Ernie Stautner and Jack Butler at the Allegheny Club at Three Rivers Stadium. They had all been named to the Steelers 50 Seasons Team.

All three men had lost their wives years earlier and all appeared somewhat lost without their mates. Most men who've had a good marriage don't fare well on their own. It's a scary prospect. I remember Nickel standing in the doorway of his home as I left to return to Pittsburgh. I thought he looked lonesome.

So many images raced through my head. I first met Judge Narick when I was a student at Pitt in the early '60s. I'd cut classes on Mondays in the fall to attend the Curbstone Coaches luncheons at the Roosevelt Hotel in downtown Pittsburgh. Players, coaches and administrators from all the local teams had representatives there. Narick was one of the men who organized the gathering. He was a football referee.

When I worked as an assistant athletic director for sports information at Pitt in the mid-80s, Judge Narick was a frequent visitor in the press box at Pitt Stadium, supervising the game officials for eastern college football. No one enjoyed the buffet offerings — food and drink — which were available to all in the back of the press box more than Judge Narick. His handshake was infamous. It was similar to a takedown move in wrestling. You had to assume a solid stance before you shook hands with Judge Narick.

I used to get a kick out of introducing Judge Narick to the stoutest of men, especially football-types, and watch them lurch forward when Judge Narick got them in his firm grip. He did not lighten up much when he met women, either, and they often left their feet and stumbled forward. If you were wearing a Pitt ring you were left with the impression of a Panther on your neighboring fingers. I scolded Judge Narick on several occasions for overdoing the handshake business. Judge Narick ignored the warning. If there were any judging to be done he'd be doing it.

I remember seeing him in church soon after his wife had died. He shook my hand, but it was a ghost of his former grip. It was a giveaway about his grief. His handshake, as Scott Simon wrote of a Chicago politician in his book *Windy City*, could crank open a Brazil nut.

Judge Narick was profiled in one of my early books, *Hail to Pitt: A Sports History of the University of Pittsburgh*. Pittsburgh artist and illustrator Marty Wolfson, who published the book, had a fine drawing of Judge Narick to go with the story. There was a great photo showing Narick and Pitt teammate Ben Kish, both handsome fellows, surrounded by five Hollywood starlets who were in Pittsburgh for a stage show. They included Susan Hayward and Jane Wyman. I wonder if Judge Narick danced with those Hollywood starlets when he met them.

Voss was a guy everyone liked. He was easy and good company. He was funny, but in a laidback way. In recent years he'd fooled around with different facial hairstyles, and wore cowboy hats and shared good stories. He worked in the Allegheny County Parks and Recreation Department for 23 years and knew a lot of people. Bob Milie, the former Steelers' assistant trainer, and I invited Voss to have lunch with us from time to time at DeBlasio's Restaurant or Atria's Restaurant & Tavern in Mt. Lebanon. Joe Gordon and Tom Averell would join us on occasion. Milie, who was still recovering from surgery, Gordon and Averell are to be admired for the way they always are there when Steelers Alumni and others are hospitalized or ailing. They are so supportive of their friends when those friends are experiencing any difficulty.

In his later years, Voss showed up with different facial hair formations, a goatee that looked like an icicle, a different beard, and some kind of dark cowboy hat.

In his playing days, Voss liked to drink vodka, according to former Steelers' lineman Bruce Van Dyke. In his latter years, Voss enjoyed a glass of Chardonnay now and then. He always had a huge cigar between the fingers of his right hand. He was fun to be around.

Lloyd looked and behaved like a good ol' boy from the South, but he was from southwest Minnesota, a farming community called Magnolia. There were only 17 kids in his high school graduating class. He played in a high school football league where the teams consisted of six players on the field at a time.

It's amazing that he was able to go from that to a starring role at the University of Nebraska. His bright red No. 71 Nebraska jersey was framed and on display near his casket at Slater's Funeral Home in Scott during his viewing. There were lots of photos of Lloyd on display, and I felt proud when I saw two of him that I had taken in recent years in a prime position.

I knew his story, so I volunteered my services to offer a eulogy on his behalf at his funeral service at Christ United Methodist Church in Bethel Park.

Bob Milie offered me a story about Voss in the vestibule of the church, just prior to the service. It was a good one.

Soon after Chuck Noll became the coach of the Steelers, he asked Voss what he might do as a gesture to please the players and to unify them. Voss said, "When I was with the Green Bay Packers, Vince Lombardi was our coach. On every road trip, he always made sure we had two beers apiece on the bus to the airport. He'd even help load the cases onto the bus."

After that, the Steelers players were always treated to two beers, usually on the airplane ride home. It may have been one of the secrets to the team's success in the '70s. Times have changed. There's no longer booze on the airplanes or in the media lounge at the stadiums and ballparks.

Our old friend, the late Bernard "Baldy" Regan, known as the Mayor of the North Side, and a regular on the Steelers' scene, used to say about such success stories, "Only in America." Yes, Lloyd Voss was very much an "Only In America" success story.

As a child, I collected bubble gum cards for football and baseball. I had a set of black and white cards with the Steelers of the '50s. Elbie Nickel wore a leather helmet in one of them. I never thought back then that someday I'd actually get to meet some of these guys, such as Ray Mathews, Bill McPeak, Jerry Nuzum, Jack Butler, Jim Finks, Bill Walsh, Lynn Chandnois, Fran Rogel and Jack McClairen. Or players from other eras such as Johnny "Blood" McNally, Bill Dudley, Bill Walsh, Gary Glick, John Baker, Dick Modzelewsi, Marion Motley and Roy Jefferson.

These were all good men. None of them got their names in newspapers for the wrong reasons. They were tough guys on the field, but humble down-to-earth guys off the field.

Anybody who ever spent time with them profited from the experience. They were from a different era. They didn't make big money, but they were rich in so many ways. They'll be missed by those who got to know them.

Pat McDonnell welcomes Lloyd Voss to Atria's Restaurant & Tavern in Mt. Lebanon.

Jack Butler, Pat Brady and Elbie Nickel enjoy reunion at Steelers' 50th Year Anniversary Dinner at David L. Lawrence Convention Center.

Norman Mailer & Co.
Writer thankful for special days in journalism career

November 23, 2007

The death of writer Norman Mailer earlier this month reminded us of a special day in our life, and a memorable period in our career. It would be one of the days to consider when counting our blessings on Thanksgiving.

The story of Mailer's death appeared at the bottom of the front page of our daily newspaper on Veterans Day, which seemed fitting since Mailer had authored one of the great novels about World War II, *The Naked and the Dead*, back in 1948. It would be considered Mailer's masterpiece.

Mailer was a monumental figure in American literature for many reasons, some good, some not so good. He was 84 when he died in New York.

It brought to mind the day I first met Mailer in New York. It was at Gallagher's Steak House in midtown Manhattan, just off Broadway.

I was there on behalf of *The New York Post* to report on a press conference featuring Muhammad Ali and Joe Frazier to promote their upcoming heavyweight championship fight at New York's Madison Square Garden. It was billed as "The Fight of the Century."

It lived up to its billing. I had one of the best seats in the house for that fight, in the first row of ringside seats reserved for the media and at mid-ring. It's the most important sports event I ever covered. I have pictures above my desk from those days. The venerable Nat Fleischer, the founder and editor of *Ring* magazine, sat next to me. Actors Burt Lancaster and Lorne Greene sat a few rows behind me, and Jack Kent Cooke, who was one of the investors in the fight, had come in from LA for the monster event. I remember seeing Diana Ross, then the lead singer for the Supremes, all dolled up that night. Men and women were wearing their finest fur coats. No one talked about bling back then, but there was plenty of bling at the Garden that evening.

Frazier and Ali were in attendance at Gallagher's that afternoon leading up to the fight, as was Joe Louis, the former and forever heavyweight champion. So three of the greatest fighters of all time were there. That's quite a ring trifecta.

I was excited about being there. This was in late February of 1971. Such gatherings were usually held at Toots Shor's, but for some reason this one was at Gallagher's, in a second-floor banquet room. Mailer was one of three great novelists there that day. I was just as excited to be in their company.

William Saroyan and Budd Shulberg, both boxing aficionados, were there with Mailer. They had drawn special assignments to write

Norman Mailer enjoys courtside seat for New York Knicks' game at Madison Square Garden.

New York Post reporter Jim O'Brien interviews Muhammad Ali in New York, at right, before "The Fight of the Century" with Joe Frazier.

Look between Muhammad Ali's white sneakers and you'll find author Jim O'Brien at ringside for "Fight of the Century" with Joe Frazier.

lengthy magazine pieces about the big fight. (I remember that Saroyan never turned in his article.) They loved the fight game and all the interesting characters that were part of the cast. Writers had more access to fighters than athletes in any other sport. The promoters needed the media to sell tickets.

Saroyan was a proud Armenian who came in from Fresno, California for the pre-fight event. Shulberg came in from the quaint Long Island community of Quogue, where he and his wife, the Broadway actress Geraldine Brooks, made their home.

I had read Saroyan's short story, *The Young Man on the Flying Trapeze*. During my student days at Pitt, I had read one of Shulberg's books, *What Makes Sammy Run?* The main figure was Sammy Glick, an ambitious young man who walked over people to get ahead. Sammy Glick became synonymous with anyone who was overly ambitious the way Shakespeare's Shylock from *The Merchant of Venice* became synonymous with usury or bad money-lending practices. Sound familiar these days?

I couldn't put Shulberg's book down. I still have a tattered paperback copy of that book that I had to put tape on to hold it together. Shulberg also wrote *The Harder They Fall* and *On The Waterfront*, and his screenplays became famous movies about the fight game and organized labor and mob influence. Shulberg's father was in the movie business, and Bud grew up around Hollywood people. I was surprised when Shulberg spoke that he had a bad stutter. He was still a champion storyteller. I had several opportunities at other big fights to spend time with Shulberg. He had a salt and pepper beard he tugged at nervously when he spoke. It was difficult for him to speak, but he had something to say, so everybody listened. No one listened more closely than I did. Whenever I covered a big sports event, such as a heavyweight championship fight, the Super Bowl, or the NBA All-Star Game, I was always eager to spend time with the best writers. They were my champions. Seeing Shulberg and hearing his stories was a real thrill.

I could envision Marlon Brando and L. J. Cobb and Rod Steiger, three actors who were to the theatre what Ali, Frazier and Louis were to the boxing business, playing their roles in the classic movie *On the Waterfront*. I could remember Brando, as a punk former fighter named Terry Malloy, crying to Steiger, his older brother, about his downfall, "I coulda been a contender."

There were also some famous sports media figures at Gallagher's that afternoon. Dave Anderson and Red Smith and Arthur Daley, who would all win the Pulitzer Prize for their work, were there, as was Howard Cosell, Pete Hamill, Jimmy Cannon, Larry Merchant, Milton Gross and Jim Murray, all giants in the sportswriting game. I probably stared at them as much as I did Joe Louis. Horace McMahon, who played the lead detective in the TV series, "The Naked City," always showed up at these boxing luncheons. As a teenager, I'd watched that TV show religiously on Sunday nights.

I remember that Mailer used to show up on occasion for a Knicks' game at Madison Square Garden. He'd have a courtside seat. I still

Author, with awful Fu Manchu mustache, sits next to Ring Magazine editor Nat Fleischer. Seated in background are Jack Kent Cooke, Lorne Green, David Merrick in celebrity-studded crowd in March of 1971 at Madison Square Garden. See if you can find them.

Syndicated sports columnist Jimmy Cannon has fight face on for Joe Frazier and Jim O'Brien during interview at Gallagher's Restaurant just off Broadway in New York City.

have a photo of him, showing him with his legs crossed in such a seat. Who sits with their legs crossed in a front row seat at a basketball game?

Woody Allen, Elliott Gould, Barbra Streisand and Dustin Hoffman would sit in front row seats at Knicks' games in the early '70s as well. It was an exciting time. The house was full for every home game. Not an empty seat in the building over Penn Station. I got to New York in time, in April of 1970, to be one of four writers assigned to cover the Knicks in the playoffs and, eventually, the championship round as they won the first NBA title in the team's history. The Long Island Railroad had a line that ran right past the first apartment we lived in out in East Rockaway, and I could catch the train and be in Penn Station in an hour's time. I'd just walk up the steps or take the escalator and I'd be in Madison Square Garden, the mecca for so many sports in America, especially college and pro basketball, boxing, wrestling, hockey and musical entertainment of all varieties.

Years later, after I had returned home to Pittsburgh, I was dispatched to Logan, Utah, the home of Utah State University, to cover the West Virginia team in the NCAA basketball playoffs. I recall that Wyoming, Fresno State and Georgetown were the other teams in that regional tournament.

I found a black book without a dust jacket in the Utah State campus library called *Obituaries*, written by William Saroyan. I read it in two days. It was an intriguing book. While Saroyan lay dying in a hospital he was given a year-end copy of *Variety*, the showbiz weekly tabloid. It contained a Necrology, listing all the people associated with show business who had died that year. Saroyan bet a nurse that he would personally be acquainted with at least 35 of them. I recall that one he knew and had an encounter with was the British actor Stanley Baker.

He wrote a book about this, going down the list, and recalling a meeting with each of the names he recognized, or making up something if that would suffice. Surely, Saroyan would have some good stories about one of his contemporaries, Norman Mailer. It was fascinating stream-of-consciousness writing by a wordsmith of the first order.

On Veterans Day of 2007, I checked out a wall unit in my living room that has one half of it devoted to bookshelves. On the very top was a red cover copy of *The Naked and the Dead*. It was up there with books by James Jones, *From Here to Eternity*, and Herman Wouk's *The Caine Mutiny*. To their left were three blue-bound books by Ernest Hemingway, including *For Whom the Bell Tolls*. Hemingway was my first literary hero. Like Mailer, he took pride in his macho bearing. But it was merely a mask. He ended up shooting himself.

Those books in my livingroom are some of the best books ever written about war. I made a mental note to try and re-read them sometime soon. Mailer, a boastful, combative sort, would have smiled at the sight, with his book at the top of the stack. He'd have thought the placement was appropriate. Like Ali, he thought he was "The Greatest."

How I Met My Fiancée in Detroit the Weekend of Super Bowl XL

By Lee Ann Prosky

January 11, 2007

Ever since I was a teenager growing up in Pittsburgh, I have always wanted to go to a Super Bowl that the Pittsburgh Steelers were in and won. I grew up in the 1970's and my dad had season tickets to the Steelers. I would go to the games at Three Rivers Stadium (Section 509 —"the sun never shines in 509") on occasion with my dad and two older brothers and became a huge Steeler fan. With winning all those Super Bowls in the 1970's, it was like the Super Bowl became another holiday for us in Pittsburgh: Thanksgiving, Christmas, New Years, and Super Bowl.

My professional career has taken me to many different locations since my teenage years in Pittsburgh, but I have always remained a diehard Steeler fan. I lived in New York City, Orlando, Atlanta and am now in Boca Raton, Florida. I currently work for Siemens Communications in the Finance Department. Despite living in these various areas, I have always found a way to come back to some of the Steeler home games and playoff games.

After the Steelers beat the Broncos in the AFC Championship game in January 2006, I knew that I had to go to the Super Bowl. Unfortunately, we did not get tickets through the season ticket holder lottery. My dad and my brothers were not interested in going & spending the money (my dad had already gone to the Super Bowl XIV in Pasadena). So, I went on to the internet to buy a weekend package/ticket. After the initial shock of ticket prices (lowest price was $2,500), I still moved forward to buy one as this has been a goal of mine for a long time and I didn't know if they would ever get back there; particularly after the previous AFC Championship games that we lost vs. San Diego, Denver and New England (twice).

On Friday, February 3, 2006, I flew up to Detroit. I got to the Hilton Garden Inn in Plymouth, Michigan around 9:00 pm and checked in. I went to the hotel bar to have a drink and this is when I met my future fiancé, John Carter. He was also there for the Super Bowl and is a huge Steeler fan. He is originally from Rochester, NY but has ties to Pittsburgh. He attended college at University of Pittsburgh and Indiana University of PA, and lived in Indiana, PA for several years. He became a Steeler fan in the 1980's, when they weren't doing so well so he really is a true fan (not jumping on the band wagon). John currently lives in Jupiter, Florida (approximately 50 minutes from where I live in Boca Raton) and works for Florida Power & Light in the Safety Department. John has also served in the military (Army) and most recently did two tours of duty in Afghanistan and Iraq. We talked about the upcoming game for awhile and learned that we both lived in South Florida (what a coincidence!). We agreed to meet up on Saturday to go to the NFL Experience.

On Saturday, February 4, 2006, John & I went to the NFL Experience together in Detroit. We got to know each other better and both had a lot of fun. The weather was cold and rainy / snowy at night as we waited for the bus to take us back to the hotel but we had fun. When we got back to the hotel, we had dinner & drinks by the fire in the lobby. It was very romantic.

On Sunday, February 5, 2006 (the Big Day!), we rode on the bus together to the Super Bowl and attended the tailgate party arranged by Primesports, the company we each bought the packages from. Again, we had a great time, but were both getting a little nervous about the upcoming game.

When you attend in person, there is always a greater emotional investment in the outcome of the game—when it is the BIGGEST GAME of the year, the emotional stakes are exponentially higher. I recall the time I went to the AFC Championship game in Pittsburgh in 1994 when we played the San Diego Chargers. Everyone thought the Steelers were going to win. At the end of that game after we lost, I actually cried leaving Three Rivers Stadium. I have since matured over the past 12 years, but I have to believe that losing in the Super Bowl is devastating!!

Fortunately, we did not have to experience this. As we all know, the Pittsburgh Steelers went on to beat the Seattle Seahawks in Super Bowl XL 21–10 and all was well with the world that day. Since John and I purchased our packages separately, we did not sit together. He was about 20 rows up from the Steeler end zone and I was on the other side of the stadium in the 200 level looking down over a corner of the Seahawks endzone (where Big Ben got the first touchdown by running it in and breaking the plane!).

As the final seconds of the game ticked off, I stood up with all the Steeler fans in the stadium (the Seattle fans had since left) and felt a wave of emotion … we did it!!! They won and I was there to witness it in person. After the celebrations on the field had dissipated, John and I met up and hugged. We were both so happy that the Steelers won!!!

The week after, John sent to me a disk with the pictures he took at the Super Bowl. He had this great camera with a zoom lens so the pictures were awesome! Then on Valentine's Day he sent me a dozen black & gold roses —very unique. That weekend, we went out on our first date in Boca Raton —dinner by the ocean and a carnival. We had a great time and started to go out on a regular basis. He proposed marriage in May on the beach at night with a full moon and I said Yes.

Our wedding will be on Saturday, June 2, 2007 in Pittsburgh. The ceremony will be at Fox Chapel Presbyterian Church and the reception will be at the Le Mont.

John & I always say that we owe our meeting in Detroit at the Super Bowl to Ben Roethlisberger. If he doesn't make "The Tackle" in the Indianapolis playoff game, then the Steelers don't get to the Super Bowl and we don't meet. It's funny how fate lends a hand in these matters.

John & I continue to be big fans despite the 8–8 season and missing the playoffs in 2006. In fact, as a Christmas present, I got John a photo of "The Tackle" signed by Ben Roethlisberger. Many other gifts that we exchanged this past Christmas also had the Steeler theme, including "Steeler Stuff" by Jim O'Brien (autographed).

Our dreams came true as a result of the Steelers winning the Super Bowl last year and we will always be thankful to them for it. Not only did they give us as Steeler fans the ultimate gift (a Super Bowl win and chance to see it in person), but more importantly they had a hand in causing us to meet the loves of our lives / soul mates. Sounds like a Hollywood movie, but it's true!

p.s. May 24, 2008

Jim, yes, in answer to your inquiry, we are still an item. In fact, we got married on June 2, 2007 in Pittsburgh and will be celebrating our 1st anniversary in a few weeks. I am sending you a couple of good wedding photos of us in front of Heinz Field and sitting by the Art Rooney statue. We're honored to be in your new book. We also moved to Pittsburgh last year and have a home in Gibsonia.

Florida residents Lee Ann Prosky and John Carter met at Super Bowl XL in Detroit where the Steelers defeated the Seattle Seahawks in February, 2006.

Lee Ann and John Carter were married in Pittsburgh on June 2, 2007 in Pittsburgh and posed for pictures at Art Rooney statue outside Heinz Field on the North Side. They are now at home in Pittsburgh.

Marshall Goldberg
His last three interviews

"I prefer to live in the present."

April 12, 2006

George Gojkovich

Icalled Marshall Goldberg on his 85th birthday—October 24, 2002 —at his apartment in Chicago. His wife, Rita, answered the telephone. She told me that Marshall was not doing too well, and that he had memory lapses.

"I don't know how reliable his responses will be," she said when I told her I wanted to interview her husband.

I told her my experience had been that old ballplayers could remember their glory days well, even if they couldn't tell you what they had that morning for breakfast. I remembered that people had warned me not to expect much from John Henry Johnson and Fran Rogel because of dementia and they were both great. So was Goldberg. He recalled little details about exchanges between him and his coach, Jock Sutherland that took place in the late '30s. "He put his hand on my shoulder," said Goldberg, "and he leaned into me and said quietly in my ear, 'Marshall, I'm counting on you to lead the way today.'" Who could ask for more?

And he never said "you know" once in our three half-hour conversations over a six-week time period.

Marshall Gavin Goldberg had been the most famous football player in the history of the University of Pittsburgh until Mike Ditka and Tony Dorsett came along in the '60s and '70s, respectively. He was known as "Biggie" and "Mad Marshall," and "The Elkins Express."

He had been a three-sport standout at Elkins High School, gaining all-state honors in 1935 in football, basketball and track & field. He was 5–11, 185, somewhere in between Dorsett and Ditka in size. He came to Pitt from Elkins, West Virginia, where his father, Sol Goldberg, owned a movie theatre and a clothing store and did a little betting on the side.

Sol Goldberg was described in an article that appeared in the Clarksburg, West Virginia newspaper as "a little, roly-poly man with the fancy vests and glittering stickpins." Sol sent telegrams faithfully to Jock Sutherland during Marshall's days at Pitt. They made Sutherland laugh, which was not easy to do.

"Biggie" Goldberg was an All-American running back who led Pitt to national championships in 1936 and 1937, and was third in the balloting for the Heisman Trophy as college football's best player in 1938. The Panthers, coached by the legendary Dr. Jock Sutherland, posted a 25-3-2 in Goldberg's three varsity seasons. Goldberg made All-America at two positions, fullback and halfback.

Pitt played Fordham in three scoreless ties in that decade — before sellout crowds — and Goldberg, who played in two of those contests, was frequently heralded in the New York newspapers for his ability. He was one of the few Jewish sports stars of that era and many of the sportswriters were Jewish. He was once referred to in a newspaper report as "a Jewish hillbilly from West Virginia." Goldberg died last week at a nursing care center in Chicago at the age of 88.

I thought about that phone call I had made to him on his 85th birthday and two subsequent calls over the following two months. He spoke slower than I had remembered him speaking, but he made sense. Sometimes he startled me by the details of his recall. His coach was regarded as dour and aloof by many, but he treated Goldberg like a father. At the end of our interview, I asked Goldberg, "What's your wife's name?" There was a pause and he said, "You got me there. Hold on a second. Oh... it's Rita." He and Rita had been married 18 years at the time. His first marriage ended in divorce after 24 years.

Rita later told me that those three interviews he did with me on the telephone were the last ones he ever did.

The year before I had visited the College Football Hall of Fame in South Bend, Indiana. The football player portrayed at the entrance is Tony Dorsett of Pitt. Bernie Kish, who was the director at the time, took my friend Alex Pociask and me on a personal tour. Kish, who hailed from Indiana, Pennsylvania and was a big fan of Pittsburgh athletes such as Roberto Clemente, showed me some scrapbooks that Marshall Goldberg had given him a week earlier. He later lent me those scrapbooks, trusting me enough to ship them to me in Pittsburgh.

There was also a bound itinerary for the Pitt football team for the 1936 Rose Bowl trip to Pasadena. It contained daily schedules, Pullman railroad car berth assignment—Goldberg was in No. 8 lower berth in Car A—and even a list of suggested reading material. The best players were all in the same car as Jock Sutherland and his top assistant, Bill Kern. A Pennsylvania Railroad train took them to Chicago, and they rode the Santa Fe Railway train from there through Albuquerque and San Bernardino before arriving in Pasadena. They stayed at the Huntington Hotel.

The Goldberg scrapbook contained newspaper clipping and photos from the '30s and '40s, when Goldberg played for Pitt and then the NFL's Chicago Cardinals. He was a four-time All-Pro defensive back for the Cardinals. To my surprise, I found a loose tear sheet from *The Pitt News* inside the cover of one of the scrapbooks. It was the first thing I came across. It contained a column I had written about Goldberg's son, Marshall Goldberg Jr., who tried in vain to follow in his father's footsteps at Pitt during my student days at Pitt in the early '60s. I had won a national collegiate journalism contest with that column that had appeared in *The Pitt News*, the campus student newspaper. I smiled when I saw it. It was an honor to be in Marshall Goldberg's scrapbook. There was also a picture up front showing him with teammate Steve Petro, one of the toughest and kindest contributors to the Pitt football scene as a player, coach and athletic department aide.

A Pitt professor told me he asked his finance class of 35 or so students last week if they had ever heard of Marshall Goldberg. Only two of them said they had. All Pitt students should know about Marshall Goldberg and Jock Sutherland and Tony Dorsett and Mike Ditka and Dr. Jonas Salk and Dr. Thomas Starzl, so they can better appreciate where they are going to school. Their success stories might prove inspirational. The Pitt family suffered another setback last week when Maggie Dixon, the sister of Pitt's basketball coach Jamie Dixon, died of a heart problem at the age of 28. She had coached the women's basketball team at Army to its first NCAA tournament at the same time her older brother's team at Pitt was in the men's tournament. It was a good story. It hurt to hear what happened to her. So suddenly. She was younger than both of my daughters. Goldberg was 88 and had led a full life. He'd become a millionaire in business after his ballplaying days. His death was easier to accept.

"I prefer to live in the present," Goldberg once said. "To me, playing sports should be a stepping stone to a career. It's not an end in itself. There's a valuable lesson for young people who play games. I'm more proud of my accomplishments off the field.

"Football taught me to look for and expect only victory. It also taught me singleness of purpose, poise, competitiveness, the ability to get along with others and the ability to sacrifice."

Goldberg led Pitt to the Rose Bowl title in 1936 and to the national championship the following season. He then played in the NFL for eight seasons, interrupted by a military service stint (he served in the U.S. Navy in the South Pacific during World War II), and he was considered one of the greatest defensive backs in the league. The legendary sportswriter Grantland Rice raved about Goldberg in many of his columns, and named him to his All-American team. "No one who ever played," wrote Granny Rice, "loves the game better." *Sports Illustrated* named Goldberg to the 1930s College Football Team of the Decade.

"We lost only three games in three years," said Goldberg. "We lost two of those to Pittsburgh teams, Carnegie Tech and Duquesne, as well as Duke. We had three scoreless ties with Fordham. We never lost to West Virginia. We beat them three times. I didn't want them to beat us. I didn't want to go home and hear about that."

He was a member of the "Dream Backfeld" at Pitt, lining up with quarterback Harold "Curly" Stebbins, and halfbacks John Chickerneo and Dick Cassiano. A newspaperman gave us that name before the '37 season," said Goldberg. With the Cardinals in 1946, he was a member of another "Dream Backfield" with quarterback Paul Christman, Goldberg and Elmer Angsman at halfbacks, and Pat Harder at fullback. In his last two seasons, Goldberg was replaced on offense by the great Charlie Trippi.

Goldberg won NFL All-Pro honors four times.

Goldberg and Emmitt Thomas, a defensive back with the Kansas City Chiefs, were both nominated by the veterans committee for induction into the Pro Football Hall of Fame in the Class of 2008. Thomas was voted in, but Goldberg didn't get enough votes for the honor.

All-American in 1937 and 1938

Author Jim O'Brien does research on Marshall Goldberg during visit to College Football Hall of Fame in South Bend, Indiana. Pitt's Tony Dorsett (No. 33) is depicted at HOF entrance

Ave Daniell, an All-America tackle at Pitt in 1936, lived in Mt. Lebanon most of his adult life and was the president at Ionics in Bridgeville. He once told me, "Marshall Goldberg was a winner by nature. He was an elusive runner like Tony Dorsett in his prime—and he was a good blocker—something Dorsett couldn't say because the system didn't call for him to block. Like Tony, Marshall had natural instincts; he was born with it. They don't coach that kind of football."

Goldberg's coach at Pitt, Hall of Famer Jock Sutherland, said, "Marshall is a football player's player. He's the first fellow on the practice field and the last one off. He was one of the finest backs I ever saw on any college team, and just about the best I ever coached."

When I paused during one of our interviews, taking time to get a comment of his down carefully in my notebook, Goldberg said, "You still there? I thought you fainted."

His sense of humor was still intact. I limited myself to a half-hour each time because I didn't want to tax him. He said that was fine.

Marshall Goldberg:

"I never broke a rule once."

First Interview:

I played for Frank Wimer at Elkins High School. He was a strong man, a man who was honest as the day is long. He did unto others as he wanted others to do unto him. He was a very knowledgeable athletic coach. He coached me in football, basketball and track. I ran the 100, 220 and I was on the 440-relay team.

I was always close to my coaches. Coach Wimer had me over to his house several times. His wife was a great woman, too. He took me under his wings and he taught me what I had to do to train to be an athlete. He taught me about conditioning, something that was all new to me. He taught me to run on the inside of the track, how to pace myself. Before that, I was just running in the dark. I was a pest in grade school, but he found a way to harness my energy in high school.

He was very rigid. Just like Jock Sutherland, I would later learn. He always wanted me to do it better. I thought he was a hero. I broke my neck to do what he wanted me to do. I was surprised. He proved to me that you could make a good athlete even better.

We were state champions in basketball. We won our division in football. Baseball wasn't a school sport but I was a catcher for our local sandlot team and pretty good at it. I learned to catch low balls and Coach Wimer helped me with that.

I had three special men in my life. My dad, my high school coach and my college coach, Jock Sutherland. I always felt I had a great responsibility to all of them. I had complete respect for them. I never broke a rule once.

None of those men ever gave me a hard time too much, but they forced me to achieve greatness. If I thought I did a real good job, they always asked for more.

You ask me what Elkins was like. It was heaven. My father had a theater. It was the Roosevelt Theater. He'd come over from Poland. He was a dapper dresser and he loved sports. I ushered in the theater in high school and it was just fun to do. I saw a lot of good movies. There were sports all the time. I played baseball all day, I played football all day, I played basketball all day. It helped my timing and development to play so many sports. Coach Wimer told me you've got to win. You've got to win and you have to do it honestly. We did everything possible to do that. Frank Wimer was our hero, just a wonderful man. When I'd score a touchdown, he just put his hand on my shoulder. He didn't say anything at all. He didn't praise me. I had to work for it.

My dad, well, he had a big mouth. He was going around town talking about me all the time. I didn't like it, but I knew my dad was very proud of me. His name was Sol Goldberg and he was a Jewish businessman. My mother was Rebecca.

We had five boys in our family, and three of us were athletes. I was next to the youngest. My brother, Isadore, was a good tennis player at Davis & Elkins College. My other brothers were Victor, Joe and William. Once I got into Pitt, I was so busy with my schooling and activities that I only got back home for two or three days at the most every so many months, and then it was back to school. I never knew much about what was going on in Elkins. Pittsburgh was the world for me.

I was into the Pirates, who were playing at Forbes Field on our campus. So were the Steelers, but they had just started up a few years earlier, and the NFL wasn't what it would become. I knew the players. I'd say hello to them when I saw them.

Second Interview:

The people at Pitt were dedicated to excellence. Sometimes in school, athletes make monkeys of themselves. But they didn't do it at Pittsburgh. Jock Sutherland was the same in his approach and demeanor as Frank Wimer.

He was an austere, strong, dedicated, serious, yet kind and appreciative gentleman. When Jock put his hand on my shoulder I could feel the warmth of his friendship. He never praised me until I got out of school. But he never said a hard word to me.

My best game at Pitt was when we beat Notre Dame (he carried the ball 22 times for 117 yards and led the Panthers to a 26–0 victory over the previously undefeated Irish as a

397

sophomore in 1936). We won at Notre Dame the next year, too. I almost went to Notre Dame, but my dad wanted me to go to Pitt so he could see me play. So it was always a thrill to play at Notre Dame, and to be able to beat them. It was a pleasure.

I had a great situation at Pitt with Jock Sutherland. I was his man. I did what he wanted me to do. He respected all the fellows. I was in the Phi Epsilon Pi fraternity at Pitt. I was popular. I never got ideas of greatness. I was friendly with everyone, from top to bottom. I didn't embarrass anybody.

I was always a good dresser. That was always important with me. I liked to be clean and have some class about me. I always wore a shirt and tie to any social affair at Pitt. My dad owned a clothes store and believed in dressing the part. I was a good student and I was involved in a lot of campus activities.

I was a pretty good football player, but I was very careful to be Marshall Goldberg from Elkins, West Virginia and not Marshall Goldberg the great football player.

I was calm, very calm. I was never antagonistic. I was not a smart aleck guy. I always said hello to everybody on the campus when I saw them. I always said hello; a lot of the fellows didn't. Some were stuck up with the rest of the students. I always thought I was a student at Pitt.

My dad liked to come around. You could always hear Sol Goldberg. He was really something. He was out there like he was an assistant coach. He'd tell me to play a great game because he had a bet on the game, and I told him he shouldn't be telling me that and that he shouldn't be betting on us. He bet on us against Notre Dame, and I told him we could be in trouble because they were that good.

Football was very different then. We were playing real tough football. A lot of guys just wore themselves out. I knew they'd be in trouble later on. I remember we trained at Windber, out near Johnstown and Altoona. It was a tough camp. We played a couple of football games a week when we were there, starting with the freshmen against the varsity.

Jock took care of everything. He was able to stimulate players mentally and physically. I never had a disagreement with him. He and I were friends. Steve Petro was a different type of person. He was a guy from overseas. He didn't know much English in the beginning. He hadn't been educated as much as some of the guys. We had to be very careful around him. He was easily offended and upset. He was a good man, and a very friendly man for the most part. He was my escort at times. He loved Pitt and so did I.

I loved playing for the Chicago Cardinals. I had great teammates there, too. Charlie Bidwill was the owner. I was crazy about him. He was very nice to me. He was like Jock Sutherland. He was ready to do anything for me. I started out making $6,500 a year and ended up making $10,000 a year. That

No. 1
CKFIELD

Pitt's Dream Backfield includes, left to right, Curly Stebbins, Marshall Goldberg, John Chickerneo and Dick Cassiano

Marshall Goldberg, Mrs. Charlotte Ditka (Mike's mother) and Joe Schmidt appeared at halftime ceremony when their jersey numbers were retired by Pitt officials.

Marshall Goldberg was a Navy officer in 1945

was good in those days. It was nothing like they have today. I started a business in Chicago and had my own machinery company for years. We did well with that. I started out in the sales department and ended up owning the company.

I was a big fan of Mike Ditka. He was a football player's football player. He was a linebacker at Pitt, and he knew how to do it. He scared half the backfield. He hit them and he hit them hard. I played against him once in one of those old-timers' games at Pitt. He didn't have any problem with me; I kept a safe distance from him.

I love to go to his restaurant here in Chicago. When I want a good meal it's the first place I go to. I head to his restaurant. It's a great restaurant. He played for the Bears and he coached the Bears to a championship, so he's still a big man in this town. He has a picture of me in one of the rooms there. He still has a special fondness for the Pitt and Pittsburgh guys. He's quite a guy. We had something else in common. He almost went to Notre Dame.

I remember George Halas. They called him "Papa Bear." He was a good man. He started the Bears and coached them for a long time. I can picture him on the sidelines, his hands on his hips. He always wore his hat. If he saw something go wrong he'd put his hands on his hips. He'd be up and down the sideline; he didn't stand still.

I have so many good memories of my days in football. I was blessed to have been a part of it.

Third Interview:

My dad wanted me to go to Pittsburgh. Notre Dame offered me a scholarship and that was a big deal in Elkins. When I showed it to my father, he said he still wanted me to go to Pitt.

I visited Pitt with my dad. Everybody was scared to death that I might go to Notre Dame, so they bent over backwards to show us the best time. My dad was a businessman and he thought it would be an advantage to his business if I were a star athlete in Pittsburgh. We lived on Kerns Avenue. We lived in a big house next door to his clothing shop. He also sold fire insurance. He was an enterprising guy.

My mother Rebecca was only 37 when she passed away. I was 13 years old and just starting high school. I missed my mother. A mother is important to you. My dad had friends and there were always people looking out for me.

The other three guys who were in The Dream Backfield with me at Pitt are all gone now. I feel sorry for the others. I'm the only one left.

I thought Tony Dorsett was a good football player, but he was a little bit aloof around me. I didn't have much to do with him. Edgar "Special Delivery" Jones was a good running back at Pitt (1939–1941). He deserves more attention. He was one of those fellows who could block and tackle and he was a good player.

Jock Sutherland was a star. I enjoyed a special relationship with him. Yes, I did. I can't remember all the details, but he talked to me a lot. I was 17 years old when I came to Pitt. They wanted to take care of me, look after me. They were babying me. Dr. Sutherland took me in and kept me on my feet, nice and steady. I loved it when we played Notre Dame and Fordham, but my favorite game was when we played West Virginia. I loved to play against them. That was my favorite game. It was wonderful. Dr. Sutherland was very dignified and stern, but I saw him cry. Everybody was afraid of him, but he was very nice to me. I did everything he wanted me to do.

I'm glad I went to Pitt. It was the perfect place for me. I always felt welcome there. I always felt important. I haven't been able to get back lately because I've had some health issues. I feel fine today. It's good to talk to you and to talk about those days when I played at Pitt. I'm glad you called.

I always felt better when I was on the Pitt campus. I always feel a little younger when I'm there.

Dr. Jock Sutherland takes a knee at Pitt Stadium, flanked by Pitt's Dream Backfield, left to right, of Dick Cassiano, Curly Stebbins, John Chickerneo and Marshall Goldberg.

Tragic Endings

The three most important men in the young life of Marshall Goldberg all had tragic endings. His father, Sol Goldberg, committed suicide. "My father shot himself," Goldberg told me. His coach at Pitt, Dr. Jock Sutherland, was found wandering through a farm field in Kentucky. He had a brain tumor and died upon being returned to a hospital in Pittsburgh. His coach at Elkins High School, Frank Wimer, was murdered. Wimer, then 86, and his wife, Eleanor, 83, were both murdered on April 11, 1961, in what amounted to a car-jacking in Randolph County, where Elkins is the county seat.

According to West Virginia sports historian Doug Huff of Wheeling, the Wimers picked up a hitchhiker, Dennis Currence, near Beverly, West Virginia. He stabbed them both to death (23 times for Frank and 10 for his wife), robbed them and stole their car. Currence was arrested for being drunk before the bodies were found. He was sentenced to life without parole. It was one of the biggest funerals in Elkins' history and was held at the National Guard Armory.

They were buried in Maplewood Cemetery on Route 219, north of Elkins where the two early senators, Davis & Elkins (for whom the local college is named) are buried.

Frank Wimer is a member of the West Virginia Sports Hall of Fame. He helped construct the football stadium at Elkins High in 1935 and it is named Wimer Stadium. He also helped build four local playgrounds. He coached football, basketball and track from 1920-1954 at Elkins High and retired from teaching in 1960.

His football record was 181–86–26 with a state title in 1928. His basketball record was 585–184 with two state titles. Besides Goldberg, he also coached Red Brown, later the West Virginia University basketball coach and athletic director, Marshall "Little Sleepy" Glenn, a WVU athlete and later football and basketball coach who is now a surgeon, and Herman Ball, who spent 31 years as an NFL coach.

PITTSBURGH

ALL AMERICAN

MARSHALL GOLDBERG   *Halfback*

Marshall Goldberg was always his hero

Jim Duratz of Meadville, the chairman of PCN (Pennsylvania Cable Network), offered a good story about Marshall Goldberg. As a fifth-grader growing up in Grindstone, Jim Duratz — then Durazio — won a contest for selling copies of *The Pittsburgh Press*, the afternoon daily. I recalled that Grindstone, near Uniontown, was also the hometown of Pat Mullin, a fine outfielder for the Detroit Tigers for ten years back in the '40s and '50s. "I knew him, too," declared Duratz.

It was an overnight trip to Pittsburgh — which was a big deal — and it included a tour of the University of Pittsburgh campus. "We were walking into the Cathedral of Learning," recalled Duratz, "and I spotted Marshall Goldberg coming out.

"He was my hero, so I stopped him and asked him for an autograph. He was very nice to me. Years later, in the late '80s, I drove my father-in-law, George Barco, to Pitt where he served on the Board of Visitors for the Athletic Department. At the meeting, I was sitting next to Marshall Goldberg. He also served on the board during Chancellor Posvar's days at Pitt. I told him, 'You have no idea what this means to me. I know you don't remember it, but I stopped you one day during your playing days at Pitt and got an autograph from you. You were my boyhood hero. You're still my hero." The Duratz Athletic Center at the UPMC Sports Complex on the South Side is named in honor of Jim and his late wife Yolanda Barco.

Three of Pitt's strongest benefactors, left to right, are John Petersen of Erie (lead gift for Petersen Events Center), Mike Ditka of Chicago and Jim Duratz of Meadville.

Ron Everhart and Bob Huggins
Mutual admiration society

"He is a big-hearted guy."
—Everhart on Huggins

R on Everhart had an interesting story to share about Bob Huggins that provided insights into their success as basketball coaches, respectively, at Duquesne University and West Virginia University.

Everhart had a winning team in his second season at Duquesne, something that hadn't happened on the Bluff in a long time, and Huggins took over a team that had been recruited by John Beilein and managed to take it all the way to the NCAA's Sweet 16.

Beilein had a terrific run as the head coach at WVU, before moving on to Michigan, but he coaches a different style than Huggins. Yet Huggins won anyhow.

Both Huggins and Everhart proved once again during the 2007–2008 season that they can flat out coach. Huggins, age 54, was rewarded by signing an 11-year contract that may keep him at his alma mater until he's 65. He'll get paid $1.5 million a year, plus incentives, and it could be worth over $20 million. Everhart, age 46, drew interest from several schools seeking a winning coach, and it may prove difficult for Duquesne to keep him long term.

Both men were guest speakers at the Coaches Corner luncheon in November of 2007, and were big hits for different reasons. Huggins looks like a bouncer at an after-hours nightclub, and plays the part. His mostly self-deprecating humor had the audience in stitches, and I believe he was the funniest speaker to ever appear at the luncheon in more than 25 years. He scolded all the high school coaches who preceded him on the dais who boasted about their players' academic records. "I don't like to have players who are smarter than me," he said. "It's tough enough coaching 'em."

Huggins has had his share of scrapes in his college coaching career, and it cost him his job after a long successful run at Cincinnati, but he is a bright fellow whose intelligence belies his reputation. He graduated with honors at West Virginia and was an Academic All-American.

Everhart told a story that showed that Huggins also had a good heart as a young player in his hometown of Morgantown.

Everhart grew up in Fairmont, West Virginia, better known as the hometown of Mary Lou Retton. Her dad Ronnie had played with Jerry West at West Virginia. When he was 10 or 11 years old, Everhart used to tag along with some older fellows — one or two of them old enough to drive an automobile — and they'd drive to Morgantown.

This was during the summer and they wanted to see the West Virginia basketball players, and perhaps fill in if they needed a player or two for a game, or even just to retrieve the ball during individual

404

Michael Dradzinski/University of Pittsburgh

Bob Huggins got off to a great start as basketball coach at West Virginia University and was rewarded with a contract extension.

Jim O'Brien

Mike Rice Jr. of Robert Morris University, Orlando Antigua of Pitt (now at Memphis) and Ron Everhart of Duquesne University swap hoop tales at 2008 Dapper Dan Dinner & Auction.

workouts. "I was a gym rat, no doubt about it," explained Everhart. "I was excited just to be there."

On one such trip, Everhart got left behind by his buddies. Huggins, who was 18 or so at the time, spotted Everhart, looking a little lost after one session. Left behind by his friends, he stayed out on the floor and shot around. "What are you doing here?" Huggins asked the youngster. "Where are you going?"

When Everhart explained his dilemma, Huggins told him he could stay in his dorm room. "You can call your parents and tell them what happened," he said. "Don't worry about it. We'll get you a ride home."

Everhart was relieved. "He watched over me pretty good. He is a big good-hearted guy. The next day, I chased after loose balls and helped Bob any way I could. That was a big thrill. I stayed overnight with him a few times that summer, telling my parents in advance what I was doing. They knew I was having a good time. For me, it was like going to a basketball camp. I just loved being in a college gym, playing the game I loved, doing anything to help out."

Everhart played three years at Fairmont West High, then transferred for his senior year to DeMatha Catholic in Washington, D.C., one of the nation's most high-powered programs. He went to Virginia Tech and captained the 1984-85 team.

He got into coaching as a grad assistant, then as an assistant coach, and, finally, landed the head job at McNeese State and then Northeastern, fast gaining a reputation for turning programs around. That's what he's done at Duquesne as well.

He invited me to come to his office at Palumbo Center on the Duquesne campus to see first-hand all the improvements they have made since he came on board in March of 2006.

"I will always be grateful to Bob Huggins for helping me in the beginning, and all the years since then," said Everhart. "He knows how to coach and how to motivate young men. You'll do anything to please him. It's phenomenal what he's done so quickly at West Virginia.

"He had a good thing going at Kansas State, and felt bad about staying there only one season, but West Virginia is the job he always wanted. It's coming home. He's one of the most intelligent coaches in the game. You can sit down with him and discuss anything. You will learn life lessons from him. He's very inspirational. His reputation and outward demeanor are misleading.

"Hugs will say stuff just to get a rise out of people. He's quick to put himself down. He's taught me a lot. He's made me realize how you have to be careful when you're a public figure. It makes you more responsible to be a good role model. He was a 4.0 student, but he found the time to look out for me. No one works harder at his job than he does. He stays involved with people he likes. He does care.

"When a kid comes into his program he's going to have to compete. He's going to have to work hard to get a college education. I was fortunate I got to know him when I did. I try to be helpful to young men in my care, the way he looked after me when I was just a gym rat."

Last-second victory sparks
memories of last-second setback

February 14, 2008

Sometimes it is difficult to distinguish between dreams and reality. Dreams often seem so real and reality often seems so unreal. I frequently have sports-related dreams. I can dunk a basketball in my dreams. I had one the other night where I was in a restaurant that had a large rectangular bar. Penn State's Joe Paterno was sitting across the way. We were all watching a basketball game in which Penn State beats Pitt. Paterno tosses a football my way to get my attention at game's end, and then he runs around the bar celebrating the Lions' victory.

Can you picture that?

My wife Kathie and I witnessed Pitt's exciting last-second victory over West Virginia in a Big East basketball game on a Thursday evening earlier this month. Pitt's backcourtman Ronald Ramon hit a 3-point field goal with two-tenths of a second showing on the game clock to win the game. The final score at the Petersen Events Center was 55–54.

For a Pitt fan, that's as good as it gets, right up there with the 13-9 victory over West Virginia at Morgantown in the final football game of the 2007 season for the Panthers.

A couple of coincidental meetings at the Petersen Events Center the night of the Pitt-WVU basketball game frame the evening's excitement.

Before the game began, I was waiting in a runway for Kathie to come back from the concession stand. That's when I spotted Calvin Sheffield coming my way.

Cal and I were classmates at Pitt. We both came to the Oakland campus in September of 1960. He was a member of an outstanding freshman basketball team and an outstanding family. I remembered that he was from New Brighton, that he was one of 17 children, and that three of his brothers played basketball at Geneva College. I knew he had owned and operated several funeral homes, including one in Pittsburgh's Manchester section.

I introduced Kathie to Calvin. "He wrote good stories about me," said Sheffield. I told Kathie that Calvin was the leading scorer on the team during his three varsity seasons. He averaged 15.3 points over that span while scoring 1,115, one more point than his teammate Brian Generalovich, who averaged 15.5 points while playing one less game.

Sheffield and Generalovich were great college players. Generalovich came from Farrell. He is a dentist in his home area these days, and has remained active in Pitt alumni affairs.

The other three starters on that freshman team were center Paul Krieger, a redhead from Uniontown; Dave Sauer, a forward from Avonworth, and Paul Martha, a guard from Wilkins Township. Freshmen were not eligible for varsity competition in those days. It was a better system. They played their own schedule. They had a chance to get acclimated to the academic side of school with less pressure on them as athletes. Krieger is now in Houston, Tex., Sauer in Bluffton, S.C., and Martha in San Diego.

I always felt fortunate to have gone to Pitt during the same period those guys were there. That's before there were three-point field goals and five to six coaches cluttering up the bench.

Martha had been recruited for football, and was also a starting infielder for the school baseball team. That's when schools had three-sport stars. Mike Ditka was a senior that year. Ditka not only played football, baseball and basketball, but he was the intramural heavyweight wrestling champion. Rex Perry, Pitt's wrestling coach, thought Ditka could have been an NCAA wrestling champion. Dr. Dick Dietrick had been a three-sport star before Ditka and captained all three varsity teams.

Martha and Rick Leeson of Scott Township were the star backs on that 1960 freshman football team. They were coached by Lou "Bimbo" Cecconi, Billy Kaliden and Steve Petro, all familiar names in this neighborhood, and they finished with a 6–0 record.

Here's where it gets a little weird.

As Kathie and I are walking across the runway to the exit after the game, I'm telling her how this game reminded me of a heart-breaking defeat Pitt suffered at the hands of West Virginia during my student days at Pitt.

That was during the 1962–63 season, our junior year.

I told her how a guard named Dave Roman hit a two-point field goal at the buzzer to beat West Virginia, 69–68, only to have one of the referees signal that the shot didn't count. Ben Jinks, a sleek senior forward from East Meadow, N.Y., had called for a timeout just before Roman released his shot. It would be a three-point field goal today.

Jinks had been instructed to do so by Coach Bob Timmons on the sideline. Timmons, an easy-going sort, never complained about the call. "I wanted a time-out," he said with that lopsided grin of his. "The ref had it right."

So Pitt lost by 68–67. Games with West Virginia were much more meaningful in those days. It was much more of a heated rivalry. Pitt would avenge that loss, a little bit anyhow, by beating West Virginia in Morgantown later that season, 69–68. Check that score. It was the same as it should have been at the Pitt Field House. That was weird, too.

I told Kathie—as we continued to head for the exit—that Dave Roman had come to Pitt from the Pitt-Johnstown campus in his hometown. He was the leading scorer for the Panthers that 1962–63 campaign, averaging 15 points a game. I mentioned that he conducted a training camp aimed at improving shooting skills. "They call him the 'Shot Doctor,'" said Dick Groat when I mentioned Roman to the Pitt basketball analyst. Roman had a deadly outside shot. Nowadays, his average would be 18 or 19 points a game with the same degree of shooting success he had in his Pitt playing days.

About ten yards short of the exit door at the Petersen Events Center, we bumped into Dave Roman. "This is unreal," I told him. "I was just talking about you. I told her about you and how we lost that game here to West Virginia."

Roman, still wearing his Pitt varsity letter jacket, smiled in return. "I thought about that, too," he said. Before he departed, he said to Kathie, "He wrote some nice stories about me."

As soon as we were outside of the Petersen Events Center, Kathie took out her cell phone and called our older daughter, Sarah, at her home in Columbus. She knew Sarah would be watching the game on ESPN. Sarah put her daughter Margaret on the telephone. Margaret will be four this May. When she was just a baby and when she was two years old she went to many Pitt basketball games with us. She even had her own Pitt cheerleader costume.

I got on the phone. "Grandpap, I saw you and Grandma on TV," Margaret said in her most excited voice. She told me what we both were wearing. "What do you say, Margaret?" I asked. "Go, Pitt!" she responded, just as she did so many times when we coached her at the Petersen Events Center.

I told Sarah we missed having them with us at the game. It was something we always enjoyed as a family. I'll tell her my Dave Roman story when I visit her in Columbus this weekend.

From University of Pittsburgh Sports Information

Dave Roman came from Pitt-Johnstown to be a shooting star for Pitt in mid-60s.

Basketball, baby-sitting
go well together

Pulling for Pitt in the
Big East Tournament

March 20, 2008

O ur family follows Pitt basketball the way most Pittsburgh families follow their Steelers. We get really involved, and we pace the floor a lot in the late going. "It makes me nervous," cried Kathie at one point in the stretch run of the Pitt-Georgetown game for the Big East Tournament title last Saturday night.

When your favorite basketball team misses 22 free throws it can make for an anxious evening. That's right, Pitt missed 22 of its 44 free throws. They still won the game, 74–65. They became only the second team in Big East history to win four games in the tournament to claim the championship. I guess it wouldn't have been as exciting if they were hitting more of their free throws. They did make 22 free throws.

We watched the first of those four games at our home in Pittsburgh and the final three games in Columbus, Ohio. Kathie and I were watching our granddaughter, Margaret, who will turn four this May.

Margaret was anxious only when she helped her grandmother when she was getting a nursery room ready for Margaret's baby sister, who is due in mid-May. Margaret is worried about her exalted status in the Zirwas home.

Her mother, Sarah, seven months pregnant though you'd hardly know it, was in Hawaii with her husband Matt at a medical conference where Matt was scheduled to speak on a dermatology matter. Sarah had her doctor's OK to make the trip.

They had to board an airplane in Oahu to fly to Maui with eight minutes remaining in the title game. "It looked like Pitt was doing its best to lose the game at that point," recalled Sarah.

They didn't know the final outcome until they got into their hotel suite in Maui and turned on ESPN that afternoon (there's a six-hour time difference). Sarah still loves her Pitt basketball even though she and her husband are on the staff at The Ohio State University Medical School. Sarah does research at the Nationwide Children's Hospital in Columbus.

Ohio State, by the way, didn't get invited to the NCAA Tournament this time, even though they played Florida in the championship game a year ago. Florida also failed to get back, after winning the NCAA title the previous two years in a row. This is the seventh straight trip for Pitt's Panthers.

I spoke to several people in Columbus. They were all aware of Terrelle Pryor, the prize athlete at Jeannette High School, and hoping he would pick Ohio State as his college choice. Pryor had not made a choice on the National Letter of Intent Day, saying he was having difficulty making up his mind. Pryor said he was going to play football only. At one point, he had talked about playing football and basketball.

During March Madness, I wondered how Terrelle could turn his back on basketball when he had such a gift for the game, and when it seemed like college basketball created such a national stir at this time of the year.

Orack Obama and Hillary Clinton were both coming to Ohio to campaign for the state primary election that was coming up, but many of the sports fans were more interested in having Terrelle Pryor come to Columbus.

I remember taking Sarah to the Big East Tournament when she was about 12 or 13, and we watched seven Big East games and one NBA game involving the Knicks in a three-day span. That's why she's like she is. That's why Margaret likes to shout, "Go, Pitt!" Or, "Let's go, Pitt!" It makes for a lot of family fun, especially when Pitt pulls off a Broadway run like it did this time around in New York.

The four of us went to the Big East Tournament in 2004 when Sarah was seven months pregnant with Margaret. So Margaret's been to Madison Square Garden as well.

The Panthers were 5–0 at Madison Square Garden this season. They had as many as five New York area kids in their lineup in the Big East Tournament and they get pumped playing in what Looie Carnesecca, the long-time St. John's coach, always calls "the mecca" of basketball.

Pitt has gotten so many kids out of New York City since Ben Howland and Dixon have been on board that I often refer to it as "St. John's West." They get kids who used to play at St. John's.

Norm Roberts, the current coach at St. John's, told me last summer, "Pitt doesn't get the best kids out of New York, but Jamie Dixon does a good job of getting some good kids, and he coaches them up."

Rick Pitino, the coach at Louisville, told me something similar about how Dixon develops his players, how they get better from one season to the next. That's why Pitt often has the most improved player in the league. This year's award winner in that category was Sam Young. He also made the diluted first team (11 players) all-conference team and, better yet, the MVP award for the tournament.

It's tough to outrecruit Pitino, UConn's Jim Calhoun and Syracuse's Jim Boeheim — they still get the best players — but Dixon does an outstanding job in coaching what he gets. I also like his style on the sideline. He's under control more than most of his coaching contemporaries.

Many members of the Pittsburgh media — quick to look for dark clouds in the sky (that's the sports reporters as well as the weather reporters) — thought Pitt's chances to be successful this season were ruined when they lost Mike Cook and then Levance Fields to crippling injuries early in the campaign.

I never bought into that doomsday dissertation. While I thought Cook was a solid contributor, I thought his absence would force Dixon

411

to play some talented youngsters. I felt the same way when Fields went down, though I knew his ball-handling and daring-do would be sorely missed. I hope Pitt goes to bat for Cook with the NCAA, in earnest, to get him another year of eligibility. They owe him that much.

I've always felt that Dixon was slow to give serious playing time to some of his talented newcomers. He did start Schenley High's DeJuan Blair right from the beginning and it's no wonder. This kid was born to play basketball. He enjoys the game and he has big man's strength and a small guy's agility and ball-handling skills. With that wide grin, he's Pitt's answer to the Steelers' Hines Ward.

With Cook and Fields sidelined, Dixon had to play the likes of veterans Keith Benjamin, who was languishing on the bench, and freshmen Gilbert Brown and Brad Wannamaker. Brown and Wannamaker will be terrific next season. Trust me, Brown is going to be the second coming of Sam Young. Behind Blair, Coach Dixon was quick to insert Tyrell Biggs and Gary McGhee. Big guys improve over the summer — ala Aaron Gray and Young — at Pitt under Dixon, so the best is yet to come for these projects.

Shooting guard Ronald Ramon had to handle the ball, and he got better at it, which proved useful to Pitt in the stretch run after Fields returned to the lineup. Ramon was, in my mind, the MVP of Pitt's final game in the Big East tournament and a steadying influence throughout the tournament. He will be missed next year.

Young was the catalyst for heroics at both ends of the court, though he seemed to be coasting at times as he made his way up and down the floor. I hope Young and Blair will be back to lead this team next season.

I love this time of the year. My son-in-law has one of those large, flat-screen DVD sets. It's like Cinerama in the family room. Kathie has been to the Big East Tournament at the Garden with me, and she admitted that you miss the excitement of being there. But it's difficult to complain when one enjoys the comforts of home, even when it's somebody else's home.

Margaret was with us, after all. We managed to read her about six books apiece each of the three days we were there. Early in the morning on Saturday, I watched a "Tom and Jerry" marathon with Margaret. The cat chasing the mouse stories are all the same, but they make Margaret smile and laugh the same way they entertained me at Saturday matinees at the theater in my hometown.

Margaret was tucked in her bed before the 9 o'clock tip-off time for the Big East championship game on Saturday night. We could hear her breathing, sometimes snoring, through one of those monitors modern-day families have now. She hollered when she had to go to the bathroom.

I wasn't thrilled to hear Pitt would be playing Oral Roberts in their first NCAA Tournament game. I remember that Pitt lost to Louisiana Tech in a first-round game in 1985 at the Oral Roberts campus. Louisiana Tech had a big guy named Karl Malone, who turned out to be a pretty fair pro player.

I love lounging around and watching all the basketball games, with a little Tiger Woods action in golf for a little variety — Tiger is such a great attraction — and some "Tom and Jerry" and "Curious George" tossed in for a different twist.

I'd by lying if I told you I thought Pitt was going to win the Big East Tournament, but I went into each game — Cincinnati, Louisville, Marquette and Georgetown — with a good feeling. I wanted West Virginia to get to the final, too, because I thought that would make for a great game at the Garden as well.

Jamie Dixon has done a fantastic job as head basketball coach at Pitt, succeeding his mentor and friend, Ben Howland, now at UCLA.

Most magic moment in
Pittsburgh sports history
still sparks memories

"It took a Polack to do it."

The New York Yankees came to Pittsburgh to play the Pirates in mid-June, 2008 for the first time in 48 years. Their return to town sparked stories and reminiscences of the 1960 World Series when the Pirates defeated the heavily favored Yankees in seven games.

Bill Mazeroski hit a home run leading off the bottom of the ninth inning to win the final game, 10–9, in what is still regarded as the most magic moment in Pittsburgh sports history.

I spent two days the weekend prior to the Yankees' visit signing my books at a special gathering of Pittsburgh athletes and displays of championship seasons for all the Pittsburgh sports entries at the Heinz History Center in the city's Strip District.

I was on the first floor and Maz was on the second floor. When any one showed me the signatures they had collected on their circuit of the History Center and the Western Pennsylvania Sports Museum, it was always easy to spot the signature of Bill Mazeroski. It stood out from the pack.

Maz's signature could win a penmanship award.

It remains the clearest and most recognizable and readable of all the local athletes. It's often difficult to identify today's players' signature because they scrawl or scribble their names as quickly as possible. Ben Roethlisberger's is one of the worst. He might be better off just signing Big Ben. The penmanship of the old-timers is much more distinct than today's players. It's a sign of the times education-wise.

Maz threw out the ceremonial first pitch in the first game of the three-game series at PNC Park and, knowing him, he was probably more nervous about doing that than he was when he strode to the plate on Oct. 13, 1960 with the score tied 9–9 against the mighty New York Yankees.

"I never thought that home run would stay with me the rest of my life," said Mazeroski.

I have two famous photos on the wall above my writing desk showing Maz from behind home plate as he hit the ball that cleared the wall to the right of the scoreboard in left field, and another that shows him being pursued by delirious fans as he nears home plate.

A woman who told me her name was Mary Margaret Zelinski when she was a grade school student at Immaculate Heart of Mary in Polish Hill back in 1960 shared a wonderful story with me regarding Maz and his home run.

It's one of those events that occurred away from Forbes Field that day that Bob Prince, "the voice of the Pirates," or any of the reporters covering the game, weren't aware of and yet it's one of those events that made it such a memorable day.

"I was walking home from school," related Mary Margaret Zelinski, "and some boys were walking ahead of me. One of them had a transistor radio pressed to his ear."

So many of the memories of that 1960 World Series make reference to transistor radios, popular at the time.

"When Maz hit the home run, one of the boys started hollering, and he told the others what had happened, and the boys all went crazy. At the same time, a man burst through the screen door of his home nearby, and came out on his stoop shouting. He kept hollering, 'It took a Polack to do it! It took a Polack to do it!'

"That night they blocked off the streets on Polish Hill and they had a block party. People brought wine and beer and they ate pierogies and all kinds of good Polish delicacies. Everyone had a great time. It was a great evening on Polish Hill." They were so proud of William Stanley "Stush" Mazeroski.

Maz once told me that he and his wife Milene, who grew up in Braddock, left Forbes Field and wanted to get away from the crowd. So they got in their car that was parked at a gas station on the corner near Forbes Field and drove up to Schenley Park.

They stood at the peak of Schenley Park and Maz said they could see the skyline of Downtown Pittsburgh from where they stood. "There was no one else where we were," said Maz. "There weren't even any squirrels. I think they all went Downtown to join the celebration."

A man from Zelienople named Alan Wilson, age 57, told me he was nine at the time, and sitting with two of his young cousins on a porch swing with their Grandpap Greer as he listened to that seventh and deciding game on the radio.

"When Maz hit the home run," Wilson told me, "my Grandpap jumped up off the swing. The three of us kids had all been sitting on the front edge of the swing and we all tipped over and spilled onto the floor of the porch. I got a bad bruise above my eye and one of my cousins cut his chin badly and had to have three or four stitches to close the wound. It took awhile before my Grandpap realized we were hurt."

If you want to learn more about Maz and his teammates, get a copy of Jim O'Brien's book, *Fantasy Camp: Living the Dream With Maz and the '60 Bucs*. The author spent a week with eleven members of the '60 Bucs at the team's Bradenton, Florida training complex in January of 2005. He had an opportunity to interview everyone in depth and get an up-to-date look at the players and what they accomplished that special summer.

Danny Murtaugh   *Casey Stengel*

Dan Marino
Always a hometown hero and still a BMOC at Pitt

"You want to look back and say, 'I was the best I could be.'"

There was a touch of irony to the appearance of Dan Marino as the featured speaker at the University of Pittsburgh's 220th commencement exercise on a beautiful, balmy Sunday afternoon, April 27, 2008.

It was the second day of the 2008 college football draft. The Steelers were pleased with their picks on the first day — they had the 23rd pick — and were hopeful of filling some needs on the second day.

Back in 1983, with the 21st pick in the first round, the Steelers selected Gabe Rivera, a defensive tackle from Texas Tech. They were the 21st team to pass up drafting Dan Marino of Pitt.

The Steelers were sure they were in great shape as quarterbacks went with Terry Bradshaw coming back (they didn't know he had an ailing throwing arm), and backups Cliff Stoudt and Mark Malone. They had made Malone their first pick in the 1980 draft.

Rivera was having a fine rookie season when he was badly injured in an auto accident on the city's North Side, not far from Three Rivers Stadium. He lost the use of his legs in the accident, careening into a car driven by a Steelers' fan. It had vanity plates boasting of being a STEELER FAN. Rivera has been in a wheel chair back in San Antonio ever since.

Marino had one of the most spectacular careers in NFL annals, and has been inducted into both the Pro Football Hall of Fame and the College Football Hall of Fame. He has been a big success on television as an analyst and commentator as well as in commercials.

Marino mentioned his grandma and growing up in Oakland and got a little choked up during his commencement address.

I had a dinner with Dan's family back in 1982, just before his senior season, at the Marino home on Parkview Avenue in South Oakland. His mother made spaghetti and a salad and I recall there was fresh Italian bread. I got the recipe for a fantastic dessert she served and, to this day, it's my daughters' favorite dessert. The glorious concoction of Veronica Marino calls for chocolate and vanilla pudding, cream cheese and whipped cream. Need I say more? Dan's mother and dad couldn't have treated me better — like family — and Dan's two sisters, Cindi and Debbie, joined us at the dinner table.

"Just eat," Dan Marino Sr. said, when I started out too rigidly perhaps. "You don't have to put on any airs for us. We're just regular people. And Danny is just one of our kids. We love them all and treat them all the same."

There was a sign on the gate in front of the Marino house that read: BEWARE OF DOG. It was a humble home, similar in appearance to one that Joe Montana and his family lived in out on Park Avenue in Monongahela. What are the odds of Marino living on Parkview Avenue and Montana living on Park Avenue? The Marinos lived across the street from St. Regis Catholic Grade School, and within a few miles — walking distance, Dan often declared — of Central Catholic High School and the University of Pittsburgh, where he continued his education and sports activities.

No one — certainly not the Steelers' scouts and not too many of the NFL scouts — knew just how good this kid was going to become. He became one of the greatest passers in pro football history with the Miami Dolphins.

The rumor had surfaced that Marino might have been fooling around with drugs during his college days. Don Shula took the time to call Coach Foge Fazio at Pitt and check into that, and Fazio assured him that he'd have no problems with Dan Marino. Fazio said he was a solid citizen. Marino turned out to be one of NFL's stellar citizens and won its Walter Payton Man of the Year Award in 1998 for his stellar character and his contributions to the community though his involvement with fund-raising activities, especially his interest in Children's Hospitals in several cities.

Marino, still so handsome, was a good man in so many ways.

Chancellor Mark Nordenberg, who'd suffered a serious shoulder injury a week earlier in a fall at his mother's home in Clearwater, Florida, ignored the pain to participate in the commencement exercise and to extol the virtues of this hometown hero.

"We recognize Dan for his accomplishments on the playing field, but also honor his broader achievements and contributions in business, broadcasting and philanthropy," said Chancellor Nordenberg. "Looking at nearly three decades, it would be difficult to identify any one person who has been a better representative of his or her university."

Marino was awarded an honorary doctorate degree in broadcast journalism by the University of Pittsburgh. Henceforth, he said with that special smile of his, he was going to insist that his colleagues on television — including Terry Bradshaw — address him as Dr. Marino.

Marino shared stories and reflections for 3,000 graduating students and 10,000 of their family and friends at the Petersen Events Center on the Oakland campus. One never knows in Pittsburgh, but it would have been a perfect day to hold the commencement on the lawn of the Cathedral of Learning. The temperature rose to 70 degrees.

It was also a great day for Pittsburgh sports fans because the Penguins beat the New York Rangers, 2–0, and the Pirates beat the Phillies 5–1 and pitcher Paul Maholm went the distance for the victory. Marino was drafted as a pitcher by the Kansas City Royals during his schooldays at Central Catholic, but chose to go to college and play football instead. It turned out to be a wise choice.

Marino's No. 13 is one of the jerseys that have been retired at Pitt. He led the team to four consecutive bowl game appearances. Who can ever forget him flinging that last-second TD pass into the end zone to John Brown to beat Georgia, 24-20, in the Sugar Bowl. It was fourth down and five yards to go at the Bulldogs' 33 when Marino threw his third touchdown pass of the game.

Jackie Sherrill declined to kick a field goal. "We were not here to tie," said Sherrill. "We were here to win."

I had a neighbor, Bob Johnson, who was a Georgia grad, and I ruined his day and possibly our relationship by calling him on the telephone right after that TD and shouting, "How 'bout them Dogs?" He promptly hung up his telephone.

That touchdown toss and catch remains one of my favorite memories in Pittsburgh sports history, right up there with Roger Kingdom's gold medal performances in the 110-meter high hurdles in back-to-back Olympic Games in 1984 and 1988. My two pro favorites are Bill Mazeroski's home run to win the 1960 World Series and Franco Harris' "Immaculate Reception" to beat Oakland in the 1972 AFC playoffs.

Marino has often returned to Pittsburgh for good causes. He's the prime source for fund-raising at his alma mater, Central Catholic High School, and he's been a regular at Mario Lemieux's Celebrity Invitational to raise money for kids with cancer challenges. There's a wing named after Marino at the Children's Hospital in Weston, Florida.

"I played 17 years in the NFL and set every passing record possible," said Marino in his Pitt commencement address. "But you know what? A lot of them have been broken. But when you touch someone's life in a positive way, it lasts forever.

"You want to look back and say, 'I was the best I could be,' that 'I worked hard and followed my dreams.' That 'I made a difference in people's lives.' If you can do that, then you will have peace of mind, no matter what you achieve in life.

"The core values of life and success remain the same: hard work, passion, integrity and, most important, family."

He said he was lucky to have the family and good fortune he enjoyed along the way. "I found my love for sports at a young age," he said. "And whether it was baseball or football, I found my true talent. I could throw it. All the hours on the practice field, all the days studying film, and all the years of working on my game, it didn't seem like work to me. Because it was fun. It's what I liked to do.

"It may take some of you longer, but it's worth the search to find your passion. It doesn't have to be about the money. I guarantee you this: If you love your life's work, the financial reward will take care of itself."

He advised everybody to give something back to their community. "It doesn't have to be money," he said. "Give your expertise. Give something of yourself."

In summing up, he said, "I was the best that I could be. Look at me, I came to Pitt with two goals, to be the starting quarterback and to get my degree. Now look at me. I'm Dr. Dan."

Jerome Bettis, the former Steelers' running back and a Notre Dame graduate, addressed Duquesne University's commencement class the following Friday at the A.J. Palumbo Center. "I believe," said Bettis, "that success is your ability to make others successful."

A week later, on Saturday, May 10, Steelers' coach Mike Tomlin delivered a commencement address at St. Vincent College, the summer home of the Steelers. He had warmed up for this appearance by offering the commencement address at his alma mater, The College of William & Mary, at an earlier date.

Tomlin spoke for 15 minutes. "I want to encourage you to trust your preparation," he said. "Trust what it is that you've done here. I tell you that you are prepared for the game of life.

"You must continue to dream the wild dreams that you dreamed when you were young. Dream, and dream big. But you have to make a daily commitment to take action to make your dreams a reality."

Dan Marino has his number (13) retired at University of Pittsburgh ceremonies with broadcaster Bill Hillgrove and athletic director Steve Pederson making presentation.

13

Oakmont Country Club
U.S. Open sparks memories

June 13, 2007

A familiar photograph graced the front page of our Sunday newspaper. It showed two of the greatest golfers, Arnold Palmer and Jack Nicklaus, coming off the 18th green at Oakmont. Nicklaus, a 22-year-old upstart from Columbus, had just beaten Palmer, the hometown favorite from Latrobe, in an 18-hole playoff to win the U.S. Open title. Palmer has always been one of my favorites because he never forgot where he came from, and he has always respected and acknowledged Arnie's Army and been graceful and honest with the media. He's been a role model for his game.

That was in the summer of 1962. I was 19, and had just completed my sophomore year at the University of Pittsburgh. I had a summer internship at *The Pittsburgh Press*, working in the city-side news department. I had won a *Wall Street Journal* scholarship worth $500 and was feeling positive about my future.

I may have written the original caption for that famous photograph that was in the paper on Sunday.

One day I overheard some discussion in our department about how the paper planned to cover the U.S. Open. Some city-side reporters would be out at Oakmont along with sportswriters. They would provide some sidebars, or "color" stories. I volunteered to tag along with a photographer to keep a roster of the pictures he'd be taking, writing down who was in the photo and describing the activity. Now you can get cameras that have recording devices in them.

It got me a first row seat, the best in the house, at the U.S. Open Golf Tournament at Oakmont. I'd be sitting on the edge of the greens, or right next to the tees. It would be the first major sports event I ever worked as a newspaperman. My press badge got me into the country club, into the clubhouse, and into the men's grill where the media hung out for the 1962 U.S. Open.

The media, so much larger now, will get no such access this week when the U.S. Open returns to Oakmont for the eighth time, the most it's been played at any one golf course in the country. They have a large tent, with tiered worktables, and lots of TV monitors, and the media won't have as much freedom to roam the grounds as they did in 1962. Security will be tight, another hangover from 9/11 that still costs us dearly. It's still a special event. It was special in 1962 as well. I worked with a reporter named Frank Christopher and a photographer named Al Herrmann Jr. Seventeen years later, I would return from New York to Pittsburgh and link up with Herrmann once again to cover the Pittsburgh Steelers for *The Press* when they won their fourth Super Bowl in the 1979 season. We were a good team.

420

Back in 1962 I was a nervous cat at Oakmont. For one thing, I had never been to a country club before. I grew up in the inner city, the milltown of Hazelwood, and I never thought there'd be a day when I'd go to a country club. To this day I still feel funny when I am invited to have lunch or to attend an event at a country club.

I was also uneasy about being with so many big-time sportswriters. They came from the big cities across the country to cover that 1962 Open. I've always enjoyed keeping company with the best sportswriters, especially my elders. I always thought I could learn something. My mother told me long ago that you'd be judged by the company you keep.

Bob Drum, who lived in Bethel Park, was the golf writer for *The Press* and he knew all the famous sportswriters. He was a pal of Palmer. Drum was a garrulous guy, a favorite among the golfers and the media. He was a funnyman, most of the time, and told good stories. He held court at Oakmont on a round-the-clock basis.

So did a nationally syndicated writer named Oscar Fraley. He and Milt Richman represented the UPI, the late United Press International, a wire service that went out of business years ago. Fraley was famous for writing the book *The Untouchables*, and there was a popular TV series based on his book. It was about Chicago mobsters such as Al Capone and federal law enforcement officials such as Elliott Ness. It was "The Sopranos" of its day.

I loved spending time with the writers at Oakmont. That famous photograph had a stately oak tree in the background. It's probably gone now, too. Oakmont this week, which I toured with my good friend Mike Hagan of Upper St. Clair, was completely different from 1962.

I had read that club officials had over 5,000 trees cut down and removed from the course landscape. The idea was to get the course back to its original design, to make it more of a links course, those bare kind where they play the British Open.

To me, in my humble opinion, it is a big mistake. The members won't be happy about this. This is Oakmont, not Baldmont; this is western Pennsylvania, not southwest America. Only seven oak trees remain at the country club layout. Most of those writers are gone, too.

On Tuesday I had a club member's pass, a gift from Bruce McGough of Geyer Printing. I was able to get into the country club. No one told me I had to leave. It was great to return to Oakmont. It brought back the best of memories.

Bob Friend, former Pirates pitcher and a long-time member at Oakmont, offers this thought:

"Every time I play Oakmont
it's like playing baseball
at Yankee Stadium."

Savoring special afternoon
at Oakmont

June 20, 2007

A friend of mine, Gerry Hamilton, has a home on Oak Street in Oakmont. She's lived there over 40 years. She lives across the street from Jim Roddey, the former county executive and the emcee extraordinaire at nearly every important fund-raising dinner in Pittsburgh these days. He lives in one of the new homes that have been built on that side of the street in recent years.

That plot of land where Roddey resides was once the site for St. Anthony's Home for Exceptional Children. A niece of mine, Reisha Marie Cook, went to school there for many years, so I know the neighborhood.

My daughter Sarah and her husband Matt lived in nearby Oakmont Commons during their respective residency programs at Children's Hospital and UPMC Montefiore about five or six years ago. It's on the outskirts of Oakmont where it meets Verona. It provides a seldom-traveled back road that gets you into Oakmont without having to traverse Allegheny River Boulevard, Oakmont's main street.

Gerry Hamilton's home is two short blocks from Hulton Road and the main entrance to the Oakmont Country Club. Everyone who lives in that neighborhood was given three parking passes for the week of the U.S. Open Golf Tournament.

Parking in Oakmont's streets near the country club was restricted to residents and their guests. Gerry Hamilton gave me one of her passes for one day. It was my ticket to a special afternoon at Oakmont.

I invited my friend Mike Hagan to go with me. We go to a lot of Upper St. Clair High School football and basketball games together. We get together for lunch on the South Side. He has been the president for 12 years of the Iron & Glass Bank, which is headquartered at a beautiful old bank building on East Carson Street.

Mike Hagan is good company, an easy traveling companion. We're pale-faced Irishmen — he's a proud Notre Dame grad (aren't they all?) — and we require the same sunscreen and ballcap to survive a day in the sun. We both wore shorts and looked like two geezers going off to senior camp.

I pride myself on knowing how to get from here to there anywhere in Greater Pittsburgh. So I avoided Route 28 and the logjam at the Hulton Bridge, and traveled to Verona and Oakmont via Bloomfield and Lawrenceville on the other side of the Allegheny River. We had lunch at Del's in Bloomfield. It's better and cheaper to eat at a restaurant you know rather than risk getting ripped off and disappointed at a concession stand at a sporting event, any sporting event.

We reached our parking spot in front of Gerry Hamilton's home without hitting any traffic. I felt like I was cheating. We didn't have to wait for a shuttle bus or the drive from any parking lot on the outskirts of Oakmont. We arrived at Oakmont around 1:30 in the afternoon.

This was Tuesday, one of the practice rounds. That's the best time, in my opinion, to go to a major golf tournament. You get to see the players up close, they're more relaxed and fan friendly. You get to see them working at their game. You can take pictures because cameras are permitted during the practice rounds, but not during the tournament. There's no better way to watch the actual golf tournament than on TV.

No sooner did we walk onto the grounds of the legendary Oakmont Country Club than we spotted an ex-Steeler and ex-Pitt football player, Emil Boures. He was one of Chuck Noll's favorites in the early '80s because he was versatile and could play every position on the offensive line.

We walked over to an area where the pros were practicing driving, chip shots and putting. The first player we recognized was none other than Tiger Woods. He was twenty yards from us. It was a genuine thrill to see him in the flesh, working at his game. There's not a bigger figure in sports these days than Tiger Woods. I'm one of his fans. "This is too good," I told Mike Hagan. "This is our lucky day." He nodded and smiled in agreement.

From there, we went to the grandstand overlooking the 18th green. I thought that was for reserved seating, but it's first come, first served. We sat on the top row, with back support, and, most importantly, in the shade of some of the few oak trees that remain at Oakmont.

We had a great view of Oakmont. We could see the 18th, 10th, 11th, 12th, 14th and 15th holes. It was quite a view of Oakmont since they cut down about 5,000 trees to restore the course to its original design and layout. The sky was Carolina blue with white puffy clouds. The weather was right. Mayor Luke Ravenstahl, who is younger than most of the pro golfers, had to be smiling somewhere on the grounds. Bob O'Connor, the late mayor, had to be smiling from somewhere above. He enjoyed such a day when the All-Star Baseball Game was held at PNC Park a year earlier.

We saw Jim Furyk — no one studied the course any closer — and Davis Love III, Ben Curtis, Bubba Watson, Steve Elkington, Sean O'Hair, Vijay Singh, Jeff Sluman, Stuart Appleby, Jerry Kelly, Justin Leonard and Geoff Olgivy among others at the 18th.

Mike Hagan always amazes me by how much he knows about the players on the opposing teams at high school football games. He surprised me by being equally informed about the touring pro golfers. He recognized some of them by their walk. I thought I was with Walter Hagen, the legendary golfer.

We stayed a few hours, bought some souvenirs, and beat the traffic home in time for dinner. It's a day that will go into the sports scrapbook of my mind and remain forever. It was that special. Mike Hagan and I agreed that when we watched the Open on TV we felt like we were still in the grandstand, in the shade, at the 18th hole.

Lackner and Luckhardt
Boxing came first and football followed

A good story should be twice told. Two of this area's finest football coaches shared similar stories at separate meetings earlier this month. I was struck by the coincidence, especially because I'd never heard these stories before.

Rick Lackner of Mt. Lebanon, the head coach at Carnegie Mellon University, and John Luckhardt of Peters Township, the head coach at California (Pa.) University, were talking about their introduction to playing the game of football.

Lackner and his lovely wife, Cindy, sneaked in behind me and Mike Hagan as we were taking in the Fox Chapel at Upper St. Clair high school football game a few Fridays back. They sat in the stands with us for the first half and then hustled over to Mt. Lebanon to catch the second half of a game there.

Lackner was on the lookout for athletic and academic standouts who could cut it at CMU. Hagan, then president of Iron & Glass Bank, was so taken with the Lackners that he later told me he has been checking out the newspaper accounts of the Carnegie Mellon games to see how the Tartans are doing. Hagan is a Notre Dame grad. The Fighting Irish lost their first three games this season, so maybe Hagan needs another college team to root for these days.

I knew that Lackner, who's 51, had gotten his start playing for St. Bernard's Grade School football team. I related a story about how when I was in eighth grade playing halfback and linebacker for the St. Stephen's Grade School football team in Hazelwood that we were intimidated by the mere appearance of the St. Bernard's team. They were one of the best teams in the Catholic Grade School Football League.

They arrived at our home field in three bright, shiny yellow buses and they just kept filing off these buses. There were so many of them. Their football uniforms were as bright as the buses and certainly better than our gear. They each had a helmet that looked like a leather helmet but had a hard veneer. Paul Hornung wore such a helmet when he won the Heisman Trophy at Notre Dame in 1956. This was 1955.

Lackner smiled as I told him my story. Then he offered one of his own. "The coach at St. Bernard's back when I was on the team was Frank "Cip" Cipriani," the CMU coach recalled. "He owned a tavern-restaurant called Cip's on Washington Road in Dormont.

"When his St. Bernard's players came to their first practice, Coach Cipriani passed out boxing gloves. They had to box first. He wanted to see how tough they were. He thought he could win if he had tough players."

I'd never heard such a story before. I knew that we had to wrestle and sometimes box with other boys in our neighborhood in a garage that belonged to a local milkman. You knew where you stood on the tough-guy ratings on your block. It was like the *Ring* magazine ratings.

Four days after I enjoyed the Lackners' company I attended the monthly Coaches Corner Luncheon at the Riverwatch on Smallman Street in the Strip District. This is a sports luncheon hosted by Iron City Brewery and KDKA-TV that features representatives of the Steelers, Pitt, sometimes WVU and Penn State, and area small colleges and high schools.

Luckhardt, age 63, who had great teams for years at Washington & Jefferson before coming to California, was telling a story to Dan McCann, the former sales chief at Iron City who coordinates the Coaches Corner confabs.

Luckhardt and McCann had the same head coach, Bob Hast, at two different high schools. Luckhardt had Hast at Scott Township High School, where one of his teammates was future Pitt star Rick Leeson, and McCann had Hast at North Catholic. Hast coached championship teams at both schools, as well as back-to-back Class A champions at Bridgeville High School in the late '40s. Luckhardt went on to play at Purdue.

"When I showed up for practice," related Luckhardt, "I had no idea I'd have to box first to show my mettle. But that's what he did. He was one of those guys who'd seen action in World War II and boxing was part of their training."

Hast, indeed, had seen action in World War II. As a captain, he was in charge of a landing craft at Normandy on D-Day.

One of my neighbors, Bill "Woody" Wolf, had been a tough two-way lineman on those undefeated Bridgeville championship teams in 1948 and 1949. Wolf went on to play for Jack Wiley at Waynesburg College. He doesn't remember having to do any boxing at Bridgeville. "If we had," said Wolf, who looks like the trainer played by Burgess Meredith in those "Rocky" movies, "I'd have been the champeen."

Boxing before football would never fly today, of course. The first kid who came home with a shiner would be coming back to school the next day with his parents and the family lawyer. Those were different days. The coaches felt they needed to know just how tough their players would be in the clinch. Or in the clutch.

Chuck Klausing

* * *

I checked with Chuck Klausing, a member of the College Football Hall of Fame and the WPIAL Hall of Fame, about the authenticity of the boxing-before-football stories. Klausing coached Braddock High School to six undefeated seasons (54-0-1) in the '50s, the same period John Luckhardt and Rich Lackner alluded to in their stories.

Klausing couldn't recall any of the coaches in the Steel Valley having their kids box before they could play football. He said Nick Kliskey at Munhall, Neil Brown at Clairton and Duke Weigle at McKeesport were all no-nonsense disciplinarians, but he didn't remember boxing being part of their training process.

Klausing, who now resides with his wife Joann in Indiana, Pennsylvania, always comes through with a related story, however. He prides himself on swimming every day, and doing some writing and reading every day, and fancies himself a good storyteller. He went to Penn State College (as it was then called) for two years, then went into the military service, and finished his college work at Slippery Rock. He was a 155-pound combatant on the boxing team at Penn State.

"I learned to box at the Wilmerding YMCA," said Klausing. "My coach was a guy named Jack Rovesta. He fought Art Rooney three times. He won once, lost once and they had a draw. I was always lucky to have good coaches. There were a lot of things you did in boxing, especially footwork, that have applications in football. I know boxing helped me with football."

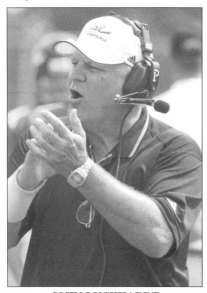

JOHN LUCKHARDT
California (PA) Coach

RICH LACKNER
Carnegie Mellon Coach

Nellie King on Paul Waner:

"Walker Cooper told me Paul liked to have a drink once in a while. One day Cooper said he could smell the alcohol on Waner's breath and said something to him about it. Waner came in to pinch-hit. He told Cooper, 'I'm going to hit the first pitch between the third base coach and the bag. I'm going to hit the second pitch between the first base coach and the bag, then I'm going to hit the next pitch to center for a single.' And that's exactly what he did."

Dwight White
A Steelers' success story

"I had to go up to hit bottom."

Dwight White was about to blow a gasket. And he was just warming up to the subject. "The Rooneys are treated like royalty in this town," said White, "but they're no better than I am. We all come from similar, humble backgrounds. I loved Art Rooney. The old man treated me and my teammates better than any other owner in the National Football League.

"But, let's get real. He was a racketeer. His dad owned a bar on the North Side. Art Rooney started out in gambling and other nefarious activities. The Steelers were a sandlot team at the start. He gained respectability when the NFL became respectable. It wasn't always the way it is now.

"I know where I came from, and I had to work real hard to improve my lot in life. My grandparents weren't slaves, but they worked on farms and they weren't much better off. I went to a college in Texas where the only blacks were ballplayers. I had to go up to hit bottom. So I know that the Rooneys and the Whites both had to lift themselves up by the bootstraps to get somewhere in this world."

I conducted extensive interviews — two and three hours long — with White over a ten-year period for stories in three different books I wrote about the Rooneys and the Steelers. He was my favorite interview of all the former Steelers I interviewed. None was as passionate and forthright as Dwight White.

Ed Kiely, who was once the Steelers' public relations man and then Art Rooney's right-hand man during the '70s and '80s, said he asked Roy Blount Jr., the author of the wonderful book *About Three Bricks Shy of a Load*, that preceded the Steelers' first four Super Bowl conquests, who was the most interesting of the Steelers he spoke to, and Blount said it was Dwight White. I would agree with Blount.

White died at age 58 on June 6, 2008 from a blood clot following back surgery at a UPMC hospital in Oakland. I learned of his death while I was vacationing and doing some interviews for this book in Chicago. It hurt to hear that Dwight White had died. He had so much going for him. White was doing a lot of good things in the community. He was a real success in the investment business on a national level. He had, indeed, made something of himself.

I thought about his wife Karen and their daughter Stacey. Dwight was so proud of them and boasted about how smart and educated they were, and how much they helped him improve his act.

White was a member of the Steelers' famed Steel Curtain. He teamed up with Joe Greene, L.C. Greenwood and Ernie Holmes to form the most feared front four in the NFL. White was best known for coming out of a hospital in New Orleans, where he was suffering from pneumonia, to play for the Steelers in their first Super Bowl. He tackled Minnesota Vikings' quarterback Fran Tarkenton in the end zone for a safety and the only points in the first half of the Steelers' triumph that day at old Tulane Stadium. White was a tough guy with a soft heart. He called me "Bookman," and some other less flattering names, no doubt, and like Jack Lambert, he always liked to intimidate me with a gruff voice during our interviews. I was intrigued by him and his stories.

He was outspoken, sometimes to a fault. I never used the Rooney story that started this column in any of my books. I told Dwight that he was working in the Pittsburgh business world and that it could come back to hurt him. I knew what he was saying, and where he was coming from, but it was the kind of remark that could be misinterpreted — or misused like so much of the rhetoric in the 2008 political race for President. "I don't care if you use it or not," said White. A few years later, when he was being difficult, I reminded him that I had looked after him when I wrote his story. Then he denied he'd ever made those remarks about the Rooneys. Now he realized they could hurt him.

White blamed Chuck Noll for Joe Gilliam becoming dispirited and turning to drugs after Noll took his starting quarterback job away from him in favor of Terry Bradshaw. White told me that he and Lambert didn't speak to each other for more than ten years during their playing days. "Lambert had a license plate that said I DON'T BREAK FOR LIBERALS and stuff like that. He wore a policeman's hat all the time. He'd come into the locker room and holler out, 'Turn that damn African music off!' I knew where he was coming from, and I didn't care for it.

"I learned to respect Lambert later on. We both grew up. When we were with the Steelers, we were both playing the role. He was 'Jack Splat' and I was 'Mad Dog.' We were both wearing masks.

"I played for one of the greatest teams in the history of the NFL. The Steelers today are living in our shadow, and they can't get out from under it. We're responsible for the rejuvenation of this city. There wouldn't be new stadiums or ballparks here except for what we accomplished. I'm proud of that."

White was full of pride and anger. He came on strong like the primal and basic beat of guitar wizard Bo Diddley who died at 79 four days earlier than White. He couldn't shake the memories of his humble childhood, "of cousins who thought comic books were serious literature," as he put it, of some of the stuff he had to put up with in college and, yes, even during his stay with the Steelers.

"I'm as proud of what I've accomplished in business as much as what I did in football," he told me. "I'm even prouder of my family. I feel good every day. When I get out of bed each day I am reminded that I played football. My back bothers me. It stays with you. Those aches and pains won't go away. Football is always there. But it becomes a smaller and smaller part of my life each day."

> *The average life expectancy for NFL players is 58, according to a study by the NFL Players Association. The average life expectancy in the U.S. for former elite athletes is 67. The average life expectancy for American men is 76.*

The Immaculate Delivery
Myron Cope's voice
stirs a baby's heart

I ran into Nancy Martinez at the VIP reception of the Mel Blount Youth Home Dinner in the King's Garden at the Pittsburgh Hilton on Friday evening, April 4, 2008. She came over to say hello and introduced me to some of her friends. She told me her daughter Bethany was going to have a baby soon. I then introduced Martinez to some of my friends and asked her if I could tell her Myron Cope story. Bethany was part of that story.

December 24, 2003

I can already hear Myron Cope cackling on the air during a Steelers' broadcast when he hears about this story. Cope can use some good cheer at this time of year, the end of the Steelers' sorry season. He, too, has struggled this season, beset with persistent back pains that three surgeries have not assuaged.

Nancy Martinez told me she has always wanted to share her remarkable story with Cope, but that she never had the opportunity. Until now. I am happy to be the Christmas angel that delivers the message for Martinez.

I was introduced to Martinez and her friend Pam Blum during lunchtime at Atria's Restaurant and Tavern in Peters Township by one of the owners, Frank Sam. The women both work at the nearby PNC Bank.

Blum, who lives in Bethel Park, told me her 10-year-old son Alex made a startling statement earlier in the week. "He told us, 'The city's bankrupt, the Penguins stink, the Pirates stink, Pitt stinks and the Steelers stink. What happened?" I thought that was pretty smart for a 10-year old, especially the part about the city being bankrupt. I didn't know how he knew all that."

Martinez, who lives in Houston, Pa., shared an even better story, one that she has been keeping from Cope these 23 years. Even Santa Claus never kept a gift from anybody that long. Nor will I.

Martinez was in Mercy Hospital on Sunday, Sept. 28, 1980. She had been in the hospital for a week because of complications in her pregnancy. Now she was in an examination room, and Dr. John J. Kane, her physician, was checking her progress.

The medical staff was concerned, however, because all of a sudden they couldn't get a heartbeat on the baby. They were checking all these monitors, but they were getting nothing. Nurses have told me that happens sometimes when the baby moves away from the monitor.

Someone, and Martinez isn't sure who did it, one of the doctors or nurses reached for a radio and placed it near her stomach. "They were switching the dial, going from one music station to another," recalled Martinez. "They were searching for a sound that might induce a sound from my baby in my belly. They were trying to stimulate the baby with a loud sound. They pressed the radio to my belly.

"All of a sudden they came upon the Steelers' broadcast. You could hear Myron Cope's voice. Everyone recognized Myron's voice. He was extremely excited about something. He was wound for sound. All of a sudden, the baby moved on me. They got a heartbeat. The nurses were cheering. I was crying. My husband was crying. Two days later, my daughter was born without any more problems.

"My daughter, Bethany Martinez, has been a football fan ever since. She loves Myron Cope. When the Steelers were on television, her dad always insisted that they turn the sound down on the TV and listen to Myron Cope on the radio broadcast. We've been Myron Cope fans ever since."

She told me further that Bethany Martinez, now 23 years old, graduated from Waynesburg College. She earned magna cum laude honors in business administration and marketing studies. She is now working as an assistant manager at Victoria's Secret at the Crown Center in Washington, Pa. Myron ought to pay her a visit there. They have lots of nice girlie things there that would rattle his cranium.

For the record, I checked the Steelers' media guide and they beat the Chicago Bears 38–3 that Sunday in September 1980, at Three Rivers Stadium.

It's a good story to share, particularly at this time of year. It's sort of Myron Cope's version of The Immaculate Reception. Mercy Hospital was always Art Rooney's favorite hospital. And mine. I was not only born there, but doctors saved my life there after I suffered serious head injuries in an automobile accident when I was three years old.

My kids, Sarah and Rebecca, used to misbehave in the back seat of our car whenever Myron Cope was on the car radio. Kathie and I always blamed Myron for their misbehavior, like it was a Pavlovian response to his voice or something.

"I know some people think he has an awful voice," related Martinez. "They say it's like the sound of chalk screeching on a blackboard. But it's a beautiful voice to me. It stays with me to this day. Every time I hear his voice, I think of what happened 23 years ago, and I get a tear in my eye."

The same thing happened to a lot of Steeler fans this year.

Bill Hillgrove, the Steelers' play-by-play man, always calls his sidekick "Dr. Cope." Now, at last, there is evidence that Myron has truly earned the title of distinction. Once upon a time Dr. Cope assisted in the birth of a beautiful baby girl.

Special letter to author Jim O'Brien

As a Special Agent with the U.S. Secret Service, I travel frequently, and often to foreign countries. A recent trip that I took to India prior to President Bush's visit there, required flights that totaled 20 hours each way. To help pass the time, I took your books "Glory Years," and "Lambert." What a treat it was to read each of them. As a native Pittsburgher, "Glory Years" was a great opportunity to relive stories of hometown heroes that I remember, and learn more about the heroes that I still hear my father speak of (my father played with Fran Rogel at Braddock Scott High School).

"Glory Years" also made me a little homesick. It was good to read about all the former Pitt players and staff who said that the stadium should have never been torn down. I agree. I have many great memories of Pitt Stadium. It was where I saw my very first college football game, and I was at the last game when the Panthers beat Notre Dame. When I get a chance to get home, I still miss seeing the old stadium there.

On the flight home, I read "Lambert." I actually had to keep myself from reading it while I was there. I was anxious to get to it, but I wanted to save it for the return flight! Jack Lambert was, and still is, my favorite Steeler. His singular focus and dedication to a task is what I admired most. Getting to relive the days of the Steelers of the '70s was like looking back in time. It was also a treat to get to read stories of where some of those men are now. It makes me look forward to reading "Steelers Forever."

Thanks for helping make a long trip go by so quickly. Thanks, also, for being the historian of Pittsburgh sports. You're a credit to our home town.

With warmest regards,

Jeff James
Secret Service
Centreville, Va.

Special agent Jeff James, his wife Julie and their daughter Delaney flank President George Bush and First Lady Laura Bush at White House holiday season reception.

Pitt's Petersen Events Center